Mrs. Shipley's Ghost

Mrs. Shipley's Ghost

The Right to Travel and Terrorist Watchlists

Jeffrey Kahn

The University of Michigan Press • Ann Arbor

First paperback edition 2014
Copyright © 2013 by Jeffrey D. Kahn

All rights reserved

This book may not be reproduced, in whole or in part, including illustrations, in any form (beyond that copying permitted by Sections 107 and 108 of the U.S. Copyright Law and except by reviewers for the public press), without written permission from the publisher.

Published in the United States of America by
The University of Michigan Press
Manufactured in the United States of America
♾ Printed on acid-free paper

2017 2016 2015 2014   5 4 3 2

A CIP catalog record for this book is available from the British Library.

Library of Congress Cataloging-in-Publication Data

Kahn, Jeffrey, 1971–
    Mrs. Shipley's ghost : the right to travel and terrorist watchlists / Jeffrey Kahn.
      pages   cm
    Includes bibliographical references and index.
    ISBN 978-0-472-11858-8 (cloth) — ISBN 978-0-472-02883-2 (e-book)
      1. Freedom of movement—United States.   2. Passports—United States.
3. Terrorism—Prevention—Law and legislation—United States.
4. Freedom of movement—United States—History—20th century.
5. Shipley, Ruth.   6. United States. Passport Office—History—20th century.
I. Title.

KF4785.K34   2013
342.7308'5—dc23

                                                2012042606

ISBN 978-0-472-03587-8 (pbk. : alk. paper)

For LaiYee, Sophia, and Nadia

There is always an easy solution to every human problem—neat, plausible, and wrong.

—H. L. Mencken, *A Mencken Chrestomathy* 443 (1949)

Contents

List of Abbreviations ix
Acknowledgments xi

Introduction 1

I. Fact
1. Travel Stories 19
2. "What's the Point of Being a Citizen?" 36

II. Law
3. Freedom of Movement and the Constitution 57
4. A Brief History of the Passport 81

III. Policy
5. Origins: The Extraordinary Mrs. Shipley 97
6. Change: Digitizing Mrs. Shipley 125
7. Growth: Mrs. Shipley's Ghost 154

IV. Principle
8. *Civis Americanus Sum* 205
9. What Is to Be Done? 232

Notes 243
Bibliography 329
Table of Cases 335
Index 339

Abbreviations

The Agencies

DHS Department of Homeland Security
   CBP Customs and Border Protection
   TSA Transportation Security Administration
      (March 2003–present)

DOJ Department of Justice
   FBI Federal Bureau of Investigation
   TSC Terrorist Screening Center

DOS Department of State

DOT Department of Transportation
   FAA Federal Aviation Administration
   TSA Transportation Security Administration
      (November 2001–March 2003)

ODNI Office of the Director of National Intelligence
   NCTC National Counterterrorism Center (formerly TTIC)

The Watchlists*

APIS Advanced Passenger Information System (1988; CBP): A system that maintains passenger and crew manifest information from commercial airlines.

CLASS Consular Lookout and Support Systems (1995; DOS): A system that vets visa and passport applications.

No Fly List (2001; TSA): A list of individuals prohibited access to commercial air travel.

Selectee List (2001; TSA): A list of individuals subject to heightened airport security screening.

TIDE Terrorist Identities Datamart Environment (2002; NCTC): A clearinghouse to centralize collection and analysis of terrorist information.

"TIPOFF" (1987; DOS): A State Department terrorist watchlist that contained approximately 60,000 names on September 11, 2001.

TSDB Terrorist Screening Database (2004; TSC): The consolidated terrorist watchlist from which specialized watchlists, such as the No Fly List, are derived.

VGTOF Violent Gang / Terrorist Organization File (1995; FBI): A component of the National Crime Information Center used by law enforcement. In 2009, this file was divided into two separate files: the Gang File and the Known or Suspected Terrorist File.

*This book references many watchlists. This list may help the reader keep them straight. Each list is identified by its commonly used acronym or initialism. The year of origin for the watchlist and the agency that is frequently associated with it follows. This is *not* a complete list of known U.S. Government watchlists, which is always in flux but would include, at a minimum, the Interagency Border Inspection System (IBIS), Treasury Enforcement Communications System (TECS), National Law Enforcement Telecommunications System (NLETS), National Automated Immigration Lookout System (NAILS), Integrated Automated Fingerprint Identification System (IAFIS), and the Automated Biometrics Identification System (IDENT).

Acknowledgments

This book owes its life to the paper edition of the *New York Times*. In October 2006, I stumbled on a short article by Randal Archibold buried on page A10 of the national edition. I doubt that I would have stopped to click a hyperlink to its title, and it is unlikely that a computer algorithm would have selected it for me based on my past reading history. But the first sentence sank its fangs into me: "Two American citizens of Pakistani descent returned to the United States on Sunday, five months after they were denied permission to fly home to California unless they submitted to an interrogation by F.B.I. terrorism investigators."[1]

I tore the story out of the newspaper and let it gnaw at me as the page yellowed on my desk. Out of the clipping, a law review article emerged.[2] While researching that article, I stumbled on a reference to Mrs. Shipley. That discovery owes its life to the Internet. Without the free, searchable digital archives of magazines and newspapers, I never would have come to know her well enough to want to seek out her files at the National Archives in College Park, Maryland. Those visits to NARA led to another law review article.[3]

So, ironically enough, I discovered Mrs. Shipley's passport-and-rubber-stamp world thanks to massive digital databases of the sort now used to power terrorist watchlists. But I found the inspiration to examine the No Fly List, an invention of the twenty-first century, thanks to the broadsheets of the Gray Lady.

While working on drafts of these articles and this book, I traveled around the country to present their arguments and gather counterarguments. I thank the faculty at the Stanford Law School, University of Minnesota Law School, University of Wisconsin School of Law, Lewis and Clark School of Law, Villanova University School of Law, University of Connecticut School of Law, and Texas Wesleyan University School of Law for their invitations to share my work with them. I am also grateful to the organizers of several conferences at which my work was also selected for presentation: the Yale/Stanford Junior Faculty Forum, the Junior Faculty Workshop at Michigan State University, the AALS National Conference in New York City, the National Security Law Junior Faculty Workshop at Wake Forest University School of Law, and the Gloucester Summer Legal Conference in Gloucester, England.

Along the way, I benefited from the generosity of many talented human beings who welcomed me into their archives and libraries. I owe special debts of thanks to Gail Daly, Director, and Lynn Murray, Head of Research Services, at the SMU Underwood Law Library; Elizabeth Gray, Finding Aids Liaison in the Archives II Reference Section, National Archives at College Park, Maryland; and Linda Schweizer, Law and Business Librarian at the Ralph J. Bunche Library, U.S. Department of State.

Michael Rolince opened an important door for me at the FBI early in this project. Dr. Mark Hove, a historian at the Office of the Historian, U.S. Department of State, and Dr. John Fox, the FBI Historian, were especially generous with their time and expertise. I also thank Assistant Director Michael Kortan and public affairs specialists Susan McKee and Trent Duffy, at the Office of Public Affairs, Federal Bureau of Investigation, and Chad Kolton, Public Affairs Officer, Terrorist Screening Center. I am grateful to these dedicated current and former civil servants, who were fully aware of my critical views of the FBI's role in this system. Not everyone shared their enlightened views about access to government officials. Attempts to meet with current officials in the Department of Homeland Security and the Transportation Security Administration in both the Bush and Obama administrations were repeatedly rebuffed.

I could not have traveled to so many archives, libraries, law schools, government offices, conferences, and workshops without the financial support of the SMU Dedman School of Law, the SMU Tower Center for Political Studies, and the Marla and Michael Boone Faculty Research Fund. Even with funding aplenty, I could not have pursued these topics without the support of my family, my colleagues, and friends. Jan Spann, my faculty assistant at SMU, was always ready to lend a hand for tasks big and small. Her proud reports about her sons, Petty Officers First Class Adam and Eric Spann, U.S.N., were frequent reminders of the gravity of the threat to our country and the dedication of those who face it daily. To single out a few individuals is only to recognize those who went out of their way to help me along my way. I thank Bruce Ackerman, John Attanasio, Joe Bankman, Jeffrey Bellin, Nancy Bielaski, Lackland M. Bloom Jr., Marion "Spike" Bowman, William

Bridge, Thomas R. Burke, Dale Carpenter, Bobby Chesney, Danielle Citron, Anthony Colangelo, Nathan Cortez, William V. Dorsaneo III, Linda Eads, Richard Thompson Ford, Kathie Hendley, David Hoffman, Jeff Hood, Alan Kahn, Andrea Kahn, Stephen Kahn, Brian Kalt, James Mangiafico, Michael Moreland, Fred Moss, W. Keith Robinson, Carl Rollyson, Meghan Ryan, Martin Saxon, Glen Staszewski, Juliet Stumpf, Jenia Turner, James Van de Velde, Rose Villazor, and Tung Yin. I also thank my students, in particular, Richelle Blanchard Campbell, Vanessa Jeffries, Vaniecy S. Nwigwe, Amber Reece, Jonathan M. Whalen, and Joseph A. Wyly. You will detect their improving hand where the evidence is strongest, the arguments tightest, the prose smoothest, and the conclusions most persuasive. The rest is my fault.

The Dahl cartoon in chapter 6 first appeared in the *Boston Herald Traveler's* September 23, 1968, edition and is reprinted with permission of the *Boston Herald*.

Too many holidays, Sundays, dinners, late nights, and early mornings were spent working on this book. Those hours did not belong to me; I took them from LaiYee and Sophia. Sometimes I despair that the debt cannot be repaid, for time is not a fungible commodity. I hope they understand why I did it, and for whom.

J.D.K.
Muskegon, Michigan

Introduction

> Experience should teach us to be most on our guard to protect liberty when the government's purposes are beneficent. Men born to freedom are naturally alert to repel invasion of their liberty by evil-minded rulers. The greatest dangers to liberty lurk in insidious encroachment by men of zeal, well-meaning but without understanding.
>
> —Justice Louis D. Brandeis (1928)[1]

> It was a righteous mission back then, and it is a righteous mission today.
>
> —Timothy J. Healy, Director, Terrorist Screening Center (2009)[2]

Imagine waiting in Hong Kong International Airport for the final leg of a long journey home to the United States. You are traveling with your family. Everyone is tired. When you reach the front of a long line at the ticket counter, the agent looks nervous: "I'm sorry, but I cannot print your boarding pass. Your name appears on a United States terrorism watchlist."

You are stunned. Obviously someone, somewhere, has made a mistake. A simple misspelling, perhaps. You ask to speak to a supervisor, but she shrugs helplessly as you show her your U.S. passport, the ticket stubs from your previous flight, even your driver's license. "There is nothing I can do. It's not our list. But we cannot board anyone who is on it. You will have to contact the Department of Homeland Security." She hands you a slip of paper with a telephone number and a website address on it. As you leave your place in line, you are stung by the nervous glances of travelers who overheard your exchange.

Waiting on hold, a slow sense of dread begins to overwhelm you. This is not going to be resolved with a simple phone call. What is this "watchlist"?

Who put your name on it? How can your name be removed from it? How can an American citizen be kept from returning home? Your thoughts turn to more immediate, practical concerns. You are thousands of miles from home. Your family received their boarding passes; should they travel without you? Can you stay here? Fly to Canada? Take a boat?

Still waiting, you open the website that the gate agent gave you: https://trip.dhs.gov/. "Thank you for contacting the DHS Traveler Redress Inquiry Program. Please check ALL the scenarios that describe your travel experience." You start to scroll down, clicking all the categories that apply: "I am unable to print a boarding pass at the airport kiosk or at home"; "I was denied boarding"; "The airline ticket agent stated that I am on a Federal Government Watch List." Some of the categories seem broad, others quite specific: "I feel I have been discriminated against by a government agent based on race, disability, religion, gender, or ethnicity"; "I believe my privacy has been violated because a government agent has exposed or inappropriately shared my personal information." Then there is the ubiquitous "other" category. Should you click that one, too? The next screen asks for personal information. The heading states: "The following information is voluntary; however, it may be needed to complete your request." But when you omit your date of birth, a message pops up to say that this information is required to proceed. This is confusing. What if you make a mistake? Who is going to read this? Will you ever learn what started all this trouble?

Do you need a lawyer?

This hypothetical is drawn from the experience of an American family split in half by the United States Government's "No Fly List." Half the family was allowed to return to their home in California, but father and son were stranded for five months, thousands of miles away, as their attorney fought against a remote and classified government program. Their story is told in chapter 2 as an example of how the No Fly List has expanded from a sharply honed tool for protecting the security of commercial aircraft to a broad and blunt instrument to pursue all kinds of government interests. For example, chapters 1 and 2 describe how it has been used to apply pressure to citizens to agree to FBI interrogations and polygraph tests as a condition of returning home to America. In fact, Richard Falkenrath, who as a senior White House official led the drive to consolidate the nation's watchlists immediately after the terrorist attacks of September 11, 2001, urged the expansive deployment of watchlists in testimony before the U.S. Senate only two weeks before this family was reunited: "The federal government needs to do a much better job of promoting the widespread utilization of watchlist screening."[3] Michael Jackson, Deputy Secretary of Transportation on September 11 and Deputy Secretary of Homeland Security from 2005 to 2007, agrees: watchlists "shouldn't be restricted to air travel."[4]

The logic behind watchlists makes the urge to expand their use practically irresistible. What should dictate the limits of expansion? For decades before September 11, the FAA maintained a system of issuing what it called "security directives" to airlines that it used to deny boarding to individuals deemed to present a "specific and credible threat" to an aircraft.[5] These directives identified only a handful of people year to year. Now, according to Director Timothy Healy, whose Terrorist Screening Center is responsible for maintaining the No Fly List, the federal government may prevent the travel of "known or suspected terrorist[s]" who "present a threat to civil aviation *or national security.*"[6] With three small words, this disjunctive phrase now justifies adding a person to the No Fly List who does *not* pose a threat to civil aviation. In early 2011, Director Healy said that the No Fly List prohibited over 10,000 people from flying, up to 1,000 of them being U.S. citizens.[7] A year later, the Associated Press reported in early 2012 that government figures showed the list had nearly doubled in size to 21,000 names, while the number of Americans on it reportedly decreased to around 500 people.[8]

So what? After September 11, who could object to a policy that denied known and suspected terrorists access to anything? But who decides that these people are terrorists, or even suspected terrorists, that they threaten national security, and that their liberty should be restricted? The watchlisters are prosecutor, judge, jury, and jailor. Their decisions are made in secret and their rules for decision—like their evidence for deciding—are classified. There is no appeal from the decision of the watchlisters, except to the watchlisters themselves.

But perhaps that, too, is tolerable in this age. Wouldn't it be foolish to be too open about the details of this list? Known and suspected terrorists could escape detection. They should not be treated as mere criminals entitled to the rights that police and prosecutors must respect, and courts protect.

There lies the problem. Who "they" are is left to the watchlisters. Not only do the new standards make that discretion broader than ever before, the pressure to watchlist someone is great. In its September 2010 report on the FBI's investigations of various domestic advocacy groups, the FBI's Inspector General criticized the practice of overclassifying matters as domestic terrorism cases.[9] It is only human nature that those who are daily confronted by a thick and terrifying threat matrix should inevitably prefer to err on the side of watchlisting.

Of course, that is the rationale for requiring that the judgment of even the most experienced police and prosecutors be evaluated by a neutral and dispassionate magistrate. But there is no such person involved in the watch-listing process—the decision is returned to the original deciders. There is an appeals *process,* of course, but the burden is on the individual to prove that he or she is not a terrorist or some other security threat. And this must be done without access to the information that led to the watchlisting in the first place. What if someone made a mistake? Or the judgment is based on evidence that is of unknown provenance or weak credibility or susceptible to multiple interpretations? In the absence of legal standards that are routinely enforced by neutral third parties (as courts routinely enforce the legal standards that govern searches, arrests, and other invasions of an individual's liberty), what institutional incentives exist that would lead an anonymous analyst to resolve ambiguous evidence in any way other than in favor of watchlisting? Who wants to be the official who erred in favor of a terrorist? As David Addington, Chief of Staff to Vice President Cheney, once angrily responded to Jack Goldsmith, a senior Justice Department official, "If you rule that way, the blood of the hundred thousand people who die in the next attack will be on *your* hands." Imagine the pressure on lower-level government officials expected to carry out orders. As Goldsmith notes, "It is hard to overstate the impact that the incessant waves of threat reports have on the judgment of people inside the executive branch who are responsible for protecting American lives."[10] Or, as TSC Director Timothy Healy put it, "The problem I've got is if I allow that person to get on a plane and something happens, what do I say to those victims that go on the plane?"[11]

The technology that facilitates these watchlists develops even faster than the changes in air travel that catalyzed their creation. When the FAA began its system of security directives in the early 1990s, the fax machine was the fastest means of distributing its short, paper list of persons considered too dangerous to fly. (The FAA should not be singled out. The State Department's list of people considered too dangerous to receive a visa was kept in a shoebox.) Today, massive government-run computer databases transmit information at lightning speed. Indeed, the state no longer need wait until the moments before departure for an airline's gate agent to determine that a person should be denied boarding. All travelers now require the federal government's express prior permission to board any aircraft (or maritime vessel) that will enter, leave, or travel within the United States.[12]

Of course, no one realizes that permission is required—or has even been sought—until it has been refused. In late January 2009, the Transportation Security Administration (a component of the Department of Homeland Security) began the phased implementation of a program called Secure Flight.[13] This program requires every person who wishes to buy an airplane ticket to submit his full name, date of birth, and gender to the airline at the time of purchase. Although the government permits the airline to sell the ticket right away, that reservation cannot be redeemed for a boarding pass without the government's assent. This Secure Flight data is sent to the TSA (and sometimes to a support office run through the FBI called the Terrorist Screening Center), where analysts determine whether the information matches entries on any of their watchlists. Long before the traveler arrives at the airport, TSA analysts can now arrive at the decision that the traveler will not receive a boarding pass. In June 2010, the TSA achieved its goal of 100 percent watchlist prescreening.[14] In other words, each time you travel by airplane in American airspace, it is by the grace of the U.S. Government.

The speed of technological change will not slow down. And that means that the pressure to expand watchlisting and screening will only grow as more and more becomes possible. Why stop at the hazards of air travel? If a person is too dangerous to fly, isn't he too dangerous to drive a truck laden with dangerous chemicals? If a No Fly List, and a No Hazmat List, why not a No Gun List? Who would want to give a terrorist easy access to a gun or a truck full of dangerous materials?[15] Certainly, this is the opinion of the controllers of these watchlists. In a PowerPoint slide shown to the author (in unclassified form) and to congressional staff (with the inclusion of sensitive security information, or "SSI"), the Director of the Terrorist Screening Center, Timothy Healy, made abundantly clear how versatile a terrorist watchlist can be.[16] A simplified version of this display appears in figure 1, but the colorful graphics on the original slide included a reproduction of 9/11 terrorist Mohamed Atta's U.S. visa and images of an American Airlines aircraft, an automatic handgun, and John Riggins's famous touchdown run in Super Bowl XVII. What do all of these things have in common?

The message was clear: this Terrorist Screening Database (the TSDB) could be used for any number of security purposes. And yet this protection comes with a price. The secrecy that shrouds watchlists—indeed, the secrecy necessary to make them useful in the first place—conflicts with our most basic instincts for an open government accountable to its citizens and checked in its inevitable excesses by a watchful, neutral judiciary.

The logic of a No Gun List or a No Hazmat List is identical to that of the list that started them all: the No Fly List, the subject of this book. Terrorists rarely self-identify; at least, they tend to prefer anonymity before it is too late to stop them. Therefore, the government must deploy its intelligence resources to find them. Once identified, those on the list should not have easy access to a wide variety of activities and things that are essentially

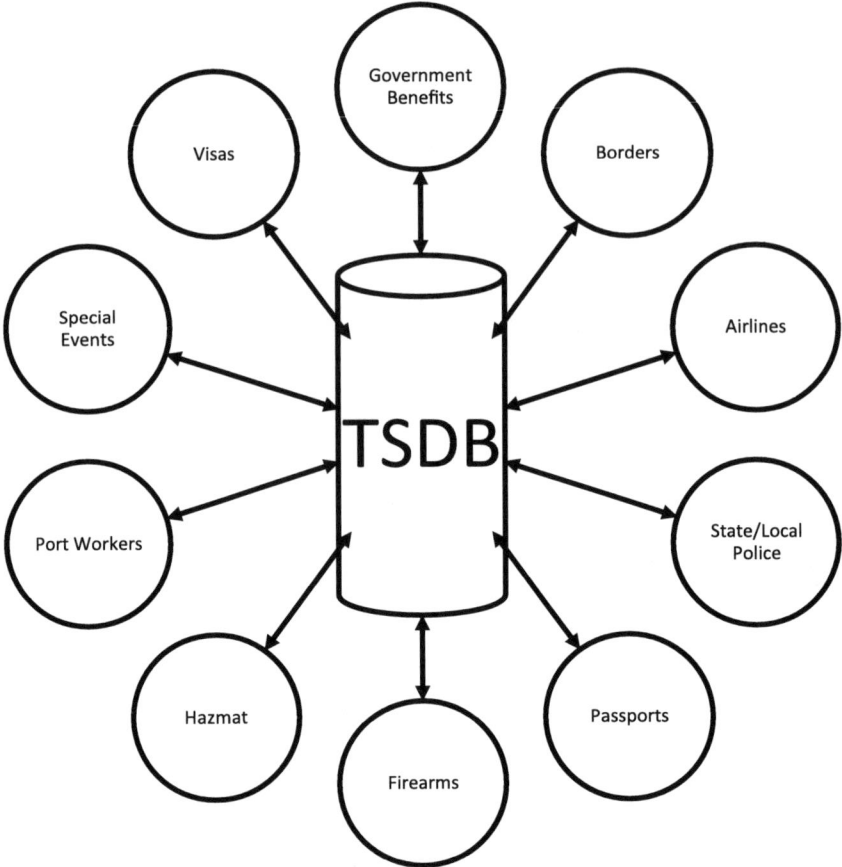

Fig. 1. A (Simplified) TSC PowerPoint Slide: The Many Uses of a Watchlist

dangerous, but also essential to modern life. And if a watchlist is to have any utility at all, it can't be widely shared. Terrorists could easily circumvent the list if they knew they were on it by inventing an alias or tapping coconspirators who are not on the list. It would be easier for terrorists to commit their horrible crimes, or escape justice, if they knew that the government was on their trail. Some predict that name-based lists will someday give way to biometric-based systems that will be much harder to trick or evade. But whether names or fingerprints or retina patterns are collected, the original concept will remain the same: a list kept by the state identifying who among its citizens may come and go freely.

Some would say the risks inherent in using terrorist watchlists to police America's borders and transportation networks (if not access to guns or dangerous materials) are worth taking. Citizens of the United States enjoy a freedom of movement at home and abroad that others have long envied. But that freedom, like so many freedoms, is not absolute. In a world in which airplanes have been transformed into guided missiles, some say that travelers should accept new limitations on their right to travel. Among those new rules: every time a citizen wishes to fly somewhere, the state must approve the itinerary.

This argument is not new. In fact, it was made, and ultimately rejected, the last time the nation's intelligence community perceived that the country faced an existential threat. The No Fly List has a historical analogue in the methods the United States used to control travel through the control of passports. Sixty years ago, communists were feared just as terrorists are feared today: they were international, ideologically driven enemies, sometimes hidden in plain sight, intent on destroying the American way of life. Restricting their travel was not just about dampening the ardor with which they spread their pro-communist sympathies. Back then, the fear was not that terrorists in league with religious extremists would kill thousands by flying jets into skyscrapers. The fear was that this international conspiracy in league with the Soviet Union would overthrow the U.S. Government, even if it meant vaporizing American cities in a nuclear Armageddon that could extinguish all life on earth.

The technology of that day was cruder, but its purpose and effect were the same. Americans whose loyalties were questioned or who were perceived as threats to the state's interests were denied passports and kept at home. Their names were put on secret lists and in files kept by the FBI, the Justice Department, and the Department of State. Others were allowed to travel, but on restricted itineraries that were monitored by requiring their passports to be renewed at embassies and consulates spread throughout the world, as if the citizen were a prisoner on parole from America for good behavior, but still under suspicion. The courts initially upheld these actions because a passport holder should not "exploit the sponsorship of his travels by the United States."[17] The Court of Appeals for the District of Columbia Circuit (the nation's second most important court) put the point more bluntly: "The Secretary [of State] may preclude potential matches from the international tinderbox."[18] The evolution of this case law is examined in chapter 3 and the transformation of the passport is explored in chapter 4. The system of travel controls that resulted is examined in chapter 5.

I reject the premise that puts a citizen's right to travel into conflict with national security. The premise is that the state has a right to restrict any citizen's travel when it frustrates the state's foreign policy or national security objectives. This premise naturally suggests a balancing test: when national security outweighs a citizen's interest in travel (and, so characterized, it nearly always can be made to seem to do so), the state should prohibit this travel. But citizens are a special type of civic creature. Citizens of a republic, unlike the subjects of a monarch or dictator, should be no more obliged to abridge their travel to serve the state's interests than they are obliged to curtail their speech when it conflicts with the state's preferences. A citizen's travel is not "sponsored" by the state. The metaphor of the traveling citizen as a "match" set to ignite an "international tinderbox" ignores the difference between a citizen and a subject. It is rarely constitutionally appropriate to weigh a citizen's travel interest against how that itinerary will affect foreign policy. Travel restriction in the service of the state is the hallmark of authoritarian regimes, not democratic republics. Citizens are not pawns on an international chessboard or proxies for their nation's foreign policies.

Of course, few rights are truly absolute. The Constitution, many like to warn, "is not a suicide pact."[19] *Some* national security reasons *should* result in curtailment of a citizen's right to travel. But these cases are rare birds. This is easy to see when the deceptively labeled balancing test is replaced by the proper constitutional test for a fundamental right such as the right to travel. The right to travel should be curtailed only to the extent that strict judicial scrutiny determines it necessary to achieve a compelling government interest. A secret, summary, executive decision to curtail all air travel for an indeterminate time and without meaningful procedures to contest that decision would not pass such review. The No Fly List must be adapted to our liberty-rich society, not the other way around.

The mistakes of the mid-twentieth century are being remade at the start of the twenty-first. Although the technology to control travel has changed tremendously, the logic behind the controls has not changed at all. To invite historical reflection, therefore, is not to minimize today's threats or to suggest that victory over them is inevitable. It is simply to ask how we got here and to pause to consider whether "here" is a good place to be.

THIS BOOK TRACES THE HISTORY of the right to travel, the dangers it faces today, and proposes a new approach to reconciling the state's security with the citizen's liberty under the U.S. Constitution. Chapters 1 and 2 present a series of travel stories, from our time and the era of the Red Scare. Chapters 3 and 4 analyze the legal history of regulating the right to travel, a freedom that every American (rightly) assumes he possesses, but no one seems able to locate precisely in the Constitution. Chapters 5, 6, and 7 uncover how this ambiguity has been exploited to restrict travel in the name of national security, first when the country felt threatened by communism in the 1950s and today when the threat is terrorism. Chapter 8 proposes an end to this ambiguity by fixing the source of the right to travel in the essence of citizenship in a democratic republic.

In short, this book is about the development of a powerful idea, first by a powerful woman in the middle of the last century, and again by a powerful federal agency at the start of our own. Here in a nutshell is that idea, that woman, and that agency, linked by a shared conceptual history.

The Powerful Idea

The idea is to make a list of people who are thought too dangerous to be allowed to move freely in society. Infringing their free movement in this way may be considered necessary because their prosecution is not yet possible (perhaps for want of evidence) or simply not desirable (perhaps out of fear of exposing sources of intelligence). What distinguishes this idea from the much older ideas of internal exile, house arrest, or preventive detention (aside from their more frequent association with authoritarian regimes than with republican democracies) is the complete absence of judicial oversight. Restraint is an exercise left to the self-control of executive officials.

The image of the plotting terrorist resonates most strongly today, but dangerous subversives have taken many forms in the past. In the twentieth century alone, we have cycled through periods when we as a nation have felt threatened by anarchists, enemy aliens, Communists, and now religious extremists. Fighting these threats, a young J. Edgar Hoover conducted the Palmer Raids in the 1920s, Japanese-Americans were interned in the 1940s, and subversives were stripped of their passports (not to mention their livelihoods and reputations) in the 1950s.[20]

In each historical instance, the threat was first seen to come from foreigners or recent immigrants organized as fifth columnists in secret cells. This perception was politically useful, for foreigners and recent arrivals are not constituencies typically possessed with politically powerful defenders. Inevitably, however, the perception of each threat turned inward, to be viewed as a domestic threat rather than only a foreign one, and the distinction between citizen and foreigner became less meaningful. Lists that may have prevented the visit, employment, or naturalization of dangerous foreigners never remain limited to policing the nation's borders. These borderlines dissolve, or move inward, to capture dangerous citizens, too. After all, the logic always goes, the threat is not the lesser for originating with an American than with a foreigner. In fact, the threat may be worse for hiding in plain sight, making more difficult the process of distinguishing good from bad.

Who could object to the most basic first step: know your enemies. In fact, a terrorism watchlist seems so obviously valuable that it seems strange to think that it didn't always exist. The federal government's first watchlist devoted to identifying suspected terrorists and keeping them out of the country was the creation of one State Department employee, John Arriza. In 1987, Arriza compiled a list of foreigners suspected of terrorism who should not receive visas to enter the United States. He kept his list—later called TIPOFF—in a shoebox of three-by-five index cards.[21]

Like past government lists, TIPOFF started with a narrow purpose: evaluating visa applications. Roughly twenty years later, TIPOFF had become the seed for a sophisticated system of records containing information about approximately 400,000 unique individuals that is now known as the Terrorist Screening Database (TSDB).[22] The TSDB, in turn, is used to spin off "downstream" watchlists for a variety of purposes: to assess visa applications, patrol our nation's borders, disrupt terrorist financing networks, investigate and prosecute terrorists themselves, and keep Americans safe when they are at home, when they travel, and when they participate in the civic life of the nation at work and at play. The No Fly List is just one of these watchlists, but it, too, has expanded beyond its original purpose. The No Fly List originated in FAA security directives intended to prevent hijackings and bombings of commercial aircraft. Now the No Fly List is tasked with protecting us against threats to civil aviation or national security, a much broader function that permits its use not just to prevent imminent threats, but to investigate or disrupt more dimly perceived future ones that may have nothing to do with civil aviation.

Like past government lists, Arriza's TIPOFF list started with a focus on foreigners outside the United States. Its successor, the TSDB, includes U.S. citizens and foreigners alike. Why shouldn't it, when one considers the American citizenship of Timothy McVeigh (executed for the 1995 Oklahoma City bombing), Ted Kaczynski (serving a life sentence for years of terror bombings as the "Unabomber"), Nidal Malik Hasan (charged with the Fort Hood massacre), and Faisal Shahzad (sentenced to life in prison for the attempted bombing of Times Square). Federal officials tasked with managing the No Fly List routinely testify to Congress that only a tiny percentage of the people on the No Fly List are American citizens—that is, the people who vote for members of Congress. That diminishes an important political

Fig. 2. The Extraordinary Mrs. Ruth B. Shipley

restraint in a democracy. And in its absence the pressure to use the list for more and more purposes grows without substantial impediment.

The Powerful Woman

The first person to fully exploit the power to control travel in pursuit of national security was one of the most powerful women in government in her day. Surprisingly, her name has been all but lost to history. Ruth B. Shipley was the chief of the State Department's Passport Office from 1928 to 1955. Figure 2 shows her at work on a passport.[23]

Ruth Shipley was not a politician or even a political appointee. She was a civil servant who rose from the ranks of World War I era file clerks to become a force in Washington whom presidents praised and to whom senators paid obeisance. Franklin Delano Roosevelt called her "a wonderful ogre," which he intended as a great compliment.

At first glance, Mrs. Shipley may seem an unlikely person to link to the difficult national security issues of our time. Ruth Shipley never heard the phrase "No Fly List," which did not exist when she was a government official. Computers did not exist either. Al-Qaeda had not been organized in her lifetime, nor had the U.S. Army's elite counterterrorism unit, Delta Force. Ruth Shipley never saw the Twin Towers of the World Trade Center in New York City, nor had ground been broken for the FBI's Hoover Building in Washington, D.C.

But this extraordinary civil servant is the intellectual ancestor of the No Fly List and of the anonymous government officials who use it to decide who flies and who is grounded. She invented the first government system to identify people whose travel was—in the idiom of her day—"not in the interests of the United States." These people were not criminals or even clearly identified enemies of the state. In fact, their seeming or even professed innocence was sometimes considered further evidence of their dangerousness. Mrs. Shipley controlled travel by issuing, or not, what became a license for their travel: a passport. It was her job to decide who could go where, for how long, and under what conditions. On the day she retired, Mrs. Shipley's office had amassed files on twelve million people.

The No Fly List, of course, embodies a power much broader than Mrs. Shipley's passport power. The No Fly List makes no distinction between domestic travel and international travel. But Mrs. Shipley's control of passports was, at the time, the only means the federal government had of monitoring and controlling the travel of its citizens. Then, as now, no national identity card or internal passport was in use. Indeed, such things were identified in her day with only the most authoritarian and undemocratic of regimes—the Soviet Union. Mrs. Shipley lacked any means other than a gumshoe to track the movement of subversives. And that job was the responsibility of J. Edgar Hoover, the head of the FBI.

The Powerful Agency

Mrs. Shipley's Passport Office was a large and powerful bureaucracy. But Mrs. Shipley's large staff rummaged through thousands of filing cabinets stuffed with paper files. Today, Mrs. Shipley's office has been digitized in a new and powerful government entity: the Terrorist Screening Center (TSC), a multiagency body administered through the Federal Bureau of Investigation. The motivation for such a center was forged in the aftermath of September 11, when it became apparent that the failure to prevent the attacks had a lot to do with the failure of federal agencies to share information. Although housed in the FBI, it is staffed by officials and analysts detailed from the FBI, State Department, Department of Homeland Security, and the Intelligence Community. Congress did not create the TSC—it is entirely a creature of executive power.

The TSC was conceived to be both a funnel and a sieve for all of the federal government's terrorist watchlists. First, the TSC is a funnel: it is the central repository for the federal government's most comprehensive, consolidated watchlist, the Terrorist Screening Database (TSDB). Information gathered by FBI agents, State Department diplomats, the armed forces, CIA operatives, signals intelligence analysts, and many others is evaluated by members of the intelligence community. Those analysts then "nominate" that information for inclusion in the Terrorist Screening Database at the TSC, where it is evaluated for compliance with generally agreed criteria that are intended to make the information capable of immediate dissemination and use to all components of the federal government.

Second, the TSC is a sieve: its specialists, many of whom are detailed or assigned from other parts of the federal government, determine to which of numerous "downstream" watchlists the information should be added. Among these downstream lists is the No Fly List. As nominations to the TSDB are accepted, the information is evaluated against additional criteria for potential inclusion in the No Fly List. That list is then sent to the Transportation Security Administration (TSA) for immediate use to screen incoming and outgoing commercial flights. If TSA identifies a "hit" on the list, the TSC serves as a liaison to the government official or agency that made the original nomination.

Today's No Fly List is no better, and in many ways much worse, than Mrs. Shipley's passport regime, a system of travel controls long since discredited and disassembled by order of the Supreme Court. It is Mrs. Shipley's ghost that inhabits today's computer systems and watchlisting databases. The idea that a citizen travels only with the government's permission is an idea that she perfected. The asserted needs for secrecy, urgency, and absolute discretion that infuse today's No Fly List decisions are echoes of her own insistence on the unabridged power of her office. And today's legal arguments, claims, and defenses of executive authority to exercise this power, especially in a time of war or national emergency, all can be traced to the arguments, claims, and defenses raised by Mrs. Shipley and her cadre of capable defenders in the courts and on Capitol Hill.

The TSC retains the most troubling aspects of Mrs. Shipley's era. But it also has injected disturbing features that even Mrs. Shipley could not have foreseen. Mrs. Shipley could be found most days on the top floors of the Winder Building at the corner of Seventeenth and F Streets, just a block from the White House. The TSC operates in an undisclosed location in northern Virginia. None of its analysts are ever identified by name. Their decision making is conducted in absolute secrecy.

In Mrs. Shipley's day, her large and well-staffed Passport Office in the State Department was the easily identifiable agency responsible. From whom should the frustrated traveler now seek redress when she is denied a boarding pass and told by the airline's ticketing agent that "the government" is to blame? The TSC creates the list, but with intelligence that originates with other agencies. It purports to have no operational role to play in the use of the lists it manages other than to serve as a liaison and clearinghouse. The TSA uses the list, but asserts that it has no authority over the listing of a name in the TSC's Terrorist Screening Database from which the No Fly List is crafted. Nor can it reveal the originating agency's information about the traveler without the permission of that source. The Department of Homeland Security operates the redress system mandated by Congress, as well as an Office for Civil Rights and Civil Liberties. But those resources have no power over the TSC or the intelligence agencies whose data the TSC funnels and sifts into watchlists. In any event, interviews with senior officials suggest how easy it is for political pressure and groupthink to circumvent these structures. Once a person is caught in this web of agencies and watchlists, the way out is pitted with administrative dead-ends, depersonalized switchbacks, and legal traps.

READER, YOU SHOULD KNOW before turning another page that every current and former government official whom I interviewed to write this book strongly disagrees with the analogy that I make between Mrs. Shipley's past and the computerized, but faceless system at work today.

Stewart Baker, former General Counsel for the National Security Agency and the first Assistant Secretary for Policy at the Department for Homeland Security, rejects this analogy:

> The Communist threat is like the Confederate threat. It's historical and easy to see as inherently improbable [and] it tends to trivialize

the threat. . . . The wars that you've won always look like you were bound to win them.²⁴

Randy Beardsworth, a distinguished Coast Guard officer and civil servant who helped set up the operational components of the Department of Homeland Security, rejects this analogy:

> The idea of making a comparison between denying passports to U.S. citizens for political reasons and denying people the ability to get on an airplane because they pose a threat is just—it's apples and oranges.²⁵

McGregor Scott, the former U.S. Attorney in whose district the events described in chapter 2 occurred, rejects this analogy:

> That was a simpler time. There is no way today that someone like Mrs. Shipley could exist.²⁶

Needless to say, the current director of the Terrorist Screening Center, Timothy Healy, who generously consented to an interview, also was not favorably inclined toward my critique.²⁷ Michael Jackson, Deputy Secretary at the Department of Transportation on September 11, 2001, and then Deputy Secretary at the Department of Homeland Security from 2005 to 2007, also disagrees with my approach. The truth, he notes, is "not easy to pitch in a book where you're looking for people who are right and people who are wrong. The truth is that if you have the responsibility to manage these types of things you have to do what you think is the most prudent thing and you have to err on the side of caution in today's world."²⁸

These current and former officials, like so many other men and women in the federal government, dedicated themselves to public service to protect our nation from terrorists. My conversations with them convinced me that their efforts to create, use, or defend terrorist watchlists like the No Fly List are based on firmly held convictions that such lists are essential to protect the national security of the United States. These are men and women of zeal, and they are well-meaning. We need such professionals in the halls of our government.

And yet Mrs. Shipley was a civil servant, too, one of equally unimpeachable integrity and deeply held principles. Her credentials were second to none, her judgment was respected at the highest levels of government, and the system of passport controls that she perfected was zealously defended for more than a decade as essential to national security. But Mrs. Shipley's system was the wrong one, administered without understanding of the relationship between liberty and security that the Constitution demands.

I did not write this book to find heroes or villains. I wrote this book to examine a particular policy choice that was made in the aftermath of September 11, 2001. I hope to persuade you that the No Fly List, as currently conceived, is as indefensible in our democratic republic as Mrs. Shipley's system of travel controls that came before it.

1 · *Fact*

CHAPTER ONE

Travel Stories

The past is never dead. It's not even past.
—William Faulkner[1]

Almost everyone has travel stories. The travel stories gathered in this chapter, however, are different. They are not stories of adventure in far-off lands or our own, or descriptions of peoples and places discovered in exotic or familiar locales in the course of work or play. These are the stories of Americans who have been forbidden to travel. They have been summarily ordered to return to the United States or refused permission to leave it. Some sought to travel within the United States, but were subjected to such constraints that their travel was rendered practically impossible. These are the travel stories of Anne, Erich, Paul, and Larry.

Consider the stories of these Americans to test your predisposition to the argument advanced in this book. Some describe an unpalatable past; others describe the experience of travelers today. But just how different are they? With the dates of Anne's story hidden until its conclusion, can you say with confidence whether it occurred fifty years ago or today?

Anne

Anne Bauer, a recently naturalized U.S. citizen, had just finished working in the military government that the United States had installed to govern territory won in a war against a dangerous dictator.[2] After four years of government service, Anne was ready for a change. With her new American passport in hand, Anne moved to Paris to work as a freelance reporter.[3]

Unbeknownst to Anne, American officials suspected her loyalty. Maybe it was an article she had written, or the company she kept. It is hard to say: no public statement was ever made, no investigation announced, no charges were ever brought against her. Instead, the State Department in Washington cabled the U.S. Embassy in Paris, authorizing officials there to seize Anne's passport "and validate it for return to the United States only."[4] Anne was summoned to the American consulate and told that her passport had been canceled. Her continued presence in France, without documents, was now in violation of French law. Travel anywhere but to the United States was impossible without a valid passport.

To say Anne was surprised is an understatement. Her passport didn't expire for another six months.[5] No warning preceded this abrupt change. The Embassy would only tell her that "her activities are contrary to the best interests of the United States."[6] Whatever those contrary activities were, suspicion about them seems to have been substantial. Anne was not trusted to retain her amended passport, now no more useful than a one-way ticket. Her passport, she was told, "is to be retained at the Embassy until you complete arrangements for your return to the United States."[7]

What could she do? Without her passport, Anne could neither stay in France nor travel elsewhere. Her journalistic career was over—what good is a foreign correspondent who is not allowed to travel? How could the government treat her this way, upending her life but refusing to say why? As her lawyer would later write, "[T]he imagination can hardly create a situation more incompatible with the spirit of our institutions than that one civil official's completely secret viewpoint should be conclusive without a hearing, as to what constitutes 'the best interests' of the United States."[8] With dwindling options, Anne sued the Secretary of State, demanding the return of her passport or, at the very least, a hearing where she could confront the secret allegations against her. In her complaint, Ms. Bauer asserted that she was a loyal American citizen and not engaged in any activities contrary to the best interests of the United States.[9]

The United States ceded no ground in its defense. The Secretary's authority to issue and revoke passports was grounded not just in statute, but in "inherent executive power to carry on the foreign relations of the United States," for which passports were "political documents" in service of that end.[10] A court should not review decisions in this international field, but rather accord the President and his officers "a breadth of discretion which would never be admissible in purely domestic affairs."[11] If more support were needed, Congress had granted additional statutory power to meet the urgent needs of war and "the existence of an unlimited national emergency" that was still in effect.[12] As the Government made this point in a later filing, "[I]n such times the resources of the country are devoted to the prosecution of war and it behooves the President and the Government generally from allowing traveling facilities to be dissipated on useless trips of citizens where their travel would not be of assistance to, but even detrimental to, the war effort."[13]

Finally, "though there may be a constitutional right to travel abroad in time of peace, there is no correlative 'right' to issuance or retention of a passport."[14] On the contrary, the Government argued, "it is clear that the Government of the United States has the power to compel the return of a citizen from abroad."[15] And all of this executive action, the government argued, was beyond any judicial power to review.

The case was heard by a specially convened three-judge panel of the U.S. District Court for the District of Columbia. Judge Richmond B. Keech, who wrote the two-to-one opinion, dismissed as "unrealistic" the glib argument that the government was only regulating passports, not any right to travel.[16] Whatever the executive's powers in the realm of foreign affairs, Judge Keech rejected the government's claim of absolute discretion to issue or revoke passports. Anne was entitled to know the government's reasons—not merely its conclusions—for taking her passport, and an opportunity to be heard before the final decision was made.[17]

In response, the State Department gradually worked out a set of procedures and institutions to hear appeals of its decisions.[18] Anne Bauer never sought her hearing, and so the State Department never returned her passport. This was not for lack of interest on Anne's part, but for lack of access. The State Department complied with the court's order, but with the speed of molasses. Fourteen months after Anne Bauer's passport was summarily revoked, the new Passport Appeals Board still awaited the Secretary of State's approval. According to the regulations ultimately approved eighteen months after the court's opinion, applicants seeking redress of a passport denial could speak at a hearing of the Board and present evidence to the Board, but would not be permitted to see the files of the Passport Office and other government agencies on which the decision had been made for reasons of national security.[19] In other words, Anne would be fighting the Department's decision blindfolded, unable to see what those who made the decision (and who would hear her appeal) had seen.

Tired of fighting, Anne Bauer married a French national and renounced her recently acquired American citizenship.[20] The year was 1952.

Erich

Leap forward half a century, to the year 2008.

Erich Scherfen is an American-born U.S. citizen. He is a combat veteran of the first Gulf War honorably discharged from the U.S. Army after thirteen years of service. His wife, Rubina Tareen, is a naturalized citizen from Pakistan. Both Erich and Rubina are practicing Muslims. They live in Pennsylvania, where Rubina operates a home business selling books on Islam and Erich, as of 2008, worked as a pilot for Colgan Air—which operates regional flights for Continental Connection, United Express, and US Airways Express.[21]

In early 2008, Erich was startled when gate agents and airport officials with the Transportation Security Administration (TSA) told him that his name appeared on the "Selectee List," one of the federal government's terrorism watchlists. This list is compiled out of a larger "Terrorist Screening Database" by the multiagency Terrorist Screening Center (housed within the FBI) but used by TSA screeners and security personnel. Anyone on this list is subject to heightened security procedures every time he or she seeks to board a commercial aircraft. These procedures can take anywhere from a few minutes to several hours. Needless to say, it was not a list on which a commercial airline pilot would want to find himself, especially one who routinely "deadheaded" commercial flights to reach his scheduled assignments on time. Gate agents for his company and even TSA officials at the airports often laughed at the irony of a pilot on a watchlist and waved him through.[22]

Erich's employers did not find his watchlisting so funny. In May 2008, he was placed on leave without pay. The company told him he had two weeks to resolve the matter before his life insurance, dental, vision, and health coverage would all be terminated. If Erich could not get himself removed from this watchlist by September 1, he would be fired.[23] In the meantime, Erich was required to return his pilot identification card. A pilot on a terrorism watchlist is a pilot who can't fly.

Erich did not find this funny either. He and his wife, whether traveling together or apart, had been stopped in this way with increasing frequency. Sometimes Rubina was held and questioned for so long that she missed her flights. First they tried to resolve the problem by writing a letter to the Department of Homeland Security (DHS), the agency that houses the Transportation Security Administration. The form letter they received in reply was uninformative: DHS could neither confirm nor deny whether Erich or Rubina was on any lists. Nevertheless, the letter invited them to submit an inquiry via the Internet to the DHS Traveler Redress Inquiry Program ("TRIP"). The progress of the inquiry, the letter explained, could be tracked with control numbers that DHS would issue them when it received their inquiry. The couple submitted their inquiries but no control numbers were sent, nor any other action apparent on their inquiries. A second attempt by e-mail (as the letter instructed for this contingency) failed, too. A third attempt, this time by their lawyer, also failed.[24] Two more months had passed. Erich was about to lose his job.

Erich Scherfen, like Anne Bauer, filed a lawsuit. Like Anne, Erich protested his innocence against unseen allegations. He had not been charged with a crime, nor told that he was the subject of any investigation. Like Anne, Erich asserted that he was a law-abiding American citizen with no ties to any unlawful activities.[25] Like Anne, Erich's livelihood depended on the secret decisions of unknown officials who were unresponsive, and seemed unconcerned, with his plight. And like Anne's lawyer, Erich's attorney alleged that her client's rights had been infringed without due process of law: she demanded that he receive notice of the reasons for government action and an opportunity to be heard before a decision was made that so dramatically changed his life.

There the similarities between the two cases ended. The Bauer case took less than five months from complaint to judgment; Erich Scherfen's case took eighteen. Anne Bauer won her case, but never received a passport and ultimately gave up on the hearing process. Erich Scherfen lost his case, but in the struggle managed to eke out what amounted to a reprieve from, if not an explanation for, the government's watchlisting.

Erich had a problem that Anne didn't—figuring out who was responsible for his legal injury. Anne sued Dean Acheson, the Secretary of State, whose department was wholly responsible for all passport matters. Erich sued an alphabet soup of defendants, each of which was responsible for a piece of his puzzle: the Terrorist Screening Center (or TSC, which compiled the Selectee List out of its larger Terrorist Screening Database, one or both of which Erich believed included his name), the National Counterterrorism Center (or NCTC, which fed the TSC intelligence it used to compile the database and the Selectee List), the FBI (which ran the TSC), the Transportation Security Administration (or TSA, which used the list to conduct its airport screening), and the Department of Homeland Security (or DHS, which ran the redress process).

The fact of so many defendants was indicative of the diffusion of responsibility that characterized the watchlist that Scherfen blamed for his troubles. Unlike Anne, Erich couldn't point to one agency as the source for his alleged injury or to demand a remedy. There was nowhere, in short, where the buck stopped. No one to call to ask the status of his case. No supervisor to whom to complain about an inattentive subordinate. It was an automated system, run by unseen analysts, in unknown places. And it didn't seem to acknowledge error.

Only a lawsuit attracted anyone's attention. Erich's complaint was filed on August 18. After more than four months spent seeking relief, he had been unable to obtain even the control number for the inquiries he made into what looked increasingly like a black hole. Along with his complaint, Scherfen sought an expedited preliminary injunction from the court, a special process to seek immediate, if temporary, relief and stave off his impending termination from work.

That request for special judicial action caught the government's attention. Within a week, David Glass, the Justice Department attorney responsible for representing the agencies named as defendants in the case, had obtained a letter from Colgan Air, Erich's employer. The letter said that Erich would be returned to flight status instead of terminated. Glass would not say who instructed Colgan to write such a letter, or why the letter should be addressed to the Office of the Chief Counsel at the TSA instead of to Erich himself. Nor would he say whether the letter indicated that Erich's status on the Selectee List might have changed. But the letter did stave off a hearing at which the TSA risked an injunction.[26]

That early salvo signaled the course of the rest of the lawsuit. In mid-October, while the defendant agencies moved for extensions of time to file their arguments, the Scherfen's four-month-old TRIP inquiries were finally answered, in a manner of speaking. This "final agency decision" was written in a style of English that combined the very best elements of George Orwell and Franz Kafka:

> Where it was determined that a correction to records was warranted, these records were modified to address any delay or denial of boarding that you may have experienced as a result of the Transportation Security Administration's watch list screening process. . . . Although we can neither confirm nor deny that DHS has records or information that prompted this inspection, if DHS has determined based on your correspondence that there is a need to make changes or corrections to any such record or information, should it exist, I can assure you such changes or corrections have been made.[27]

What did this mean? Were any records inspected? Was a correction to them—if they existed—actually made or determined to be unwarranted? What was the correction, change, or modification, anyway? Why was everything written in the passive voice? Where was the action, and who took it?

Erich Scherfen never found answers to those questions. After months of delay, the defendants moved to dismiss the case. Their primary argument was that Erich had not suffered any injury that required a court's remedy.[28] After all, DHS had now responded to his TRIP inquiry and, following the mysterious letter from Colgan Air to the TSA's Chief Counsel, Erich had been returned to flight status. What did he have to complain about now? Anticipating the answer, the defendants argued that Erich had not shown that there was any real chance that his experience would soon repeat itself. Without irony, the defendants noted that their own unresponsiveness to Erich's inquiries, which had driven the Scherfens to sue in the first place, made it unlikely that they could ever prove such a future claim of injury, "in view of the considerations of national security that preclude their being given access to protected information."[29] The defendants offered to show the judge that information, but only if the court would agree not to share it with the plaintiffs.[30]

Judge Thomas I. Vanaskie took the defendants up on their offer and reviewed government documents that the plaintiffs were not allowed to see.[31] On the basis of those documents, Judge Vanaskie concluded that the plaintiffs had lost whatever standing to pursue their lawsuit that they might originally have had. Although the voluntary cessation of unlawful conduct is generally not enough to warrant dismissal of a case (such a rule would make it easy for the government to avoid litigation when its actions were challenged), Judge Vanaskie concluded that it was unlikely that his court could render meaningful relief. The immediate injuries that had brought the Scherfens to court—threats to his job status and lengthy delays at airports—seemed to have abated. Whether their names were removed from the watchlist, the larger database, or both, absent "the *continuing* existence of a live and acute controversy," the court dismissed the case.[32]

Did Erich Scherfen nevertheless win his case? He would never know the reason he was watchlisted, or why his name was later cleared (if indeed that was what occurred). Could it happen again? Erich Scherfen was licensed to fly commercial aircraft. He now knew that anonymous officials at an uncertain number of agencies could render that license useless simply by adding his name to a list he could not see, on the basis of information he could not know.

Paul

Return back in time to the 1950s.

In July 1950, the State Department issued a "stop notice" at all U.S. ports to prevent the planned international travel announced by the entertainer and civil rights activist Paul Robeson. By "urgent" teletype, FBI Director J. Edgar Hoover ordered his agents to find Robeson and confiscate his passport. When Robeson, on the advice of his attorney, refused to hand it over, the State Department declared it to be "null and void," explaining that this "will prevent Robeson leaving the country on any airplane, ship, bus, automobile or in any other manner at points at which Immigration or other Federal officials concerned with travel are stationed."[33]

Robeson's attorney wrote to Secretary of State Dean Acheson to ask why the passport had been canceled. The reply came from Mrs. Ruth Shipley, the head of the State Department's Passport Office, who wrote that "the Department considers that Robeson's travel abroad at this time would be contrary to the best interests of the United States."[34] But this was just a conclusion, Robeson's attorney replied, not a satisfactory explanation. At a meeting between the parties, the State Department officials explained that his criticism of racial inequality in the United States was a "family affair" that should not be given voice abroad. If Robeson would agree in writing not to give speeches abroad, his passport application might receive more positive evaluation.[35]

Rather than agree to a prior restraint in exchange for permission to leave the country, Robeson sued, and quickly lost. Although it was clear that applying for a new passport would be an exercise in futility, the court dismissed the case for Robeson's failure to do so before filing suit; since the passport that had been invalidated by order of Mrs. Shipley had also passed its natural expiration date, the court could not reinstate it.[36] Nevertheless, the lawsuit did lead the Department of State to provide a more detailed explanation for its action: "if Robeson spoke abroad against colonialism he would be a meddler in matters within the exclusive jurisdiction of the Secretary of State."[37] Considering that Robeson spoke out, vigorously and routinely, against most American foreign policies—from the Soviet Union to Korea to Africa—and was bombarded with speaking invitations from audiences all over the world, the State Department's statement showed considerable restraint. Nevertheless, the opinion of the court was the same in each case.

A passport was not required for travel between the United States and Canada. Aware of that fact, Robeson accepted an invitation in late January 1952 to speak and perform at a labor union convention in Vancouver. Border officials, however, would not let Robeson cross into Canada.[38] By long-distance telephone jerry-rigged to a public address system, Robeson told the crowd that he seemed to be under "a sort of domestic house arrest and confinement."[39] The union officials whose invitation was thwarted in January invited him to perform at the Peace Arch that May. Robeson performed while standing atop a platform truck backed up to the American edge of the U.S.-Canadian border.[39]

Robeson continued to fight for his passport. He applied again in 1953 and 1954, and was told both times that the application would be rejected unless he submitted an affidavit describing any past or present affiliation with the Communist Party or appeared for an informal hearing where he must do the same. When he brought suit to challenge the regulations, the suit was dismissed. Notwithstanding the obvious futility, the law required Robeson to exhaust these administrative remedies: "We cannot assume the invalidity of a hearing which has not been held or the illegality of questions which have not been asked."[40] That was as close to departing the country that Robeson managed to come until 1957, when he finally received a passport as a result of the Supreme Court's landmark decision in *Kent v. Dulles*.

Larry

As fall turned to winter 2002 in Washington, D.C., Chad Wolf opened his e-mail, and a can of worms. "Chad, thanks for the help. Attached is the article about this gentleman. . . . Please note, Mr. Mussara [sic] is a retired Coastie."[42] The message was from Cori Sieger, the Associate Director for Legislative Affairs in the Transportation Security Administration, a new component of the Department of Transportation less than a year old. Chad's title was Special Assistant to the Associate Under Secretary for Security Regulation and Policy at TSA. In other words, he was a fixer of problems. Larry Musarra, a retired Lieutenant Commander in the U.S. Coast Guard, was the problem. Or, rather, he and hundreds of other Americans were the victims of a new problem. Now he was Chad Wolf's problem.

Sieger had attached to the e-mail an Associated Press story about Musarra.[43] It described a white male in his late forties, Italian-Irish, who now worked for the U.S. Forest Service near Juneau, Alaska. While attempting to fly to Portland with his wife and their disabled twelve-year-old son, he found that he couldn't print his boarding pass at the Alaska Airlines electronic kiosk. Neither could the desk clerk. Or her supervisor.

"We are having trouble clearing your name," the supervisor said. "Actually, we can't clear your name. You are on an FBI list." The family only got to Portland after an exhaustive, and highly intrusive, security screening. The way back home was even worse and the family barely made the flight. "Everyone has been really nice," Mrs. Musarra said. "But if you are traveling with children who have special needs, this circumstance produces tremendous anxiety." Musarra's brother had the same trouble. As did an uncle. And another relative, ninety-one years old and in a wheelchair. Every time they flew. And no one—not the airlines, not the FBI, not the TSA—seemed capable of doing anything to get their names off that list, or even explain why their names were on it in the first place.

This was Chad Wolf's problem. There were very good reasons to be circumspect about the government's new terrorist watchlists. Not all of them were the same, or had the same purpose. And revealing even seemingly innocuous information to help the Musarra family could give a clue to terrorists about how to evade the system. Still, harassing a retired "Coastie," his disabled son, and elderly relatives was not good press for a new agency. Hence Sieger's e-mail.

Larry Musarra in Juneau was not alone. As post-September 11 watchlisting increased, government officials like Sieger and Wolf heard more and more complaints. Congresswoman Louise Slaughter wanted TSA to help a constituent in upstate New York who suddenly found himself denied permission to take weekly flights between Rochester and Harrisburg, Pennsylvania.[44] Antiwar activists in Wisconsin accused the federal government of targeting them, but couldn't figure out exactly *who* in the federal government should be the target of their criticism. "What's scariest to me is that there could be this gross interruption of civil rights and nobody is really in charge," one told the *San Francisco Chronicle*. "That's really 1984-ish."[45]

Chad Wolf e-mailed Cori Sieger a week later. The problems were piling up and attracting attention on Capitol Hill. Damage control was needed. "I believe the best way to answer the questions is by an informal phone call rather than a formal letter," Wolf wrote. "[A]s you know, this is a sensitive matter and it would be best for all if communication on this subject could be kept verbal."[46] The sensitive matter was the problem of "false positives"— all of the Larry Musarras sprinkled throughout the country. Wolf proposed a stock answer to the question increasingly being asked: "How many 'false positives' occur and does TSA keep track of them?" The answer he proposed exposed more than just bad judgment in dealing with the Hill. Chad had decided to pass the buck:

> While a few carriers keep track of "false positives," the majority do not. Consequently, TSA does not have the ability to record this data

nor is there a pressing need to do so. TSA believes the most effective way to avoid "false positives" is to be sure the intelligence organizations provide sufficient biographical information about an individual before that person is placed on either watchlist—No-Fly or Selectee. TSA is working to develop clear guidelines to this end.[47]

In other words, it wasn't TSA's fault. Blame the Intelligence Community for submitting insufficient data. Or the airlines for mismatching passenger names to names on the lists. But whose responsibility was it to decide how to use the data? Or detect and resolve errors on them? Wolf's answer suggested that TSA could not figure out just how big this problem was. Nor should TSA be expected to do so. That was someone else's problem. Most of all, the Musarra family, who resigned themselves to their new, seemingly unshakeable status.

The problem would only get bigger. In spring 2004, an increasingly frustrated Senator Edward "Ted" Kennedy was stopped on five separate trips. Each time, airline officials refused to issue him a boarding pass, saying his name appeared on the No Fly List.[48] A senior administration official (speaking on condition of anonymity) claimed this was the result of a suspected terrorist's use of the alias "T. Kennedy."[49] It took Kennedy's staff three weeks to resolve the problem, with Senator Kennedy announcing that he finally had to contact his friend, Secretary of Homeland Security Tom Ridge, to do so.[50]

That fall, Yusuf Islam, formerly known to millions as the musician Cat Stevens before his conversion to Islam, was as surprised as the other passengers on board his London-to-Washington flight when the announcement was made that they would make an unscheduled stop in Bangor, Maine. The man who brought the world "Moonshadow" and "Morning has Broken" was traveling with his daughter to Nashville for a recording session. He never made it. Instead, he was taken off the plane, separated from his daughter, and interrogated by FBI agents before being sent back to London. In a break with protocol, a DHS spokesman confirmed that he was on the No Fly List, but said that he had been allowed to board the plane by mistake.[51] In the end, the mistake was determined to be a spelling error—Yusuf Islam (aka Cat Stevens) had been confused with Youssouf Islam, a watchlisted person.[52] The incident drew a rebuke from British Foreign Secretary Jack Straw delivered personally to Secretary of State Colin Powell.

Catherine "Cat" Stevens, wife of former Senator Ted Stevens, found that she was frequently the subject of heightened scrutiny, which prompted her husband to act. As Chairman of the powerful Senate Commerce Committee, he summoned TSA administrator Edmund "Kip" Hawley for questioning at a hearing his committee held on watchlisting:

THE CHAIRMAN. I don't want to embarrass anybody, and I don't want to get in any trouble at home, but we have people like Ted Kennedy being stopped, my wife, Catherine Stevens, being questioned whether she's "Cat Stevens."
[Laughter.]
THE CHAIRMAN. How do people get off these lists? How do they prevent [sic] from being approached in a redundant way once that's been established?
MR. HAWLEY. There is a process called the Redress Office, where we have a phone number and website, that the people who have familiar names—or names that are close to those of terrorists. They provide additional data. We give them a special number that then goes into their passenger record, and that list is actually kept, so that if they show up, they are removed from that confusion. And when it comes into Secure Flight, into the government, the system will run a little bit better, because it will be totally automated, whereas, now it is part of the airline process.[53]

If only it were that simple.

It would be tempting to think that the problems Larry Musarra faced were the problems of a new security system still shaking out the kinks. True enough, the most egregious flaws of the watchlisting process—mistaking senators and their wives for terrorists—gradually disappeared. Now redress numbers are automatically assigned to individuals who file their travel complaints electronically.[54] And new procedures have removed the likelihood that blatant false positives would occur with as much frequency.[55]

Nevertheless, nine years after the attacks that led to the creation of the No Fly List, exasperated plaintiffs continued to complain of the same injuries and empty remedies. In fall 2010, the ACLU filed suit on behalf of thirteen Americans, three permanent resident aliens, and one asylum seeker against the Justice Department, the FBI, and the Terrorist Screening Center.[56] Conspicuously enough, the ACLU did not bother to name the Department of Homeland Security or Transportation Security Administration as defendants.[57] The ACLU lawyers apparently believed that neither DHS nor TSA had any power to remedy their clients' injuries, even though TSA administered the No Fly List and DHS administered its redress procedures. The real power was perceived to lie with the gatekeepers of the No Fly List itself: the FBI and the TSC housed within it.

The allegations also suggested that the plaintiffs believed that the No Fly List had changed from a security tool to stop specific and credible threats to civil aviation to a much more general investigative tool for federal law enforcement and the Intelligence Community. The diversity of plaintiffs made such a conclusion hard to avoid. Among the thirteen plaintiffs who were U.S. citizens was Ayman Latif, a disabled veteran of the Marine Corps who lived in Egypt with his wife and two daughters. When airport officials in Cairo refused to permit them to board a return flight to the United States, Latif sought help from the U.S. Embassy. Latif waited a month for FBI agents to travel to Egypt to subject him to lengthy interviews, only to be told by the embassy's legal attaché that FBI Headquarters was still not sufficiently satisfied to permit him to fly home.[58] While waiting for more FBI agents to come to interview him and administer a polygraph test, Latif learned that his disability benefits as a Marine Corps veteran had been cut for failure to attend scheduled disability evaluations in the United States.[59] Finally, twelve weeks after being denied boarding, the embassy's legal attaché told Latif that he "would be permitted to fly to the United States as a 'one-time thing,' but that he could not guarantee that Mr. Latif would be able to return to Egypt by commercial air after this trip."[60] Like Anne Bauer, Ayman Latif declined the one-way ticket home.

He was not alone. Three other plaintiffs were also U.S. citizens with military records, including Raymond Knaeble, who traveled to Bogota to marry a Columbian national and to visit relatives only to find that he was not permitted to return to the United States.[61] Like Latif, he alleged that his request for help at the U.S. Embassy resulted in lengthy FBI interrogations over the course of the next month, including a series of meetings with an FBI agent from the Dallas Field Office, Rodney Sanchez.[62] When Knaeble, exasperated after a prospective employer rescinded a job offer for failure to appear at a physical examination in Texas, told Agent Sanchez that he had retained an attorney to help return him home, Sanchez said he would no longer help Knaeble return home, since the attorney's involvement was "closing all doors in the investigation."[63] When he sought to fly to Mexico and then proceed by land to Texas (where his daughter was waiting), he was stopped by Mexican authorities and deported back to Columbia. Knaeble suspected that the Mexican authorities acted on behalf of American officials "because of his inclusion on the No Fly List, as there was no known legal barrier to his being permitted to transit through Mexico."[64]

Perhaps the most amazing allegation concerned plaintiff Steven Washburn, a U.S. Air Force veteran whose travel story rivaled that of Odysseus:

> Mr. Washburn was born and raised in Las Cruces, New Mexico. He was denied boarding by the Defendants on a commercial flight from

the United Kingdom to the United States. Mr. Washburn thereafter attempted to fly from London to Mexico in order to enter the United States by land, but his flight was diverted back to London several hours after take-off. Upon information and belief, the airline diverted Mr. Washburn's flight from London to Mexico because of his inclusion on the No Fly List, as there was no known legal barrier to his being permitted to fly to, or transit through, Mexico. Mr. Washburn thereafter undertook a journey that lasted over fifty hours and required him to travel by plane from Dublin to Frankfurt, Frankfurt to São Paulo, São Paulo to Lima, Lima to Mexico City, and Mexico City to Ciudad Juarez; to endure hours of detention and interrogation by Mexican authorities in Mexico City and Ciudad Juarez; and to travel over land from Ciudad Juarez to Las Cruces, where he currently resides. He cannot see his wife, a Spanish citizen who is located in Ireland and is currently unable to secure a visa for travel to the United States, because Defendants have barred him from boarding commercial flights to or from the United States or over U.S. airspace.[65]

Of course, Latif, Knaeble, and Washburn's allegations were just that, as yet unproven claims in a complaint, the first document filed in a lawsuit.[66] They hoped for a chance to confront officials from the agencies they blamed for their problems in discovery depositions and as witnesses at trial.

They never got the chance. In early May 2011, a federal judge dismissed their complaint, citing Erich Scherfen's case, for failure to include the TSA as an indispensable party to the lawsuit.[67] In other words, the court did not agree with an essential premise of the plaintiffs' case: the real source of their injuries was the TSC, which cleverly passed its decisions through another agency whose orders were statutorily exempt from the district court's jurisdiction.

The plaintiffs promptly appealed. Oral argument on the appeal was heard on May 11, 2012, before a three-judge panel of the United States Court of Appeals for the Ninth Circuit. On July 26, 2012, the panel issued its unanimous opinion reversing the district court. The court of appeals held that the district court was not barred from joining the TSA as a defendant alongside the TSC to respond to plaintiffs' substantive and procedural claims. The appellate court's opinion, a breakthrough in litigation against the No Fly List, is examined in more detail in chapter 7.

NOT EVERYBODY HAS THE CONNECTIONS of a Senator Kennedy or a Senator Stevens to solve their travel problems. Much more common were the experiences of Larry Musarra, Erich Scherfen, and the ACLU plaintiffs, many of whom alleged that their attempts to travel were followed by lengthy meetings with FBI agents whose questions revealed their focus on general investigations and intelligence gathering, not airline security.[68] Their experiences were beginning to look a lot like the experiences of Anne Bauer, Paul Robeson, and many others from a long time ago.

As a *Washington Post* editorial conceded, "In a time of stress such as the present it is no doubt necessary to place some restraints on the traditional American freedom of travel."[69] But when was that editorial written?

The *Post* was not talking about terrorism. This editorial was written almost fifty years before the events of September 11, 2001, in response to Anne Bauer's lawsuit. Without minimizing the threat, the *Post* took issue with the government response to it. "Americans may refrain from seeking the right to travel—because of fear that a capricious State Department denial would stigmatize them as disloyal. The fear itself is incompatible with freedom."[70]

The year was 1952 and the "time of stress" that the *Washington Post* referenced was a gross understatement. The Soviet Union had successfully tested three atomic bombs. The Korean War was entering its third year, with hundreds of thousands of military and civilian casualties. President Truman's proclamation of a national emergency to fight the "world conquest by communist imperialism" led Congress to pass the Emergency Powers Continuation Act, extending the statutory duration of a wide variety of exceptional presidential powers.[71] Senator Joseph McCarthy had discovered communists infiltrating the U.S. Government. The House Un-American Affairs Committee revealed in February how American youths deceived U.S. officials to receive passports to attend a Communist youth festival in Soviet-controlled East Berlin.[72] The year before, the Supreme Court had upheld the lengthy convictions handed down to eleven Americans who, as Dean Erwin Chemerinsky observed, were tried not "for overthrowing the government or conspiring to do that, not even tried for advocating the overthrow of the government, but [for] conspiracy to advocate the overthrow of the government."[73] In other words, they were teaching the doctrines of Marxism-Leninism. At the time, their actions were considered part of an existential threat to the United States. The distinguished judge Learned Hand, who rejected the eleven defendants' first appeal, described the defendants in terms that resonate today:

> The American Communist Party, of which the defendants are the controlling spirits, is a highly articulated, well contrived, far spread organization, numbering thousands of adherents, rigidly and ruth-

lessly disciplined, many of whom are infused with a passionate Utopian faith that is to redeem mankind. It has its Founder, its apostles, its sacred texts—perhaps even its martyrs. It seeks converts far and wide by an extensive system of schooling, demanding of all an inflexible doctrinal orthodoxy. The violent capture of all existing governments is one article of the creed of that faith, which abjures the possibility of success by lawful means.[74]

The Supreme Court adopted Judge Hand's test, finding that the defendants' discussion groups posed a "clear and present danger" to the United States:

The formation . . . of such a highly organized conspiracy, with rigidly disciplined members subject to call when the leaders, these petitioners, felt that the time had come for action, coupled with the inflammable nature of world conditions, similar uprisings in other countries, and the touch-and-go nature of our relations with countries with whom petitioners were in the very least ideologically attuned, convince us that their convictions were justified on this score. And this analysis disposes of the contention that a conspiracy to advocate, as distinguished from the advocacy itself, cannot be constitutionally restrained, because it comprises only the preparation. It is the existence of the conspiracy which creates the danger. If the ingredients of the reaction are present, we cannot bind the Government to wait until the catalyst is added.[75]

It was this case and this language that Secretary of State Dean Acheson cited to uphold the State Department's passport policy.[76] The enemy was invisible, inside the United States, bent on the overthrow of its government, and backed by a nuclear-armed world power whose leaders were ideologically committed to world revolution. They were an existential enemy who didn't play by the rules. And their agents—sometimes alleged to be closely controlled and sometimes "lone wolves" inspired by their ideology—had been perceived to be a growing threat in the United States since before the Bolshevik Revolution. Indeed, their criminal convictions, sustained by the Supreme Court, formed the foundation of the Court's first doctrines on the First Amendment and subversive activities.

The Supreme Court and the Executive Branch were not alone in reaching this conclusion. Congress led the way. In 1950, Congress had concluded that Communism was "a world-wide revolutionary movement whose purpose it is, by treachery, deceit, infiltration into other groups (governmental and otherwise), espionage, sabotage, terrorism, and any other means necessary, to establish a Communist totalitarian dictatorship in the countries throughout the world through the medium of a world-wide Communist organization."[77]

It was in this environment that Anne Bauer and Paul Robeson lost the right to enter and leave their country at will. They were far from alone. In 1952, the eminent chemist Linus Pauling was denied a passport to attend scientific meetings at the Royal Society of London and receive an honorary degree in Toulouse because the "proposed travel would not be in the best interests of the United States."[78] Permission to travel was granted only following an angry speech by Senator Wayne Morse, international media coverage, and Pauling's agreement to sign a statement that he was not and never had been a Communist.[79]

In 1954, the playwright Arthur Miller was denied a passport to attend the Brussels opening of *The Crucible* because such travel "would not be in the national interest."[80] Another passport application, pending while Miller was called to testify before the House Un-American Affairs Committee in 1956, was held up by "derogatory information" leading the State Department to request "an affidavit concerning past or present membership in the Communist party."[81] Miller was later convicted of contempt of Congress during this hearing ostensibly called to examine "the fraudulent procurement and misuse of American passports by persons in the service of the Communist conspiracy."[82]

These passport cases, like those of many other ordinary citizens, have faded into obscurity. But the tenor of the time in which they occurred has a ring in common with our own. Both then and now, the country felt itself under attack by international forces that did not play by the agreed rules of sovereign nation-states. Both then and now, new and aggressive measures to counter the threat were demanded. Both then and now, the enemy seemed first to come from abroad, only to surprise us deep within our borders. Both then and now, many argued that national security had to take precedence to individual liberty. Both then and now, well-intentioned public officials reacted with government programs that went too far.

Reader, as a simple test, ask yourself whether the words of one of the country's most successful Supreme Court lawyers, writing in a well-known American periodical, describe that world or our own:

> In short, several officials gather secretly behind closed doors, peruse secret intelligence reports and purport to arrive at a fair judgment affecting not only the citizen's right to travel but also his reputation and possibly his livelihood and financial well-being.[83]

CHAPTER TWO

"What's the Point of Being a Citizen?"

Oh Lord, stuck in Lodi again!
—John Fogerty, "Lodi"

Lodi is a small town in San Joaquin County, California, about thirty-five miles south of Sacramento. Drive down Highway 99 toward Lodi and you will see vineyards, cherry orchards, and walnut farms as far as the eye can see. There are more cabernet sauvignon, merlot, chardonnay, zinfandel, and sauvignon blanc grapes grown here than in all of Napa and Sonoma counties combined.[1] Modern life has brought other sources of employment to Lodi—there is a big Blue Shield HMO calling center, and General Mills runs a breakfast cereal plant. But the canneries and fruit-packing plants that shadow the railroad tracks on the east side of town are still busy reminders of Lodi's origins. So are street names like Vine and Tokay, and the Lodi Grape Festival, going strong since 1907. The misson-style arch that spans Pine Street was built that year for the first celebration and remains Lodi's proud symbol.[2] It's an all-American town.

In June 2005, sleepy Lodi became nationwide news, but not for its wine. FBI Special Agent Keith Slotter, in charge of the FBI's Sacramento Field Office, announced: "We believe through our investigation that various individuals connected to al Qaeda have been operating in the Lodi area in various capacities."[3] In particular, Agent Slotter said, those individuals "have received terrorist training abroad, with the specific intent to initiate a terrorist attack in the United States and to harm Americans and our institutions."[4] One man, Hamid Hayat, was convicted of providing material support to terrorists on the basis of his statements during a marathon FBI interrogation and the testimony of an undercover informant. Two imams at the local mosque were deported for immigration violations. But the U.S. Attorney later conceded that there was not, and never had been, an Al-Qaeda cell in Lodi, California.[5]

The Hayat trial received national attention. It may never be known whether he was a jihadist in the making duly convicted by a jury, or, as he and his family have always maintained, a lazy and foolish young man coerced into a false confession. But while the nation's attention focused on Hamid's trial, the FBI's attention turned to his eighteen-year-old cousin, Jaber Ismail.

On April 21, 2006, as Hamid Hayat's jury entered its seventh day of deliberations, Jaber, his parents, brother and sister—all American citizens—were returning home to Lodi from a family visit to Pakistan. Someone in the FBI, however, ordered that Jaber and his father, Muhammad, not be allowed to fly back to the United States. They were never charged with a crime; no warrant was ever issued for their arrest, nor any public statement made to suggest that they were under investigation for any wrongdoing. In fact, if their exclusion was based on criteria routinely applied to all international travelers, those criteria are what the federal government calls "sensitive security information" and not published. And, whether theirs was a routine case or a special one, the analysts who made the final decision were operating behind a screen of anonymity, in an undisclosed location somewhere in northern Virginia.

Jaber and Muhammad were on the No Fly List. Five months, and the hard work of a dedicated lawyer, would be required to reunite them with their family in Lodi. To reunite, that is, not to learn the reasons why they were separated in the first place, or even to receive an apology if, in the language of government, "mistakes were made." This is the story of how two American citizens fought the U.S. Government to win the right to return home. What would their citizenship have meant if they had lost?

THE FRUIT OF SAN JOAQUIN COUNTY drew waves of immigrants from China, the Philippines, and what became Pakistan. Today there are about 2,000 Pakistani residents in Lodi. Many came in a wave of farm laborers that peaked in the 1920s. The modest, well-tended bungalows clustered near the packing sheds and railroad tracks are still home to the descendants of that first wave and subsequent laborers drawn like a magnet to join them. Most trace their roots back to one of two small villages on the eastern banks of the Indus River, just off the Islamabad-Peshawar Motorway.

A second wave of Pakistani immigrants came in the 1960s, now mostly composed of engineers, doctors, and other professionals. They tended to assimilate to American life faster, dispersing into the heterogeneous community of professionals they joined, their children adopting American styles of dress, their religious observances influenced by their new environment. They left Pakistan with dreams of a new life in America, happy to let the old ways fade into memory. The second wave sometimes clashed with the first, with fault lines reflecting their class, educational, and religious differences.

Unlike later waves of immigrants, the families who live near the railroad tracks did not disperse, or assimilate, or forget the customs and practices of the country they left behind. They built a small mosque on Poplar Street, a stone's throw from the railroad tracks. They do not tend to spend their hard-earned money on the conspicuous consumption of material goods that typifies modern American life. Instead, money is saved for the long anticipated and often lengthy return visits to those villages in Pakistan. Land is acquired there and homes are built. Ties are maintained, as are the dress and conservative religious customs of that region. These immigrants are as proud of their American citizenship as any other, and given their experiences may value it more than many do. But they and their children have not lost their connections to their other homeland.

In one of those small bungalows on Acacia Street, close enough to the tracks to hear the trains rumble past, lives the Ismail family. There is father Muhammad, mother Nusrat, and their four children. In 2006, Usama, Jaber, and Sarah were teenagers, and little Abubakr a boy of seven. Chronic illnesses had always made it difficult for Muhammad to find work, and money was always tight. Nevertheless, for as long as Usama and Jaber could remember, the family had saved what it could for a trip back to their father's village, Behboodi, one of the two villages that claim the Pakistani residents of Lodi. This trip was important to Muhammad and Nusrat, who wanted their children to have a proper religious education. That meant studying and memorizing the Holy Koran in a madrassa, a religious school. And Usama was approaching a marrying age. Both needs beckoned to be filled by a return to Behboodi.[6] Although the typical age for boys in their community to begin that study is six or seven, the family did not have enough money for that trip until Usama was fifteen and Jaber was fourteen.

The Ismails stayed in Behboodi for several years. Usama, the eldest son, returned home to Lodi first, in March 2005, now engaged to be married and approaching his twentieth birthday. The rest of the family left Islamabad the following year, after Jaber completed his religious schooling. On April 21, 2006, Muhammad, Nusrat, and their children began the first leg of their long trip home to Lodi. They had purchased the cheapest tickets possible, bracing themselves for an exhausting journey from Islamabad to Hong Kong on Pakistan Airlines, then flights to Seoul and San Francisco on

Korean Airlines. As the family woke early that Friday morning, Jaber, now eighteen, was looking forward to the trip. As he later expressed his feelings, with teenage candor, "I was excited because I am going back to America . . . who doesn't want to go back? You been stuck in a country for five years doing religious studies, you know."[7]

Without incident, the Ismails boarded their PIA flight in Islamabad for the first leg of their journey home, via Hong Kong.[8] But when they changed planes in Hong Kong for the Korean Airlines flight to Seoul and then, finally, home, the trouble began. As Jaber recalls, an airport official was waiting as the family disembarked, holding a sign with their names on it. Jaber was puzzled by the special treatment, "I'm like thinking, what the heck, you know, we're not celebrities or anything."[9] The official beckoned the family to follow her to the Korean Airlines counter, where attendants printed boarding passes for Nusrat, Sarah, and seven-year-old Abubakr.

Jaber's puzzlement turned to unease as he watched the Korean Airlines agents attempting to print the remaining two boarding passes for him and his father. Repeatedly, and apparently unsuccessfully, the agents scanned their passports in their computer. Jaber, whose fluent English made him the family spokesman, asked what was wrong. The agent stated that "no record" existed of Muhammad and Jaber Ismail in the United States and that their passports did not "come on" to their computers.[10]

That was beyond odd. Muhammad Ismail, born in Pakistan, was a naturalized U.S. citizen.[11] Jaber was born in Lodi, and was thus an American citizen by birth.[12] Neither father nor son holds dual citizenship.[13] Unsuccessful attempts to persuade the authorities that Jaber and Muhammad were bona fide American citizens followed. "I showed them my birth certificate, my school ID, but they wouldn't listen," Jaber later reported.[14] Initial puzzlement passed unease to become frustration. Frustration was about to turn to fear:

> So we're waiting, waiting and then we see a bunch of people like, they look like Hong Kong soldiers and they come with big guns, you know, like AKs and stuff and they tell us, "Ismail family, make a circle." And we're in a circle and they said, "Raise your hands." And they are pointing the guns at us and my mom is crying.[15]

Sarah and little Abubakr were now crying, too. Jaber turned to the agent, "Is there anything you guys can do?" "No," came the reply, "we have no clearance, you have no record there, so you can't fly." Muhammad and Jaber were refused boarding passes.[16] Mrs. Ismail turned to her husband and son, "Are they going to send you to jail?" It was a fair question: they had neither permission to remain in Hong Kong nor to return to Pakistan and, apparently, could not return to the country of their citizenship.

Faced with few options and high travel costs, the family divided: mother and young children continued to the United States, while father and son returned to Pakistan.[17] Little did they know that spring would turn to summer and then to fall before they would see each other again.

Seven hundred dollars cash (money cobbled together from the remains of their savings and money borrowed from an elderly traveling companion from Behboodi) bought Muhammad and Jaber seats on the next PIA flight returning to Islamabad, though boarding passes were never issued. Father and son found themselves back in Pakistan as dawn broke on Saturday morning, wondering what to expect from the Pakistani authorities who had stamped their American passports with exit visas only the day before.[18] Exhausted, they made their way to a cousin's home in Islamabad, for quick access to the U.S. Embassy there when it opened on Monday morning.

Meanwhile, Jaber and his father made frantic and tearful phone calls back home to Usama waiting in Lodi for their return. "I felt their helplessness," Usama said later. "It was such an emotional point at that time. I didn't know what to do."[19] Usama sought help from Basim Elkarra, the director of the Sacramento chapter of the Council on American-Islamic Relations (CAIR), and Richard Pombo, their member of Congress.

Early Monday, Muhammad and Jaber went to the Embassy in Islamabad.[20] There they met Steve Perry, a consular officer. Perry advised booking a direct flight home, suggesting that connecting flights had caused similar problems for other families.[21] Father and son took this advice, borrowing money from family members.[22] About two weeks later, when their lost luggage arrived from Hong Kong, they returned to the airport.

Again Jaber woke early. Again the excitement grew as he and his father arrived at the airport. And again, Jaber remembers the same terrible routine:

> So we get to the airport and we get through; we just, we just say good-bye to our cousins. And we get inside and then we were just waiting you know and we're gonna go get our boarding pass. And the guy goes, well they are trying to scan our passports again and oh, I was just praying, oh, come on, man, I just want to go back, you know. We're standing there and then he keeps on scanning it again and again. I was oh, shoot man, we're not gonna—we're not getting out of here anytime soon. So he goes in the back and takes our passports and he tells us to sit down.[23]

Thirty minutes before the scheduled departure, the PIA gate agent showed Jaber and his father their names on a two-page list. Next to each name were the letters NFL. "What does NFL mean?" Jaber recalls asking. "I was like, it's not a football thing or anything like that."[24]

No, the agent told him, you are on the U.S. Government's No Fly List. Permission to board the aircraft would be denied unless and until a clearance could be obtained from the U.S. Embassy. What could they do? Their own country seemed to have barred access to the most common and direct way to return home. And they could not remain in Pakistan save through the continuing grace and consent of that government.

Back to Steve Perry at the Embassy on another Monday morning. This time, Perry admitted that he didn't know what was going on and promised to call them back. Two days later, on Wednesday, Perry called, inviting them back to the Embassy for a third time the next day at three o'clock.[25] Waiting there for the Ismails were two special agents from the FBI.

The FBI agents, Janelle Miller and "Steve" (Jaber never caught his last name), didn't introduce themselves as FBI agents right away. They told Muhammad Ismail to wait while they took his son Jaber into a small room and closed the door. It was only then that Jaber was informed that these two officials represented the FBI. The agents announced that they had some questions for him. The agents didn't say why they wanted to ask Jaber questions, or what their questions had to do with going back home. But they were detailed questions, asking about every aspect of his time in Pakistan, and implying that Jaber was not being truthful with the agents. The questioning continued for an hour and a half. As the session wrapped up, the agents told Jaber that his father would be interviewed the next morning. Jaber would need to come back, too, to take a polygraph test.

But then, oddly, the FBI seemed to lose all interest. Jaber and Muhammad went to stay in Rawalpindi, at the family home of Usama's fiancée, much closer to the Embassy than their own home in Behboodi. By the time they got there, however, Janelle Miller had called Jaber to cancel the next day's interview, vaguely saying only that something had come up. Several weeks passed with no word. Exasperated, Jaber called Special Agent Miller to find out what was going on with their case. Miller assured Jaber that she hadn't forgotten about him or his father. But she was now hundreds of miles away in Karachi and would call soon.

No call came. Three weeks later, Jaber called again. And again a week and a half after that. But Special Agent Miller was always busy. Finally, on his fourth call, Miller explained that some people were coming to Islamabad from Sacramento to conduct the interview. It was mid-July when Special Agent Miller called to say she was ready to talk again.

By this time, Jaber was fed up. He told Miller he didn't want to talk to her. According to Jaber, Miller warned him, "Your window of opportunity is running out." "I was like, I don't care," Jaber remembers. "There's other ways I can get back. And I just hung up on her." Now Agent Miller was calling Jaber, but Jaber wasn't taking her calls. Muhammad also refused to return to the Embassy, where the family had first sought help as citizens only to find themselves subjected first to a surprise interrogation and then abandoned.

The Ismails didn't seem to realize how much they needed the help of a lawyer. In the end, Jaber figured out for himself what any competent lawyer would have told him: nothing was to be gained by talking to the FBI. Some time after Jaber stopped returning the FBI's calls in mid-July, Usama's call for help to Basim Elkarra at CAIR bore fruit. CAIR contacted the American Civil Liberties Union of Northern California and in late June or early July, the ACLU was retained as counsel to the Ismails.[26] Julia Harumi Mass, an ACLU staff attorney, began work on their case a short time later. Jaber Ismail would later call Ms. Mass the family's "angel," for she was the one that finally managed to bring the Ismails back home and reunite the family.[27] But it would take her two more months to do so.

BY THE TIME MASS TOOK the Ismails' case, it was almost August. She began, as any lawyer would, by asking questions. Why were Muhammad and Jaber Ismail kept from traveling home with their family? Who put the Ismails on a No Fly List? How could Muhammad and Jaber be too dangerous to fly to the United States, but apparently too dull to interest the FBI in Islamabad for weeks at a time?

Most of all, who was in charge? Mass realized that her first task was to figure out who was responsible for stopping the Ismails' return home. Logic suggested that whoever claimed the power to stop their travel was likely in a position to permit its resumption. As it turned out, however, she was wrong. Names were easy enough to add to the No Fly List, but surprisingly difficult to remove.

Ultimately, Mass discovered that neither the Korean Airlines officials in Hong Kong nor Pakistani Airlines officials in Islamabad had acted on their own initiative. Nor did the order to keep Muhammad and Jaber Ismail from returning to the United States come from the Pakistani government, or the U.S. Embassy in Islamabad, or even U.S. officials in Washington, D.C. To her surprise, the source was much closer to home, as Special Agent Miller had hinted in her penultimate conversation with Jaber. The order originated just fifty miles up Highway 99 from Lodi, in the Sacramento Field Office of the FBI, at the desk of Special Agent in Charge Drew S. Parenti.[28]

Mass started with Steve Perry, the consular official in Islamabad. His off-the-cuff advice had already cost the Ismails money they could ill afford to spend on tickets the U.S. government forbade them to use. Perry confirmed what the PIA ticketing agent had told the Ismails. According to Perry, Muhammad and Jaber Ismail had been placed on the U.S. Government's No Fly List. However, he said, the State Department had no power to change that status. Mass would have to talk to FBI Special Agent Janelle Miller, who was on detail to the Embassy.

Mass contacted Miller on August 8, 2006.[29] Miller said that she could not speak to Mass on the subject. The right person to call was a federal prosecutor, an Assistant U.S. Attorney in California. Miller promised to arrange for the prosecutor to call Mass. No one called. Taking matters into her own hands, Mass called the Special Agent in Charge at the FBI's Sacramento Field Office, Drew Parenti, on August 14, 2006.[30] What she heard took her breath away.

Special Agent Parenti told Julia Mass that the request to keep the Ismails in Pakistan had come from him as the person in charge of the Sacramento Field Office.[31] Mass then asked what her clients had to do to return home. According to her contemporaneous notes of their conversation, Parenti said that the Ismails had agreed to an interview and polygraph exam but that after the FBI set one up "at great taxpayer expense," they had decided not to show up for it. In order to come home, he said, all they needed to do was submit to the polygraph and interview.

Mass asked whether the Ismails could take a ship home, or were they forbidden to return no matter their mode of travel? Special Agent Parenti said that the Terrorist Screening Center was tasked with implementing his decision. It was his understanding, he said, that the Ismails were prohibited from coming back into the country, but added the caveat that he was not an expert, "so don't quote me."

Mass was stunned. Under what authority, she asked, did he have the power to do this? Parenti demurred, saying that he was not going to have that conversation. In that case, Mass asked, was there somebody else with whom she could talk about it. No, Parenti said, "it comes out of this office." Parenti confirmed that Muhammad and Jaber had not been indicted, but would not share any information about the FBI's investigation of them, including whether anyone had accused them of anything or the substance of the FBI's questions for Jaber.

It was not surprising that Special Agent Parenti would not say much about his investigation. At a press conference the previous summer announcing the arrest of Hamid Hayat and his father, Umer Hayat, McGregor Scott, then the U.S. Attorney in Sacramento, had noted that the Lodi investigation was a major one: "Every step we have taken—and will take—is examined, reexamined and vetted by the highest levels of the Justice Department."[32] Scott later recalled his first meeting with Attorney General John Ashcroft after being nominated to serve as a U.S. Attorney. The AG made crystal clear that counterterrorism was to be his focus. "This is your number one priority," Ashcroft said. "If someone spits on the sidewalk, you throw him in jail."[33]

Since December 2001, the Sacramento Field Office had been conducting a high-level investigation of the Pakistani community in Lodi, which the FBI suspected of harboring individuals and groups sympathetic to foreign terrorists.[34] Parenti was a late arrival to the investigation, having taken command in mid-June 2005, just two weeks after the investigation produced its first—and as it turned out, only—successful arrest: the arrest of Jaber Ismail's twenty-three-year-old cousin, Hamid Hayat.[35]

Like the Ismails, the Hayats are U.S. citizens.[36] Hamid, who had only a sixth-grade education and did not speak or understand English well (having spent half of his life in Pakistan), worked in a cherry-packing shed when he worked at all. His father drove an ice cream truck for a few years before seeking state disability payments.[37] The two men were arrested on terrorism-related charges in early June 2005, following their own return to the United States from Pakistan.[38] Just as the Ismails would be stopped in Hong Kong, Hamid Hayat had been stopped in Tokyo. Announcing Hayat's arrest, Mr. Scott noted that Hamid Hayat "had been on the 'No Fly' list, but was downgraded to the 'Selectee List' after having been interviewed in Japan."[39]

After Hamid arrived in the United States, both men were brought to the FBI's Sacramento Field Office for voluntary questioning, after which they were arrested. Hamid was charged with having provided material support to terrorists in violation of the USA PATRIOT Act, and with three counts of making false statements about his activities.[40] Specifically, the Government alleged that "during a period of months" Hayat had sought "jihadist training at a training camp in Pakistan."[41] His father was charged with two counts of making false statements, to wit, with lying to law enforcement officials about his son's activities. In the end, a jury would convict Hamid Hayat on all counts and a judge would sentence him to twenty-four years in prison.[42] (His father fared better: his trial ended with a hung jury.)[43] On April 21, 2006, the same day that the Ismails' travel odyssey began, Hamid Hayat was awaiting the jury's decision.[44]

During Jaber's surprise meeting with the FBI in Islamabad, one of the FBI agents asserted that Jaber had been put on the No Fly List because he had listed his uncle Umer as an emergency contact on his passport application.[45] But the connection ran deeper than an incidental reference on a passport application. During a marathon interview session with FBI agents in June 2005 that ultimately led to his arrest, Hayat had made rambling references to several Pakistani teens in Lodi, whom he speculated may have attended terrorist training camps in Pakistan.[46] When asked who had attended the camps, Hayat answered, "I can't say 100 percent, but I have a lot of, you know, names in my head. . . . [Jaber Ismail] went, like, two years ago."[47] Asked if Jaber had attended the same camp as Hamid, he said, "I'm not sure, but I'll say he went to a camp."[48] In addition, Hamid named several other Lodi teens, including Jaber's brother Usama and the sons of several other prominent members of the Lodi Muslim community.

In the week following the Hayats' arrests, the FBI's Sacramento Field Office and U.S. Attorney's Office were in a state of high alert. "We didn't know what we had," McGregor Scott, the U.S. Attorney, later recalled. According to Scott, "an army of FBI agents were in Lodi" in the days after the arrest, in part because Scott's office and the FBI agreed that "a show of strength was needed to deter anything that might have been planned."[49] FBI agents ostentatiously parked cars outside of several of the boys' homes.[50] Some reported seeing low-flying aircraft making passes over Pakistani neighborhoods.[51]

Tracking down each teenage Pakistani male named by Hamid Hayat became a top investigative priority. All but one were easy for the FBI to find because all but one were in Lodi. One by one, the FBI sought them out for questioning. Sometimes their approaches were casual and friendly; sometimes they could be quite threatening. Usama Ismail remembers one incident:

> My cousin, his name is Sohel, he was walking to the park, and the FBI came and they grabbed him by the arm and they say, you're coming with us. And he said the F word and he said get off of me. He goes, "I'm an American citizen," and that's when they backed off. They thought he was a paper. They didn't think he was a citizen.[52]

Some of the teens agreed to speak to the FBI, while others refused.[53] As parents watched their sons being followed and stopped by federal agents, they wondered if their children would be arrested like Hamid Hayat.

The exception was Jaber Ismail. To the FBI agents, the pieces of their puzzle, the results of a long investigation, now seemed to be coming together. Hamid Hayat had confessed to training at a terrorist camp. One of the people he named was not only his cousin, but still in Pakistan. Suspicious, and aware of a powerful tool to find out more information before a suspected jihadist could return home, Drew Parenti ordered Jaber Ismail and his father added to the No Fly List. They would leave Pakistan when his agents were satisfied, not before.

Meanwhile, back in Lodi, Usama Ismail remembers one FBI Special Agent, Sean Wells, who repeatedly showed up on the Ismail family's doorstep. When Jaber refused to participate in any further interrogations back in Islamabad, Usama received a telephone call. According to Usama Ismail, the agent asked him to convince his brother to speak with the FBI agents at the Embassy:

> Sean Wells, and I don't know who else it was, they called me and they were on the other line with my dad and my brother, I think. And then they said, tell your dad and brother to come and take a polygraph test or talk to us or whatever. And Sean was telling me, or I don't know if it was Sean or if it was Steve—I forget his last name though—he's telling me, look, I'm going to be in Karachi or Islamabad on so-and-so date. Tell your brother to talk with us and we'll [get] everything [ ] taken care of. So that's when I told him no.[54]

Presciently, if saltily, Usama put his finger on at least one constitutional issue: "I said, 'You guys screwed my uncle over, and now you want to screw my brother over?' They're treating them like foreigners or something. What's the point of being a citizen?"[55]

ON AUGUST 9, 2006, Julia Mass sent a letter complaint to the Office for Civil Rights and Civil Liberties at the Department of Homeland Security (DHS). Still unsure exactly who was responsible for the Ismails' exile in Pakistan, Mass's letter to DHS was written in broad language, describing the Ismails as having been "denied clearance to board an airplane to return to the United States," an action "carried out by the U.S. Department of State in conjunction with the Federal Bureau of Investigation."[56] The complaint summarized the Ismails' experience as citizens seeking help from their embassy:

> The following Monday, the Ismails went to the U.S. Embassy. The consular officer they spoke to told them he would contact them with information about how to proceed. Later that week, the Ismails were instructed to return to the Embassy. When they returned, Jaber was

interrogated by two FBI agents. The FBI agents told him that he would need to submit to a polygraph test before he would be permitted to return to the United States. At the end of the interrogation, the Ismails were told to return the next day. However, the next morning one of the FBI agents called and cancelled the appointment. She said that she would call again for an interview. After three weeks, Jaber Ismail contacted the FBI agent to find out what was going on. After several more weeks passed, the FBI agent called Jaber Ismail and told him that he needed to submit to further interrogation in order to "clear up" the situation before he would be permitted to return to the United States.[57]

The ACLU's complaint requested a full investigation, an explanation for the government's actions, clearance to return to the United States, removal from the No Fly List, and compensation for the costs incident to their delayed travel home.[58] The same day, Ms. Mass also filed Traveler Identification Verification Forms (TIVF) and identity documentation with the Transportation Security Administration (TSA).

As the Ismails' story drew media attention, the FBI and DHS declined to comment on the actions apparently being conducted overseas with their knowledge, if not at their instigation.[59] The U.S. Attorney's Office in Sacramento acknowledged that FBI agents wanted to speak with Muhammad and Jaber Ismail.[60] McGregor Scott, then U.S. Attorney for the Eastern District of California, was the most candid, confirming that the Ismails were on the No Fly List.[61] Rather euphemistically he described the condition placed on their return: "They've been given the opportunity to meet with the FBI over there and answer a few questions, and they've declined to do that."[62]

Communication by DHS directly to the Ismails' attorney was stilted and vague. On August 28, 2006, Mass had tried to get answers over the telephone from a DHS employee named Sara Lilly.[63] Mass asked whether her clients were precluded from entering the United States by any means of transport or route of travel (e.g., by ship or over land), or if the travel ban merely extended to air travel.[64] Ms. Lilly declined to answer, but said she would reach out to both TSA and Customs and Border Protection (CBP) to find out.[65] Next Mass asked what the relationship was between the FBI's Terrorist Screening Center and the TSA. Lilly had no ready answer, but said that she would check on that, too.[66] Although she said that she would call back by the end of the week, no call came. Instead, the next day, August 29, DHS sent Mass a written acknowledgment of her complaint.[67]

Ironically enough, these were questions being asked in the U.S. Attorney's Office in Sacramento, too. A former official in that office recalled seeking advice from Washington about the legal implications of keeping a citizen out of the country using the No Fly List. The official was surprised to discover that Washington had no ready response to this important question, instead answering, in essence, "We're looking into it."

On September 6, Mass received a call from Rebekah Tosado, an attorney in the DHS Office for Civil Rights and Civil Liberties.[68] Ms. Mass describes the call as "very cryptic."[69] Ms. Tosado would only state that review of the complaint had been completed and that "changes have been made as appropriate."[70] Ms. Mass asked for more information, including whether alternative means of transport home were possible. The DHS representative declined to answer or even say whether that question had been investigated. When Mass asked what the phrase "changes have been made as appropriate" actually meant for her clients, Tosado responded with a question: Had the Ismails recently tried flying again? When Mass said no, Tosado suggested they might try flying again.[71]

The phone call was followed by two faxes dated the same day, identical with the exception of one word: the names Muhammad and Jaber. The faxes were sent from the TSA Office of Transportation Security Redress. Read one for yourself (see figure 3). Try to determine what, exactly, was done.

Did "any applicable records" exist? Was their review deemed by TSA to be "appropriate"? What "other federal agencies" were consulted and who had the final say? Was any determination made "that a correction to records is warranted"? Had TSA acknowledged that the Ismails "may have experienced" a five-month exile in Pakistan "as a result of the watch list screening process"? What exactly was "TSA's final agency decision," which the letter purported to constitute?[72]

Still uncertain whether TSA, DHS, FBI, or the U.S. Attorney's Office was really in charge, Mass left messages for both Drew Parenti and McGregor Scott, seeking to confirm that her clients would be cleared to fly home before they bought their fourth pair of international airline tickets. Mass does not recall receiving a return call from either one; Scott thought he might have left a voicemail message in reply, but only to say that the Ismails' travel delay was simply not his issue.[73]

The DHS Office for Civil Rights and Civil Liberties sent Ms. Mass a longer fax dated September 8. It recounted the timeline of her complaint, adding one operative part identical to the sentences in the Ismails' faxes: "Where it has been determined that a correction to records is warranted, these records have been modified to address any delay or denial of boarding that Messrs. Ismail may have experienced as a result of TSA's watch list screening process."[74]

U.S. Department of Homeland Security

Office of Transportation Security Redress
Arlington, VA 22202

September 6, 2006

Mr. Jaber Ismail
Lodi, CA 95240

Dear Mr. Ismail:

The Transportation Security Administration (TSA) has received your Traveler Identity Verification Form (TIVF) and identity documentation. In response to your request received on August 9, 2006, we have conducted a review of any applicable records in consultation with other federal agencies, as appropriate. Where it has been determined that a correction to records is warranted, these records have been modified to address any delay or denial of boarding that you may have experienced as a result of the watch list screening process.

TSA cannot ensure that your travel will always be delay free as this redress process does not affect other standard screening procedures in place at the security checkpoint. For example, an individual may be selected by TSA for enhanced screening in order to resolve a walk-through metal detector alarm, because of random selection, or based on certain non-identity based factors reflected in reservation information. Additionally this process may not eliminate the need to go to the ticket counter in order to obtain a boarding pass. For instance, an airline might still require a brief period of time to comply with identity verification requirements prior to issuing a boarding pass.

This letter constitutes TSA's final agency decision, which is reviewable by a United States Court of Appeals under 49 U.S.C. § 46110.

If you have any further questions, please call the TSA Contact Center Office of Transportation Security Redress (OTSR) toll-free at (866) 289-9673 or locally at (571) 227-2900, send an E-mail to TSA-ContactCenter@dhs.gov, or write to the following address:

Transportation Security Administration
TSA-901
601 South 12th Street
Arlington, VA 22202-4220

Sincerely,

James G. Kennedy, Jr.
Director
Office of Transportation Security Redress

GP-33501

Fig. 3. TSA Letter to Jaber Ismail

The complaint, aggressive lawyering, and widespread media coverage ultimately paid off.[75] Speaking on condition of anonymity, a federal law enforcement official told the *San Francisco Chronicle* only that "There's been a change," and that the change came from DHS.[76] A DHS spokeswoman was willing to state on the record that the Office for Civil Rights and Civil Liberties "did some research on the case and did make appropriate changes," but declined to say what those changes were.[77]

Some might say the DHS complaint process worked. But if the Ismails' experience is evidence of a well-functioning complaint process, then the bar for success is apparently quite low. On October 1, 2006, Muhammad and Jaber Ismail returned home to the United States.[78] Said Jaber: "I never imagined that the country I was born in would stop me from coming home for five months and separate me from my family, especially when I was not even charged with a crime."[79]

Jaber finished high school and is now in college. He works part-time at the Lodi Boys and Girls Club, in an after-school program for kids. But for years the Ismail family feared what could happen if they again attempted to board an airplane. It took four years and the enticement of Usama's wedding before anyone in the family flew again. "We want to," Jaber said, "but a little thought in the back of our mind that, you know, what if it happens to us again." Usama unwittingly hit upon a common legal metaphor to describe the feeling: "It's like we get the chill now thinking about flying, traveling anywhere."[80]

THE EXPERIENCE OF JABER and his cousin Hamid as Americans placed on the No Fly List makes one thing clear. Official claims to the contrary notwithstanding, the No Fly List is not limited to keeping bombers and hijackers off airplanes. It has become an investigative tool that the state can deploy at will to further purposes other than aviation security. At the time of Hamid Hayat's arrest, U.S. Attorney Scott explained that his No Fly List status had been downgraded after an interview in Tokyo with federal agents. A year later, in an interview with *New York Times* reporter Lowell Bergman, Scott provided more details:

> BERGMAN: How did [Hamid Hayat] get on a plane in 2005 if he was on the no-fly list?
> SCOTT: He mistakenly was allowed to board that plane. Once the plane was airborne, his presence on that plane was determined, and it was rerouted to Tokyo, where he was pulled off the plane

by the FBI and interviewed. . . . He was interviewed by the FBI in Tokyo and was allowed to return on his journey to the United States following that interview. . . .

BERGMAN: Because [the FBI] wanted to talk to him, or because they didn't think he was a danger anymore?

SCOTT: Well, I think the fact that they did interview him extensively within a very short period of time after coming back in the United States shows that there was a concern, that we wanted to find out what this guy was up to.[81]

Back in private practice years later, McGregor Scott reflected on how these choices had unfolded at the time, and stood by them. His U.S. Attorney's Office had obtained a conviction of Hamid Hayat for material support for terrorism. The jury's verdict seemed to him good evidence that the decision to put the Ismails on a No Fly List was a rational one. Drew Parenti's FBI field office had been thorough and careful in its investigation of the Lodi community. "An army of FBI agents were in Lodi" in the days after the arrest, both for continued investigation and out of concern that "a show of strength was needed to deter anything that might have been planned."[82]

Government officials involved with the case continue to suggest that there remain unanswered questions about the long stays in Pakistan by both the Hayats and the Ismails. If this is not so, then these families have been unjustly maligned. The former U.S. Attorney involved with the case alluded to information that came out neither at trial nor in the media. "We know things the public will never know," Mr. Scott said.[83] In hindsight, one could look back on these events and see only a sleepy California farm town. But Attorney General Ashcroft had made crystal clear to all ninety-three U.S. attorneys in the country that preventing another terrorist attack was their number one job. How would the Lodi investigation be perceived now if there had been another terrorist attack? Monday morning quarterbacks often forget how it feels to be down on the field, without the luxury to reflect and with great pressure to act.

Drew Parenti and McGregor Scott are honorable men with long and distinguished careers in public service. These are not men given to rash or thoughtless action. But their words and actions reveal two pernicious defects in the power asserted by federal officials to decide which citizens they will permit to travel, and by what mode of transportation. First, watchlists originally conceived and justified for the narrow purpose of securing the safety of civilian aircraft succumb to the inevitable pressures of "mission creep."

Second, leaving the keepers of these watchlists to police themselves is as dangerous a practice in this field as in any other.

First, the pressure to expand the uses of watchlists is uncontainable within a single branch of government. The Office of Inspector General of the Department of Homeland Security reported in July 2009 that the No Fly List is "not for use as [a] law enforcement or intelligence-gathering tool[]."[84] The facts of the Ismail case, and many others, throw doubt on such claims. Jaber Ismail was the only young man named by Hamid Hayat during his long FBI interrogation who was not in Lodi and therefore available for questioning or surveillance. The hearsay statements of an FBI agent in Pakistan (people are coming "from Sacramento to interview you"), FBI agents in Lodi ("Tell your brother to talk with us"), and the Special Agent in Charge in Sacramento, Drew Parenti (the order "comes out of this office"), do not support the conclusion that Jaber Ismail and his father were stopped from boarding their flight home and separated from their large family because they were a threat to the safety of their fellow passengers. After all, they were allowed to fly—unescorted—back to Pakistan, and then ignored by the FBI for weeks at a time. Father and son were forced to return to Pakistan by an FBI that thought it could coerce an American citizen to answer its questions and submit to a polygraph test in exchange for permission to return to the country of his birth.

The No Fly List was used as a blunt tool of coercion in an ongoing investigation, not to secure the safety of passengers on a particular flight. It may well be that government officials, well-meaning and full of zeal, acted as they thought necessary to pursue the best interests of the United States. But should the power they exercised—so absolute and unchecked—belong to anyone in the government of the United States of America? What keeps the watchlist from further expansion?

Second, leaving decisions about the balance that should be struck between liberty and security to executive branch officials inundated with daily reports of threats to our national security is a recipe for trouble. What Jack Goldsmith observed of policymakers in the top echelons of the Bush Administration holds true for the officials in charge of terrorist watchlists: "Their want of actionable intelligence combined with their knowledge of what might happen to produce an aggressive, panicked attitude that assumed the worst about threats and embraced a 'better safe than sorry' posture toward them."[85] No official or agency of the federal government has ever offered a public explanation for the Ismails' experience. But there has been a common refrain to the thoughts of retired senior officials asked about this episode. When your tool is a hammer, everything looks like a nail. Randy

Beardsworth, who helped set up the operational components for border and transportation security in the Department of Homeland Security, reflected on the No Fly List decisions he saw between 2003 and late 2005: "There was almost always a good, articulable reason for these things to happen, which you may never, and the individual may never, get visibility on."[86] Michael Jackson, who at the time of these events was Deputy Secretary of the Department of Homeland Security, recalled the concerns U.S. Attorney Scott raised about the Lodi investigation.[87] "If you are a U.S. citizen and you don't have anything to hide about illegal activities and the FBI comes to you and says, look, here's a relative, deep trouble," Jackson began by way of introduction. "Wouldn't you as a U.S. citizen feel like it would be in your interest to sort of cooperate with the FBI and try to help deflect any concern about your own personal activities? I mean, I would. I would be happy to take a polygraph under those circumstances and say take me off."[88]

In Jackson's mind, the Ismails were to blame for their own exile, for resisting rather than cooperating with the FBI. After all, if you have nothing to hide, you have nothing to fear. But why should a citizen, even one with nothing to hide, speak to government officials who conduct themselves in such a rough fashion? Why should citizens be separated from their families and threatened with de facto exile as the price for exercising their rights as citizens of a democratic republic? In the opinion of Jackson, one of the most senior officials in the federal government's homeland security apparatus at that time, the relationship between citizen and state was one in which the state should be free to decide which citizens, although breaking no law, should be summarily denied the right to travel:

> When you look at the massive numbers of people flying in and out of the country, there's always going to be some number of cases, hopefully a small number of cases, where you need intervention to be able to sort out who's really right and what's fair and just in these cases. And it seems like almost never is it the case that someone's totally innocent. There's some nexus of reason why they come to the attention of law enforcement. And by being fully candid with law enforcement, you increase by a substantial magnitude the likelihood that you can get it resolved and get on about your business.[89]

Who decides which cases need "intervention" and when that euphemism should be subject to the oversight of a neutral magistrate? Who decides what's "fair and just" and when someone is not quite "totally innocent"? As the pages of this book reveal, when it comes to the travel of citizens, those decisions are made by a small group of anonymous federal officials, the keepers of the watchlists. They oppose the interposition of any neutral magistrate between them and their judgments about who may travel and how. They resist the notion that the lists they compose should be subject to the checks and balances that normally protect individuals from the power of the state.

Instead, the view from the keepers of the watchlists is simply stated: trust us.

II · *Law*

CHAPTER THREE

Freedom of Movement and the Constitution

Travel is a part of America's DNA. There would *be* no America without the explorers, settlers, slaves, revolutionaries, and wave after wave of immigrants who all traveled (if not always freely) from a known world to an unknown one, and then continued westward across an uncharted continent. For much of American history, travel was difficult, expensive, and inordinately time-consuming. The flow of travel was therefore primarily unidirectional: it followed the international currents of immigration and the domestic economic needs of American homesteaders and those who traveled west in search of a better future. The idea of such travel was so crucial to the American dream that it is commemorated by the most famous landmark in New York Harbor, with a poem by Emma Lazarus at its base and an outstretched torch high overhead lighting the way.

Travel is still at the heart of the American idea, but its manifestations are strikingly new and different. The technologies that render our world ever smaller have made travel faster, cheaper, and more accessible. The harrowing journey of the immigrant is no longer its primary manifestation. In an era of globalization, it is no longer the province of the very rich; millions of Americans travel within the country's borders and abroad for work and play. Nor is the typical transoceanic journey a unidirectional one. Millions of Americans journey back and forth between their old and new homes. In 2006, the year the Ismails struggled to return home, more than 39 million Americans traveled to foreign countries aboard commercial air carriers.[1] In 2010, according to the Bureau of Transportation Statistics, domestic commercial aircraft transported 629,521,640 passengers in the United States.[2] That is more than 1.7 million people in the air every day. In other words, if every man, woman, and child in Philadelphia boarded a plane each day, there would still be over 198,000 airplane seats to fill.[3]

How, then, does the Constitution protect this freedom, so intrinsic to the idea of America? The text itself says nothing at all about it. One searches in vain for any "right to travel" expressly protected in the way that the freedom of speech or right to a speedy and public trial are protected. In fact, the only explicit textual reference to a right of "free ingress and regress" in American constitutional history was found in the Articles of Confederation.[4] But that clause was *removed* from the final draft of the Constitution without any recorded debate at the convention that met in Philadelphia in the summer of 1787.[5]

Does that mean that the Founding Fathers did not intend to recognize any such right? Though some have strained to make this argument, it goes too far.[6] The importance of freedom of movement, and especially the right to enter and leave one's own country, was well known to that generation of Americans, who could easily locate it in the common law of England and railed against its denial to the American colonies.[7] Hadn't the early colonists exercised that very right to flee religious persecution and make fresh starts in the New World? Indeed, restriction of freedom of movement was one of the "injuries and usurpations" listed in the Declaration of Independence.[8] Several early colonial charters and bills of rights in the states also referenced the right to exit or otherwise travel freely abroad.[9]

The logic of the original document also made explicit protection of the right to travel, considered so essential to the life of a free citizen, seem unnecessary.[10] After all, the government established by the new constitution was to be one of limited and enumerated powers. Since the text of the Constitution gave Congress no power to abridge this right, what need was there of explicit textual protection for it? This, of course, was Alexander Hamilton's logic concerning a Bill of Rights: "why declare that things shall not be done which there is no power to do?"[11]

Perhaps, then, it is understandable that a freedom felt so essential to citizens of this new democratic republic should have been left without explicit reference in the founding text. Although the words may have been absent, the right was solidly felt. In fact, the country's early foreign policy was shaped by a strong defense of the right of expatriation (arguably the most extreme form of freedom of movement).[12]

Though understandable, omitting explicit protection had the consequence of leaving the basis for it unclear. It fell to the Supreme Court to set the boundaries for that protection. This chapter presents a theory to explain the sharp distinction that resulted: the Supreme Court developed a body of case law that treated the rights to engage in domestic travel and international travel very differently. This jurisprudence undervalues the right of citizens to engage in all forms of travel. And the Court has not adapted this case law to the extraordinary technological changes that made travel over ever increasing distances an ever more commonplace aspect of American life. An alternative, unified and modernized approach, based on the Citizenship Clause of the Fourteenth Amendment, is presented in chapter 8.[13]

The cases raising issues of domestic travel came first. The Court found strong constitutional protection for travel between the states. The case law that developed held such travel to be a *fundamental* right. That meant that the state could only infringe the right to travel to achieve the most compelling of government interests and, even then, subject it to only the least restriction necessary to accomplish that interest. Years later, such a formulation would come to be known as the "strict scrutiny" test, the highest level of protection.

Foreign travel, on the other hand, received far less protection. It was *not* found to be a fundamental right. The right to international travel, the Supreme Court concluded, was merely an "aspect of liberty" to be protected like any other liberty interest, by due process of law. Rather than subject government regulation of foreign travel to strict scrutiny, the Court settled on a test that merely weighed the competing interests of the state and the citizen, a much weaker test than "strict scrutiny."

Why the difference? The answers lie, at least in part, in the fact that the domestic travel cases arose first. Few Americans traveled abroad in the country's early history and America's relative isolation in world affairs until the dawn of the twentieth century meant little pressure to regulate such travel, or perceive threats to the nation's security from it. Without any reason to focus on all aspects of the right to travel, the Supreme Court adopted a very functionalist approach to protect the right to domestic, interstate travel that was easy to state but hard to find in the Constitution's text. So the Court found justification to protect the right to travel as a means of protecting other rights, powers, or designs that were more directly expressed in the Constitution. Thus, travel between states received heightened protection because it functioned to add value to *other* rights and freedoms more easily identified in the text: associational freedoms, the participation of citizens in federal governance, and the pursuit of individual and national economic prosperity.

This approach had an unintended consequence that went unnoticed at a time when unregulated foreign travel was taken for granted and cases did not arise to contest unchallenged assumptions. This functionalist approach transformed travel from an *intrinsic* right of citizenship into a *contingent* right of citizenship. As a result, the Supreme Court has afforded heightened protection to the freedom of travel *within* the United States—where the other rights and interests that travel may strengthen are most clearly exercised—but not to travel *outside* the United States, where such contingent interests historically have seemed more difficult to find. This contingency also led some courts to hypothesize a strange distinction: protection for the abstract right to travel but little or no protection for the use of any particular mode of transportation that would give that right real meaning.[14]

The implications of such contingent logic did not become fully apparent until more and more Americans began traveling within a more and more technologically sophisticated system of mass transportation, one sophisticated enough to create a No Fly List. The unforeseen consequence of these arguments has been the erosion of the practical protection for the right to travel, at home and abroad.

1. Domestic Travel

Government attempts to restrict interstate travel have occupied the Supreme Court since the early part of the nineteenth century. It is a curiosity of this line of cases that the Court has never seemed troubled by its difficulty locating in the Constitution the source of a right to interstate travel. "Freedom to travel throughout the United States has long been recognized as a basic right under the Constitution," Justice William Brennan wrote in an opinion in 1986, but quickly conceded that the textual source of the right "has proved elusive."[15] Rather, the Court has journeyed among arguments based on different parts of the Constitution as well as arguments made by examining the structure of the Constitution as a whole. As a result, this right of domestic travel has largely been upheld indirectly and contingently, not as a right with an intrinsic value but one necessary to the full functioning of other rights and interests. A closer look at each of these sources of support in the order that the Court adopted them—the Privileges and Immunities Clause in Article IV, the Interstate Commerce Clause in Article I, the federal structure of the document as a whole, and the Privileges or Immunities Clause of the Fourteenth Amendment—makes this clear.

The Privileges and Immunities Clause of Article IV

The right to interstate travel was first defended through the Privileges and Immunities Clause in Section 2 of Article IV. It provides: "The Citizens of each State shall be entitled to all Privileges and Immunities of Citizens in the several States." The argument relied upon a belief prevalent among many judges in the early nineteenth century that certain natural rights, though unspecified in the Constitution, nevertheless limited the reach of the new government.[16] In *Corfield v. Coryell,* an early case that sought to discern its content, U.S. Supreme Court Justice Bushrod Washington (nephew of George Washington) described some of the "fundamental" rights "which belong, of right, to the citizens of all free governments; and which have, at all times, been enjoyed by the citizens of the several states which compose this Union, from the time of their becoming free, independent, and sovereign."[17] Although he found it "more tedious than difficult" to name them, he began his list with the right "of a citizen of one state to pass through, or to reside in any other state, for purposes of trade, agriculture, professional pursuits, or otherwise."[18]

This would have been an unexceptional textual argument had Justice Washington been interpreting Article IV of the Articles of Confederation. It begins: "The better to secure and perpetuate mutual friendship and intercourse among the people of the different States in this Union, the free inhabitants of each of these States, paupers, vagabonds, and fugitives from justice excepted, shall be entitled to all privileges and immunities of free citizens in the several States; and the people of each State shall have free ingress and regress to and from any other State, ..." But, as noted above, the "ingress and regress" clause had been deleted from the new Constitution.

State and federal judges were undeterred by this omission. Well into the 1860s, this phantom clause was cited for the right to interstate travel as one of the privileges and immunities referenced in the Constitution, often paraphrasing this original language of the Articles of Confederation.[19] Thus, unlike the majority of cases concerning interstate travel, which ultimately rested protection of the right on the need to protect other fundamental rights or national interests, the first references to free travel grounded the right in what was seen to be the very essence of citizenship. These opinions defend that purpose for the clause in strong terms: "No provision in that instrument has so strongly tended to constitute the citizens of the United States one people as this."[20] Although this provides some historical support for the theory advanced in chapter 8, these cases have all but blinked out of existence today.

In 1873, this approach came to an abrupt end with Justice Samuel Miller's opinion for the Court in *The Slaughter-House Cases.* That case is most widely known for the narrow interpretation it gave to the Privileges *or* Immunities Clause of the Fourteenth Amendment. But the case also sealed the fate of any further attempt to use the Privileges *and* Immunities Clause of Article IV in the same way that Justice Washington and others had used it: to find and protect natural rights or rights intrinsic to the concept of citizenship.

Writing for a narrow majority, Justice Miller initially seemed to take a very expansive approach, observing that although the clause in Article IV of the Constitution is a much shortened form of that which appeared in the Articles of Confederation, "[t]here can be but little question that the purpose of both these provisions is the same, and that the privileges and immunities intended are the same in each."[21] Had he stopped there, the right to travel would have found far greater security in this part of the Constitution, for it implied the Hamiltonian logic that the absence of the phrase protecting "ingress and regress" from the Constitution's text was no great matter.[22]

But Justice Miller continued, rejecting the argument that the federal government protected these privileges and immunities if a state should equally restrict the privileges of both its own citizens and citizens of other states within its jurisdiction.[23] With the exception of a few express limitations imposed on the states by the text of the Constitution (in Art. I, § 10), "and a few other restrictions," Justice Miller held that "the entire domain of the privileges and immunities of citizens of the States, as above defined, lay within the constitutional and legislative power of the States, and without that of the Federal government."[24]

The limited restriction placed on states by this "Golden Rule" theory—that states could only "do unto" others as the state would "do unto" its own citizens—would seem to destroy any protection the clause could afford to a right to travel. Under this reading, if a state chose to close its borders to "ingress" by citizens from other states, that restriction would not violate this part of the Constitution (although it may offend other parts) if the closure equally applied to its own citizens' "regress" across those same borders. What is more, this reading seems to belie the assertion a few paragraphs earlier that the essential purpose of the clause was the same as that found in the Articles of Confederation, which quite explicitly did provide for a right of "free ingress and regress" into and out of states.

Justice Miller's phrase, "and a few other restrictions," however, left him some room to protect this particular privilege and immunity (which the Court had already identified). Citing his own opinion in a case called *Crandall v. Nevada,* Miller described the rights of citizens to come to the seat of government and to free access to the nation's seaports as protected by "implied guarantees" of the Constitution that owed its existence to "the Federal government, its National character, its Constitution, or its laws."[25]

In preserving this right, however, Justice Miller did a two-step evasion of the Privileges and Immunities Clause as the source for it. First, Justice Miller's reference to *Crandall* to protect a right to travel was inapposite: that case did not rely on the Privileges and Immunities Clause. Protection of such a right apparently fell into Justice Miller's category of "a few other restrictions" on state sovereignty, in this case the national character and federal structure of the country's government. Second, Justice Miller distinguished the Privileges *and* Immunities Clause in Article IV from the Privileges *or* Immunities Clause of the then new Fourteenth Amendment and held that neither worked a broad check on a state's broad legislative jurisdiction over its citizens. Indeed, in a move caught by Justice Joseph Bradley, one of the dissenters, Miller misquoted Article IV, Section 2 to read, "The citizens of each State shall be entitled to all the privileges and immunities of citizens *of* [rather than *in*] the several States,"[26] and then concluded his discussion of the lack of federal protection for privileges implied by Article IV, which he held resulted from *state* citizenship, with a refusal to define what was protected by Section 1 of the Fourteenth Amendment.[27]

Thus, Justice Miller preserved some federal protection for a right to interstate travel under very limited circumstances, such as access to seaports or federal offices. Not for another 126 years, in a case called *Saenz v. Roe*, would the Court partially revive this definitional argument (*Saenz* is discussed below). Until then, the right to travel lacked an independent textual source for even that small "component." Instead, the right to travel was defended through consequentialist reasoning and contingent argument. The strongest set of cases in that line rested on the Interstate Commerce Clause.

The Interstate Commerce Clause

Cases in this category based the right to engage in interstate travel on the need to protect the workings of the national economy. Thus, these cases are unabashedly consequentialist in their reasoning: the right to travel is protected against infringement by the states because free movement is essential to the promotion of a desirable national objective, interstate commerce. This argument also initially appeared to contain an inherent limitation: it protects a citizen's right to travel within the United States from interference by different *states* but does not protect the citizen from *federal* restrictions imposed on his interstate movement. (As will be seen, however, this argument was rejected in *Saenz v. Roe*.)

Ironically, the first Commerce Clause case to protect travel within the United States concerned not citizens but foreigners. In *The Passenger Cases,* the Court invalidated state laws that taxed passengers arriving in ports on foreign ships.²⁸ The tax was defended on a variety of grounds, including the general police power of the states to maintain quarantine and inspection laws, as well as to protect the public fisc from immigrating paupers and other undesirables.

In a splintered five-to-four decision with each justice writing separately, the Interstate Commerce Clause provided the basis for the majority to hold that these state taxes were unconstitutional as applied to foreign passengers. Concern that such a tax could be extended from foreigners to citizens, or lead to higher rates or more frequent instances of taxation, drove the justices in the majority to conclude that states could not be left to thus regulate their own ports without destroying the advantages of uniform regulation of commerce. That uniformity, protected by granting exclusive power over interstate and foreign commerce to the federal government, was a novelty of the Constitution that the Articles of Confederation lacked.²⁹

Justice Robert Grier found the commercial consequences of such divisive state taxes in conflict with the Constitution. But it was a conflict he saw with Congress's plenary power to regulate interstate commerce, *not* a conflict with a citizen's right (let alone a foreigner's) to move freely within national borders.³⁰ Thus, states could not tax passengers (whether citizens or aliens) for their travel into or among the states of the Union. The unconstitutionality of such state laws was not premised on violation of any right to travel. Rather, such laws infringed the ability of people to engage in commerce and, indeed, to be part of the stream of commerce themselves. Travel was seen as a concomitant aspect of commerce, and therefore perceived to require only derivative protection under the Constitution's protection of interstate commerce. Perhaps that is unsurprising in an era when few had the means to travel for travel's sake and most commerce was local.

Roughly eighty years later, the Great Depression and Dust Bowl led to "the spectacle of large segments of our population constantly on the move," and to the "anti-Okie" legislation that was at issue in *Edwards v. California.*³¹ California sought to stem the flow of indigent migrants by criminalizing the transport of such nonresidents into the state, lest they become public charges.

As in *The Passenger Cases,* the Court considered multiple theories for the unconstitutionality of the state statute, including conflict with the structural principles of federalism and freedom to exercise political pressure, before settling on the Interstate Commerce Clause as the source of the constitutional violation.³² Again, the advantages of exclusive federal regulation of interstate commerce were seen to be at risk if states followed California's "open invitation to retaliatory measures" by sealing themselves off from national economic crises. The Court reaffirmed that transportation of persons was a form of commerce. Fred Edwards' conviction for transporting his destitute brother-in-law out of the Dust Bowl was reversed, but only because of this secondary and contingent protection for a right to travel.[33]

The Structure of Federal Union

The right to travel within the United States has also been recognized to occupy "a position fundamental to the concept of our Federal Union."[34] Even when the right was found implied in a textual provision of the Constitution, such structural arguments have provided further support.[35] An early and clear articulation of this approach came from Chief Justice Taney, dissenting in *The Passenger Cases*. Taney would have upheld the tax at issue there as to foreigners, but not if the case had presented a citizen's claim. Although Taney could not find a right to interstate travel explicit in the Constitution, he found contingent protection for travel in the federal structure of the Union. In a lengthy passage concluding his opinion, he nominally reserved judgment on the rights of citizens to travel:

> Living as we do under a common government, charged with the great concerns of the whole Union, every citizen of the United States, from the most remote States or Territories, is entitled to free access, not only to the principal departments established at Washington, but also to its judicial tribunals and public offices in every State and Territory of the Union. And the various provisions in the Constitution of the United States—such, for example, as the right to sue in a federal court sitting in another State, the right to pursue and reclaim one who has escaped from service, the equal privileges and immunities secured to citizens of other States, and the provision that vessels bound to or from one State to another shall not be obliged to enter and clear or pay duties—all prove that it intended to secure the freest intercourse between the citizens of the different States. For all the great purposes for which the Federal government was formed, we are one people, with one common country.[36]

Justice Taney's reasoning remained as contingent as other arguments for free interstate movement. All of these clauses were merely indications of the Framers' intent "to secure the freest intercourse between the citizens of the different States." Were that not the desired consequence of federal union (for instance, and counterfactually, if the Framers had espoused a more confederal union), the "right to pass and repass through every part of it without interruption" would not necessarily be implied by the various rights Taney enumerated.[37]

Sometimes the Court has been more explicit. Eighteen years after *The Passenger Cases,* the Court examined a tax on all passengers transiting by rail or coach through Nevada.[38] Relying first and foremost on the Court's opinion in *The Passenger Cases* (including Chief Justice Taney's dissent),[39] Justice Miller's opinion for the Court held the statute unconstitutional, but not for infringing any particular federal power (although the Interstate Commerce Clause, Declare War Clause, and Imposts and Duties Clause were all considered).[40] Rather, the tax on passengers was held to interfere with the structure and exercise of federal government across a large territory by making essential conduct (*e.g.,* transporting troops, assembling legislators, or summoning petitioners to federal courts or agencies) dependent on payment of a state tax. As a result, the felt national *need for* citizens to travel and participate in government, much more than the individual *right of* citizens to freedom of movement, drove him to invalidate the tax. As Justice Miller explained for the Court:

> But if the government has these rights on her own account, the citizen also has correlative rights. He has the right to come to the seat of government to assert any claim he may have upon that government, or to transact any business he may have with it. To seek its protection, to share its offices, to engage in administering its functions. He has a right to free access to its sea-ports, through which all the operations of foreign trade and commerce are conducted, to the sub-treasuries, the land offices, the revenue offices, and the courts of justice in the several States, and this right is in its nature independent of the will of any State over whose soil he must pass in the exercise of it.[41]

Justice Miller's conditional language is unmistakable.[42] He refers to "correlative rights,"[43] and does not refer to the citizen's "right" to travel except in the conditional tense.[44] Justice Miller clearly viewed the right to travel, "[i]f the right . . . is one guaranteed to him by the Constitution,"[45] as one based not on its value to the individual citizen but on its utility for the collective good of the nation. The power of the state to tax passengers is held unconstitutional only because "its exercise has affected the functions of the Federal government," not because it infringed the inalienable rights of the citizen to travel.[46]

Indeed, all of the references to the "citizen" are clearly intended to emphasize the importance of an open union of states in which the federal government "has a right," "demands . . . services," and "is entitled" to compel its citizens to travel to meet their obligations to it.[47] The correlative rights of a citizen to come to the seat of government are part of the smooth operations of government, and valued for *that* reason. While the value of such travel to the citizen is obvious, this passage grounds the right itself in contingency, for if the states could tax citizens called to service by their government: "the government itself may be overthrown by an obstruction to its exercise."[48] Thus, the right to travel through states of the union is protected only because a federal union depends on such unimpeded internal channels. Prohibition of a tax on interstate travel was derived from the structural need for successful government, not from any intrinsic value the citizen might obtain in the freedom to roam.

Although Justice Miller refers in *Crandall* to this "right of passing through a State" as one "guaranteed" to the citizen of the United States by the Constitution, it is clear that he was not foreshadowing an interpretation of the Fourteenth Amendment's Privileges or Immunities Clause that would be adopted in *Saenz v. Roe* many years later.[49] Justice Miller repeated this argument in dicta in *The Slaughter-House Cases*. Citing directly to *Crandall v. Nevada,* he recited the "correlative rights" (although without labeling them as such) to travel to the seat of government, conduct business there, access seaports and federal offices and found them "protected by implied guarantees" of the Constitution.[50] Justice Miller wrote (again quoting Chief Justice Taney in *The Passenger Cases*) that these were "privileges and immunities of citizens of the United States which no State can abridge" because this right of citizenship enabled "all the great purposes for which the Federal government was established."[51] No reference was made to the fact that Nevada's tax was not assessed on *citizens,* but on "every person leaving the State." Thus the holding could not have been grounded on a right of citizenship without being fatally underinclusive.

Miller's emphasis on the relationship between the "rights," "demands," and "entitle[ments]" that the federal government could expect a federal union to facilitate over the "correlative rights" of citizens was meant to illustrate a fundamental element of the structural theory of a federal system: the necessity of open, internal borders. These benefit the citizen as much as the visitor. But they are somewhat easier to illustrate through the citizen's relationship with the government than that of the visitor. Indeed, the foreigner (as a person protected by the Fifth Amendment), is guaranteed the right to come to the seat of government and transact business when his or her life, liberty, or property is threatened. But to link a "correlative right" to travel to the advantages it accrues for "the functions of the Federal government" is a risky business. It diminishes the right with a contingency that is rightly absent from what might be termed free-standing rights found in the Constitution, such as the protection against suspension of the privilege of habeas corpus, prohibitions on bills of attainder and ex post facto laws, protections against conviction for treason, and the Bill of Rights itself.

Justice Miller's selective quotation of *Corfield v. Coryell* in his opinion in *The Slaughter-House Cases* supports his contingent view of the right to travel. Justice Washington's *Corfield* opinion included "[t]he right of a citizen of one state to pass through, or to reside in any other state, for purposes of trade, agriculture, professional pursuits, or otherwise" as one of the privileges and immunities found in Article IV that were "more tedious than difficult" to enumerate. Indeed, Justice Washington had asserted that this right numbered among those "in their nature, fundamental" and belonging "of right, to the citizens of all free governments."[52] In *The Slaughter-House Cases*, Justice Miller quotes from that same passage of *Corfield*, but ends his selected citation one sentence short of the reference to travel as a free-standing privilege and immunity![53]

No reference to *Corfield* appears in Justice Miller's earlier opinion for the Court in *Crandall v. Nevada*. Nor would one expect it to appear, since Justice Miller found a limited value to the "correlative right" to travel only to the extent that it buttressed the effective administration of federal government. Justice Bradley, on the other hand, described in his dissenting opinion in *The Slaughter-House Cases* a "perfect" constitutional right to "go to and reside in any State" the citizen chooses, which he found lodged in the Fourteenth Amendment's citizenship clause.[54] Even more telling, Justice Bradley fully cited Judge Washington's argument in *Corfield,* including his reference to "[t]he right of a citizen of one state to pass through, or to reside in any other state, for purposes of trade, agriculture, professional pursuits, or otherwise."[55] The difference between Justice Miller's view of the right to travel and Justice Bradley's view is nothing short of the difference between viewing travel as a contingent right or as an intrinsic, or fundamental, right.

The Privileges or Immunities Clause of the Fourteenth Amendment

Foreshadowing the Court's action fifty-eight years later in *Saenz v. Roe,* Justice Douglas stated his view in *Edwards v. California* that the right to travel was a fundamental right to be found in the Privileges or Immunities Clause of the Fourteenth Amendment.[56] Justice Douglas expressed his revulsion for the contingency implied by attachment to commerce: "I am of the opinion that the right of persons to move freely from State to State occupies a more protected position in our constitutional system than does the movement of cattle, fruit, steel and coal across state lines."[57] Justice Jackson, writing separately, also found the right to "enter any state of the Union, either for temporary sojourn or for the establishment of permanent residence" to be a privilege of citizenship of the United States.[58] This view was shared by many of their brethren on the Court.[59]

In *Saenz v. Roe,* the Court made a surprise return to the Fourteenth Amendment as a source for the right to interstate travel.[60] *Saenz,* decided in 1999, concerned a California law that capped the first twelve months of welfare benefits for new residents at the level of benefits that the applicant would be entitled to receive in the state of previous residence.[61] California's cost-savings measure had federal statutory approval.[62] The case seemed destined for decision on one or more of the standard, if ambiguous, approaches the Court had adopted to assess durational residency requirements in the past.[63]

Writing for the Court, Justice John Paul Stevens sought more precision. He divided the right to travel into three components, each with different constitutional sources of protection. The first component was the "right to enter and leave another state," for which the opinion cited *Edwards v. California* and *U.S. v. Guest* as precedents. Although those cases lodged the right to travel in the Interstate Commerce Clause, Justice Stevens concluded that for purposes of the case before the Court, "we need not identify the source of that particular right in the text of the Constitution."[64] The second component, the right "to be treated as a welcome visitor rather than an unfriendly alien when temporarily present in the second State," the Court found firmly protected by the Privileges and Immunities Clause of Article IV.[65]

Saenz presented an issue concerning the third component, the right "to be treated like other citizens" when a traveler elects to settle in a new state.[66] The Court found protection for this component in Section 1 of the Fourteenth Amendment, relying on both its Citizenship Clause and Privileges or Immunities Clause.[67] That both clauses were employed should not be surprising given that the Court was deciding the constitutionality of a federal matching-grant program. That program provided a benefit (a "privilege") primarily intended for citizens of the United States, while the case was framed in the context of the broader question of a constitutional right to travel.[68] The Citizenship Clause "expressly equates citizenship with residence," which the Court held to mean that this third component of the right to travel "embraces the citizen's right to be treated equally in her new State of residence, [and thus] the discriminatory classification is itself a penalty."[69]

Referencing many of its durational residency opinions, the Court added something new: the federal government's approval of this short-term discrimination against new state residents made no difference to the constitutionality of the state's program. In fact, such federal consent was itself unconstitutional. The reason was that Congress's acquiescence violated the Citizenship Clause: "[T]he protection afforded to the citizen by the Citizenship Clause . . . is a limitation on the powers of the National Government as well as the States."[70] (This conclusion supports my argument in chapter 8 that the Citizenship Clause is a sound source of protection for the right to travel.)

THE RIGHT TO INTERSTATE TRAVEL, long defended for the contingent value it added to other constitutional interests, became a fundamental, albeit unenumerated, right sometimes to be found through the Citizenship and Privileges or Immunities clauses of the Fourteenth Amendment.[71] How did this happen? When did this come to pass? The most straightforward statement of this (new or renewed?) constitutional fact was made by Justice Stewart:

> The Court today does *not* "pick out particular human activities, characterize them as 'fundamental,' and give them added protection. . . ." To the contrary, the Court simply recognizes, as it must, an established constitutional right, and gives to that right no less protection than the Constitution itself demands. . . . This constitutional right . . . is *not* a mere conditional liberty subject to regulation and control under conventional due process or equal protection standards. . . . [I]t is a virtually unconditional personal right, guaranteed by the Constitution to us all.[72]

In his short concurrence, Justice Stewart responded to a provocative dissent by Justice Harlan. The concurrence summarized much but explained little, laying claim to the new ground like an explorer, but without describing how he arrived there. Thus, the right to travel "finds constitutional protection that is quite independent of the [Due Process and Equal Protection Clauses of the] Fourteenth Amendment."[73] This is undoubtedly true, and Stewart's citation here to *The Passenger Cases* is meant to confirm it.

The Court has evaded conclusive statement of where to find the right to interstate travel in the Constitution. In fact, it can and has been found in many parts of the text as well as in the structure of the document as a whole. State action that has been judged to abridge the right of a particular class to travel must pass strict scrutiny to avoid violating the Equal Protection Clause. Or travel restrictions may violate the Interstate Commerce Clause, or the Privileges and Immunities Clause, or principles of federalism, or the Fourteenth Amendment, or some combination of them all. Notwithstanding federal plenary authority over interstate commerce and the unique position of the federal legislature as a body representing the interests of all citizens, the Citizenship Clause also prohibits Congress from complicity in action by states to restrict the right to travel.

The "Mode of Transportation" Cases and the No Fly List

Interstate travel enjoys robust constitutional protection against restrictions by the states, and perhaps if *Saenz* is read for all it is worth, against restrictions by the federal government, too. If that were the end of the case law, one might wonder how the No Fly List could remain a control over domestic air travel. There are, of course, myriad ways that the state or the federal government might be perceived to infringe the right to such travel. When does interference work a violation of this constitutional right? The Supreme Court has said that: "A state law implicates the right to travel when it actually deters such travel, when impeding travel is its primary objective, or when it uses any classification which serves to penalize the exercise of that right."[74] Leaving aside whether the test for a state law would be the same as for a federal law that implicated interstate travel, the No Fly List would surely seem to deter the travel of those watchlisted—it is an outright ban. Indeed, "impeding travel" is its primary objective.

A line of cases has emerged, however, that the Justice Department has embraced in an effort to limit the power of this broad language. These cases hold that "burdens on a single mode of transportation do not implicate the right to interstate travel."[75] Many in fact display a certain mockery of the idea. One court derisively noted that the plaintiff "does not have a fundamental 'right to drive.'"[76] Another court characterized the argument before it as the "feeble claim that passengers have a constitutional right to the most convenient form of travel. That notion, as any experienced traveler can attest, finds no support whatsoever in [the Supreme Court's right of interstate travel jurisprudence] or in the airlines' own schedules."[77]

There are two flaws in using this line of cases to insulate the No Fly List from constitutional challenge. The first is the unstated premise that all modes of travel are interchangeable. Being equivalents, the argument goes, the loss of one sort of vehicle cannot violate the right to travel when so many alternative vehicles exist. If that premise is accepted, it is hard to see how even an absolute ban on a particular mode of transportation could "actually deter[]" travel or have impeding travel as its "primary objective."

This premise is flawed, and grows more so with each advance in transportation technology. The case law, which draws on cases from the 1970s and 1980s, has not kept up with the times. In 1999 and again in 2006, for example, the Ninth Circuit Court of Appeals relied on a 1972 case about profits from charter flights for the conclusion that "burdens on a single mode of transportation do not implicate the right to interstate travel."[78] But modes of transportation are not interchangeable; indeed, they are hardly comparable. In the twenty-first century, many Americans traverse the nation for business or pleasure with the insouciance of a cross-town jaunt. The volume of such traffic is immense, and reliance on this mode of transportation is growing. In September 2010 alone, 777,000 domestic flights were scheduled on U.S. airlines, transporting over fifty million passengers.[79] At the start of this century, air travel accounted for 16 percent of all business trips.[80] Excluding airplanes from the protection of the right to travel is like excluding telephones from the protection for freedom of speech. After all, quills and parchment, though less convenient, are an available mode of communication.

The second flaw is the failure to note a fundamental difference between the state action in this line of cases and the state action that characterizes the No Fly List. In other words, these cases are easily distinguished. The "mode of transportation" cases all concern individuals who oppose generally applicable requirements that are publicly known and openly and neutrally administered. Consider the plaintiffs in those Ninth Circuit cases noted above. Donald Miller refused to provide his Social Security number as part of a required driver's license application.[81] Ronald Tutor was denied permission to land a private jet that exceeded an airport runway's weight limit.[82] The other plaintiffs in this line of cases are no different. Dennis Love lost his driver's license after repeated traffic convictions and after he elected not to pursue an additional postsuspension hearing; the law that took his license away made special exceptions for individual cases of hardship or loss of a commercial license.[83] And in the more recent Second Circuit case, *Town of Southold*, a particular type of ferry service was canceled by a permit requirement adopted after public hearings.[84] In *City of Houston*, the issue was an FAA rule, subject to notice-and-comment rulemaking that affected the entire nation.[85]

Compare these restrictions on travel—all of them individualized, public, and process-oriented cases—with the restriction that the No Fly List imposes. As the stories told in chapters 1 and 2 suggest, and as chapters 6 and 7 detail, the No Fly List accords no process that is remotely comparable to these cases. It operates in total secrecy. And its effect is sudden, unpredictable, and absolute. It is hard to fathom how such case law could sweep away the strict scrutiny required for such a substantial infringement on the right to travel as the No Fly List. And yet *Miller, Southold, Houston,* and cases that cite to them are the source of the argument advanced by the Justice Department in defense of the No Fly List.[86]

2. International Travel

American citizens have a fundamental right to interstate travel that is based on its importance to the life of the individual and the life of the nation. One might expect similar defenses of the right to travel internationally. As the Supreme Court explained in its first substantial case on the question:

> Travel abroad, like travel within the country, may be necessary for a livelihood. It may be as close to the heart of the individual as the choice of what he eats, or wears, or reads. Freedom of movement is basic in our scheme of values.[87]

Nevertheless, international travel has not enjoyed the same protection. At its most supportive, the Supreme Court has assumed that the right to travel abroad may have some limited protection under the liberty prong of the Due Process Clause of the Fifth Amendment.[88] This is the "balancing test" described below. Until recently, the typical case involving a right to international travel was brought to compel the issuance of a passport. In many ways, these Cold War–era cases resonate—in both the fears they articulate and the deference they advocate to executive authority—with more recent cases catalyzed by the "War on Terror."

The Supreme Court's analytical approach to domestic travel weakened its appreciation for the right to foreign travel. The freedom to engage in interstate travel was routinely upheld not for any intrinsic value accorded to it, but as a necessary correlate to other constitutional interests. Few of these interests are advanced by foreign travel. Thus, a right to foreign travel was left without clear foundation and appeared to be deserving of *less* protection under the Constitution. A review of the foundations for domestic travel make this clear.

The Court's first foray into protecting a right to interstate travel, through the Privileges and Immunities Clause of Article IV, had no logical application to foreign travel. That clause was viewed as a means of promoting harmony between the states by requiring the equal treatment of visitors from one state in another. With the waning influence of Justice Washington's natural law approach, the protection it offered shrank. For the citizen interested in travel outside of the United States, the clause offered no support.

In fact, early interstate commerce analysis worked *against* protection for foreign travel. In *The Passenger Cases* and again in *Edwards v. California,* the Court prohibited the states from infringing on the power given to Congress to regulate commerce among the several states. But, at least before the Court decided *Saenz v. Roe* in 1999, these cases gave no protection against restriction of interstate travel by the federal government itself.[89] Indeed, the same would be the case for any attempt to ground protection for foreign travel in the foreign commerce clause. Justice Black observed as much in *Aptheker v. Secretary of State*, emphasizing that his concurring vote was *not* based "on the ground that the Due Process Clause of the Fifth Amendment, standing alone, confers on all our people a constitutional liberty to travel abroad at will."[90] Rather, he explained, "[w]ithout reference to other constitutional provisions, Congress has, in my judgment, broad powers to regulate the issuance of passports under its specific power to regulate commerce with foreign nations."[91] Congress had been quick to do so. Under legislation passed back in 1803, masters of merchant vessels were required to deposit lists identifying the ship's company of seamen in order to receive clearance to depart on a foreign voyage, and could forfeit a substantial bond for failure to return with the same crew.[92] One might consider this the precursor to post-9/11 rules requiring federal clearance for international passengers on commercial aircraft and maritime vessels.

Structural arguments from the nature of federal union present the same problem for foreign travel. In *Crandall v. Nevada,* the Court articulated the need to prevent states from infringing a right to travel to the seat of government, or to a courthouse, or a seaport. The temptation of states to do so was only made possible by a federal form of government. Obviously, that argument has no traction in the context of travel across *international* borders. Once the traveler reaches those seaports, this logic says nothing about the federal authority to limit his foreign travel.

Professor Charles Black's groundbreaking analysis of that decision's structural arguments might at first glance suggest a more hopeful reading. Professor Black argued that the Court had based its holding "on a reciprocal relation between the national government which might have need for its citizens to travel, and their right to travel."[93] Surely the federal (if not state and local) government might have similar need for its citizens to travel abroad—to promote an informed citizenry, extend commerce, expand the arts and sciences, and so forth.

But these might be called luxuries for the state, as compared to necessities: travel to vote, to seek access to courts, to petition at the seat of government for a redress of grievances, and so forth. That is why a structural argument like the one advanced in *Crandall*—just like textual arguments from the Commerce Clause—is shaky ground on which to base a fundamental right to foreign travel. The right to international travel is not really a reciprocal right at all. As argued in chapter 8, the right to international travel is one that citizens qua citizens need to keep their status from descending into something less than citizenship—to become a subject or, worse, an object of the state's hegemony.

Evolution of the Balancing Test

The Supreme Court issued its first opinion on the right to travel abroad in 1958 in *Kent v. Dulles*.[94] In *Kent*, the Secretary of State had denied passports to the petitioners due to their alleged Communist sympathies and affiliations. The Court held that Congress had not delegated the Secretary such authority. Writing for the five-to-four majority, Justice Douglas cited both to *Crandall* and to *Edwards* for the general proposition that "[f]reedom of movement is basic in our scheme of values."[95]

Protection for the right to foreign travel was thus off to a shaky start. Neither of these two cases, of course, concerned international travel. *Crandall* based protection for interstate travel on the structural framework of federal union. *Edwards* upheld its protection under the Interstate Commerce Clause. And neither case conditioned state restrictions on interstate travel on the outcome of a balancing test between the citizen's need to travel and the state's interests. Nevertheless, the *Kent* Court held that these separate interests should be weighed in the context of foreign travel. The Court found the right to foreign travel to be "part of the 'liberty' of which the citizen cannot be deprived without the due process of law under the Fifth Amendment."[96] Just how much a part of liberty, and the "extent to which it can be curtailed," the Court found unnecessary to decide, since the case turned on the statutory question of how much discretion Congress had granted the Secretary of State to make passport decisions under the Immigration and Nationality Act of 1952.[97]

The first case to assess the constitutionality of a statutory restriction on the right to travel came six years later, in *Aptheker v. Secretary of State*.[98] At issue was Section 6 of the Subversive Activities Control Act of 1950, which made it unlawful for any member of a suspect class of Communist organizations to apply for, use, or attempt to use a U.S. passport.[99]

Echoing its analysis in *Kent v. Dulles*, the Court observed that freedom of travel is a constitutionally protected liberty guaranteed by the Fifth Amendment.[100] Although the Court held that Section 6 violated appellants' Fifth Amendment liberty by "too broadly and indiscriminately restrict[ing] the right to travel," the opinion said little about what the parameters of that protected liberty interest in fact were.[101] That analysis was left to the dissenters, who found that Congress only needed (and, in their view, clearly had articulated) a rational basis to find that a worldwide Communist conspiracy threatened national security, that foreign travel was essential to the advancement of that conspiracy's goals, and therefore that the restraint Congress had placed on some citizens' ability to travel was "outweighed by the dangers to our very existence."[102] Criminalizing the attempt of a Communist-conspirator to obtain the travel documents necessary to further the conspiracy's purpose was therefore a "reasonably tailored" remedy.[103]

Thus, although the Court commented that its earlier decision in *Kent* "did not examine the extent to which [the right to travel] can be curtailed," the Court did not meaningfully fill that void in *Aptheker* either.[104] The case had more to do with associational rights than with travel rights. The Court rejected the statute's "irrebutable presumption" that a passport would be used to further the unlawful aims of the illicit organization, which consequently criminalized innocent travel (such as "to read rare manuscripts in the Bodleian Library of Oxford University").[105]

The Court's travel docket grew as Congress and the Executive Branch increasingly sought to prevent travel perceived to interfere with foreign policy goals. In *Zemel v. Rusk,* decided less than a year after *Aptheker,* the Court upheld sections of the Passport Act of 1926 used to prevent citizens from traveling to Cuba.[106] The Court held that the legislation amounted to a grant of authority by Congress to the President to adopt so-called "area restrictions" on the issuance of passports.[107] The Court's assumptions were clearly on display. The regulatory scheme at issue was "designed and administered to promote the security of the Nation."[108]

The Court sought to distinguish its analysis in *Kent v. Dulles,* which rejected passport restrictions based on the "character of the applicant" as unauthorized by Congress, from its acceptance in *Zemel* of Executive Branch authority to prohibit travel by Americans to Cuba. Such area restrictions, the Court argued, were not based on individualized criteria but on "foreign policy considerations affecting all citizens."[109] The Court's summary history of such area restrictions, however, belied any such clear-cut distinction between a passport regime driven by selective assessments of whose travel was deemed friendly to U.S. interests abroad and a purely geography-based policy. Area restrictions were actually riddled with holes and exceptions based on individualized assessments by the Executive Branch of the perceived urgency for such travel.[110]

Nevertheless, this false dichotomy was adopted by the lower courts. The D.C. Circuit was called to consider the appeal of a journalist whose application to renew his passport had been rejected on grounds of his repeated disregard for area restrictions placed on its use. The court's opinion began by noting that "refusal of the passport rested in no part upon Worthy's personal beliefs, writings or character. It was an application of the Secretary of State's general policy of refusing Government sanction to travel by United States citizens in certain areas of the world, presently under Communist control and deemed by him to be trouble spots."[111] The appellant, Dr. William Worthy, had traveled extensively in China and Hungary, both of which were under area restrictions. The court did not consider that by lodging in the Secretary of State a power to *waive* those restrictions for reasons of urgency, exigency, or other exceptions to the rule, Congress made it impossible to say whether a *refusal* to exercise that discretion was a function of a general policy about dangerous areas or an individualized assessment of this particular journalist's "personal beliefs, writings or character."

The D.C. Circuit in *Worthy* also conflated the state's discretion to refrain from issuing travel documents that adversely affected its foreign policy (e.g., such as undesired recognition of a foreign state or unwillingness to extend the state's protection to travelers there) with the state's power to prohibit citizens from traveling to places of their own accord and at their own risk. The court did not avoid hyperbole in assessing the government's interests in denying a passport to visit Communist China or Warsaw Pact Hungary:

> Unless almost the whole of our foreign policy and the titanic domestic burdens being presently borne by our people are devoid of factual foundation, there is presently in the world a deadlock of antagonistic forces, susceptible of erupting into a fatal cataclysm. The capacity of incidents arising from the conduct of individuals to ignite that conflagration is well proven. Worthy says the reasons averred by or available to the Secretary are insufficient to support the restriction of his passport. We hold they are ample.[112]

By "ample," the court meant an ample demonstration of the Executive Branch power to conduct foreign affairs. A travel restriction was at least "an instrument of foreign policy" if not a foreign policy "in and of itself."[113] The court also evoked the Hostage Act as grounds to keep citizens out of "trouble spots" or "danger zones" in which the President would be pressed to come to their rescue.[114] The court then held that the "refusal of the Executive to accord Government approval for a citizen to travel in such a designated area [was] also a foreign affair."[115] The court reasoned:

> History establishes that either the behavior or the predicament of an individual citizen in a foreign country can bring into clash, peaceful or violent, the powers of his own government and those of the foreign power. This is a fact, not a theory. The nub of the problem at bar revolves about a fact, not a suppositious theorem. The acts of individuals do cause clashes; the prevention of such acts does prevent clashes. Such clashes, whether diplomatic or military, involve 'foreign affairs' . . . In foreign affairs, especially in the intimate posture of today's world of jets, radio, and atomic power, an individual's uninhibited yen to go and to inquire may be circumscribed. A blustering inquisitor avowing his own freedom to go and do as he pleases can throw the whole international neighborhood into turmoil.[116]

The court was confident that the President possessed the power to act in loco parentis for American citizens willing to risk danger abroad.[117] What is more, as the court had previously explained, citizens are "potential matches" in an "international tinderbox."[118]

The D.C. Circuit refused to acknowledge that this was a predicament of the state's own design. Were individuals permitted to depart without a passport, or with one that did not claim to provide the protection of the state, such foreign policy interests would be far less implicated. And if a foreign power demanded recognition by the United States in the form of a passport requirement for entry into its territory, then U.S. refusal on foreign policy grounds would not infringe the travel rights of its citizens, whose inability to travel to such places would then be due to the demands of a foreign government not their own. (Chapter 4 charts the evolution of the passport as a travel control device now adopted by virtually all states.)

In a sense, then, it was an easy case for the Supreme Court to hold that Philip Agee, a rogue ex-CIA operative who threatened to reveal the identities of secret agents abroad, could be deprived of his passport notwithstanding the absence of explicit statutory language conferring that power on the Secretary of State.[119] Agee's conduct, though surprisingly not illegal at the time,[120] was deemed so extreme as to warrant revocation of his passport.[121]

Thus, the right to enter and leave the country was protected only by the requirements of Fifth Amendment due process.[122] The process due to someone whose travel abroad the state wished to restrict was first described as "a function not only of the extent of the governmental restriction imposed, but also of the extent of the necessity for the restriction."[123] In *Zemel v. Rusk,* restrictions on the right to travel to Cuba were upheld because the area restriction was held to be narrowly drawn ("Cuba is the only area in the Western Hemisphere controlled by a Communist government")[124] as well as urgently needed (since "the Cuban missile crisis of October 1962 preceded the filing of appellant's complaint by less than two months").[125]

It is strange to consider that the right should be deemed one protected under the shield of the Fifth Amendment, which extends protection beyond citizens to any person within the jurisdiction of the United States. Perhaps this is because international travel cases have almost always raised a controversy over passports, the issuance of which has never been limited solely to citizens. But locating protection under the Due Process Clause, not the Citizenship Clause, diverted attention from the essential characteristics of the relationship between citizen and state in a democratic republic.

The Separation of Powers and Foreign Travel

The Executive Branch has long argued that its control of foreign travel is a natural, necessary extension of its constitutional authority over foreign affairs and national security. Indeed, the first secretaries of state assumed the discretion to issue passports under their own signatures without any statutory authority at all.[126] Thus, less than a month after the first Supreme Court opinion challenged this heretofore unbridled authority of the Secretary of State to issue passports, President Eisenhower sent an urgent message to Congress seeking clear statutory authority to do so. He made clear in his message, however, that "[s]ince the earliest days of our Republic," this authority derived first from the President's responsibility to conduct foreign affairs, with only "additional statutory authority" supplied by Congress.[127]

Congressional grants of authority to control travel, until recently, were explicitly linked to wartime necessity and automatically terminated upon the cessation of hostilities. Thus, late in the War of 1812, Congress forbade citizens from crossing into enemy-held territory, or even linger near the frontier, without a passport.[128] The statute contained a clause providing that it would continue in force "during the continuance of the present war between the United States and Great Britain, and no longer."[129] Likewise, during World War I, Congress granted the President the power "when the United States is at war" to make it unlawful for citizens to depart or enter, or attempt to depart or enter, the United States without a valid passport.[130]

The Supreme Court has frequently accepted with relatively little scrutiny the political branches' assertion that restrictions on travel were necessary to protect national security. Thus, in *Zemel v. Rusk,* for example, the Court held that "the Secretary has justifiably concluded that travel to Cuba by American citizens might involve the Nation in dangerous international incidents, and that the Constitution does not require him to validate passports for such travel."[131] That is true as far as it goes, but it blurs the distinction between the *demand* of a citizen for the protection of his government while abroad, and the *right* of the citizen to assume the risks of traveling even to places where his own government has urged him (on the grounds of his own safety or the government's own preferences) not to go. While the former protection may well be within the discretion of the government to deny, the latter freedom should be left to the individual autonomy of the citizen. The citizen is not a pawn on a geopolitical chessboard, but free (because of that status as citizen) to choose to come and go as he pleases.

The *Rusk* Court implied that because the President was required by the Hostage Act "to 'use such means, not amounting to acts of war, as he may think necessary and proper' to secure the release of an American citizen unjustly deprived of his liberty by a foreign government," the citizen could not realistically claim that his travel was solely his own private affair.[132] The prodigal citizen might entangle his government in dangerous, embarrassing, or expensive diplomacy by bumbling into a dangerous country whose leaders were either eager to hold an American citizen for ransom or powerless to stop those who wished to do so. But the statute granted the President the discretion to use such means short of acts of war "as he may think necessary and proper" in that circumstance. It is entirely consonant with that congressional directive for the President to find that when a citizen knowingly or recklessly travels into an area in which the Secretary of State has issued a warning not to travel, he or she does so at his or her own peril.[133] Freedom is a two-way street.

Nevertheless, the view persisted that the decision to issue a passport should be left to the discretion of the Executive Branch. This argument was based on the claim that the passport, which indicates the Secretary of State's request to foreign officials to assist the American traveler, is an aspect of foreign policy and national security. A judicial order to an executive official to issue a passport would violate the separation of powers because it would tread on this authority. Interestingly enough, although U.S. passports contain language entreating the assistance of foreign officials, the statutory definition of the passport nowhere references this function.[134] The citizen of the American democratic republic does not travel under the sponsorship of the sovereign. Why it should nevertheless appear that she does is the subject of chapter 4.

CHAPTER FOUR

A Brief History of the Passport

To fully appreciate the power that Mrs. Shipley once held, one must understand the ever-sharper tool of control she wielded so authoritatively: the passport. From the moment of its creation, the U.S. Government issued passports.[1] Their original form and purpose, however, would not be recognized by travelers in Mrs. Shipley's day or our own.[2] And although passports are no longer the method of travel control that they once were, a survey of how passports changed is a useful addition to the argument of this book. That history shows that a state certificate of modest value, originally issued for the convenience of travelers, gradually changed into a license by which the state could prohibit travel altogether. This story is told here and in chapter 5. Change happened gradually, did not affect the outward appearance of the document itself, and was catalyzed by technological change as much as by changes in politics and society. The same tale can be told about government watchlists. How those influences affected the development of the No Fly List is the subject of chapters 6 and 7.

Gaillard Hunt, the U.S. Passport Clerk at the end of the nineteenth century, began his monograph on the American passport by noting that the word originally meant the very opposite of its current understanding. "Passport" came from the French *passer* and *port,* literally "to pass through a port or harbor." The term was intended to identify a document that granted the *foreigner* permission to pass into or out of one's ports.[3] Transit across the frontiers of many countries obliged the foreigner "to obtain a new passport at the boundaries of each nationality, and each national authority might subject him to an examination to ascertain his character and citizenship."[4] To avoid such inconvenience, the practice emerged whereby one's own country provided the passport in which to affix visas from the countries through which the traveler sought to pass. Such visas thus served an authenticating function, indicating that the passport to which they were affixed had been evaluated in advance to the satisfaction of a representative of the sovereign in whose name they were issued.

Thus, initially, a passport was issued by the sovereign authority of the country the traveler sought to enter, not the traveler's own country. In times of war, this permission was sought by enemy aliens, not citizens: "In the strict nomenclature of international law, passports were classed with those documents known as safe conducts or letters of protection, by which the person of an enemy might be rendered safe and inviolable."[5] It was precisely this meaning that described General Washington's issuance of a passport to allow the ship *Amazon* to deliver supplies to British and German prisoners of war.[6] When the supplies were seized in Pennsylvania by "sundry persons" enforcing a state licensing law, it set up a preconstitutional debate about the proper breadth of the central government's powers.[7]

Outside of wartime, early American border controls were extremely lax.[8] "In time of peace a law-abiding American citizen has always been free to leave the country without the permission of the Government; and, under the same conditions, foreigners have always been permitted to travel or sojourn within our boundaries without a permissive document."[9] Indeed, at the start of the twentieth century, international travel was generally indistinguishable as a matter of law from any other travel. With only a few exceptions, passports were not required for entry into most foreign states.[10] This may be due to the small number of people who possessed the means to travel overseas; international travel was the province only of the elite and the desperate.[11] As Professor Chafee observed:

> To jump on a steamer in Boston and go to Liverpool was as easy as boarding the night-boat for New York. During the horse and buggy age, in which I was happily brought up, a passport was unknown except for Baedeker's remark that it might help you get permission to look at a private collection of paintings. The only country which required passports was Czarist Russia, and few Americans wanted to visit that despotic domain.[12]

The U.S. Government even lacked monopoly control over the practice of issuing passports.[13] State and local officials as modestly ranked as a notary public issued them.[14] As one can imagine, recognition of these documents by foreign officials was spotty at best. This tended to frustrate federal officials who feared for the authenticity and value of the passports they issued. Only in 1856 did Congress respond to this chaos by passing the first statute authorizing the Secretary of State alone to issue passports.[15] The division of the State Department tasked to do this employed only ten people, and "most of the year time hung heavily on their hands."[16] It took ten more years to limit issuance of passports only to U.S. citizens.[17]

More than one Attorney General rendered the opinion that these statutes created no right to a passport should the state decline to issue one.[18] But since few states required passports, few people cared. Only in times of war did the United States attempt to restrict foreign travel by its citizens. Such restrictions were almost always imposed by act of Congress.[19] It is not surprising, therefore, that the Executive Branch "claimed unbridled discretion over the issuance of passports" during this time.[20] The need for regulation, after all, was minimal: few people traveled abroad and the passport itself was really nothing more than a rather formal note of introduction, occasionally a convenience, rarely a necessity.

In this milieu, in which passports were not *required*, the passport could be considered a genuine instrument of foreign affairs issued by one government to request the assistance or protection of another government for its citizens abroad. Eventually, the passport would shed this purpose, but its foreign policy gloss lingered. This disconnect between reality and its misperception gave courts a basis to uphold passport denials on the grounds that foreign policy decisions were political questions that a court was ill-suited to adjudicate.

1. World War I

The passport radically changed during the "Short Twentieth Century."[21] Passports slowly became licenses for international travel. At first, the pressure was external: European countries engulfed in World War I demanded that foreigners present passports for travel through their war-readied ports and war-wearied provinces.[22] Foreshadowing events in the United States, these provisions started as temporary measures limited to areas affected by the outbreak of war but gradually became permanent requirements for all travel anywhere in the state.[23] Thus, although passports were not required for travel by American citizens under U.S. law, they became a requirement for travel due to the laws of an increasing number of other countries.

The laissez-faire approach to travel before the war resulted in substantial problems for Americans without passports who found themselves trapped abroad at the outbreak of war. These travelers faced difficulties obtaining passports for travel through warring Europe back to their American homes.

American officials worked under pressure to quickly repatriate their fellow citizens. At the same time, these officials faced a rash of passport frauds perpetrated by enemy agents. The two problems were symbiotic. This may have accounted for the delay in imposing restrictions, which did not emerge until eighteen months into the war.[24]

The Travel Control Act, as it was popularly known, authorized the President to limit the entry into and departure from the United States of both aliens and citizens alike.[25] As one might expect, the President was given a relatively free hand to control the travel of aliens.[26] But Congress was more careful to limit executive discretion when it came to citizens, even during wartime. First, the power was delegated by statute, which implied that Congress could revoke the power in the same way. Second, the power was delegated for use only when the United States was "at war." Third, even in the midst of war, the power could not be used until a presidential proclamation expressed the written finding that public safety required exercise of such controls. Only after such public proclamation did it become unlawful for any citizen to depart from or enter, or attempt to depart from or enter, the United States without a valid passport.[27]

The statute worked just as intended. President Wilson issued a proclamation implementing these restrictions on August 8, 1918, in which he ordered that no citizen would receive a passport "entitling him to leave or enter the United States, unless it shall affirmatively appear that there are adequate reasons for such departure or entry and that such departure or entry is not prejudicial to the interests of the United States."[28] By executive order, the President established a system of travel controls over all persons seeking to enter or depart from the United States.[29] Unless and until the appropriate official was satisfied, inter alia, that the passport holder's "departure or entry is not prejudicial to the interests of the United States," the individual stayed put.[30] As the State Department's confidential guidance document on administering the law instructed: "Passport of citizens known to be disloyal or reasonably suspected of disloyalty should not be verified [an official act that rendered passports valid for return to the United States] without authority from the Department of State."[31] Satisfaction was achieved by interrogation. "If, as the result of such questioning and examinations, the Control Officer decides that the entry or departure of the holder of the passport or permit would be prejudicial to the interests of the United States, such person shall not be allowed to enter or depart."[32]

The statute privileged the foreign interests of the United States over the private interests of the citizen. That is hardly surprising, given the history of the passport. What was once merely an identity document of no legal value was becoming what Attorney General Hoar described in 1869 as "a certificate of citizenship, and that person receiving it is certified to be entitled to such protection as the Government can give to its citizens in foreign countries."[33] If the passport entitled the bearer to the protection of his government when abroad, then the government had an interest in its careful issuance to travelers worthy of such protection going to lands where such protection was possible. At that time, however, passports were still certificates, not licenses. Their use was optional, not required. Even after entering the First World War, Congress felt strongly enough about the importance of freedom of movement to heavily encumber the President's power to control it. While the urgency of war might necessitate its infringement, the expression of responsibility made in a public proclamation with written findings was meant to safeguard this freedom in the long run. But the utility of such travel controls had not gone unnoticed by the Executive Branch, as Attorney General Knox had earlier observed: "Circumstances are conceivable which would make it most inexpedient for the public interests for this country to grant a passport to a citizen of the United States. For example, if one of the criminal class, an avowed anarchist for instance, were to make such application, the public interests might require that his application be denied."[34]

The Travel Control Act of 1918 was the first significant step in the conceptual move to the Internal Security Act of 1950, which finally changed travel restrictions from temporary controls in wartime to permanent controls in what amounted to a perpetual state of emergency in peacetime. The distance between these two approaches was shortened by the shift in thinking about the passport, from a diplomatic letter of introduction to a license to control mass travel. As will be seen, long after Congress rescinded the Internal Security Act and the fears that motivated its passage have been largely forgotten, current travel restrictions are possible because of the lingering conceptual remnants that remain.

2. Between the Wars

The Travel Control Act and Wilson's implementing orders worked a sea-change in the nature of American travel. As David Riesman observed, "After the War, in this field as in others, a desperate and doomed attempt was made to return to pre-war 'normalcy.'"[35] In 1917, when the passport was optional, the number of passports issued was 37,615.[36] By 1920, that number had more than quadrupled, to 160,488.[37] More significantly, the idea had been planted by law and practice that the State Department must ultimately decide whether the traveler's reasons were "sufficiently adequate to warrant issuing his passport."[38] The war had indelibly grafted the passport to the idea of international travel. Regulation of the one was regulation of the other. This bureaucratic shift was noted by the American poet Ezra Pound, who recalled his wandering through a prewar Europe that "still 'groaned under tyranny'" where he "went on foot into its by-ways for sixteen years with no 'papers,' that is to say with no brass checks, no government's petty officials' permission, nothing in fact, but . . . an unstamped membership card to the Touring Club de France." But those days were gone:

> The war produced, if not a new ruling class, at least a new zealous bossiness. I had my first meeting with the new civic order during the armistice. I was living in London. I was told that I "could not go to France unless I had business." I naturally had business. I received a lot of other improbable information from the under-sub-vice-assistant. My wife could not possibly accompany me unless she were ill. I naturally produced doctors' certificates. I could not move about in France; I must go to one place and stay there. At this point I was rescued by an elderly intelligent official from another department who took two hours off and swore to several contradictory statements in a manner showing great familiarity with the mind-ersatz of officialdom.[39]

By November 1919, the American business press could advise its readers that "restrictions on travelers have been lightened bit by bit," with passport applicants "no longer required to furnish documentary proof of the urgent necessity of the contemplated trip."[40] Congress ultimately made use of the sunset provision it had placed on these controls, passing a joint resolution in 1921 declaring that the law and its implementing materials should be "construed and administered as if such war . . . terminated on the date when this resolution becomes effective."[41] The Executive Branch complied.[42]

Between 1921 and 1941, a citizen did not require a passport for exit from the United States.[43] This did not mean an end to passports, however, or their regulation. In 1926, Congress passed the Passport Act, which repealed the first statute regulating passports (the 1856 law that begat § 4075 of the Revised Statutes) and delegated exclusive authority to the Secretary of State to issue and validate passports "under such rules as the President shall designate and prescribe."[44] The default duration for a passport was two years, although the Secretary could limit or lengthen this period within certain statutory bounds.[45] This was not rollback enough for free spirits like Ezra Pound, who was willing to concede that war and armistice left Europe "confessedly, in a mess, and errors might be exceptions. But what in heaven's name has that temporary confusion to do with 1924, 1925, 1926, 1927? What has it to do with the unending boredom of waiting an hour, a half-hour, three hours, in countless bureaus, for countless useless visas, identities, folderols?"[46] Pound was not alone: the editorial pages of the *New York Times, Boston Globe, Baltimore Sun,* and *Newark News* all called for the abolition of the passport.[47]

It was not to be. In 1930, a high-water mark was reached: 203,174 passports were issued.[48] In New York alone, there were over 51,000 applications for new or renewed passports.[49] Although that number dropped substantially in 1933 (to 106,991 passports issued), it rose and fell in 1937 (168,016) and 1938 (134,747).[50]

With the war over, and with it the end of a mandatory passport regime, what explains the proliferation of passport applications? The system had taken on a life of its own, for even if the United States no longer required its citizens to carry passports to depart or return home, other countries required passports in which to stamp entry and exit visas to cross *their* borders. Europe, in particular, retained the passport rules adopted there during the Great War, tinkering at the margins to create passports for refugees abandoned by their homelands rather than abolishing controls no longer justified by war or famine.[51] States realized the power passport requirements gave to them over both foreigner and citizen alike (not to mention the revenue raised by visa and passport fees). This realization was not limited to non-democratic regimes like Soviet Russia or Nazi Germany, which wielded the passport as one more tool for control of suspect subjects. Nearly all states succumbed to the temptation to use passports to restrict travel for political purposes. Whatever value more precise legislative instruments of foreign policy might offer (such as arms embargoes or criminal sanctions for foreign enlistment), governments worldwide seized on the passport as a most useful, if blunt, tool of social control. Reaction to the Spanish Civil War provides a good example:

> All the great powers of Europe declared passports to be invalid for travel in Spain. Although the United States was not a member of the Non-Intervention Committee, the State Department, on its own motion, stamped all passports "not valid for Spain," required an affidavit from applicants for passports that they did not intend to go to Spain, and refused passports altogether to any who it believed would go to Spain in defiance of the restriction.[52]

The international passport regime that war introduced, peace could not repeal.

By executive order, President Roosevelt issued rules under the 1926 Passport Act only in 1938.[53] Only those owing allegiance to the United States ("whether citizens or not") could be granted or issued a passport, which occurred only following the swearing of an oath of allegiance before an official lawfully able to hear it.[54] Each citizen or a resident of an insular possession of the United States, was obliged to indicate on his passport application a detailed description of his proposed itinerary. This included the port of departure, name and sailing date of the outgoing vessel, the countries to be visited and the object of each visit (subject to the Secretary's discretion to demand "satisfactory documentary evidence" of this object), and the expected return to the United States.[55]

Even if all this and other information were provided and the oath of allegiance sworn, the President authorized the Secretary of State "in his discretion to refuse to issue a passport, to restrict a passport for use only in certain countries, to restrict it against use in certain countries, to withdraw or cancel a passport already issued, and to withdraw a passport for the purpose of restricting its validity or use in certain countries."[56] Secretary of State Hull issued Departmental Order No. 749 the same day as President Roosevelt's executive order.[57] The departmental order made extension of a passport that had been restricted for a period less than two years dependent upon the express authorization of the Department (not its passport agents, diplomatic or consular officers in the field).[58] Section VII.25 of the order stated, "An applicant for the renewal or extension of his passport may be required to submit satisfactory documentary evidence of the necessity and purpose of his journey abroad."[59]

Of course, one may ask just how onerous a burden or intrusion into the privacy of the traveler this really was if passports were not required by law for entry or departure other than in time of war and presidentially proclaimed emergency. In many cases, perhaps not much of a burden at all. But as war clouds gathered, the value of an American passport increased. The point is that the new understanding of the passport remained in place while these regulations sat dormant. Like Chekhov's gun, lying on the table in Act I, it was only a matter of time before they were put to their intended use.

War broke out across Europe on September 1, 1939, with the German invasion of Poland. Declarations of war by France and the United Kingdom against Germany soon followed. How could the United States protect its citizens abroad? What was to be done with those Americans who were abroad without passports who sought to return, now out of or through belligerent countries? Should applications for passports to travel to places of present or perceived imminent danger be granted?

American policymakers wanted to preserve American neutrality. This was reflected in the new passport rules. Thus, travel was prohibited aboard ships flagged to the belligerent nations in much of the North Atlantic and other waters in or bordering Europe.[60] On September 4, a day before President Roosevelt issued a proclamation regarding U.S. neutrality,[61] Secretary of State Cordell Hull issued Departmental Order No. 811. The order prohibited the use of any issued passport for travel from the United States to Europe unless the passport were resubmitted to the State Department for validation. The likelihood of validation (which expired in six months or less) depended on the ability of the would-be traveler "to submit documentary evidence concerning the imperativeness of his proposed travel."[62]

How much these regulations truly focused on the foreign policy goal of maintaining neutrality was not always clear. Some questioned the favoritism and preferential treatment that came with the power to grant exceptions to the general rule. Both by the terms of the regulations and their actual implementation, the State Department was more receptive to business travelers than those wishing to engage in travel for other reasons.[63] The ability of women and children to travel on the passports of husbands and fathers, previously a relatively easy matter, now required special pleading.[64] As one scholar contemporaneously observed: "It is not easy to discover the ways in which the Act works out in practice. Buyers and commercial travelers seem to have no trouble in making the necessary documentary showing, . . . But personal needs of the greatest importance have in some cases been thought not 'imperative necessity.' American women married or engaged to French or British citizens who wished to join their husbands or fiancés in Europe have found their passports withheld. . . . Journalists have complained that the State Department practice of limiting passports to one or two countries prevents them from reporting effectively."[65] The regulations warned of criminal penalties for false or misleading statements made to evade these regulations.[66] Those who evaded validation or disregarded limits placed on the validated passport were also warned that "the protection of the United States may be withheld from him while he is abroad," and prosecution may follow his return to the United States.[67] Other regulations required American citizens "to surrender their passports upon their arrival in the United States. The passports are sent direct by the immigration authorities to this Department, where they are filed pending a request for their return for further use."[68]

The Neutrality Act was a joint resolution of Congress approved on November 4, 1939. As the short title implied, and the full title categorically announced, the objective was to keep the United States out of war.[69] The failure to achieve that objective in April 1917 was in no small part due to submarine warfare against American merchant fleets and passenger lines in the Atlantic Ocean.[70] Therefore, the act generally prohibited American vessels from carrying "any passengers or any articles or materials" to any states proclaimed by the President to be at war (with steep criminal penalties for any violation).[71] American citizens and vessels were also prohibited (with equivalent penalties) from proceeding into or through designated combat areas.[72] Nor could Americans travel on vessels flagged to designated belligerent states.[73] The exceptions were sufficiently complicated and evanescent to render busy and powerful the agency delegated authority to issue restrictions, rules, and regulations.

That agency was the Department of State, which was well aware of its power and well-versed in wielding it. As described in a summary of Mrs. Shipley's office prepared in support of a recommendation that she receive the Medal for Merit, the act transformed the Passport Division into "a travel control office."[74] After passage of the Neutrality Act,

> [T]here were areas to which Americans generally could not go and routes by which they could not travel. The regulation of travel was enforced mainly through the withholding of passport facilities or the limitation of the passport as to time or countries and waters in or over which it was not valid for travel. But the law and regulations permitted certain exceptions and it was Mrs. Shipley's responsibility to ascertain when the travel fell within an exception and to document accordingly.[75]

This power was augmented by the Nationality Act of 1940.[76] Under the act, both native-born and naturalized American citizens (and persons seeking merely to be considered "nationals" but not citizens) lived under additional restraints on their travel and stays in foreign countries.[77] Mrs. Shipley enforced these limitations, too.[78]

3. World War II

Six months before Pearl Harbor, Congress took the next step toward peacetime travel control. The Travel Control Act of 1918 had required that there exist *both* a state of war *and* a presidential proclamation of the need to preserve public safety.[79] This conjunctive protection was weakened by changing it into a disjunctive statement. Now, *either* a state of war *or* the existence of a national emergency (which the President had already proclaimed the previous month) would suffice to impose passport controls on a citizen's travel.[80]

President Roosevelt issued a proclamation and regulations under the amended act in mid-November 1941.[81] The Secretary of State was delegated authority to act under the statute.[82] Ten days later, Secretary Hull issued Departmental Order No. 1003 establishing regulations that limited travel by American citizens and nationals by itinerary, mode of transport, and purpose of travel.[83] Thus, travel without a passport was strictly prohibited to "any foreign country or territory in the Eastern Hemisphere."[84] Travel in the Western Hemisphere was somewhat more lenient, allowing passportless travel to Canada, Mexico, and selected Caribbean islands, but retaining restrictions on travel in the North Atlantic established under the Neutrality Act.[85] Merchant seamen and members of the military were specially excepted. An attempt by a citizen or national to enter the United States without a valid passport would result in the traveler's immediate detention.[86]

Besides limitations on where Americans could travel and for what purposes, there were also procedural checks established by the system of passport controls itself. Mere possession of a passport was now sufficient to depart the United States. But to enter or return to the United States, the passport must have been "verified" by an American diplomatic or consular official in the last foreign country from which the traveler departed.[87] Through foreign service officers stationed worldwide, the State Department had the power to "verify, review, amend, extend, and cancel" passports.[88] The Department also retained the authority to refuse to permit the departure from or return to the United States by a citizen or person owing allegiance to the United States whose travel the Secretary or his representative considered prejudicial to the interests of the United States, even if a passport had already been issued to the person.[89] This was in keeping with the penultimate, elastic clause of Secretary Hull's order, preserving his discretion "to refuse to issue a passport, to restrict its use to certain countries, to withdraw or cancel a passport already issued, or to withdraw a passport for the purpose of restricting its validity or use in certain countries."[90]

This authority, in turn, was delegated to the chief of the Passport Division.[91] As the State Department itself later characterized the purpose of the legislation, it was "to curb unnecessary travel and particularly to prevent the travel of irresponsible people, adventurers, saboteurs, criminals, and others who might harm the United States or its Allies, and to make the limited transportation facilities available only to persons whose reasons for travel were legitimate and important to the war effort."[92]

As the war continued, control of travel expanded. Mrs. Shipley thought that the "exigencies of the present international situation" made it desirable "to document all American citizens who travel between the United States and Mexico."[93] In October 1943, Acting Secretary of State Stettinius issued Departmental Order No. 1207, which modified Order No. 1003 (issued in November 1941). No longer would travel across the U.S.-Mexican border be uncontrolled. A valid "card of identification" was required of citizens desiring to make frequent crossings. Cards remained valid for two years, unless the issuing officer had reason to limit the card to a shorter period.[94]

Mrs. Shipley's discovery of the utility of passport controls was not her exclusive epiphany. Her counterparts in governments throughout the world recognized their same value, as George Orwell lamented in words that echoed Ezra Pound's jeremiad almost twenty years earlier. Even discounting the effects of world war, Orwell complained that the counterintuitive effect of technological advances like the airplane had been "to make travel enormously more difficult" as countries threw up more and more bureaucratic barriers to free movement to replace those that had been broken down by new inventions.[95]

4. The Cold War

The conclusion of World War II and the gradual return to the peacetime conduct of foreign affairs resulted in only a superficial lifting of travel restrictions. On the one hand, the number of countries to which American citizens were now permitted to travel grew and grew with the end of the war. On the other hand, the premise had been firmly implanted in the minds of both government officials and the traveling public that the United States had the authority to deny or permit travel based on the state's concerns about the nature of the traveler or his intended itinerary. In 1951, *Reader's Digest* published a glowing story about Mrs. Shipley that described without criticism (if it did not endorse) her power: "No American can go abroad without her authorization. She decides whether the applicant is entitled to a passport and also whether he would be a hazard to Uncle Sam's security or create prejudice against the United States by unbecoming conduct."[96]

Thus, countries could be added or removed from the list of permitted destinations by government notice. Such decisions were sometimes grounded in paternalism—the United States had determined that it was not "in a position to accord normal protection" to travelers in some country, for example, due to the absence of a diplomatic mission there.[97] Other times, the decision was based in a calculation of realpolitik or concern that rambunctious, naive, or contrarian travelers could interfere with American foreign policy interests. In the metaphor of one court, such persons were dangerous matches who could be kept by the state out of the international tinderbox.[98]

In the early 1950s, travel controls were broadened again in order to assist in the fight against the international Communist conspiracy. Congress passed the Internal Security Act of 1950 over President Truman's veto. The act contained two titles, the Subversive Activities Control Act and the Emergency Detention Act.[99] Congress had concluded that Communism was "a world-wide revolutionary movement whose purpose it is, by treachery, deceit, infiltration into other groups (governmental and otherwise), espionage, sabotage, terrorism, and any other means deemed necessary, to establish a Communist totalitarian dictatorship in the countries throughout the world through the medium of a world-wide Communist organization."[100] Congress noted the evils of totalitarianism and the manifest success in "numerous foreign countries" of the Communist Party and "the most powerful existing Communist dictatorship" (i.e., the Union of Soviet Socialist Republics) in establishing "Communist totalitarian dictatorships, and threaten[ing] to establish similar dictatorships in still other countries."[101]

The Subversive Activities Control Act of 1950 required Communist organizations to register with a new entity known as the Subversive Activities Control Board.[102] Once the Board issued a final order to such an organization to register itself, it became unlawful for any member of the organization to apply for, renew, use, or attempt to use a passport.[103] If convicted of violating this section, a person faced a fine of up to $10,000 and/or up to five years imprisonment.[104] These prohibitions and penalties were necessary, Congress found, because of the unusual transnational nature of the Communist menace: "Due to the nature and scope of the world Communist movement, with the existence of affiliated constituent elements working toward common objectives in various countries of the world, travel of Communist members, representatives, and agents from country to country facilitates communication and is a prerequisite for the carrying on of activities to further the purposes of the Communist movement."[105]

The act, although draconian in its restrictions and penalties, required no great leap from existing theory or practice in the administration of passports. Since passports were not held to be a *right* of citizenship, and since the passport was seen as obliging government protection for its holder, someone whose travel was not only contrary to the interests of the United States but actually in defiance of them could expect no help from the state. The act itself made this clear in its congressional findings: "In the United States those individuals who knowingly and willfully participate in the world Communist movement, when they so participate, in effect repudiate their allegiance to the United States, and in effect transfer their allegiance to the foreign country in which is vested the direction and control of the world Communist movement."[106] From the perspective of the U.S. Government, if a passport was desired by a Communist, he or she was welcome to seek one from the Union of Soviet Socialist Republics.

In 1952, the McCarran Act expanded the justification for travel controls to include either war or "*any* national emergency proclaimed by the President."[107] It was now unlawful during such times for a citizen to depart from or enter the United States, or attempt to depart or enter, without a valid passport.[108] By 1978, all conditional language on imposing travel controls was struck out. Neither a state of war nor a presidentially proclaimed national emergency was necessary to initiate temporary travel controls. The controls were permanently installed for all peacetime travel.[109]

It is not hyperbole to say that "[o]ne of the first casualties of the Cold War was freedom of travel."[110] The growing power of the United States in the second half of the twentieth century corresponded with an almost complete inversion of the original meaning of a passport. The passport ceased to be merely a document that provided evidence of the bearer's identity and a request for comity and aid to citizens abroad. The passport had become a license issued by a government permitting its own citizens to travel abroad. As the Supreme Court observed, it emerged as a device to restrict the liberty to leave one's own country and to monitor citizens in foreign lands.[111]

III • *Policy*

CHAPTER FIVE

Origins: The Extraordinary Mrs. Shipley

To describe Mrs. Shipley's career is to restate the legal history in chapter 4 in human terms. It is also to tell the story of a remarkably talented woman who rose to great power in male-dominated corridors of power.

Ruth Bielaski was born in 1885 in Montgomery County, Maryland, the daughter of a Methodist minister, and the granddaughter of a Civil War hero and friend of Abraham Lincoln.[1] She had a high school education and what was then called "business training" before she took a competitive civil service exam at age eighteen to qualify for a position copying assignments of patent rights in the Patent Office.[2] She began there in 1903, where she worked as a clerk until she married in 1909.[3] She spent several years in the Canal Zone, where her husband held a government post. His ill health returned them to Washington, but it was the ill wind blowing through Europe in August 1914 that landed her in the State Department's Passport Division.

Mrs. Shipley was appointed a clerk on August 25, 1914, just as World War I was beginning in Europe.[4] Thus, her career began just as modern travel controls did. She seems to have quickly become the protégée of then Second Assistant Secretary of State A. A. Adee, whose portfolio at the time covered passports.[5] In time she became Assistant Chief of the Office of Coordination and Review.[6] In 1928, Mrs. Shipley was appointed Chief of the "particularly prickly" Passport Division; a job known in Washington to be "full of responsibility, open to the constant critical attack of an impatient public, it was said to have killed one man who was formerly its chief."[7] She held that position for twenty-eight years, during which time she made "a record outstanding in the annals of the Department."[8] In figure 4, Mrs. Shipley is shown receiving an award from Secretary of State John Foster Dulles.[9]

In describing this steep career trajectory, it is worth pausing to remember the special difficulties official Washington presented for women. Women in

97

Fig. 4. Secretary of State John Foster Dulles presents the Distinguished Service Medal to Ruth B. Shipley, Diplomatic Reception Room, Department of State, April 28, 1955.

high office (considered at that time to be any civil service position salaried at over $5,000) were such a rarity that Mrs. Shipley's elevation was viewed as precedent-setting.[10] She became part of what was known as the "women's cabinet"—the small cohort of other women in positions of power.[11] Even after arriving as Chief of the Division, Ruth Shipley had to contend with condescension unimaginable for her male counterparts. The *New York Times* described her as the "slender, dark-haired head" of the Passport Division. In a Sunday feature on "The Women Who Man Our Ship of State," the *Times* marveled at the rise of career professionals sharing "a common sex which has aroused curiosity ever since Eden's gates were shut."[12] Even after five years on the job, at least one congressman congratulated the Secretary of State on "the efficiency shown by the Chief of your Passport Division, Mr. R. B. Shipley."[13] A woman in such an important position was hard for many to fathom.

Notwithstanding these difficulties, Mrs. Shipley's career was a glorious success.[14] As this chapter reveals, she laid the groundwork for future government controls on travel that she scarcely could have imagined (but would not have hesitated to use). Mrs. Shipley rose to become the No Fly List of her day.

1. World War I

When Ruth Shipley first joined the State Department, all hell was breaking loose. War trapped many Americans in Europe. Since passports were not required for travel, few possessed them. Now they were desperate for documents that could return them home.[15] It was during the "hysterical days of 1914" that Mrs. Shipley was assigned to help "locate American citizens marooned abroad, whose relatives were frantic to get them back to safety."[16] Ironically enough, Mrs. Shipley began her career working to *facilitate* travel.

While many Americans lacked passports, putting great pressure on the State Department to issue them quickly for safe voyages home, a mirror-image problem emerged in the form of passport frauds. The virtually unregulated passports of then neutral America were a tempting target for passport frauds by agents of belligerent nations, particularly Germany. By clothing German reserve officers in the neutral guise of American travelers, their travel across an Atlantic Ocean patrolled by the British fleet was considerably easier.[17] It was in this environment that Mrs. Shipley began to learn her craft. No doubt the difficulties presented in time of war by a largely unregulated travel system made a profound impression on her.

2. Between the Wars

By 1924, Mrs. Shipley had risen to the position of Assistant Chief in the Office of Coordination and Review, working under Miss Margaret M. Hanna.[18] There she worked essentially without supervision, developing a particular expertise enforcing the Immigration Act of 1924, for which she helped write regulations.[19] It seems that she was held in high enough regard that the Acting Secretary of State was willing to fight with the Personnel Classification Board to elevate her position to "a classification commensurate with the duties and responsibilities" she performed.[20] The appeal was granted.[21]

Mrs. Shipley became Chief of the Passport Division in 1928. At this time, the Passport Division had a staff of more than seventy.²² Mrs. Shipley quickly realized, however, that she was woefully understaffed and sought permission to employ passport writers on a piecework basis outside of the regular civil service. During the "rush season" of 1928, she complained, "passports were written on an hourly basis" at a rate paid on the expectation of twenty passports an hour.²³ Demand for passports grew and grew between the wars. Mrs. Shipley reported that 1930 was a banner year, with 203,174 passports issued or renewed.²⁴

By her fifth year as Chief of the Passport Division, Mrs. Shipley had exceeded the salary of her former boss, Miss Hanna.²⁵ This reflected, in part, what Mrs. Shipley characterized in an internal memo as public service "exceedingly profitable to the Treasury."²⁶ This was not puffery. During the fiscal year that ended in June 1933, passport fees collected at home and abroad totaled over $1.2 million (the equivalent of almost $20 million today).²⁷ The Passport Division maintained passport agencies in New York, Chicago, Boston, San Francisco, Seattle, and New Orleans; establishment of an agency in Los Angeles was in the works.²⁸ These operated as intake centers, not autonomous decision-makers, since all cases had to be cleared by Washington.²⁹ Mrs. Shipley quickly learned that part of overseeing her growing empire of passport agents required mastery of the art of bureaucratic turf fighting with other federal agencies. In this capacity, too, Mrs. Shipley excelled.³⁰ Nor was any decision too small for Washington (i.e., Mrs. Shipley) to address, right down to the hanging of pictures on the walls of passport agencies.³¹

As she mastered her art, Mrs. Shipley grew ever busier and, perhaps surprisingly in cutthroat Washington, more popular.³² She even felt sufficiently established in the social scene to feel comfortable inviting Eleanor Roosevelt to address the annual meeting of a service organization of which Mrs. Shipley was the local chapter president.³³ Two examples from Mrs. Shipley's early years colorfully illustrate influences on her practical education and her deft hand at creative problem-solving.

EXCURSUS I: THE CASE OF THE KIDNAPPED G-MAN

Did a terrifying event early in the professional life of Mrs. Shipley affect her views of the risks presented by even the savviest of American travelers to U.S. interests abroad?

On June 25, 1922, Mrs. Shipley's brother was kidnapped in Morelos, a small state south of Mexico City.³⁴ Her brother had traveled to Mexico with his wife to defend his business interests in a property dispute with a Mexican oil company.³⁵ This would not necessarily have been newsworthy to those outside the family had her brother not been Alexander Bruce Bielaski, the former director of the FBI. This made the story front-page news. There was initial speculation in the media that the kidnappers were linked to Communist radicals who were "tired of inaction and were planning for this Fall a campaign of terror,"³⁶ but Bielaski later dismissed the theory as very unlikely.³⁷ It was enough, however, to lead President Alvaro Obregon of Mexico to order the immediate arrest and deportation of a colony of American and Russian radicals in Cuernavaca, the capital of Morelos.³⁸ Bielaski orchestrated his own sensational nighttime escape after three days in captivity.³⁹

Ordinary tales of kidnapping would end there. But the case took an even more sensational turn a week later, when a judge in Cuernavaca ordered Bielaski's arrest pending judicial investigation of a charge that Bielaski had arranged his self-abduction to embarrass the Mexican government.⁴⁰ President Obregon traveled from Mexico City to personally oversee the investigation.⁴¹ A few weeks later, newspapers reported that the State Department was "losing patience in the Bielaski case" and had delivered a note to the Mexican authorities to wrap up the investigation.⁴² By that point, conclusion of the affair Bielaski had turned anticlimactic. It was back-page news when the local court absolved him of all charges and cleared him of any complicity in his own kidnapping.⁴³ By the time Bielaski reached Brownsville, Texas, in mid-August, the affair was fully behind him.⁴⁴

The press never reported any suspicion that Ruth Shipley used her office to help her brother and, given her low position at the time, it is hardly likely that she could have done so if she had wanted to.⁴⁵ But did the episode, hitting so close to home, leave its mark on her? One wonders how the twists and turns of the affair affected her thinking years later, as head of the Passport Division. Clearly, even innocent travelers (not to mention anarchists, Communists, and social undesirables) could find themselves suddenly mired in political scandal with the potential to influence the nation's foreign policy and international relations. Her brother's kidnapping, after all, resulted in protests at the highest levels of the American government, the personal involvement of the Mexican President, and then weeks of bizarre claims and counterclaims in the Mexican and American press.⁴⁶ Why risk dragging the United States into awkward circumstances that could have been avoided had permission to travel abroad been denied? Or, as an en banc panel of the Court of Appeals for the District of Columbia Circuit put it many years later, "The Secretary [of State] may preclude matches from the international tinderbox."⁴⁷

EXCURSUS 2: THE CASE OF THE LESS VIRTUOUS BALLERINA

Mrs. Shipley could exercise her power with a delicate touch. This delicacy, however, could not obscure her resolute decision making or its essential paternalism. One example is found in her solution to a problem described with evident frustration by the American Consul General in Valparaiso, Chile. The Consul complained in a cable to Washington that yet another "American ballet and revue company" was planning to descend on his outpost with predictable results:

> During the writer's nine years tour of duty as Consul General in Valparaiso he has been called upon so many times to assist stranded American theatrical companies to obtain return passage to the United States that he is thoroughly convinced that if Mr. Austin goes through with his announced intention of bringing a ballet and revue company to Chile he is merely courting serious financial reverses and the entire venture will end up in the company being stranded in some West Coast port.
>
> As the Department is aware, American theatrical companies stranded in Latin American ports are anything but desirable emisaries [sic] of the United States, and particularly so when the company is largely made up of single girls. It is always a difficult task, as this Consulate General knows from a great deal of experience, to repatriate the female members of such troupes, and oftentimes before this becomes possible some of the less virtuous of them are likely to become public nuisances.[48]

Although the Consul readily conceded that there was no way to stop the company from touring Chile, "nor are there any reasons why the Department should endeavor to do so," he suggested that the Department refuse to issue passports to the company unless some sort of bond was posted to cover its predicted need for return passage.[49]

The Consul was right: passports were not required to visit Chile in 1929. And there was no law or regulation that expressly authorized the refusal of a passport on grounds of predicted penury.[50] On the other hand, the economic and social costs of ill-planned ventures seemed to weigh as heavily on the United States as on even the "less virtuous" youthful ballerinas who appeared (at least to the American Consul and Mrs. Shipley) in need of protection.

Mrs. Shipley's solution was delicate but effective. She directed her passport agent in New York to refer passport applicants in this category to the

Actors Equity Association before processing their applications. Actors Equity was to be relied upon to educate aspiring artists "whether the employer is a reputable person and can be relied upon to keep them employed and provide them with return transportation."[51] Each applicant would then "be advised to ascertain the financial responsibility of her employer and [] further advised not to accept such a position unless favorable advice is received from the Actors Equity Association."[52] Her faith in the marketplace notwithstanding, Mrs. Shipley took no chances: she directed a special agent in New York to make informal inquiries about this particular theatrical venture.[53] Mr. Austin's troupe never left port.[54]

MRS. SHIPLEY ACQUIRED a well-deserved reputation for toughness in response to complaints. A municipal judge in California wrote to complain that clerks of court doubling as passport officials in Los Angeles were "rude, uncivil and so officious that you leave the department division in disgust and shame." He described the treatment he witnessed of a teacher refused service after driving twenty-five miles to make a passport application. Because she reached the office a few minutes after the four o'clock closing time, a return visit was needed for an application that took just a few minutes to handle. "Why on earth those men feel so secure and independent and discourteous is beyond me," the judge wrote. "They should realize that it isn't everyone who can stop work at 4 o'clock in the afternoon, and it certainly would not be going out of the way to help a citizen when that citizen is a public servant and must travel 50 miles in order to have the attention of a Passport clerk for three minutes."[55]

In reply, Mrs. Shipley conceded nothing, noting (with less than complete candor) that "your letter is the first one of its kind that we have received."[56] Mrs. Shipley then confronted the judge's criticism head on: "I do not think that I need to assure you that the hours of official work in the Clerk of Court's office extend beyond four o'clock." Asserting that clerical and other work would consume another hour, Mrs. Shipley ignored the details of the unhappy applicant. It was only an incidental suggestion of the judge to improve the efficiency of paying passport fees that attracted her attention. Mrs. Shipley thanked him for it and wrote to the offending clerk the same day, forwarding the judge's letter. Mrs. Shipley let his primary complaints speak for themselves, choosing only to highlight the opportunity for greater efficiency.[57]

Mrs. Shipley took no guff on the eastern seaboard either. Responding to a husband's complaint that a clerk in the New York Passport Agency treated his wife "as a criminal endeavoring to get into the country by unfair means rather than as an American citizen merely asking a courtesy of her own Government,"[58] Mrs. Shipley riposted that "[t]he Agency at New York transacts an enormous amount of business with some of the most important people in the country and probably some of the most difficult and a complaint of discourtesy in that office is very rare indeed."[59] In any event, Mrs. Shipley concluded, no harm was done. The New York agency was able and willing to process the application on July 15 "in ample time for your sailing on the 17th."[60] This was no idle claim. A year later, the passport agent in New York, Ira Hoyt, boasted in a letter seeking to secure a larger budget that "[w]e have a record of having prepared an application for passport, prepared the passport itself, and obtained telephonic authorization from the Department, all in ten minutes time."[61]

The passport was important, combating fraud was a serious matter, and the books were filling up with statutes and rules for the acquisition and use of these travel documents. But passports were not required by U.S. law for the departure or return of citizens to the country. Nor were they viewed as the unalloyed tools of national security that they would soon become.[62] At least they do not appear to have been viewed that way by the Chief of the Passport Division, who in 1936 willingly provided a visiting counselor from the Chinese Embassy copies of canceled blank passports and the loan of her personal copy of the organization plan of her division. This must have seemed eminently reasonable to Mrs. Shipley, who also invited him to call on the Commissioner of Immigration and Naturalization (then at the Department of Labor) to quench his thirst for knowledge about American practices.[63]

Further evidence of Mrs. Shipley's capacity for tolerance can be found in the interpretation she gave to the oath requirement for receipt of passports. In a series of naturalization cases (later overruled), the Supreme Court had held that conscientious objectors could be denied citizenship if they refused on religious grounds to swear an oath to defend the Constitution and laws of the United States "against all enemies, foreign and domestic." The Supreme Court interpreted this phrase to require an oath-bound obligation to take up arms if called to do so.[64] Because the respondents in these cases refused to swear to such a duty, their naturalization petitions were declined. Some feared that these cases would lead to passport denials on the same grounds; after all, the passport had acquired its importance through war. Thus, when the executive secretary of the Women's International League, Dorothy Detzer, sought a passport to attend her organization's congress in Prague, she felt compelled to include with her application an admission that "I cannot, without a very distinct mental reservation, swear to support and defend the constitution if by the word 'defend' the bearing of arms is implied, or the support of war."[65]

It was peacetime, however, and Mrs. Shipley appears to have used her discretion to allow modification of the oath. Responding to Miss Detzer, Mrs. Shipley wrote, "The department will consider the matter of issuing a passport to you upon your swearing to the statements contained in your application for a passport and taking the same oath of allegiance as was taken by Roger N. Baldwin in 1926."[66] This was a reference to a founder and then chairman of the ACLU, who was issued a passport after taking a modified oath to "support the Constitution of the United States and will, as far as my conscience will allow, defend it against all enemies, foreign and domestic."[67]

Was Mrs. Shipley motivated by her own personal views as the daughter of a Methodist minister? Would she have used her discretion in the same way for adherents to disfavored groups? Those questions were soon to be answered. Already clear, however, was Mrs. Shipley's mastery of her post. She was an agile, dedicated, and patriotic civil servant.

3. World War II

The winds of war were felt by Mrs. Shipley and her superiors, who prepared for its outbreak. It was not difficult to foresee that, as escape from Europe became more difficult, American passports would become more valuable and subject to more fraud.[68] If the Passport Division was too liberal in issuing passports, trust that their holders were truly American citizens might diminish, as would their power to extract Americans from dangerous places. In a memorandum to the Passport Division and the Division of European Affairs just days before the outbreak of war, Assistant Secretary of State George Messersmith warned, "Should hostilities break out, or even should these disturbed conditions continue further without the actual outbreak of hostilities, it is all the more important that the value of the American passport should be safeguarded in every possible way so that it may serve its purpose for bona fide American citizens and that our passport may not be abused."[69] This was, in his words, "no time for this Government in any way to relax its procedure here or in our establishments abroad with respect to the issue of passports."[70]

Mrs. Shipley played a pivotal role. As described in a memo to the President recommending her for the Medal for Merit:

> Prior to entry of the United States into World War II, Mrs. Shipley directed all outstanding passports be voided and be replaced on a world-wide basis with a new type of passport which was infinitely more difficult to alter or counterfeit. The safeguards surrounding the

issuance of these replacement passports insured their being issued to bona fide American citizens who were the rightful holders of old-type passports.[71]

Mrs. Shipley's redesigned passports were quite successful at reducing the rate of counterfeiting, which Mrs. Shipley put at less than 0.5 percent in 1939.[72] In her words, these passports were "duplicated successfully only about as often as money is, and the rate of convictions for such offenses is gratifyingly high."[73] One solution was the distribution to each diplomatic mission and consular office of equipment to take fingerprints. This early adoption of biometrics, however, was not used to take the fingerprints of travelers for verification by the Department, but to place the thumb or fingerprint of a Foreign Service officer on each validated passport![74]

The series of proclamations and regulations promulgated in the first few days of September 1939 created what became known at the State Department as the "Emergency Program." The regulations prohibited travel on vessels flagged to belligerent nations and required passports intended for use in Europe to be validated by the Department. When citizens returned to the United States, their passports were surrendered to immigration authorities for return to the State Department. No exception to these regulations for its own diplomatic and special passports, at least officially, was tolerated by the Department.[75]

Pressure from business interests led the Department to use a light touch in validating passports for business travelers.[76] A telegram dated September 14, 1939, above the name of Joseph Kennedy, Ambassador to the United Kingdom, warned of the "considerable uncertainty" of American businessmen in Britain who "complain that their situation is being considered like that of the casual traveller." Secretary Hull replied the next day: "Department has no desire or intention to hamper legitimate American business with European countries but encourages it. New Regulations merely require commercial travellers to submit documentary evidence showing necessity of traveling in European country for substantial business purpose. Since issue of new regulations passports have been issued promptly for this purpose. Department, of course, does not wish to encourage unnecessary travel on the high seas. Regulations with regard commercial travellers similar those in effect during our neutrality last war. You may assure American business men, principally those who are assigned permanently to Great Britain, that statement that their situation is considered by Department like that of the casual traveller is incorrect."[77]

Others were not so lucky. The same day that the Department received the anxious telegram from the American Embassy in London, Mrs. Shipley responded to a telegram received from a representative of parents of about 500 medical students "unable to return to Scotland to finish their studies," in some cases for their final year of training. The parents complained that their sons had been refused passports "and though educated will be thrown on a country already glutted with unskilled labor."[78] Mrs. Shipley was unmoved: "The Department has given very careful and sympathetic consideration to this matter but has concluded that the situation is so grave and the hazards involved so great as to render it inadvisable for the students to go abroad at this time."[79] Entering her second decade in command of the Passport Division, Mrs. Shipley's views were set. Whether businessman, medical student, or a less virtuous ballerina, Americans traveled only if their government approved. And it was from Mrs. Shipley's office that approval must come.

When the Department paused to assess its work over the course of the previous two hectic months, Mrs. Shipley expressed overall satisfaction: "I think the Department has handled an extremely difficult situation very well and the pressure from certain individuals for special treatment is just one of those things that is bound to occur as long as Americans are what they are."[80] All this work naturally augmented the importance of the Passport Division. By Christmas 1939, the Passport Division had a staff of eighty-two.[81]

This assessment, however, exposed the opposing forces operating on the Passport Division. The Emergency Program was just that—an operation quickly established to deal with a genuine emergency. The State Department had no desire to see American neutrality undone by harm to Americans living and working in Europe. The *Lusitania* was a fresh memory. But if the Department prohibited travel completely, it would feel the backlash of American business interests in Europe. Assistant Secretary of State George Messersmith noted in a memorandum to Mrs. Shipley the razor's edge on which the Emergency Program operated. The memo also reveals the paternalism inherent in the Department's conception of the right to travel and how removed national security or foreign policy concerns could be from its decision making:

> It is quite obvious that we must continue to validate, for instance, the passports of American citizens who desire to proceed even to belligerent countries on important business or for residence there in connection with their business. I do not see any reason for changing our present practice of not permitting the wife of such a businessman who is now in this country to proceed with him on a trip which he is making. . . .

> On the other hand, there are American businessmen who have been established abroad for a number of years and whose residence abroad is necessary for the firms which they represent or for the business which they conduct on their own account. It seems to me that the wife of such an American businessman should be permitted to leave with him and, if in this country, to proceed there even though it may be in belligerent territory. She would, of course, have to be informed on the validation of the passport that she would be proceeding on her own risk, that we might not be able to accord certain protection under given circumstances, and that we could not assume any responsibility for evacuation, et cetera. I know that such a declaration would not entirely relieve this Government of its obligations, but, on the other hand, I believe that if it were known in this country that such persons had proceeded at their own risk this Department would be absolved of any blame or responsibility should harm come to them.[82]

The situation was even more dire for American women married to citizens of belligerent countries. Responding to an inquiry from the American Consul in Calcutta, Secretary Hull ordered that the passports of such women not be endorsed for travel into combat areas "except in cases of imperative necessity such as critical illness or other impelling cause," and that American women who traveled to such areas on foreign passports rendered themselves liable under the Neutrality Act.[83]

With the passage of the 1941 amendments to the Travel Control Act, Mrs. Shipley's office acquired more power. Mrs. Shipley played a central role lobbying Congress for the changes.[84] The purpose of the amendments was to limit travel to essential persons only, as determined by the State Department. As an internal memorandum makes clear, much of this power remained unshared in the person of Mrs. Shipley herself:

> This placed tremendous responsibility on the Chief of the Division. While many applications could be refused immediately on the ground that the purpose of the travel was not urgent or essential, a goodly proportion of the applicants had to be cleared both as to security and as to purpose. . . . The direct contacts with representatives of the agencies, branches of the Armed Services, and foreign missions, which were necessary in order to develop procedures, policy, reconcile differences and exchange confidential information, were made by Mrs. Shipley with consummate skill, tact and diplomacy. She also personally passed upon a great many borderline cases daily. . . . She

handled personally the cases in which great pressure was brought to bear upon the Department by influential persons or organizations on behalf of persons who desired to travel abroad for personal reasons and who had been able to convince their sponsors of the validity of pseudo claims that their travel would be in the interests of the United States or some other country.[85]

By the end of 1942, Mrs. Shipley not only controlled the issue of passports but was also vested with authority to take action connected with official and private requests for assistance in obtaining visas.[86]

Administrative records from this period show how closely involved Mrs. Shipley was in the work of her office, from the most extraordinary tasks to the most routine. In March 1944, Mrs. Shipley was dispatched to New York to welcome into port the S.S. *Gripsholm* and repatriate American citizens returning home as part of an intergovernmental exchange of nationals with Nazi Germany.[87] In April, an American Catholic priest, Stanislaus Orlemanski, caused a national scandal by traveling to Moscow for an unprecedented private meeting with Joseph Stalin to plead for a free and democratic postwar Poland.[88] At a press conference, President Roosevelt was forced to defend the decision to issue Orlemanski an American passport. His defense was Mrs. Shipley. President Roosevelt "implied that the action was taken in ordinary course after proper consideration solely by Mrs. Ruth B. Shipley, chief of the Passport Division of the State Department."[89] According to the *New York Times* coverage of the press conference:

> Mr. Roosevelt made this point by remarking that Mrs. Shipley, veteran chief of the division, has long been known for the care with which she has had applications investigated and for issuing passports only when there were good and sufficient reasons. When anyone has got by Mrs. Shipley, the President emphasized, one can be sure the law has been lived up to. This means, he added, that in this case she must have been satisfied with the reasons that Father Orlemanski gave for requesting a passport.[90]

During the summer and fall of 1944, the Passport Division hovered between 200 and 235 personnel. The workload was relentless. A memo sent to the Acting Chief of the Division of Departmental Personnel, Robert Ward, noted the high level of attrition at the Passport Division: "I went directly to Mrs. Shipley in PD and told her that, in view of the existing shortage of qualified personnel, it would never be possible for us to fill her positions if this separation rate continued as it had in the past three months."[91] Whether the workload was oppressive or there were other reasons for resignations, the frustrated official declared the rate "inexcusable."⁹² But Mrs. Shipley led by example, working as hard as anyone on her staff. Records for a one-month period in 1944 tally over $1,000 in long-distance calls between the Passport Division and customs collectors at various ports to verify that seamen were authorized to sail under new security regulations.⁹³ In 2009 dollars, that was a one-month telephone bill exceeding $13,000.⁹⁴ In the vast majority of these calls, the telephone receiver was held to Mrs. Shipley's ear.⁹⁵

The Emergency Program aimed to protect and return citizens trapped in Europe at the start of the war and to prevent the unnecessary travel of citizens to or through belligerent countries. Acts of Congress during the war augmented and regularized that emergency authority. The end of the war brought little respite from Mrs. Shipley's iron control. Even the powerful Eleanor Dulles, whose personal accomplishments and family connections made her a force to be reckoned with in diplomatic Washington, was denied passports for her family to join her in postwar Austria to work for the U.S. military delegation there in 1945. Mrs. Shipley felt that postwar Europe was no place for children:

> The formidable Mrs. Shipley looked at her as if she was mad and said:
> "Nothing doing, Mrs. Dulles. You can't take the children with you."
> "I'm not going without my children," Eleanor said.
> "Then you're not going," said Mrs. Shipley.⁹⁶

Eleanor Dulles did not mince words about her encounter with Mrs. Shipley: "She was a tartar and a despot. It was a harrowing experience."⁹⁷ It took three months of pressure by the powerful Dulles clan, and the personal offers of both the British and Swiss ambassadors to provide visas on their official stationary (Mrs. Shipley had confiscated Mrs. Dulles's passport), before Mrs. Shipley accepted the inevitable.⁹⁸ This was one of few recorded instances of successful opposition to Mrs. Shipley. More often, the hapless traveler found Mrs. Shipley "completely immovable . . . once a decision has been reached . . . [W]hen she has once said 'no,' the disappointed applicant might as well save himself further conversation."⁹⁹

4. The Cold War

Demand for passports began to rise with the end of the war. In 1947, the Passport Division issued 202,424 passports, second only to a prewar peak in 1930.¹⁰⁰ Still, Mrs. Shipley's office maintained its control over travel. In an article in the *New York Times* about her office, in which she was the only person quoted or referenced by name, a delicate version of her office's power was publicized:

> Difficulty is experienced by those who seek to visit the Old World. Some hopefuls tell Mrs. Ruth B. Shipley, chief of the Passport Division, who has controlled American civilian world travel during the war, that they'd like to go to Europe to "see what it looks like." They are gently discouraged and are warned not to head in that direction unless it is necessary.¹⁰¹

About six weeks prior to this article, the *Times* reported a starker statement of travel controls: "the Passport Division is still working under the regularly provided wartime system of controls, with limited travel allowed only in the instances which will contribute to the national interests of the United States or the country visited and under certain conditions for business persons whose presence in the country to which they are going will contribute to the restoration of trade."¹⁰² Mrs. Shipley determined whose travel and which purposes met these criteria. New standards, catalyzed by new fears, would soon be added.

The fear of Communism that surged through the United States in the 1950s dramatically affected international travel. A population used to wartime restrictions on travel was slow to react to new controls that had the same effect on travel, if based on a very different perception of threat and different legal grounds. A few examples suggest the growing "mission creep" of travel control in the early years of the Cold War.

In June 1950, the State Department issued a "stop notice" at all U.S. ports to prevent the international travel of the entertainer and civil rights activist Paul Robeson.¹⁰³ He was denied a new passport on the vague ground that his foreign travel would not be "in the best interests" of the United States.¹⁰⁴ The Department of State later elaborated that "if Robeson spoke abroad against colonialism he would be a meddler in matters within the exclusive jurisdiction of the Secretary of State."¹⁰⁵ Robeson refused to sign an affidavit that he was not a Communist and challenged the denial of his passport in federal court. Leo Rover, the U.S. Attorney for the District of Columbia, then detailed the government's grounds for prohibiting Robeson under the Internal Security Act from traveling abroad, including Robeson's opposition to antisubversive legislation, criticism of racial segregation, and his penchant for singing Communist anthems. In addition, Rover told the court, "in April, 1949—see if this sounds like a loyal American citizen—he delivered a speech before the Communist-sponsored World Peace Congress in Paris in which he stated that the American Negroes would never fight against the Soviet Union. A cruel, criminal libel against the members of his own race."[106]

In 1952, the eminent chemist Linus Pauling was denied a passport to attend scientific meetings at the Royal Society of London and receive an honorary degree in Toulouse.[107] The State Department rejected his application, stating only that the "proposed travel would not be in the best interests of the United States."[108] Permission to travel was granted only following an angry speech by Senator Wayne Morse, international media coverage, and Pauling's agreement to sign a statement that he was not and never had been a Communist.[109] This routine continued for two more years, with passports granted (if at all) at the last minute, validated only for limited travel for limited time periods and only after Pauling signed repeat affidavits that he was not a Communist.[110] After dozens of letters, affidavits, and personal visits, Mrs. Shipley advised Pauling that his applications were denied because the Department had concluded, based on evidence never shared with Pauling, that he was "a concealed member of the Communist Party."[111] Only after Pauling won the 1954 Nobel Prize for Chemistry did the State Department grant a normal, unrestricted passport.[112]

In 1954, the playwright Arthur Miller was denied a passport to attend the Brussels opening of *The Crucible* because such travel "would not be in the national interest."[113] When the Belgian audience exclaimed "Author, author!" on opening night, it was the American ambassador who appeared onstage.[114] Another passport application, pending while Miller was called to testify before the House Un-American Affairs Committee in 1956, was held up by "derogatory information" leading the State Department to request "an affidavit concerning past or present membership in the Communist party."[115] Miller was later convicted of contempt of Congress during this hearing, which was ostensibly called to examine "the fraudulent procurement and misuse of American passports by persons in the service of the Communist conspiracy."[116]

To these vignettes could be added the travel stories of many other prominent and unknown Americans alike. The well-known Protestant pacifist J. Henry Carpenter was denied a passport to Japan in 1952 because, according to Mrs. Shipley, "his presence in the Far East is considered undesirable at this time."[117] The eminent physicist Martin Kamen (libeled as a Communist spy and subversive, but never prosecuted) fought from 1947 to 1955 for a passport, at great expense financially and professionally, until it was granted just half an hour before an oral argument in his lawsuit to obtain one (a case that, as will be seen below, other litigation increasingly forecast that the State Department would lose).[118]

Nevertheless, Mrs. Shipley could sometimes surprise. The playwright Lillian Hellman devotes several pages of her book, *Scoundrel Time,* to her interview with Mrs. Shipley in 1953, when Hellman sought a passport to work on a movie script in London.[119] After her own testimony before the House Un-American Affairs Committee, this seemed "a useless visit" to her, but one she nevertheless undertook at the suggestion of her lawyer, Joseph Rauh (a leading civil rights lawyer who would later represent Arthur Miller before the same body).[120] Hellman describes the arrival of a "fat folder" that Mrs. Shipley examined during their meeting. After briefly assaying her opinion of the work of the Committee, and eliciting a promise from Hellman to write a letter averring not to engage in political activities while abroad, Mrs. Shipley agreed to issue a limited passport.[121] A stunned Hellman met Rauh in the hallway. "Why were you so sure I would get it?" she asked. According to Hellman, a grinning Rauh replied, "Because one Puritan lady in power recognized another Puritan lady in trouble. Puritan ladies have to believe that other Puritan ladies don't lie."[122]

Rauh couldn't have been that sure, for Hellman's interactions with Mrs. Shipley were a mixed bag. Mrs. Shipley had previously denied Hellman passports in April 1943, on the grounds that she was "reported to be an active Communist," and in May 1944, despite the prodding of Metro-Goldwyn-Mayer Studios, "because of the present military situation."[123] But by fall 1944, Mrs. Shipley relented, granting her a passport to visit the Soviet Union despite a two-page memo from the FBI detailing Hellman's suspected membership in various pro-Communist organizations and her "pro-Soviet and pro-Communist point of view."[124] Mrs. Shipley also approved a visit to Tito's Yugoslavia in October 1948.[125] In August 1951, Hellman was allowed to sail for England after she wrote what one respected biographer called "one of the most galling letters of her life" to Mrs. Shipley, seeking a passport to recover from the shock of the arrest and jailing of her longtime companion, Dashiell Hammett, for contempt of court.[126] Hammett had refused to give testimony that might lead to the arrest of four men who had jumped bail, bail that he and others had raised after their convictions under the Smith Act were upheld by the Supreme Court in *Dennis v. United States* that June.[127]

Based on a thorough examination of Mrs. Shipley's files, Robert Newman concludes that, although under pressure not to issue Hellman a passport, Shipley concluded that her office's investigators were right and the FBI was wrong: Hellman was not a Communist.[128] Although she was unusually tardy in fulfilling her promise to send a passport within a week, and (according to Newman) she felt "compelled to use an administrative dodge" to protect her bureaucratic flank in doing so, Mrs. Shipley renewed Hellman's passport.[129]

The international Communist conspiracy against the West quickly emerged as the main threat to the United States. Travel controls continued to be seen as an essential weapon in the fight against this conspiracy of subversives and spies. This was not merely an effort to squelch dissenting speech or unpopular opinions. The United States was understood to be fighting a concrete threat to its national security. In fall 1959, Assistant Secretary of State Macomber wrote to Senator McClellan (Chairman of the Committee on Government Operations) that the State Department still believed "that the most critical problem in the passport field is the lack of legislative authority in the Secretary of State to deny passports to dangerous participants in the international Communist conspiracy."[130]

Mrs. Shipley was perceived to be far ahead of the curve. She did not wait for legislative permission to transform her wartime powers into Cold War controls. An internal memorandum supporting a recommendation that she receive the Medal for Merit summarized her views:

> Long before the top Communists in the United States were convicted of conspiracy in the trial before Judge Medina and the enactment of the Internal Security Act of 1950, Mrs. Shipley was alert to the dangers inherent in the travel abroad of Communists and other subversives and steadfastly adhered to the policy of refusing a passport when evidence and information respecting prior actions of the applicant indicated that the proposed travel would be inimical to the best interests of the United States. She has never deviated from this position and after the convictions in the New York trial were sustained by the Court of Appeals, and the Congress set forth its findings concerning the Communist organization in the United States in the Internal Security Act of 1950, she gained acceptance of her view that, in keeping with the spirit of the Act, passports should be refused to Communists as such.[131]

Although Mrs. Shipley figures prominently in these stories, the enormous bureaucracy she managed should not be forgotten. Her ever-expanding office worked like a powerful, well-synchronized machine. The Passport Division was located at this time in the Winder Building, across the street from the Old Executive Office Building and the White House.[132] Mrs. Shipley kept close watch on passport activities abroad, and her office was well staffed to confront all of these issues at home. Autumn 1950 opened with Mrs. Shipley on a seven-nation European tour of fifteen American diplomatic and consular offices "to review and seek advice on citizenship and passport problems."[133] By

1951, her office occupied all six floors of the Winder Building.[134] By 1953, she administered an office in Washington, D.C., that employed approximately 225 people.[135] In addition, satellite offices in the form of passport agencies had been established in New York, San Francisco, Chicago, Boston, and New Orleans, and almost 300 Foreign Service posts worldwide completed a finely wrought web of travel controls at the center of which sat Mrs. Shipley.[136]

Overall, this system impressed Congress. Some members of Congress grumbled that, at the apparent direction of Mrs. Shipley, Passport Division clerks refused to give their names to Capitol Hill staffers who telephoned for passport information for constituents.[137] Much more common than criticism, however, were the letters of praise that flowed into Foggy Bottom from Capitol Hill.[138] Mrs. Shipley had powerful supporters, although one suspects that this may have derived as much from fear as from love.[139] Mrs. Shipley was quite aware of her power, as she ominously suggested in a sharp, public exchange with Senator McCarran: "The bulk of the American traveling public are reputable, law-abiding citizens and are probably above the average in education, intelligence, and stability. The Department does not feel in view of its experience over many years that it is warranted in treating this large group of citizens as potentially subversive by establishing *at this time* procedures which would delay and hinder bona fide travelers in an effort to detect cases such as those mentioned by the Subcommittee."[140]

A blanket refusal to issue a passport was not the only arrow in Mrs. Shipley's quiver. Passport restrictions could also be used in a more nuanced way. As one contemporary State Department official observed, "The passport is an ideal device for the control of the movements of American citizens."[141] The Passport Act of 1926 delegated the Secretary of State the power to impose travel restrictions in conformity with American foreign policy.[142] The act limited the validity of a passport to two years, with a shorter period possible at the Secretary's discretion.[143] Alternatively, limits could be placed on the use of the passport in particular places or for particular itineraries.[144] In 1938, President Roosevelt issued an executive order expanding the discretion of the Secretary of State to impose area restrictions and expressly granting the power to cancel or withdraw passports used in defiance of those restrictions.[145] The executive regulations derived from that statutory authorization were broad in scope: "The Secretary of State is authorized in his discretion to refuse to issue a passport, to restrict a passport for use only in certain countries, to restrict it against use in certain countries, to withdraw or cancel a passport already issued, and to withdraw a passport for the purpose of restricting its validity or use in certain countries."[146] In 1952, the State Department began stamping all passports as not valid for travel in countries behind the Iron Curtain, rendering them useless for such a purpose unless specifically endorsed by the Department.[147] Travel to some countries quite literally required the government's imprimatur.

This was no small power, particularly as it concerned Americans who wished to live abroad.[148] Mrs. Shipley did not hesitate to use it. She brooked no opposition when she felt that her office's resolution of a complaint or issue was satisfactory. For example, a clergyman from Detroit wrote an angry letter to Under Secretary of State Herbert Hoover, Jr., to complain that the Passport Division, "supposedly directed by Mrs. R.B. Shipley," had ignored his written requests for a copy of an old passport application, in his view "MOST ABOMIBLE [sic] treatment to give any respected American citizen."[149] Threatening to take the matter up the chain of command to President Eisenhower himself, if necessary, the complainant demanded action.

Mrs. Shipley was satisfied that her office had accomplished the task as expeditiously as possible. The search for older records required additional time. In an internal memorandum to which she attached her correspondence with the man of the cloth, Mrs. Shipley summarized her view of the matter: "Dr. Gordon has received excellent service and I think for a clergyman, and I say it as a daughter and granddaughter of clergymen, he shows very little Christian spirit."[150]

Oddly enough, the State Department initially kept "[n]o particular record . . . as to how often, or on how many different grounds, passports have been refused to citizens who met all the usual requirements."[151] But a July 1951 memo responding to a request for information from the State Department's Deputy Legal Adviser summarized the practice:

> It may be stated generally, however, that from time to time passports are refused under the discretionary authority of the Secretary of State to persons in the following categories: persons whose past actions raise doubts as to their loyalty; persons suspected of an intention to commit a crime or otherwise to bring grave discredit upon the United States as, for example, international swindlers and gamblers; persons engaged in the white slave traffic; opium smugglers; confidence men; international spies; and other persons whose habitual practices are such as to bring discredit upon the United States and things American; evaders of justice, including persons "jumping bail" or quitting the country to escape the payment of alimony, or the jurisdiction of a court, or in violation of a writ of *ne exeat*; and political adventurers, which would include persons desiring to go abroad to take part in the political or military affairs of a foreign country in ways which would

be contrary to the policy or inimical to the welfare, of the United States.[152]

It is striking that the State Department felt competent to prejudge the future dangerousness and propensity to commit crimes of individuals who were under no restrictions placed on them by the criminal justice system. But all of these categories were consistent with the belief that a citizen's right to travel could be restricted if Mrs. Shipley's office deemed its exercise "not in the interests of the United States."

This memo was written after the Subversive Activities Control Board had been organized, but before it had issued any final orders. The Board became the source of the next major restriction on passports and one of the few that was ultimately prohibited as unconstitutional by the Supreme Court: restriction on the basis of membership in a Communist organization. In 1950, the McCarran Act (the Internal Security Act) made it unlawful for members of organizations ordered to register with the Subversive Activities Control Board to apply for or attempt to use passports.[153]

Only in the early 1950s, the last years of Mrs. Shipley's reign, did the winds begin to shift against her unreviewable discretion. The issue was cast in its starkest light by Eugene Gressman, the future distinguished Supreme Court scholar and litigator, who asked "whether the 700,000 Americans who travel abroad each year do so by right or by the grace of the Secretary of State."[154] In late August 1952, the State Department issued new regulations on passports that established a process by which disappointed applicants could seek a more formal review of their cases than supplication before Mrs. Shipley.[155] This was, at best, a modest procedural reform. Although the new rules required the Passport Division to notify the applicant in writing of the reasons for refusing to issue a passport, these reasons needed only to be stated "as specifically as within the judgement of the Department of State security limitations permit."[156]

The new regulations also created a Board of Passport Appeals.[157] This reform gave applicants the right to appeal an adverse decision at a hearing where the applicant could be represented by counsel.[158] The Board would decide appeals based on the preponderance of the evidence, as in a civil trial.[159] But the new regulations took away at least as much as they gave. They began with a statement of purpose:

> In order to promote the national interest by assuring that persons who support the world Communist movement of which the Communist Party is an integral unit may not, through use of United States

passports, further the purposes of that movement, no passport, except one limited for direct and immediate return to the United States, shall be issued to (a) Persons who are members of the Communist Party or who . . . continue to act in furtherance of the interests and under the discipline of the Communist Party; (b) Persons, regardless of the formal state of their affiliation with the Communist Party, who engage in activities which support the Communist movement . . . as a result of direction, domination, or control exercised over them by the Communist movement; [and] (c) Persons, regardless of the formal state of their affiliation with the Communist Party, as to whom there is reason to believe, on the balance of all the evidence, that they are going abroad to engage in activities which will advance the Communist movement for the purpose, knowingly and willfully of advancing that movement.[160]

The appellant was not permitted access to any part of his passport file or other files on which the Board would make its decision, with the exception of the copy of his initial application and other submissions.[161] A finding by the Board of "consistent and prolonged adherence to the Communist Party line" was declared to be prima facie evidence of unfitness to receive a passport.[162] If any doubt remained at any stage of its proceedings, the Board could require the applicant to declare under oath or affirmation the state of his affiliation to the Communist Party. "If applicant states that he is a Communist, refusal of a passport in his case will be without further proceedings."[163] The combination of these provisions effectively denied review by the Board to anyone unwilling to execute a sworn affidavit concerning his or her Party membership.[164] These provisions fit Mrs. Shipley's view of the world: "I intend to stay and fight for what I believe in. One of the things I believe in is refusing passports to Communists."[165] In any event, the Board seemed a dead letter: ten months after it was invented, it still hadn't met for want of appeals.[166]

A catchall regulation was also promulgated to deny passports to individuals on grounds of suspicion of future unlawful activity. The regulation only required a "reason to believe, on the balance of all the evidence," that future unlawfulness could occur.[167] This regulation was amended in 1956 to make its application even broader. The previous standard for refusal of passport facilities was lowered to instances "when it appears to the satisfaction of the Secretary of State" that a person's activities abroad would "violate the laws of the United States."[168] Two even broader grounds expanded this power further. Passports would also be denied if the Secretary of State was satisfied that the person's activities abroad would either "be prejudicial to the orderly conduct of foreign relations" or "otherwise be prejudicial to the interests of the United States."[169] Neither ground was new, nor was the bar for the determination of those grounds lowered in 1956 from where it had been before. The only change was to formally promulgate the description of what Mrs. Shipley had been doing since 1928 and "infiltrate the passport procedure with all the inanities and unfairness of the federal employee loyalty program."[170]

Two events explain the sudden promulgation of rules that cosmetically formalized procedures while keeping the substance of Mrs. Shipley's work well insulated from outside inspection.[171] First was the denial of a passport to Linus Pauling, winner of the Presidential Medal of Merit, to travel to London and France for scientific purposes. As noted above, this decision brought the wrath of Senator Morse to bear on the State Department. Mrs. Shipley's unvarnished record of implacability suggests that this alone would not have been enough (Pauling, after all, never received his passport). But shortly after the harsh press from the Pauling spectacle, a three-judge panel on the U.S. District Court for the District of Columbia held that a final order denying a passport without a hearing violated due process of law.[172] That was Anne Bauer's case, described at the beginning of chapter 1.

The Cold War policy was summarized by Louis Jaffe in terms that resonate today: "Nearly every passport denial has been a decision to keep the citizen here within the high walled fortress where he can be isolated, neutralized, kept, let us say, to his accustomed and observable routines of malefaction. It has been simply one facet of our tactic of domestic security, and only incidentally a matter of foreign policy."[173] At the start of the Cold War, as now in the so-called War on Terror, travel restrictions were deemed necessary in "this age of crisis," a response by America and its allies "to a world in fear of atomic war and planned insurrection."[174]

5. Dénouement

Mrs. Shipley retired on April 30, 1955, after forty-seven years of government service.[175] Twenty-eight of those years had been spent as Chief of the Passport Division.[176] To celebrate her retirement, Mrs. Shipley announced that she would take a long European vacation.[177] No one doubted that she would obtain her passport without delay.

In many ways, Mrs. Shipley left government just in time. Her successor, Frances Knight, was plagued with increasing scrutiny of passport policy from Capitol Hill, litigation assaults against the Internal Security Act and other sources of the Passport Division's power, the investigations of private bodies (most notably the Association of the Bar of the City of New York),[178] and the emergence of the Warren Court. Knight presided over a Passport Division of ever-diminishing power. An era had ended with the departure of Ruth Shipley.

The most important case concerning passports up to that time was one that began under Mrs. Shipley but ended—badly for the Department—under Miss Knight. Otto Nathan sought a passport in December 1952 to travel to Switzerland as the sole executor of the estate of Albert Einstein. His application was denied in July 1954, "[a]fter several months of informal interrogation and correspondence."[179] Nathan filed suit the following month and won a nearly unprecedented court order to the State Department to hold a hearing that conformed to what "the law contemplates and guarantees."[180] In response to the Government's argument that Nathan failed to exhaust his administrative remedies, to wit, the Board of Passport Appeals, Judge Schweinhaut concluded that this was unnecessary: "I think as a matter of practical fact he had none."[181]

Nor did the court believe other parts of the 1952 regulations provided what the law required. The same day that he issued his opinion and order concerning Dr. Nathan's case, the same judge decided *Clark v. Dulles*, concerning the denial of a passport to federal judge William Clark.[182] He dismissed the Government's contention that the law had been satisfied: "It is urged by the government that the plaintiff had a 'hearing' in that he personally talked to and corresponded with the then Under Secretary of State. I do not believe that that was a hearing in the sense that the law has in mind. I think, therefore, that the plaintiff should have a hearing in the State Department but I do not suggest or direct the manner in which the hearing should be conducted."[183]

The Passport Division delayed its compliance with the judge's orders in Nathan's case. On the Ides of March 1955 (forty-five days before Mrs. Shipley's retirement), the court ordered the Secretary of State to "promptly afford plaintiff an appropriate hearing."[184] Two and a half months later, Mrs. Shipley had retired and the hearing still had not occurred. The court then ordered the Secretary of State to issue Dr. Nathan a passport of standard form and duration.[185] The Department appealed the order to the Court of Appeals for the District of Columbia Circuit the same day. An affidavit from the Assistant Director of the Passport Division averred that "it would be contrary to the best interests of the United States" to issue Dr. Nathan a passport.[186] In response, the appellate court ordered the Department to comply with the district court's order and hold a "quasi judicial hearing" within four days, adding additional reporting requirements to both the court and Nathan.[187] The day before that deadline, rather than comply with those unprecedented requirements, the Department issued the passport after a further *ex parte* review by its Passport Board of Appeals.[188] As the circuit court described this surprise reversal, the Department did not

> say what the Board reported or recommended, or why. It does not suggest that the Board had new information. It does not say what the Board thought about information referred to in the affidavit of the Assistant Director of the Passport Division. However, since the Department of State has issued the passport, it must be assumed that its issuance was not "contrary to the best interests of the United States."[189]

It is likely that the State Department weighed the "best interests of the United States" and determined that issuing a passport to Dr. Nathan was a lesser evil than establishing further precedent for judicial review of State Department passport decisions. Mooting the appeal was therefore a strategic decision.

The very same day that the D.C. Circuit decided the Nathan case, it held that the Department's stated reason for denying a passport in a different case worked a violation of substantive due process beyond the procedural violations identified in the Nathan case.[190] The court held that Max Shachtman's passport application had been denied because he was chairman of an organization that the Attorney General had listed as subversive without giving Shachtman meaningful opportunity to contest that listing despite his repeated attempts to do so. The State Department's reliance on that conclusion was therefore arbitrary and unconnected to the otherwise nonjusticiable decision making integral to foreign affairs. As in the Nathan case, the court remanded the matter to the district court for further proceedings. In the end, as with Otto Nathan, the Department issued Shachtman a passport rather than risk generating even worse precedent.[191]

The Nathan and Shachtman cases were followed in short order by a rain of judicial blows to the Passport Division, blows that had not landed in Mrs. Shipley's day. Five months later, a federal court held that Leonard Boudin (the lawyer who had represented Otto Nathan and was developing a niche practice in passport cases but now found himself the victim of a passport denial) was entitled to an opportunity to refute a written record that included all evidence on which the Department based its decision.[192] Judge Youngdahl expressed evident frustration with the secret methods of the State Department: "How can an applicant refute charges which arise from sources, or are based upon evidence, which is closed to him? What good does it do him to be apprised that a passport is denied him due to associations or activities disclosed or inferred from State Department files even if he is told of the associations and activities in a general way? What files? What evidence? Who made the inferences? From what materials were those inferences made?"[193] Seven months later, a court of appeals affirmed the lower court's ruling and ordered the Secretary to "state whether his findings are based on the evidence openly produced, or (in whole or in material part) on secret information not disclosed to the applicant."[194] If the latter, the court intimated that it would have the power to evaluate that judgment. Rather than reveal information from its confidential files, or risk a precedent firmly establishing the power of the courts to determine whether the Department could rely on secret evidence not included in the record, the Department issued a passport.[195]

These cases emboldened others. Paul Robeson, who had repeatedly been denied passports and had repeatedly refused to sign an affidavit disavowing Communist ties, now sued to compel issuance of a passport without filing such an affidavit. At the oral argument over the motion, the U.S. Attorney painted the government's picture of an un-American loose cannon whose speeches and appearances abroad were detrimental to U.S. foreign policy. The U.S. Attorney dismissively summarized the other side: "We have listened to an argument here that, in effect, says because of the Nathan case and the Shachtman case, the law of the land is that all you have to do is to walk in the Passport Office, fill out an application and get your passport—go where you want to go, do as you please, the Secretary has no control over you. Now, of course, that is not so."[196]

Judicial challenges to the Passport Division's authority, growing in number and severity, began to attract interest in Congress. Only months after Mrs. Shipley's retirement, the State Department in general and the Passport Division in particular drew the unwanted attention of Senator Thomas Henning, the Chairman of the Senate Judiciary Committee's Subcommittee on Constitutional Rights.[197] The targets of the Senator's attack were the security programs of which travel controls were only a small part. The testimony of R. W. Scott McLeod, Assistant Secretary of State for Security and Consular Affairs, in November 1955 before the "Henning Committee" was the subject of particular consternation at the highest levels of the State Department. The fear was that Senator Henning would demand to know who precisely was responsible for various (and increasingly publicized) cases of passport denials. In other words, the senator struck at the very essence of the Passport Division: the unreviewable discretion of one person, such as Mrs. Shipley, or perhaps a small committee, to decide that the national interest outweighed the individual interest in travel. What the State Department considered an inherently executive prerogative grounded in the conduct of foreign policy, Senator Henning perceived to be an assault on the individual rights of citizens by calloused bureaucrats. Congress presented a danger to the Secretary's decisional autonomy that the Department had thus far avoided in the courts. Lawsuits could always be mooted by the tactical issuance of passports to successful plaintiffs. Congress, on the other hand, might not be so easily mollified.[198]

The Supreme Court issued *Kent v. Dulles,* its first opinion on the right to international travel, on June 16, 1958.[199] The Court held that Congress had not delegated the Secretary the authority he claimed to deny passports to the petitioners due to their alleged Communist sympathies and affiliations (Rockwell Kent, an artist and author, and Walter Briehl, a psychiatrist, had separately refused to complete affidavits concerning their membership in the Communist Party).[200] The Court found only delegated power to deny passports on the grounds of questions about the particular traveler's citizenship, allegiance, or unlawful conduct at home or abroad. Justice Douglas therefore concluded that Congress did not intend to give the Secretary of State "unbridled discretion to grant or withhold a passport from a citizen for any substantive reason he may choose."[201] Given Mrs. Shipley's record of having done just that for almost thirty years, Justice Douglas seems to have made a veiled and not entirely accurate reference to her work: "One can find in the records of the State Department rulings of subordinates covering a wider range of activities than the two indicated. But as respects Communists these are scattered rulings and not consistently of one pattern."[202] Finding international travel to be part of the liberty protected by the Fifth Amendment, the Court refused to see the question as a political one for the discretion of the Executive Branch. The passport's diplomatic function was "subordinate" to another. "Its crucial function today is control over exit. And, as we have seen, the right of exit is a personal right including within the word 'liberty' as used in the Fifth Amendment."[203]

The *Kent* case was a shocking blow to the State Department, which considered the use of affidavits sworn under oath that these cases invalidated to be "most effective in administering a passport control program."[204] The Department sought to introduce an oath requirement into draft legislation under consideration in Congress in 1959. This was a targeted effort to respond to the holding in *Kent,* one that would "strengthen the Government's defense of the requirement by giving a clear expression of Congressional intent."[205] The Department also sought to add to draft legislation the power to deny passports when these would "seriously impair the conduct of the foreign relations of the United States; or be inimical to the security of the United States."[206] After *Kent,* and in light of activity on the Hill that it feared could inadvertently cabin power that the Department always assumed that it possessed, the Department was taking no chances.

The same day that *Kent* was decided, the Supreme Court also handed down its decision in *Dayton v. Dulles.* If *Kent* was a death blow to the unreviewable discretion of the Department to decide passport questions, *Dayton* was the first strike on the final nail in the coffin. Weldon Dayton, a physicist, sought permission to travel to India to conduct research. His passport application originated in 1954, during Mrs. Shipley's reign. She had denied it because "it would be contrary to the best interest of the United States to provide you passport facilities at this time."[207] Dayton, unlike Kent or Briehl, was willing to swear an affidavit that he was not a Communist, but to no avail.[208] Justice Douglas described at length the use by the Department of confidential material to deny the application and then remanded the case for consideration in light of his opinion in *Kent.* Since the issue in *Kent* was the breadth of a statutory delegation of power by Congress, not the constitutional question of using confidential evidence to deny a passport, this lengthy digression could only be interpreted as a warning.

In due time, that warning would be partially sustained by the *Aptheker* case (discussed in chapter 3).[209] The State Department continued to enjoy considerable deference to set general restrictions on passports for foreign policy reasons. But the passport cases and legislative activity of the late 1950s made clear that the Passport Division was unlikely ever again to enjoy the unlimited, unreviewable discretion that Mrs. Shipley had exercised for almost thirty years.[210] This is not to say that open records and judicial-style hearings became the norm. Quite the contrary, the due process protections that emerged from these cases gradually evolved into a balancing test that accepted a heavy thumb on the side of government interests in foreign affairs and national security against individual interests in travel. As chapters 6 and 7 demonstrate, the result has been to replace Mrs. Shipley with automated processes that would satisfy only the most formalistic understanding of due process of law.

There was a certain irony to be found in the Supreme Court opinions in the *Kent* and *Dayton* cases. They were both written by Justice Douglas who, in 1959, was obliged to write to Deputy Undersecretary of State Robert Murphy seeking his "personal consideration and if necessary to discuss . . . with Secretary [of State] Herter and President Eisenhower" the Department's decision not to validate his passport for travel to China.[211]

CHAPTER SIX

Change: Digitizing Mrs. Shipley

The lessons of the past have been wasted; history not only repeats itself, it seems to be laboring under a neurotic compulsion to do so.

—Arthur Koestler[1]

When Mrs. Shipley began her career, barnstorming was the most common use of an airplane in America. The pictures that hung in Mrs. Shipley's regional passport offices displayed ocean liners, not aircraft. This reflected the most popular mode of travel, which remained ships, not planes, until 1954, the year before Mrs. Shipley retired.[2] And by the time the wide-body Boeing 747 and McDonnell Douglas DC-10 jumbo jets revolutionized international air travel with their first flights in 1970, Mrs. Shipley had been dead for four years.

Only when air travel was in its infancy was Mrs. Shipley there to control it, as she did the international travel of all U.S. citizens. Mrs. Shipley was resolute that her power was based on American interests in foreign affairs and national security. But although passport fraud was a top priority of her office, the national security reasons were espionage and pro-Communist activism, not terrorism. In a world pitched on the brink of nuclear Armageddon, such concerns resonated clearly enough: the travel and activities abroad of those suspected of Communist Party sympathies, even seemingly innocent ones, could set off an international crisis.

Nonetheless, the anxieties of the Red Scare sometimes seem inchoate and shifting compared to the current fear of terrorism. Mrs. Shipley forbade travel for many reasons, but never for the concrete one that originally inspired the No Fly List: to protect aircraft from hijackers and bombers. Paul Robeson, Arthur Miller, and Linus Pauling might have been suspected of undermining American interests abroad, but they were never suspected of planning to blow anything up. And although she kept meticulous files to prevent the departure of Americans whose international travel was "not in the interest of the United States," Mrs. Shipley never kept a No Fly List and she never used a computer.

And yet it was Mrs. Shipley's system that was reconstituted after the attacks of September 11, 2001. To be sure, her name was never mentioned. Indeed, it is doubtful that anyone closely involved in creating new agencies and policies after September 11 had ever heard of her. Nevertheless, the approach to controlling the travel of American citizens that these policymakers crafted was unmistakably hers. It is Mrs. Shipley's ghost that inhabits the new American counterterrorism machine. This chapter describes that return to Mrs. Shipley's system of controlling the travel of her fellow citizens. It also begins to explain how the No Fly List shifted from an original mission that focused on the physical safety of the traveling public to one that looks increasingly to stop the travel of individuals who do not present an immediate physical danger to anyone, but whose travel someone has concluded would "not be in the interests of the United States."

1. After Mrs. Shipley, but before 9/11

The Invention of Hijacking

On September 11, 2001, Americans were shocked by the evil demonstration that commercial aircraft could be converted into guided missiles.[3] In retrospect, the lethality of a fuel-filled, wide-bodied passenger aircraft now seems as obvious a means of terrorism as the "old-fashioned" crime of hijacking. But there was a time when hijacking an aircraft was itself a new idea, and its origins are far removed from the political act (whether a crime of civilians or an attack by combatants) that today we recognize as terrorism. In fact, when Congress began studying the problem in the late 1960s, its first report referenced Webster's Dictionary to explain what the word "hijack" meant in this new context.[4]

Fifty-five years ago, American law had no precise crime to fit the act. After all, hijackers did not typically intend to steal the plane or contraband in its hold in the way that the Prohibition-era origins of that term described the work of smugglers and bootleggers.[5] Nor did "air piracy" really fit, although that was ultimately the term of art used to categorize the crime.[6] Hijackers were not pirates as understood in international law because they typically did not intend to plunder passengers and vessel.[7] Typically, they "only" wanted to alter the scheduled route for personal or political reasons. The common law might have called the act a combination of the tort of conversion (the intentional wrongful use or possession of another's property) and the crime of kidnapping (which originally required the element of forcibly taking the person to another country).[8]

The end of America's "golden age of flight" might well be said to have coincided with the rise of Fidel Castro's Communist regime in Cuba. On May 1, 1961 (May Day), National Airlines Convair 440 became the first plane owned by a U.S. airline to be hijacked when Antulio Ramirez Ortiz forced it to fly to Cuba while carrying six passengers and three crew members.[9] Mr. Ramirez bought his ticket under the name "Elpir Cofrisi." At the last minute, he insisted that the ticket agent add the letter cluster "ata" to his first name. As "El Pirata Cofrisi"—a reference to Roberto Cofresi, a notorious pirate who roamed the Caribbean in the early nineteenth century—Ramirez used a knife and a gun to hijack the Key West–bound plane and divert its passengers and crew to Havana.[10] In the absence of any law criminalizing piracy in the air, however, the United States brought charges against him for theft of an aircraft in foreign commerce, kidnapping, and assault on the high seas.[11]

A few months later, Leon Bearden, along with his teenage son Cody, tried to hijack Continental Airlines Flight 707, a multistop flight that departed Los Angeles carrying seventy-one passengers. They, too, wanted to go to Cuba. The pistol-wielding father and son were duped into permitting the flight to make a scheduled stop in El Paso to take on fuel. Government agents then chased the plane down the runway, shot out its tires and engine, and captured the hijackers.[12] In the absence of any specific law against hijacking an aircraft, however, the prosecution ran into a series of problems. First, the flight across the high Arizona desert from Los Angeles to El Paso made "piracy on the high seas" a bit of a stretch. Therefore, the government charged Bearden with the federal crimes of obstruction of commerce, kidnapping, and interstate transportation of a stolen airplane.[13] But since the flight hadn't altered course and the passengers had been delivered to their destination on time, an appellate court ordered a new trial on the first two charges. It was error, the court of appeals said, for the trial court to have failed to instruct the jury on key elements about who was actually in control of the aircraft.[14] After a wild ride, Bearden was finally sentenced to twenty years in prison, but only for obstructing interstate commerce.[15] Clearly a change was needed in the law. In the meantime, armed federal border guards—the precursor to air marshals—were for the first time periodically sent onto commercial aircraft.[16]

These were not freak events; they were the tip of the iceberg. Fifty out of fifty-one U.S. registered aircraft hijacked between May 1961 and September 1969 had their flight plans forcibly rerouted to Cuba, with which government the United States had severed relations.[17] Of the sixty-five perpetrators or accomplices to these hijackings, twenty-four were U.S. citizens (more than from any other country).[18] The general counsel of the Air Transport Association estimated the hijack rate for American-flagged aircraft during January 1969 to be one hijacking every seventy hours.[19] A series of hijackings in Europe in autumn 1970 led President Nixon to respond with a wide range of security and diplomatic measures announced on September 11, 1970.[20]

Although terrifying, these hijackings were generally considered to be nonlethal, nonpolitical phenomena that a passenger could expect to survive.[21] In fact, hijackings to Cuba grew to be so common that they became the punch line in jokes and cartoons, like the one in figure 5.[22]

The gap in the criminal law that these hijackings exposed was no laughing matter. In fact, the first rash of hijackings served as the catalyst for the new federal crime of "aircraft piracy," which was made punishable by death in 1961.[23] These hijackings also led to amendments and regulations prohibiting various weapons on board aircraft and stimulated interest in the development of magnetometers and other security devices at airports. Of most interest to this study, however, was the grant of a new "Authority to Refuse Transport" (subject to the FAA's reasonable regulation). Airlines were now expressly granted the power to refuse to transport passengers or cargo when, "in the opinion of the air carrier, such transportation would or might be inimical to safety of flight."[24]

This was an exception to the usual requirement that common carriers serve all who could purchase a ticket. It was also the legal seed from which authority to devise the No Fly List would ultimately sprout. Although the FAA was authorized to administer this exception from the usual requirements of common carriers, the FBI was given the authority to investigate suspected crimes.[25] This was the beginning of a division of responsibility between agencies that was only partially joined up after September 11, 2001. Their different priorities (aviation safety and law enforcement) could sometimes lead to interagency tensions. The centralization of watchlisting that 9/11 produced was meant to tamp down these tensions (which could sometimes lead one agency to resist sharing information with the other) by managing all databases through a single source agency.

Despite this rash of hijackings, not one American passenger died in a hijacking incident until June 1971.[26] But 189 people were killed on U.S. and Canadian flights by bombs hidden in luggage, under seats, or in lavatories

Fig. 5. "On Voyage," by Dahl

between 1949 and 1971. These horrible acts, however, were never found to be instances of terrorism. Invariably, each was determined to be a crime of passion, the planned murder of a relative, or suicides linked with attempts to collect life insurance policies.[27] Aircraft security then was not what we have come to expect. A predeparture search of passengers and their bags was considered "heavy-handed" and pregnant with constitutional implications we do not even think about today.[28] For example, John Gilbert Graham was executed for destroying a United Airlines flight in order to kill his mother for the insurance proceeds.[29] In the aftermath of the midair explosion that caused the deaths of forty-five people, a *New York Times* journalist asked, "How can a saboteur intent on destroying a plane be intercepted?" The blithe tone of dismissal is hard to understand today:

> Security police of one major airline frankly admit there are few useful precautionary measures that can be taken. They hasten to add that saboteurs can just as easily blow up trains, buses or ships. They have some detectives' tricks for anticipating trouble, but they decline to disclose them.

> As for mechanical gadgets, they have rejected several. Customs officials use an inspectroscope to ferret out hidden compartments in luggage or the heels of shoes. But, the airlines assert, only a limited number of people come through customs. It is just not feasible, they say, to inspect the suitcase of every salesman on a short business trip and every wife flying home to see mother. Incidentally, they point out, X-ray devices ruin any film contacted.
>
> Magnetic devices that detect the presence of metal are no better. What suitcase does not contain an electric shaver or a traveling iron? Is each click of the detector to mean a suitcase opened and rifled top to bottom? The rigmarole involved in merely running the detector over every suitcase and hat box going aboard a plane would make present baggage routine, a frequent annoyance, seem like the essence of convenience.[30]

This thinking was pervasive. For example, the U.S. Postal Service routinely used commercial airlines to transport mail but did not regulate its inspection prior to loading.[31] Even as late as the bombing of Pan Am Flight 103 over Lockerbie in December 1988, the Post Office maintained the position that without a search warrant and absent extraordinary circumstances, mail sent "sealed against inspection" could neither be X-rayed nor otherwise subjected to security screening before loading it onto a passenger flight.[32] This category of mail, required by law, could include parcels weighing up to seventy pounds.[33]

Other solutions proposed in the 1960s and 1970s are identical to those proposed today: electronic pass-through detectors, locked cabin doors, armed pilots, judo-trained air marshals, and profiling for the "typical" hijacker.[34] This last suggestion was quickly dismissed by one author, who noted that the "preparation of a guide to known subversives" who were considered probable hijackers was a nonstarter "at least in the United States," because of possible legal problems "attendant to a common carrier's turning away a harmless passenger on the sole basis of suspected political affiliation."[35] Not every idea proposed in 1969 was worthy enough of reconsideration thirty-two years later. One solution proposed to the FAA was "maneuvering the hijacker over a trap door in the floor of the cabin and pressing a button to open it."[36]

New Threats, New Solutions

Hijackings continued. A rash of extortion attempts in late 1971 and early 1972, some including bombs hidden on planes, led the FAA to require airlines to create passenger and baggage screening systems and security programs.³⁷ With the passage of the Air Transportation Security Act of 1974, passengers were required to submit to a personal search of their persons and carry-on luggage if they wished to travel by air.³⁸ But after a brief lull, hijackings continued into the 1980s, with a new threat emerging that made American nationals hijacking planes to Cuba appear quaint. The new danger came primarily from foreign terrorist organizations. Their modus operandi initially focused on hijacking planes and ransoming the passengers. As the threat changed from ransoming passengers to bombing planes, so did the government response—but it was a terrifying dance in which the American reaction always seemed a beat behind the terrorist's tune.

The hijacking of TWA Flight 847 on June 14, 1985, was the first major catalyst for aviation security reforms.³⁹ In Athens, two Lebanese men (widely believed to be Mohammed Ali Hammadi and Hassan Izz-Al-Din, both members of the Shiite terrorist organization Hezbollah) boarded the Rome-bound plane. Their carry-on bags hid a 9 mm pistol and hand grenades wrapped in fiberglass insulation, weapons they used to divert the plane first to Beirut and then back and forth between Beirut and Algiers.⁴⁰ Over the course of the next seventeen days, more hijackers boarded the plane and terrorized the passengers with beatings and the murder of a U.S. Navy diver, Robert Dean Stethem. The hijackers gradually released their hostages while making their own demands, including the release of Israeli-held Lebanese prisoners, followed by their own escape.

Congress responded to the hijacking of TWA 847 with the Foreign Airport Security Act.⁴¹ As its name implied, the law focused on threats to U.S. citizens and American-flagged aircraft, but only those threats that occurred at *foreign* airports. This was hardly surprising given the then fairly accurate, but shortsighted perception that terrorism was a foreign-based threat. Among its provisions were sections calling for an expansion of the air marshal program, evaluations of security at foreign airports, and associated sanctions for inadequate compliance. There was also an authorization to the Executive Branch to immediately suspend, without notice or comment, the right of an air carrier to provide international transportation service or otherwise operate in foreign commerce upon finding that the public interest so demanded, and that "a condition exists that threatens the safety or security of passengers, aircraft, or crew traveling to or from [that] foreign airport."⁴²

TWA 847 also led the FAA to create an Intelligence Division in March 1986.⁴³ Prior to this reform, the FAA "had no ability to receive, analyze or disseminate intelligence," all of which came from other agencies of the federal government.⁴⁴ Its small cohort was staffed with officials culled from the

DEA, Defense Department, and other agencies.[45] That unit issued Security Bulletins (known as "SBs") to the airlines. These contained unclassified information about long- and short-term threats to airline security. After TWA 847, these warnings tended to be directed at specific threats placing specific airlines' routes at risk because of identified vulnerabilities.[46] But SBs were recommendations only; that is, they were advisory, not obligatory.[47] Their dissemination was quickened, but not by much; since 1987, SBs were being sent by fax to the airlines' security offices.[48] And what attention these received—even whether they *had* been received—was impossible to know. Since the airlines themselves were responsible for any action in response, not the government, this was a significant black hole.

Prior to the establishment of the Intelligence Division, the FAA relied entirely on the State Department and FBI for its intelligence. With the creation of this new office, the FAA now established liaisons throughout the Intelligence Community. Although the FAA now had its own in-house analysts, it remained a consumer of the raw intelligence produced by others and, as such, was required to engage in a time-consuming process of permission-seeking to release information in each of the twenty to thirty SBs it sought to distribute to commercial airlines each year.[49]

The next major catalyst for reform came three and half years later with the bombing of Pan Am Flight 103 over Lockerbie, Scotland, on December 21, 1988. This tragedy shifted the focus from preventing *hijackers* from backing up their demands with the threat of explosives they carried on board to preventing *terrorists* from using hidden bombs to cause high-altitude death and destruction on planes they never intended to board themselves.[50] The deaths of 270 people were caused by a bomb hidden in a radio/cassette player.[51] The bomb was in luggage in the cargo hold, most likely loaded in Frankfurt, where Pan Am's security was particularly lax, especially with regard to personnel servicing aircraft and bags being transferred for passengers in transit from one airline onto another. Two months before the bombing, an FAA inspector described an overwhelmed system in Frankfurt held together by "a very labor intensive operation and the tenuous threads of luck," but one nevertheless in compliance with FAA requirements.[52]

The presidential commission established after the catastrophe described the FAA's Intelligence Division as "the conduit for intelligence information collected and evaluated by the intelligence community and the FBI for dissemination to the private air carriers and/or airports that must ultimately take defensive action."[53] This was a polite way of saying that the FAA remained a mere recipient of whatever information the Intelligence

Community chose to share with it. As a *consumer* of intelligence produced by others, the FAA needed authority from the source agencies to distribute information to the industry—permission that was often delayed or refused by agencies cautiously guarding their sources, methods, and, sometimes, their political turf. No surprise, then, that the Commission concluded that the FAA was a "reactive agency."[54] Inside the FAA's intelligence office, there was suspicion that the Intelligence Community did not provide FAA with as much intelligence as it could because it did not take the threat as seriously as it should. As a result, FAA officials felt themselves frequently forced to prove their "need to know."[55] But all they could do was seek a greater flow of information by detailing liaisons to different intelligence agencies.[56] Unless they could persuade those agencies (mostly the CIA and FBI) to declassify information for distribution by the FAA to the airline industry, disagreement meant silence.[57]

The Commission recommended that the FAA provide more direction to the aviation industry than the merely advisory recommendations in its Security Bulletins. Baseline security measures were established as a result. Another result was the creation of "Security Directives" (SDs) and Information Circulars to replace Security Bulletins. SDs were obligatory orders (not advisory notices) to airlines to take specific action. Twenty or thirty SDs might be circulated to airlines each year as gap-fillers to augment standard security plans already in place.[58] This was considered a "clear refinement."[59] The standard for issuing an SD was focused narrowly on identifying a "specific and credible threat" to civil aviation.[60] This phrase had a particular meaning. It was understood in the Intelligence Community to mean an actual threat to a particular aircraft or carrier or route.[61] When an SD was dispatched, the reason was the detection of a serious threat based on specific evidence that a hijacking or terrorist attack on an identified target was imminent. Information circulars were informational in nature, not obligatory, and dealt with matters such as training, travel advisories, and updates on general security measures, explosives, known modi operandi, and the like.[62]

Security Directives could be cumbersome and slow. As a regulatory vehicle, they were susceptible to the coordination and vetting problems that afflict all administrative systems, although in an emergency one could be prepared within hours. They were faxed to the corporate security directors of the air carriers. These were manually checked lists—there was no automated system pre-9/11.[63] Airlines were obliged to acknowledge their receipt within twenty-four hours and report their compliance with specific instructions within seventy-two hours.[64] The infrequency of hijackings that led to loss of life, especially domestically, and the costs associated with heightened security made airlines skeptical of FAA security directives, lowering their compliance.[65] Airline executives testified before the 9/11 Commission that they came to rely on SDs, rather than proactively make their own assessments of security, in part out of fear of lawsuits.[66] Although the criteria for issuing a person-specific SD were high—a "direct and credible threat" to civil aviation—the FAA's position as a receiver, not a generator, of intelligence could also slow the process.[67] FAA had to seek the approval of the Intelligence Community, which was concerned to protect its sources and methods, before it could watchlist an individual with an SD.[68] Perhaps as a result, name-based "do-not-carry" SDs composed only a small fraction of the total library of security directives.[69]

Nevertheless, the creation of the Security Directive was an important development. For the first time, the federal government could use an SD to order a private airline not to transport a particular individual. That power was derived, in part, from the exemption from the ordinary obligation of common carriers to accept all passengers that Congress enacted in 1961: no airline was obliged to transport a person if "in the opinion of the air carrier, such transportation would or might be inimical to safety of flight."[70] FAA issuance of an SD was prima facie evidence that this standard had been met. Hence the criteria: a direct and specific threat to civil aviation.

Although SDs identifying particular individuals were the precursor to the No Fly List, and therefore their importance for what followed after 9/11 cannot be overstated, other agencies also gathered intelligence on travelers to fulfill their own legal mandates. These systems also influenced the ultimate creation of terrorist watchlists. After the 1993 World Trade Center bombing, Immigration and Naturalization Service Commissioner Doris Meissner worked with Mary Ryan, head of the Consular Affairs Bureau of the State Department, to create an automated terrorist watchlist that could be used by both agencies to achieve the same goal: excluding suspected terrorists from the United States.[71] They were building on the work of a State Department official named John Arriza, who in 1987 had designed TIPOFF, a list that collected biographical and derogatory information from State Department and other sources for use in evaluating visa applications.[72]

The origins of the TIPOFF database were not exactly auspicious. This first watchlist didn't even take the form of a list: it started off as a shoebox full of three-by-five index cards.[73] TIPOFF was only launched in a meaningful way after the Intelligence Community reluctantly agreed to allow the declassification and distribution to consular officials of four biographical elements: name, date of birth, nationality, and passport number.⁷⁴ Although the TIPOFF database had been computerized by 1993, the lists it produced were still distributed on paper when the first World Trade Center bombing occurred that year.⁷⁵ In fact, Sheikh Omar Abdel-Rahman, the "blind sheikh" now serving a life term in prison for his role in the bombing, was issued a visa in Khartoum despite his name appearing on the State Department's watchlist—nobody had checked the microfiche on which the list was stored in the U.S. Embassy in Sudan.⁷⁶

TIPOFF became part of a massive database called CLASS (for Consular Lookout and Support Systems) that the State Department's Bureau of Consular Affairs used to vet and filter out those deemed suspicious or undesirable. On September 11, 2001, CLASS contained approximately 10 million records that identified individuals who had previously been denied a visa, were wanted by federal law enforcement officials, or who otherwise had attracted undesired attention by the U.S. Government.⁷⁷ Aside from the slow speed of technological progress, CLASS and TIPOFF suffered from the same problem that the FAA's Security Directives faced: agencies reluctant to share information. The contributions of documents to TIPOFF by other agencies in 2001 could best be described as miserly.⁷⁸ Nevertheless, it was TIPOFF that served as the kernel from which the Government's new Terrorist Screening Database (TSDB) would grow.⁷⁹

No federal office or agency seemed to realize the value of watchlists more than the Customs Service, tasked with solving the devilish problem of preventing contraband from flowing into the country without inhibiting the flow of international trade on which our free market depends. The war on drugs was the catalyst for intelligence innovations like the Advanced Passenger Information System (APIS), which gradually began operating in 1988. With the cooperation of the domestic airline industry, this computerized system was fed biographical data from the airlines' reservations systems. This included not only information that any customs official could eventually obtain from a passport once the traveler had landed, but also information that only the airlines possessed: for example, credit card information gathered at the time of the ticket sale and phone numbers or addresses provided by the passenger to the airline.⁸⁰ In 2000, 80 percent of inbound passengers were screened through APIS.⁸¹

Although Customs (and the INS, which also used the system) was legally responsible only for border controls, the data from international flights could not be cordoned off from domestic flights. Nor did the government have an incentive to self-censor its access: the investigative interest in breaking up a suspected drug ring did not stop at the border. Inevitably, exigent circumstances would excuse this use.[82] Thus began the creeping expansion of watchlists, in size, scope, and power.

2. September 11, 2001: Regenerating Mrs. Shipley

On September 10, 2001, the latest FAA Security Directives prohibited the boarding on commercial aircraft of twelve named individuals who were deemed to pose a "direct" threat to civil aviation, none of whom were U.S. citizens.[83] The foreign focus was understandable. "[T]he history of the FAA was dramatically more focused on safety than security," recalled Admiral James Loy, who in November 2002 became the first administrator of the new Transportation Security Administration.[84] Not since 1991 had an airplane been hijacked inside the United States; the last time a U.S. carrier had been hijacked, anywhere, was in 1986.[85] The small size of the list was in large part because standards for inclusion on SDs were evaluated through "aviation glasses."[86] Only those persons considered a "direct and credible threat to aviation" were identified and prohibited from flying by SDs.[87]

The hijackers were nineteen foreigners whose visas, travels, and activities in the weeks and months prior to September 11 seemed to expose one failing and hole after another in American immigration and law enforcement. Their visas were obtained despite numerous problems. Several were issued speeding tickets by local law enforcement whose access to immigration data was too limited to note their violations.

Not surprisingly, the immediate focus after the attacks was oriented outward. The nation's borders had to be secured and its net of visa and other immigration controls tightened. Immigration in particular offered a fast way to arrest suspects and hold them much longer than the criminal justice system would have allowed. These efforts did not catch terrorists. Edward Alden's seminal book on the restructuring of border security after 9/11 reports that not a single one of the 762 people detained for an alleged immigration violation in those first few months "was ever charged with terrorism or a terrorist-related offense."[88]

9/11 Commissioners John Lehman and Timothy Roemer were particularly infuriated to discover that the FAA seemed to consider only twelve people in the world too dangerous to fly in American airspace.[89] This number seemed small to them compared to the State Department's TIPOFF database, which had grown out of its shoebox of index cards to identify about 60,000 suspected terrorists who should be denied admission into the United

States. By September 11, 2001, this TIPOFF terrorist watchlist had been incorporated into the larger CLASS database that the State Department's Bureau of Consular Affairs used to assess all visa applications. It had also been shared with the Justice Department's Immigration and Naturalization Service, a partnership that was catalyzed by an interest in preventing Iraqi spies from entering the United States prior to the first Gulf War.[90] But the FAA had not been included in this partnership. The Commissioners' wrath grew when Admiral Cathal "Irish" Flynn, the FAA's Associate Administrator for Civil Aviation Security, admitted under questioning that he was unaware of the existence of the TIPOFF database until the day before his testimony before the Commission, more than two years after September 11.[91]

The Commission's investigation led to two sharp criticisms. First, the FAA was not up to the task of ensuring aviation security. The agency was criticized for falling prey to the classic problem of agency capture. Its triple mandate to foster air commerce, advance aviation safety, and protect aviation security established goals that sometimes conflicted. The rarity of domestic hijackings (let alone suicide attacks), combined with the high costs to airlines of more security measures, created pressure to focus on goals more agreeable to the industry the FAA was tasked with regulating.

This criticism combined with a second one directed at the Intelligence Community. Agencies hoarded their information. This resulted in duplicated effort instead of economies of scale. Worse, it meant that agency turf battles kept intelligence from being used intelligently. The FAA was particularly affected by this problem. Its intelligence office relied on the generosity of other agencies to provide it with information. And, when information was provided at all, this intelligence could not be shared with the airlines without the permission of the originating agency, which often preferred to protect its sources and methods rather than risk exposing them to deter a threat held to be of minor significance. Combined with the airlines' own reluctance to spend money on behind-the-scenes security that inconvenienced their customers and that they considered unnecessary anyway, it is no wonder that the FAA's Security Directives identified only twelve people worldwide too dangerous to fly in American skies.

First Response: Building the System

President George W. Bush and Congress did not wait for the advice of the 9/11 Commission to begin a major overhaul of American counterterrorism policies, anticipating the Commission's recommendations concerning both the Intelligence Community and aviation security. Almost immediately, the

White House responded to the weaknesses in civil aviation security exposed by the 9/11 terrorists with the fervor of a recent convert. "We had nothing on 9/11. We had nothing. And then, what we had was pathetic," recalled Michael Jackson, who on September 11 was deputy to Secretary of Transportation Norman Mineta. "The obvious facts were that what had been done at this juncture was wholly inadequate and totally messed up."[92]

On September 20, two days after Congress authorized the use of military force against Al-Qaeda and the Taliban, President Bush announced to a joint session of Congress the creation of an Office of Homeland Security in the White House, to be headed by Tom Ridge, then governor of Pennsylvania.[93] The announcement was followed by an executive order creating that office within the Executive Office of the President and a Homeland Security Council modeled after the National Security Council.[94] The USA PATRIOT Act was signed October 26, 2001.[95]

Expansion of the APIS system was one of the first post-9/11 policy steps. It was APIS, after all, that had correctly identified all nineteen terrorists within an hour after the attack on 9/11. Customs successfully pressed for legislation passed in November 2001 that required APIS information from all airlines, domestic and foreign, that routed into the United States.[96] Edward Alden notes the pressure placed on foreign airlines to comply with those data sweeps even in advance of the deadline set by Congress. If an airline resisted this demand, it could expect every one of its passengers on every flight to be delayed for hours in secondary screening, every time. A few airlines nevertheless challenged the request to comply; when an example was made of Saudi Airlines, its opposition collapsed within two days after Customs officials demonstrated the long delays passengers outside the APIS system could now expect upon arrival into the United States.[97] The threat of lengthy screening upon arrival was an effective pressure point to compel compliance with prescreening.

But, above all, it was Security Directives used by the FAA's Civil Aviation Security Office—the neglected tool of a neglected office—that now came into their own. Senior officials desperate to prevent another attack seized on the watchlisting power embedded in the concept of "do-not-carry" security directives. As Michael Jackson recalled, "it's hard to underestimate the personal sense of responsibility that the senior government leaders felt in trying to do everything that was reasonable and yet doable to prevent another attack. And the watchlist was a core tool in that effort. So it would have been irresponsible not to develop and actively manage a watchlist of the sort that we ended up with. And there was no disagreement about that, really, amongst the team."[98]

According to Richard Falkenrath, who became the Special Assistant to President Bush and Senior Director for Policy and Plans in the White House's new Office of Homeland Security,

> [I]t was just accidental that the authority originated in their authorizing statute, I assume, and then some pre-9/11 security directive. It was really grabbed a hold of by the White House, which was driving everything back then—FBI, CIA to a certain extent. And it just became, with every single case that came into the White House post-9/11, and there were lots, we got into the habit of just asking, Is he no-flied? Is he no-flied? Is he no-flied? And the bureaucracy at first would respond, "We don't know," and they couldn't keep track of all these lists.[99]

In November, President Bush signed the Aviation and Transportation Security Act, creating the Transportation Security Administration (TSA) within the Department of Transportation.[100] (The Homeland Security Act of 2002 later transferred the TSA to the newly created Department of Homeland Security.)[101] As the name implied, the act transferred responsibility for aviation security to TSA, leaving the FAA with responsibility for aviation safety. TSA acquired the authority to issue Security Directives prohibiting airlines from transporting certain individuals deemed too dangerous to fly. In particular, TSA now also acquired the power, "in consultation with other appropriate Federal agencies and air carriers," to require air carriers "to use information from government agencies to identify individuals on passenger lists who may be a threat to civil aviation or national security and, if such an individual is identified, notify appropriate law enforcement agencies, prevent the individual from boarding an aircraft, or take other appropriate action with respect to that individual."[102] Deputy Secretary of Transportation Michael Jackson, who believed watchlisting was "a core tool," was largely responsible for starting up that new agency within the Department of Transportation.[103]

For Admiral James Loy, one of the TSA's first administrators, "keeping bad guys off airplanes was at the top of the list" of issues to accomplish when he was tapped to lead the new organization in late 2002.[104] Congress had given TSA statutory authority to use SDs, of which the name-based "do-not-carry" variety soon became the operative vehicle for the No Fly List, but left unclear exactly who was ultimately in charge of this emerging watchlist.[105] Whatever aspirations Admiral Loy and his TSA policy team had for the No Fly List, e-mail traffic between FBI agents suggests a high degree of confidence within the FBI that TSA was merely the administrative agent through which the FBI conducted some of its investigations and operations. This confidence appears to have lasted long after the TSA was up and running. On December 17, 2002, one FBI Supervisory Special Agent wrote, "We are putting the target on the TSA No Fly List here at FBIHQ. I will be getting with TSA tomorrow (12/18) to accomplish this."[106] Another e-mail, dated February 4, 2003, tersely asks: "We've got a guy we want to no-fly. Do you have a copy of the last one we gave you?"[107]

Nor was this a matter exclusively for headquarters. The process for adding names was initially so lax that, according to Edward Alden, "almost any FBI agent could add a name to the list with little scrutiny."[108] The e-mails from the field mirror those from headquarters: "Boston has subject that we would like to add to the TSA 'No Fly List.' Do you know who I address the EC [electronic communication] to?"[109] Each of these e-mail requests were answered with language cut-and-pasted from one reply to the next. The process was as easy as it was formulaic: "To place an individual on the No-Fly we ask that you state in the EC that the FBI believes that the listed individual is a threat to Civil Aviation Security. We ask also that any bio data on the No-Fly be at the For Official Use Only (FOUO) [level of classification]."[110]

The FBI's confidence that the No Fly List was at its disposal was not unfounded. Claudio Manno, who became the Acting Associate Under Secretary at TSA for Transportation Security Intelligence, wrote an internal TSA memorandum that set out the history of FBI involvement. Early on September 12, 2001, he explained in his memo,

> [A]t the request of the FBI, the FAA issued SD-108-01-06/EA 129-01-05, which included a list of individuals developed by the FBI as part of the *Pentbom* investigation. . . . The FBI "controlled," both administratively and operationally, the contents of the list and added or removed names in accordance with the *Pentbom* investigation. The FAA received the list from the FBI and disseminated it to air carriers, without any format or content changes. FAA, in essence, acted as a conduit for the dissemination of their "watchlist."[111]

This arrangement continued until November 8, 2001, when, again at the request of the FBI, the FAA "assumed full administrative responsibility for the 'watchlist' and issued SD 108-01-19." Still, the FBI seemed to want the best of both worlds: an FAA that would take responsibility for the list while still compliant enough to follow FBI instructions to add or remove names at its direction. In his memo, Manno refers with ironic quotation marks to the shift from a "FBI watchlist" to the "FAA watchlist," which by mid-

December had been divided into a No Fly List (which prohibited travel by commercial aircraft) and a Selectee List (which increased security measures but allowed travel).[112]

The growth of the watchlists led to increased conflict between rival federal agencies, especially between the well-entrenched FBI bureaucracy and the fledgling TSA. In late October 2002, almost a year after the TSA took over the FAA's responsibility for aviation security, the FBI was still adamant that "TSA is the agency which actually makes the entries and removals" from the No Fly List, although the FBI was working with TSA "to develop protocols to facilitate entry and/or removal of FBI subjects to/from the No Fly or Selectee Lists."[113] The FBI wanted the power but not the legal or political headaches associated with the lists: "It should be noted, the air carriers and/or local airport authorities are responsible for preventing a passenger on the No Fly List from boarding an aircraft, not the FBI."[114]

TSA was careful to protect its bureaucratic interests. In interagency communications, TSA noted that it would not remove any name from its lists without a written request from the agency that originally asked for the name to be listed. Meanwhile, the FBI grew increasingly frustrated with what its agents perceived to be growing TSA imperiousness in administering the watchlists while leaving the FBI to handle the public relations fallout from those bureaucratic decisions. In a May 2002 e-mail to Arthur Cummings, then at FBIHQ's Counterterrorism Division, the Supervisory Special Agent in charge of the Civil Aviation Security Program there offered "some background, if you have the patience to read it":

> Since 10/2001, when the TSA No Fly and Selectee lists came into being (aftermath of the FBI Watchlist), I have been attempting to make the updated lists available to the field agents [redacted] on a timely basis, i.e., when they are issued, because TSA has made the agents responsible for responding to possible name matches. . . . TSA also fails (except on one occasion) to coordinate with us when they tell [redacted] (the FBI) or when they change the Security Directives concerning responses which affects FBI offices. Despite my best efforts, the TSA just motors along and I and the agents are being whipped around the flagpole trying to do the right thing. . . . Example—today List 51 was issued; Lists 49 and 50 were issued on Friday. I believe I was here, but no mail from TSA, and I check every hour. I have raised this issue with people in TSA and here, and told the agents that getting the lists from me is now a luxury instead of a certainty.[115]

A month later, the same SSA wrote that TSA "maintains that they still act only as a conduit for the FBI and make no decisions about who or what to put on the list, but they refuse to coordinate the procedures with the FBI. The lack of coordination issue has been raised up pretty high now in the FBI due to questions posed to the Director for the hearings."[116] By July, the SSA was fed up. With the subject line "Info for TSA Legal Request," the angry FBI agent e-mailed: "[Redacted] seems to believe that he is entitled to an immediate response to his issues, when the FBI has been waiting since Nov 2001 for resolution to our issues asking them for [redacted] and to cooperate on crafting the Security Directives. They ignored [redacted] January letter, and have yet to act, based on discussions held at a meeting in early June to go over these issues again. Therefore, I don't know that we should be in any rush for him, but you have to keep letting him think you're working on 'it'—same tactic they use with us."[117]

As Randy Beardsworth, a distinguished Coast Guard officer who joined DHS in 2003 as Chief Operations Officer for Border and Transportation Security, observed, part of the problem was a clash of institutional cultures:

> And part of the situation was that FBI is feudal. . . . Each SAC [special agent in charge] is completely independent and powerful. So the SAC in one city will look at cases and information a certain way. They don't want to share information, and put it into a system that everyone has access to: their sources and methods, investigations, and grand jury information. TSA comes in as the new kid, very little knowledge of law enforcement, trying to administer a list. And so there's this natural tension between the two of them.[118]

According to Beardsworth:

> TSA was the kid that had the football on the football field but weighed fifty pounds and had no clue how to play the game. TSA is trying to assert its role and FBI and other agencies are sort of laughing at it. And then abusing it. Because, remember, it's not a centralized, single FBI. But you would have cases of agents who would say, "I don't know, I'm not going to be the one that lets somebody in the country. This goes on the No Fly List." But there was nobody who was adjudicating the No Fly List.[119]

Removing names from the No Fly List could be as frustrating as adding them. "It appears that there is no more [redacted] on either of the two lists

(No Fly 73 or Selectee 44), so Mr. [redacted] should have no more problems for now," the SSA in charge of the FBI's Civil Aviation Security Program wrote in a July 2002 e-mail to colleagues at State, FAA, and FBI.[120] "However, if another [redacted] should be put on the list, his name would trigger something. Your advice was the best that could be given under the circumstances. I don't know if FBI put him on the list or not."[121] Officials seem to have preferred to err on the side of watchlisting. After all, why take a risk? The e-mail exchange on the next page, between an FBI SSA in Hawaii and FBIHQ was typical.[122] Given Hawaii's geography, the resident in figure 6 was essentially stranded after being placed on the No Fly List.

The White House response had been as predictable as the infighting between agencies. It is cliché but true that armies prepare for the last war, a truth the 9/11 Commission extended to describe the early years of the war on terror.[123] America's responses to attacks on airliners in the 1980s were reactive, not proactive. The hijacking of TWA 847 led to the creation of an intelligence office at the FAA and the tightening of security requirements for foreign airports. But the FAA remained a dependent consumer of the intelligence it was fed by established members of the Intelligence Community. Since the threat of domestic terrorism still seemed remote, the focus was on foreign airports. Likewise, the bombing of Pan Am 103 led to mandatory Security Directives. But FAA's ability to act speedily to prevent a direct and credible threat to an aircraft remained hampered by its dependence on rival agencies, CIA and FBI, to declassify and permit use of their intelligence.

These interagency rivalries continued and worsened. In August 2001, both agencies were investigating troubling leads about flight training undertaken by Zacharias Moussaoui, often labeled the "twentieth hijacker." Although the CIA reached out to foreign intelligence services for information about Moussaoui—describing him as a possible suicide hijacker—and the FBI engaged in a spirited internal debate about whether to arrest him, neither agency fully shared its information with the FAA.[124] This was typical. By the time permission to use intelligence to issue a security directive was granted, the individual blocked from flying by the SD was unlikely to be flying anymore.[125] That was the case with Moussaoui, too; by the time the FBI briefed the FAA, Moussaoui had been under arrest for more than two weeks.[126]

In testimony before the Joint Inquiry into Terrorist Attacks against the United States, Director of Central Intelligence George Tenet admitted that this failure had become systemic. Speaking about the CIA's failure to seek the timely watchlisting of two 9/11 plotters, al-Mihdhar and Nawaf al-Hazmi, whom CIA knew had entered the country as early as January 2000,

From: [redacted]
To: [redacted]
Date: 9/17/02 8:01:50 PM
Subject: [redacted] and No Fly List

Wow, that is the most interesting explanation I've heard yet. I'm not sure it's valid - it just doesn't sound right. However, I will forward this to the airport agents so they know why he is still on the list. thank you for your efforts.

>> [redacted] 9/17/02 1:21:56 PM >>>
[redacted] I wanted to get back with you concerning our conversation, 09/17/2002 and your request to have [redacted] removed from the no fly list. I have spoken with several individuals concerning this, TSA, and others, to try to get to the bottom of this. [redacted] no longer a threat. However, Unfortunately we are not going to be able to remove [redacted] name from the list. [redacted] Therefore, we do not want to be faced with this risk. If you have any other questions please feel free to get back with me. Thanks!
training camps the [redacted]
>> [redacted] 08/21 1:05 PM >>>

[large redacted block]

Anyway, can you and the Terrorist Watch List Unit and [redacted] revisit this matter and see if you can get [redacted] off the list?

Thanks,

SSA [redacted] (fax)
Civil Aviation Security Program, Room 11795
Domestic Terrorism Counterterrorism Planning Section   b2
Counterterrorism Division
[redacted]@leo.gov   b7C

>> [redacted] 8/20/02 3:41:04 PM >>>
[redacted]

Attached is an e-mail documenting concerns of a Hawaii resident by the name of [redacted] who is being frequently stopped and questioned at various airports based upon the similarity of his name with that [redacted] Can you offer any suggestions as to how this Hawaii resident can obtain some relief from this scrutiny. Can a computerised entry be made on the no-fly list that [redacted] with the particular biographical descriptors is not identical to [redacted]

Thanks,

SSA [redacted] Counterterrorism Squad, Honolulu

                                                               b7C
CC: [redacted]

ALL INFORMATION CONTAINED
HEREIN IS UNCLASSIFIED
DATE 9-5-03 BY UC 60267 NLS/AG/CAC
CA# 03-1779

Gordon/Adams pg-255

Fig. 6. FBI E-mail Exchange Regarding No Fly List

Tenet observed: "The fact that earlier we did not recommend al-Hazmi and al-Mihdhar for watchlisting is not attributable to a single point of failure. There were opportunities, both in the field and at Headquarters, to act on developing information. The fact that this did not happen—aside from questions of CTC workload, particularly around the period of the disrupted Millennium plots—pointed out that a whole new system, rather than a fix at a single point in the system, was needed."[127]

Richard Falkenrath, who as Deputy Assistant to President Bush and Deputy Homeland Security Advisor claims credit for the creation of the Terrorist Screening Center, attributes his decision to focus on the watchlisting issue to that speech: "It was George Tenet's admission that the one thing they clearly screwed up was the watchlisting function of the two guys, al-Mihdhar and al-Hamsa. . . . I started every meeting by quoting from Tenet's testimony. And I'd say, all right, this can't stand. Does anyone disagree? No, we all agree. Okay. What are we going to do about it?"[128]

It was in response to this breakdown that Falkenrath and his allies at the White House displayed some creative thinking.[129] That coordination problem would be resolved, counterintuitively, by creating two *more* players in the intelligence sharing game: the National Counterterrorism Center (NCTC) and the Terrorist Screening Center (TSC). Falkenrath did not realize that in the latter office he was reconstituting a more powerful, and less accountable, Mrs. Shipley.

Refining the System: The NCTC and the TSC

The rapid accomplishment of this creative function was not left to the cumbersome process of lawmaking.[130] Speed was at a premium and the delicate task of forcing long-established agency bureaucracies to share the fruits of their intelligence activities would not be easily accomplished in open public forums. The White House therefore did much of the work behind closed doors, issuing policy directives through its Homeland Security Council (which was based on the model of the long-established National Security Council).[131]

As the FBI and TSA fought their turf war over control of the No Fly List, other new agencies were quickly "stood up," in the lingo of the federal bureaucracy. This turf battle, with another agency—the Department of Homeland Security—about to join it, was ample evidence that the information hoarding that marked the pre-9/11 era had not everywhere been replaced by an era of cooperation.

The first step was centralizing the data stream. During his 2003 State of the Union Message, President Bush announced that he had ordered the FBI, CIA, Defense Department, and Department of Homeland Security to develop a Terrorist Threat Integration Center "to merge and analyze all threat information in a single location."[132]

The Terrorist Threat Integration Center (TTIC) was the precursor to what in 2004 became the National Counterterrorism Center (NCTC).[133] On May 1, 2003, the TTIC opened its doors for business at CIA Headquarters at Langley, Virginia, and began centralizing and analyzing information from an alphabet soup of federal databases and watchlists.[134] This multiagency organization comprised officials from FBI, CIA, Defense, State, and Homeland Security and is funded by these participating agencies, but under the administrative umbrella of the Office of the Director of National Intelligence.[135] It was intended to be the clearinghouse and central repository for the nation's primary terrorist database. The TTIC aimed to integrate all of the U.S. Government's foreign terrorist threat information and analyze it in a single location. TTIC would have access to all intelligence and be given the responsibility for producing the daily reports and other analytical products on which the President and his advisors would rely.[136]

The computer database developed to assist in these tasks became known as the Terrorist Identities Datamart Environment (TIDE).[137] This database was to include "to the extent permitted by law, all information the U.S. government possesses related to the identities of individuals known or appropriately suspected to be or have been involved in activities constituting, in preparation for, in aid of, or related to terrorism, with the exception of Purely Domestic Terrorism Information."[138] (Purely domestic terrorism information would continue to be gathered and analyzed by the FBI.) The seed for the TIDE database was the State Department's TIPOFF database, which was transferred to the control of the TTIC (along with a portion of the TIPOFF staff at the State Department) on November 17, 2003.[139] Federal agencies were directed to submit all of their information about known or suspected terrorists to the TTIC for inclusion in the TIDE. TIDE contained both biometric and nominal identifying data (names, aliases, etc.) as well as so-called "derogatory information," *i.e.,* the collected substantive intelligence deemed to constitute terrorist information. While there was no new data, the value added by the TIDE (and its assembly by the TTIC) was to centralize this data for use by all appropriate parts of the Executive Branch. More colloquially, according to journalist Ronald Kessler, one former director of the NCTC described the TIDE as "the mother of all databases . . . if there's a piece of derogatory information on a known or suspected terrorist, it goes in that database."[140]

Once the TTIC began its task of consolidating the nation's foreign terrorist threat intelligence and analysis, the second step was the reorganization and consolidation of the nation's watchlists and screening systems, foreign and domestic. The TTIC had no role in setting watchlisting standards or exercising any operational controls over the growing number and size of watchlists being developed at different agencies.[141] This was again done by the Executive Branch acting through the Homeland Security Council. President Bush signed Homeland Security Presidential Directive 6 (HSPD-6) on September 16, 2003. Its subject was the integration and use of terrorist information for screening and other purposes. Terrorist information was carefully, albeit broadly, defined to be everything in the TIDE plus the FBI's purely domestic terrorism information.

HSPD-6 ordered that an organization be established "to consolidate the Government's approach to terrorism screening and provide for the appropriate and lawful use of Terrorist Information in screening processes."[142] That organization became the Terrorist Screening Center (TSC). The man who helped set up the TSC and who would later become its director, Timothy J. Healy, succinctly expressed the problem the TSC was to address: "There was no bucket that had them all in there."[143] The "bucket" became the Terrorist Screening Database (TSDB), aka the Consolidated Terrorist Watchlist. TSC was tasked with establishing the TSDB and developing a team of expert analysts who would use it to create "downstream" watchlists for customer agencies that drew from this single source and which adopted standardized criteria and formats. The most well-known of its products is the No Fly List. A "call center" at TSC was planned that would facilitate communication between government officials (such as airport personnel or local police) who encountered watchlisted individuals in their daily operations and the agencies that submitted the substantive intelligence used to create the particular watchlist involved.

Although HSPD-6 was issued on September 16, 2003, Healy was not named project leader to set up the TSC until October 27, 2003.[144] This left only slightly more than one month to organize the Center, which began operations on December 1, 2003.[145] Healy faced issues that would be familiar to anyone involved at that level in creating a federal entity from scratch. Initially, for example, personnel were largely drawn from the FBI. Gradually, criteria were established for different types of personnel to be drawn from different agencies.

The TSC is housed in the FBI but staffed by officials from agencies throughout the federal government that have a stake in counterterrorism.[146] In fact, the first director of the TSC, Donna Bucella, had been a TSA official detailed to the FBI for this purpose.[147] A decision was reached and memorialized in an early memorandum of understanding to reserve the position of principal deputy director for an official from the Department of Homeland Security; similarly, one of the assistant director positions is reserved for an official from the Department of State.[148] Although this multiagency staff is expected to represent the interests of their respective agencies, they report to the TSC Director.[149]

The TSC is entirely a creature of the Executive Branch. It has no organic statute or other Act of Congress that defines its responsibilities, structure, or limits.[150] HSPD-6 (and, to the extent applicable, HSPD-11 and HSPD-24) are the sole legal authority for the TSC.[151] The TSC is a component of the National Security Branch of the FBI. The Director of the TSC reports to the FBI Director through the Executive Assistant Director of the National Security Branch.[152] The TSC does not promulgate regulations; it operates under applicable FBI regulations and is funded through appropriations made for its operation that are administered by the FBI. In its first year of operation (fiscal year 2004), the TSC grew to a $27 million budget and 175 staff; in FY2007, those numbers had grown to $83 million and 408 staff.[153] Among those staff, eight positions were created and filled with representatives from TSA.[154]

The TSC and the TTIC were intended to work closely together.[155] In fact, the startup staff for each came, in part, by dividing up the staff responsible for TIPOFF at the State Department.[156] Both were well funded, well staffed, and well supported by patrons in different parts of the Executive Branch. The vast majority of the information in the database that the TSC used to craft and distribute watchlists to customer agencies came from the TTIC. The TTIC (reconstituted in 2004 as the NCTC) soon outgrew its original space at CIA headquarters at Langley. It is now housed just to the southwest in a state-of-the-art building complex in McLean, Virginia, known as "Liberty Crossing," a picture of which is provided on the NCTC's own website.[157] Until recently, the building was identified as NCTC headquarters on Google maps. The TSC, on the other hand, remains more cryptic about its location, somewhere in Crystal City, near Reagan National Airport; its website describes its headquarters only as "housed in a nondescript building in Northern Virginia."[158]

How the Consolidated Watchlist Works Today

President Bush's directives required all executive departments and agencies to provide the NCTC with a continuous stream of terrorist information subject only to any legal restrictions concerning information about U.S. persons.¹⁵⁹ NCTC was to act as the primary pipeline for this terrorist information.¹⁶⁰ The TSC, on the other hand, was to function as the funnel and the sieve for this information, evaluating its sufficiency for watchlisting purposes and distributing it to different government actors in the form of watchlists created for their specialized functions. A memorandum of understanding signed on June 4, 2002, by CIA, DIA, NSA, State, and the FBI established four unclassified data elements that could be used in the TIPOFF database; this was the starting point for negotiating similar ground rules for information sent from the TTIC/NCTC to the TSC.¹⁶¹ (This number was increased by subsequent memoranda of understanding.)

Today, the TSC serves three functions. First, it assembles the names of all known or suspected terrorists into a Consolidated Terrorist Watchlist, aka the Terrorist Screening Database (TSDB), along with a "handling code" that provides information about what should be done if the watchlisted individual is encountered.¹⁶² The TSDB is an unclassified but law-enforcement-sensitive database that serves as a sort of index to rapidly find all information that the Federal Government possesses about a suspected individual.¹⁶³ Entries into the TSDB can come from many different federal agencies and government offices.¹⁶⁴ If the information concerns an international terrorist, it is sent to the NCTC for preliminary review; indeed, much information comes from TIDE. If the information concerns a domestic terrorist, it is first routed through the FBI. Both the NCTC and the FBI are then responsible for submitting this information in the proper form to the TSC for final review. This process became known as the nomination process.

Once TSC analysts are satisfied that the information proposed by various agencies for inclusion is sufficiently detailed to be entered into the TSDB, other TSC analysts perform the second function. The entries on the TSDB are then sifted and sorted into discrete "downstream" watchlists tailored to the particular needs of different agencies (called "customers"), such as the TSA's No Fly List.¹⁶⁵ The TSC explained this process to Congress with the help of a PowerPoint slide (a rendering without color or graphics is made in figure 7).¹⁶⁶

These first two functions take place on an established schedule. Every night and twice on Fridays, the biometric and identifying data from TIDE is sent to the TSC for inclusion in the TSDB.¹⁶⁷

The third function occurs round the clock. The TSC coordinates and helps to respond to the inquiries of frontline officials who encounter individuals whom they perceive to be positive hits on these lists. Any federal, state, or local government agent can contact a TSC-staffed "Call Center" twenty-four hours a day, seven days a week, to seek further information after

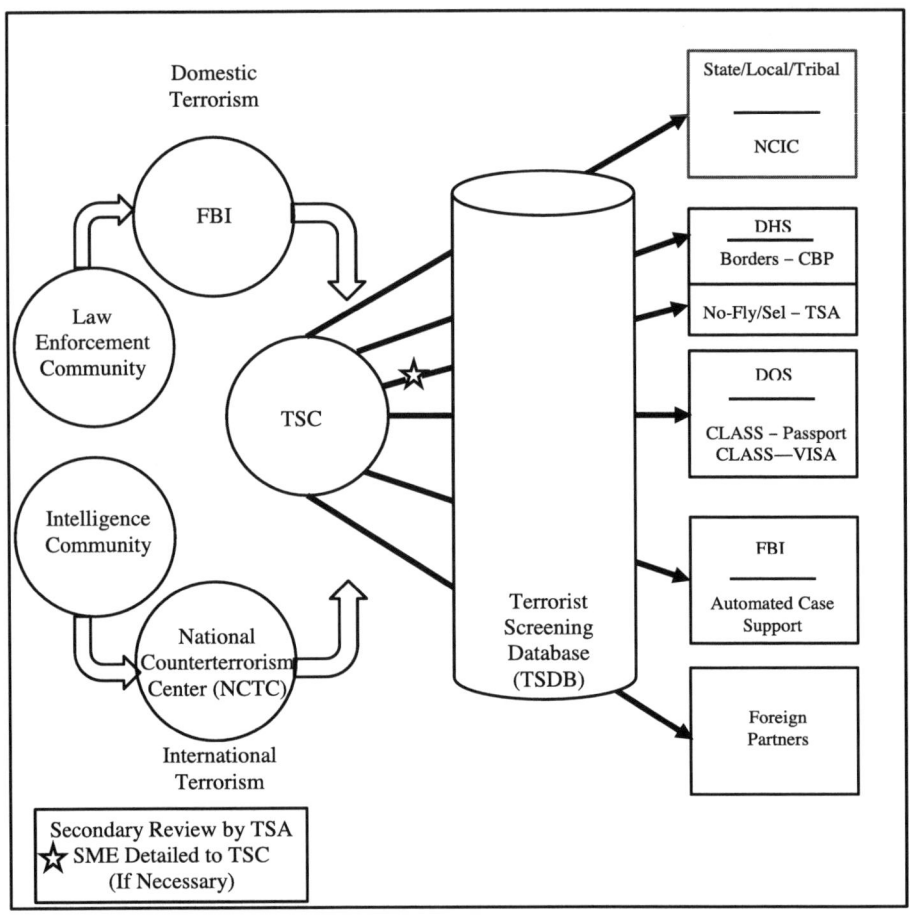

Fig. 7. TSC PowerPoint Slide: U.S. Government Integrated Terrorist Nominations Process

an encounter is made with someone on one of these lists. The TSC verifies whether the individual is indeed a positive match on the particular watchlist and, if so, advises on how the encounter with the individual should be handled. If necessary, TSC officials can quickly connect the encountering agent with the agency or official (whether an FBI special agent, a customs official, etc.) that originated the record in the TSDB or the downstream watchlist. In its first fourteen months, the TSC recorded a 1,045 percent growth in the volume of calls it handled from Customs and Border Protection, the most frequent caller.[168]

The TSDB faced a defining issue from the moment of its conception:

how rigorous should the criteria be to add a name to it? On the one hand, the very name "Terrorist Screening Database" suggested a list with a narrow focus. One could reasonably expect that such a database should only contain the names of individuals whom rigorous screening has determined to be actual terrorists. From a policy perspective, a terrorist screening database that contains the names of nonterrorists is worse than unhelpful—it is a resource-consuming distraction. And the consequences for an individual included on this list are quite serious. Individuals on the TSDB are more likely to be listed on one or more "downstream" watchlists that could restrict their travel, professional licensing, ability to engage in commerce, or receive government benefits. What is more, since the TSC's "ultimate goal" is a TSDB that is in real-time connection to its customer agencies and that contains more and more biometric data, the power of the watchlist is certain to increase.[169]

On the other hand, the TSDB is a sensitive but unclassified list that is not intended to replace other watchlists and databases maintained in classified form by other agencies.[170] Its purpose is consolidation of enough information to permit interagency coordination, a core recommendation of the 9/11 Commission. Since this consolidated list is the source of many other downstream lists used by different agencies for different purposes, it might seem reasonable to keep criteria for inclusion on it relatively broad. Further evaluation could pare back or refine downstream lists at a later stage. After the information-sharing mistakes revealed by 9/11, there was considerable zeal to err on the side of overinclusion. Even as late as 2005, Justice Department auditors reported that the then-director of the TSC, Donna Bucella, told them that "to err on the side of caution, individuals with any degree of a terrorism nexus were included" on the consolidated watchlist so long as minimum identifying data were available.[171]

As Bucella's comments suggest, the originators of the TSC chose to resolve the choice in favor of breadth and inclusion at the level of the TSDB, leaving the filtering function to those downstream lists. That puts a lot of pressure on defining what to collect. The foundational definition of what the TSDB was designed to collect—terrorist information—is established by HSPD-6. The presidential directive begins by stating the policy of the United States to be the collection and use of "Terrorist Information," defined as information about "individuals known or appropriately suspected to be or have been engaged in conduct constituting, in preparation for, in aid of, or related to terrorism."[172] In late 2009, the Terrorist Screening Database contained the names of approximately 400,000 people.[173]

In fact, the minimum criteria for inclusion in the TSDB is quite bare indeed: "at least a partial name (e.g., given name, surname, or both) and at least one additional piece of identifying information (e.g., date of birth)," and some "evidence of a nexus to terrorism."[174] What that nexus might be is suggested by the executive order that established the NCTC (which is the primary source of information sent to the TSC), which defines "terrorism information" to mean

> all information, whether collected, produced, or distributed by intelligence, law enforcement, military, homeland security, or other United States Government activities, relating to (i) the existence, organization, capabilities, plans, intentions, vulnerabilities, means of finance or material support, or activities of foreign or international terrorist groups or individuals, or of domestic groups or individuals involved in transnational terrorism; (ii) threats posed by such groups or individuals to the United States, United States persons, or United States interests, or to those of other nations; (iii) communications of or by such groups or individuals; or (iv) information relating to groups or individuals reasonably believed to be assisting or associated with such groups or individuals.[175]

The different government agencies that nominate individuals for inclusion on the TSDB have different reasons for doing so.[176] There is no requirement, for example, that the person be the subject of an open FBI investigation; an FBI legal attaché at a U.S. embassy abroad may therefore nominate an individual for inclusion in the TSDB on the basis of information supplied by the foreign country in which the attaché is stationed.[177] As Randy Beardsworth notes, the TSDB "is a database of unadjudicated information that is terrorist related and obtained by any law enforcement agency."[178] By "unadjudicated," Beardsworth meant that nobody has evaluated the opinions of the source who sponsors its nomination for inclusion on the TSDB—whether an FBI agent, a customs agent, a city policeman, or someone else. By way of example, Beardsworth observed:

> So if you or I go into the restaurant across the street, and I just happen to be unfortunate enough that known terrorists or highly suspect terrorists are meeting there for lunch and I happen to walk in the door behind them and bump into them and talk to them or sit at the table and the FBI guy is out there watching this occur and takes down my license plate number, I might end up in the database. It's a piece of information, it doesn't mean anything, but it's a piece of information that associates me in some way with terrorist activity. And it's conceivable that information as innocuous as that may be in the FBI file someplace.[179]

Watchlisting is not an action that affects only the individual nominated for inclusion on the TSDB. As the FBI's Inspector General later concluded: "A subject's inclusion on the consolidated terrorist watchlist could also have consequences for associates of the subjects [sic], even though they are not themselves the subject of any investigation."[180] This was readily admitted by Donna Bucella when she was the TSC Director in 2005. According to the Justice Department's Inspector General:

> The Director further explained that one of the benefits of watchlisting individuals who pose a lower threat was that their movement could be monitored through the screening process and this could provide useful intelligence information to investigators. In addition, she stated that watch listing lower-threat individuals that have associations with higher-threat level terrorists may lead to uncovering the location of higher watch listed individuals."[181]

There can scarcely be an objection to the Government's interest in seeking to identify terrorists, whether considered a high or low threat. But watchlisting has consequences. In many ways, the TSDB is a sticky list. Once on the list, it is hard to get off the list. What is more, one's friends and acquaintances are at greater risk of being watchlisted themselves.

The lists are sticky in another way, too. Despite the TSC's assurances to auditors that its watchlists were routinely checked and purged of names that never did or no longer belonged on them, repeat audits found that such entries had a persistent quality to them. More than a year after the first round of assurances was received, Justice Department auditors identified 2,682 records in the TSDB that appeared to be stuck there—not sent to downstream lists but not deleted from the consolidated watchlist either. Alerted to these records, the TSC investigated and concluded that 2,126 "had not been appropriately watchlisted and needed to be renominated to the TSDB."[182] Notice the stickiness: once in the TSDB, the expectation was to renominate the individual and reload the information back into the system.

Listing on the TSDB is only the first function performed by the TSC. The TSC's second function is to sift these names onto specialized lists for use by different agencies, such as the No Fly List that is used by the TSA. How this process is accomplished is the subject of the next chapter. In short, the process is astonishingly similar to Mrs. Shipley's methods of deciding to whom she would give a passport. As Yogi Berra once said, "It's déjà vu all over again."

CHAPTER SEVEN

Growth: Mrs. Shipley's Ghost

By the very act of denying the existence of the ghost in the machine . . .
we incur the risk of turning it into a very nasty, malevolent ghost.

—Arthur Koestler[1]

In 1925, the State Department's Division of Passport Control accomplished its work with an index card system.[2] By 1953, Mrs. Shipley's office maintained 1,250 filing cabinets of data on 12,000,000 people.[3] In light of this mountain of information, the efficiency of her office was amazing. She made state control over who could travel abroad appear to be a public service—few complained because most people received passports quickly and without onerous restrictions.[4] Of course, when Mrs. Shipley decided that a traveler's itinerary was "not in the interests of the United States," that was the end of the matter. The traveler stayed put. Nevertheless, many (successful travelers, at least) viewed Mrs. Shipley's reign as beneficent, if autocratic, and she successfully fended off meaningful judicial review of her discretion until she retired from office.

Mrs. Shipley's unchecked power to decide which citizens could leave home came to be seen as the gross infringement on liberty that it really was. There is no doubt that the judgments of this capable and experienced civil servant were sincere assessments of national security. But her sincerity could not mask the un-American principle she defended: that the state should have the power to control the movement of its citizens whenever their travel was secretly found to be, not unlawful, but simply not consonant with a government official's view of foreign policy or national security. Nor could her skill excuse a decision-making process kept behind a wall of unreviewable discretion buttressed by impregnable bureaucratic secrecy. Just as her passport controls reached the peak of their perfection, the courts and

Congress began to restore the individual liberty that had been sacrificed in pursuit of national security. Passport decisions were subjected to judicial review, although the government left its heavy thumb on the judicial scales, to tip them when necessary with claims of grave threats to national security.

Mrs. Shipley's passports were ultimately abandoned as the primary tool to control a citizen's travel. But her ghost still lingers in the machine. Just as her empire grew from index cards to rooms full of filing cabinets, today's watchlisting system has grown from a dozen or so names typed in a security directive that fit on a single piece of thermal fax paper. Today a massive database operates on a budget of tens of millions of dollars, employing hundreds of officials. Travel control is now done remotely, using networked computer systems to sort the good from the bad. In the blink of an eye, it can stop travel into, out of, or through the airspace of the United States. Mrs. Shipley's spirit has been digitized. It flows through these computers and watchlists with a power greater than the real Mrs. Shipley could possibly have imagined.

That shift from corporeal form to digital avatar accomplished a neat trick, even if those who created the new system did not realize just who they had regenerated. There is no single Mrs. Shipley anymore. Her power was certainly not transferred to the singular discretion of the Director of the Terrorist Screening Center. But Mrs. Shipley's spirit did not entirely disappear. It has been diffused into the databases and computers of scores of analysts working in a systematic, multilevel process. This makes decision making appear scientific, rigorous, and technologically sophisticated. Data points are parsed and assessed at different stages according to set criteria by dedicated professionals in the "watchlisting community." The involvement of multiple agencies with a stake in the results would seem to prevent any single person from amassing the power that Mrs. Shipley did. What could be more objective and dispassionate? Isn't the current system the well-designed antidote to the reign of Ruth Shipley, which Dean Acheson called in his memoirs her "Queendom of Passports"?

Though it may seem counterintuitive, diffusing Mrs. Shipley's power in fact magnified it. The new system makes it much harder to identify just who is responsible for the final decision to ground a citizen. An attempt to reach the decision makers with meaningful controls through our traditional system of checks and balances on government power is a journey down the rabbit hole. No single agency now takes responsibility for the decision to ground a traveler; authority to compose the list is split from the ministerial power to implement it. As a result, the agency action that matters most is hidden from view and, so far, effectively shielded from judicial review. Many analysts at many different decision points in the process have strong incentives to err on the side of including a name in the database. Who wants to be the one to let a terrorist slip onto a plane? When the buck stops with no one, no one has a reason to stop.

Meanwhile, the multiplication of secret criteria and threshold standards obscures the fact that nearly any decision rendered by this hidden process may later be justified by it. "This is not an exact science," Russell Travers, a deputy director at the NCTC, told journalist Ronald Kessler.[5] That is a meek admission, if it was even intended as such. Terrorist watchlisting is no more a science than Kremlinology was during the Cold War. That is not to disparage Kremlinology, the earnest attempt to identify the secret pathways of power that ran the closed system of the Soviet Union. Specialized Sovietologists analyzed the sequence of leaders lined up on Lenin's Tomb on May Day, read between the lines of *Pravda,* and hunted for clues as much in arcana as in the everyday. Then as now, the goal was to piece together an intricate mosaic made of tiny fragments of information.

But that mosaic-restoring task assumes that the pieces fit together, that there is indeed a coherent picture to uncover. That assumption makes the watchlisters poor judges of when their work has gone too far. And behind the facade of analytical rigor, the system has expanded beyond its original purpose. No longer is the No Fly List limited to protecting the physical safety of those who fly on commercial aircraft. The system now permits decisions to target someone for watchlisting as an investigative tool, or as part of a tactical operation to protect interests that may have nothing to do with the plane in the air. What is more, this decision can be hidden in plain sight—just add the name and enough speculative derogatory information into the TSDB and watchlisting may be justified under the lowered criteria for unspecified national security threats. The limit placed on the watchlisting power by the original requirement of a "specific and credible threat to civil aviation" has been rendered meaningless by the addition of a phrase that can sweep all other limits aside. Now the No Fly List prevents the air travel of those the watchlisting community believes "may be a threat to civil aviation or national security."

Mrs. Shipley's ghost threatens a freedom of movement that Americans often take for granted. Her ghost is more powerful than the flesh-and-blood Mrs. Shipley ever was. Mrs. Shipley worked—through wars hot and cold—at the Winder Building, a Washington landmark that sits across the street from the White House and the Old Executive Office Building; it now houses the U.S. Trade Representative. The Terrorist Screening Center, on the other hand, elects to remain mysterious about its location; its website describes its headquarters only as "housed in a nondescript building in Northern Virginia."[6] This difference is not without meaning. Authority, responsibility, and accountability are all diffused and dispersed among different agencies, officials, analysts, databases, and systems. Thus, while judicial review is in theory available to those who challenge their inclusion on the No Fly List, in practice, plaintiffs discover that they are playing an expensive and frustrating shell game. To date, no plaintiff has won a judicial remedy.

In a sense, it doesn't matter where the Terrorist Screening Center is located. Although that is where officials make the ultimate decision to add a name to the No Fly List, there is no one there from whom to seek redress. Reporting on Mrs. Shipley's operation, a *New York Times* reporter observed:

> Although she has ninety assistants in the passport division, Mrs. Shipley examines each application personally. Despite this extra work she never seems hurried. The door to her office is always open, and any applicant with a grievance can see that she is there and can walk right in, and people of high and low degree do. While I was talking with her the other day a housewifely woman came in about her passport troubles and later Bernard M. Baruch timidly peeped into the doorway.[7]

Mrs. Shipley's ghost is locked behind hidden doors at the Terrorist Screening Center. And those doors remain firmly closed to any traveler who wishes to contest the executive decision to deny him both the right to travel like any other American or even a statement of the reason to single him out.

Many policymakers and operational specialists reject this analogy between the War on Terror and the Cold War. They particularly disagree with the analogy between Mrs. Shipley's passports and the No Fly List. Dismissing this recent past has a profound consequence for today and tomorrow. For in refusing to believe that the past has lessons to teach, the last remaining constraint is removed on a system that strains against artificial and self-imposed limits, as its steady expansion demonstrates. It is a small step now from a list that prohibits travel to one that prohibits other potentially dangerous but routine activities, all in the name of national security.

The Passport Division kept files on individuals whose travel would concern the United States enough to consider denying or restricting a passport. The information in these files came from the FBI, the Foreign Service, the intelligence services, and other agencies.[8] Secretary Acheson fended off criticism of the secretive nature of his subordinates' decision making by describing the legal standard used to determine whether a passport application should be denied:

When an application is received for a passport at the Passport Division, the files of the Department are examined, and if there is nothing in those files to raise any questions regarding the person concerned, the passport is issued immediately, as a matter of routine.

Then we come to the second step. If there is adverse information, this information is reviewed at a higher level in the Passport Division, and if the information is not such as to provide reasonable grounds for belief that the passport should be denied—and the reasons for denial I have already mentioned to you [fugitive status, mental illness, travel adverse to the national interest]—if there are not reasonable grounds from the totality of its evidence to indicate the applicant does not fall within any of the categories mentioned, then the passport is issued.[9]

The Terrorist Screening Center receives nominations from the NCTC and the FBI to place individuals in its Terrorist Screening Database, the main terrorist watchlist from which subsidiary lists are created for particular uses by different agencies (such as the No Fly List that is used by the TSA). The TSC's Director, Timothy Healy, described the legal standard his organization uses to add a name to that consolidated watchlist:

[T]he facts and circumstances pertaining to the nomination must meet the "reasonable suspicion" standard of review established by terrorist screening Presidential Directives. Reasonable suspicion requires "articulable" facts which, taken together with rational inferences, reasonably warrant a determination that an individual is known or suspected to be or has been engaged in conduct constituting, in preparation for, in aid of or related to terrorism and terrorist activities, and is based on the totality of the circumstances.[10]

Note the similarity between the two legal standards. The few differences are largely due to the fact that Mr. Healy's standard is modeled on the standard set forth by the Supreme Court in a post-Shipley era case, *Terry v. Ohio*.[11] (How this standard also affects No Fly List nominations is discussed below.) Work on the TSC's standard began in summer 2008 in a working group cochaired by DHS and TSC that produced a policy paper called a "guidance document" for TSDB nominations, informally called the "bible" because it is considered the authoritative source on watchlisting issues.[12]

Only reasonable grounds from the totality of the evidence were required to deny a passport. Only a reasonable suspicion based on articulable facts and the totality of the circumstances is required to add a name to a watchlist. Neither standard presents much of a bar to desired action. In any event, the standard to approve a nomination to the TSDB is not policed by any court. When the State Department lost that battle concerning passports (though it fought tooth and nail to avoid judicial review of its determinations), its travel control program became untenable. In 1955, secrecy had the same defense as it does today: "State Department lawyers feel that, if they are compelled to open up security files to the public and reveal confidential sources of information, the whole antisubversive operation will be crippled."[13] The Terrorist Screening Center currently fights just as hard for the same autonomy and seeks the same protection from judicial review. Officials in both eras have emphasized the careful vetting and professional judgment used in their departments. But the answer boils down to the same two words: trust us.

The "us" now includes two separate units of government, the TSC and the Transportation Security Administration (the TSA). This division creates a new difficulty not faced by the travelers who sought out Mrs. Shipley. What can be known from published sources indicates a hierarchical relationship that puts the TSC on top of all significant decision making about composing the No Fly List. This structure is not always easy to pin down. The legal documents that describe it are riddled with delegations of authority, special exceptions, and abstract references. Still, this is a strange and shifting hierarchy. The relationship is often described by the agencies themselves as one in which the TSC delivers a "product" (the No Fly List) to its "customer," the TSA. Both agencies have good reasons to seek consensus over the crafting of that product, within agreed parameters, to satisfy both producer and consumer. But the recursive effect of this interaction can make it difficult to pin down who is in charge of what.

It is clear that the TSC is in charge of crafting the end product, with an eye toward satisfying its customer. When it comes to responding to external demands for redress, on the other hand, the relationship appears to shift depending on the vantage point of the observer. Observed from within the agencies, the TSC still appears to retain the same dominance in the redress process that it exercises in the process of composing the list. But to outsiders—the private citizens who seek review of a No Fly List decision and the few courts that have heard their complaints—the agencies project a different relationship. TSA is first presented as the sole relevant agency, the only one with a redress office accessible to the public. If pressed further, however, the response shifts to reveal a bit more: TSA is presented as a coequal decision maker with the TSC (and sometimes other agencies), or so inextricably intertwined in the work of the TSC that untangling the two entities is impossible.

One is forced to speculate that litigation concerns drive efforts to try to shield the TSC's work behind a facade of TSA authority. By claiming that the substantive work at the TSC is "inextricably intertwined" with the legal authority of the TSA, its "customer," the TSA takes advantage of a statute held over from the days of the FAA's old system of security directives. This law, found in section 46110 of Title 49 of the United States Code, transfers jurisdiction to hear a civil action concerning these orders from the federal trial courts (where discovery may be possible) to the federal courts of appeal (where only an agency's administrative record normally would be reviewed).[14] This law made sense when the civil actions were filed by airlines contesting the routine issuance of licenses and regulations, in which the only relevant evidence would be contained in a voluminous administrative record. Of course, the administrative record of the TSC—where the relevant decision-making is to be found—is not easily obtainable because of the classified nature of its content and the secret criteria that govern its work. This jurisdictional argument, routinely made by government lawyers in No Fly List cases, adds another layer of insulation to TSC decison making.

The TSA argues that the statute applies because the No Fly List acquires legal force as a security directive. No litigant has yet succeeded in reaching the point where either a trial court could order discovery of the evidence behind a decision or an appellate court could evaluate the completeness of any administrative record that would be produced to support a decision. As noted later in this chapter, a decision handed down by the United States Court of Appeals for the Ninth Circuit as this book went to press may change that litigation strategy by opening access to the TSC in the same way that courts forced open the black box of Mrs. Shipley's Passport Office.

1. Compiling the No Fly List

Who Decides?

One of the primary purposes of HSPD-6 and the establishment of the Terrorist Screening Center was to consolidate control over the nation's watchlists. In the memorandum of understanding that provided detail to the broad objectives of that presidential directive, DHS Secretary Tom Ridge agreed that his agency would "discontinue or transfer to the Terrorist Screening Center, to the extent permitted by law and with appropriate consultation with the Congress, those operations that are duplicative of the Terrorist Screening Center's mission to provide continuous operational support to users of the terrorist screening database, including . . . the Transportation Security Agency's [sic] No-Fly and Selectee list program."[15] What did all that mean? To what extent was TSA "permitted by law" to transfer the No Fly List to the TSC?

According to Richard Falkenrath, one of President Bush's advisors closely involved with the drafting of HSPD-6 and its accompanying interagency memorandum of understanding, that language meant that, in the event of conflict over whether to place an individual on the No Fly List, the call belonged with TSC to make, not TSA.[16] Admiral James Loy, who as the TSA's second Administrator was the first to operate under HSPD-6, agreed that the final decision would belong to TSC.[17] As Falkenrath described the objective: "We weren't creating TSC to just be an overlay on everything else they were doing. We wanted these other agencies to stop doing their kind of solo, isolated, uncoordinated things."[18]

That might have been the intent of the drafters of these policy documents, but did the law permit the transfer of authority and control they envisioned? Yes. When Congress created the TSA, Congress made clear that some of the functions being assigned to TSA were not to be delegated to others. For example, TSA "shall be responsible" for the day-to-day "screening operations" (such as hiring and training security personnel) for passengers and cargo at airports, and has broad authority over many aspects of that duty.[19] But when it came to who should control "screening information," Congress reduced that previous language of authority ("shall") to language of mere managerial support. In a separate subsection of the statute titled "Management of security information," Congress gave the TSA considerable latitude to decide which of these functions to hold close and which to share or delegate to other agencies. The TSA was directed to "enter into memoranda of understanding" with other Federal agencies concerning the use of screening databases, and establish procedures for submitting information to the database and relevant agencies.[20] Congress also authorized the TSA, "in consultation with other appropriate Federal agencies and air carriers," to establish policies and procedures "to use information from government agencies to identify individuals on passenger lists who may be a threat to civil aviation or national security."[21] If such an individual is identified, the TSA—again in consultation with others—shall establish policies and procedures to "notify appropriate law enforcement agencies, prevent the individual from boarding an aircraft, or take other appropriate action with respect to that individual."[22] Congress told the TSA to establish policies with the assistance of other Federal agencies, not to seize unilateral control. In other words, this was power that TSA was free to disperse.

And disperse the power TSA did. The Department of Homeland Security conceded the fight over controlling the TSC to the FBI.[23] Now the TSA took the same backseat role that the FAA had occupied when the Intelligence Community was driving the relationship before 9/11. FAA had remained the junior partner with the FBI in creating a No Fly List after 9/11. It then was hardly a surprise that TSA delegated to TSC the final authority over nominations. This delegation occurred in an FOUO ("for official use only") memorandum of understanding.[24]

A good metaphor to describe this relationship is the commercial one chosen by the TSC and TSA themselves. The TSC provides specialized watchlists to its "customers," who then put the product to use. Both Kip Hawley and Gale Rossides, in their respective tenures as TSA administrators, referred in favorable terms to the "one-stop shopping" that TSC provided to customers such as TSA.[25] But it is the TSC that crafts the product. As TSC Director Timothy Healy explained the relationship in his testimony to the Senate in the wake of the 2009 "Christmas Day" bomber, Umar Farouk Abdulmutallab:

> When submitting a nomination to NCTC, an originator may, but is under no obligation to submit recommendations regarding specific screening systems the nomination should be exported to (e.g., inclusion on either the no-fly or selectee list). If an originator submits a nomination without a recommendation, NCTC may make an appropriate recommendation based on the totality of associated information. Recommendations made by NCTC will be passed to the TSC for final disposition.[26]

Director Healy muddied the waters a bit as he detailed the process after a TSDB nomination is accepted. Who decides whether the identity should be added to the No Fly List?

> If the [TSC] analyst reviewing the no-fly nomination determines that there is insufficient information to warrant inclusion on the no-fly list, the nomination is forwarded to the TSA (Office of Intelligence and/or the Federal Air Marshal Service [FAMS]) subject matter experts at the TSC for further analysis and a final recommendation. The TSA subject matter expert will review the nomination and all accessible derogatory information associated with the individual and

apply the no-fly and selectee list criteria to that information. Based upon that review and analysis, the TSA/FAMS subject matter expert will then decide based upon that criteria whether the individual will be included on either the no-fly or selectee list.[27]

This makes it sound as if TSA may have the final decision, through "subject matter experts" overseeing the TSC. The impression is misleading. First, the "TSA subject matter experts" are "at the TSC," not the TSA. The Director does not specify whether they are detailees (temporary employees of the TSC and therefore under its control) or assignees (representing the TSA at TSC and thus still controlled by the TSA).[28] But location tends to follow power, and that fact is made clearer by the Director elsewhere in his testimony:

> TSC makes the final decision on whether a person meets the minimum requirements for inclusion into the TSDB as a known or suspected terrorist and which screening systems will receive the information about that known or suspected terrorist. In the end, however, TSC works with NCTC and the originators to ensure a nomination is exported to as many screening systems as the nomination information supports.[29]

TSA is seldom an "originator" of information. And it is the TSC that makes the final decision. "The watchlisting and nomination process," the Director stated, "can best be described as a watchlisting enterprise because it requires constant collaboration between the originators, NCTC, and the TSC."[30] It is telling that the customer agencies—like TSA—were not included by the Director in his description of that enterprise. Customers are usually not found behind the counter.

Admiral James Loy, Administrator of the TSA from November 2002 to November 2003 and then Deputy Secretary of Homeland Security under Michael Chertoff until March 2005, confirmed this relationship.[31] When detailing his people from TSA and DHS to work in the TSC, Loy challenged them "to be thoughtfully representative of quote unquote our position on these issues," but also warned them that "as soon as you're perceived to be a spy for TSA in that conference, you will be discounted in a heartbeat." Loy recalled his typical meeting in his office the day before someone departed for TSC, telling them: "You are being challenged in a collaborative forum to forge the policy necessary to best protect the interests of our country, and I will back you up by telling you in advance that we will, as the operators and the executors, we will execute what you all put together at the TSC."[32]

TSA's supporting role to TSC's dominion over watchlisting was confirmed by Michael Jackson, who helped organize the TSA as Deputy Secretary of Transportation between May 2001 and August 2003, and then succeeded Loy as Deputy Secretary of Homeland Security from March 2005 through October 2007. While emphasizing that the TSC was part of an "interagency mission that required an unusual degree of coordination and accommodation in how you manage that institution," Jackson noted that, prior to the creation of the "Secure Flight" program in 2004, "TSC has been delegated legal authorities that exist in both agencies. So when you're the head of that entity [TSC], you draw upon legal authorities that exist in both agencies. But you're still acting as the head of that organization."[33] As detailed below, however, Secure Flight did not in fact change this dynamic.

The same TSC control—and TSA lack of control—is manifest in the auditing and revision of the No Fly List. In July 2006, the Deputies Committee of the White House's Homeland Security Council provided additional guidance on the criteria that should be used to determine the composition of the No Fly List. The Justice Department's Inspector General evaluated the implementation of that guidance, noting that the TSC began a review of the No Fly List, which at that time contained over 71,000 records.[34] The review occurred at the TSC, not the TSA.[35] Six months later, the TSC recommended that the No Fly List contain slightly more than 34,000 records and recommended a transfer of slightly more than 22,000 records to the Selectee List. Slightly more than 5,000 records were considered properly included on neither the No Fly nor Selectee list. In other words, 44 percent of the records were shifted or removed.[36]

How involved was the TSA in this reconstitution of the No Fly List? Although the Inspector General's auditors examined the review process in detail, the acronym "TSA" appears only once in its account: describing TSA's role disseminating the list to commercial airlines.[37] The reason is clear: it is the TSC, not the TSA, that has expertise evaluating terrorist information against the criteria and guidance set by the Homeland Security Council. It was the TSC's Nominations and Data Integrity Unit (NDIU) that undertook the review and made the final recommendation.

It is true that this review was assisted by the temporary assignment of ten federal air marshals from DHS to TSC.[38] And it is possible that future TSC reviews could be assisted by officials assigned to TSC from TSA. In 2007, seven members of the thirty-four-member NDIU staff were subject-matter experts, one or more of whom could have been TSA officials who retained roles as agents of their TSA principal.[39] But that is a far cry from consulting, let alone seeking the permission of, the TSA about what records should go in, and what records should come out. The process was a TSC one, as always, with TSA in the role of the "customer," perhaps expressing its preferences at times, but waiting for TSC to deliver the product.

Perhaps the best evidence of TSC's control is to be found in the statements of other government agencies about the relationship. In 2005, the Department of Justice defended the TSA in a lawsuit brought by Robert Gray, a commercial pilot who sought permission from TSA to pursue flight training for larger aircraft.[40] In a series of e-mails, he was denied permission because he was considered to "pose a threat to aviation or national security." When Gray's efforts to determine the basis for this conclusion were unavailing, he filed a lawsuit. About two months later, Gray amended his complaint to allege that TSA had added his name to the No Fly List as an act of retaliation. The Justice Department's argument in opposition to Gray's motion for a preliminary injunction was revealing:

> [Gray's] assertion belies a fundamental misunderstanding of how individuals are placed on the No Fly List. That list is maintained not by TSA, but by the Terrorism Screening Center ("TSC"), which was created by the Attorney General in response to the Homeland Security Presidential Directive (HSPD-6) . . . [I]t is not within TSA's province to place individuals on the No Fly List; to the contrary, individuals who are placed on either list must be nominated for inclusion by the FBI or the National Counterterrorism Center, subject to meeting criteria established by TSA. To be sure, after an individual has been placed on the No Fly List, TSA will issue a Security Directive directing air carriers to implement specific security procedures and to take specific security measures with respect to those individuals who appear on that list. But TSA does *not* have authority to designate individuals for inclusion on the No Fly List.[41]

Outside the litigation context, the Department of Homeland Security's Inspector General concluded that following the release of the Homeland Security Council's guidance on criteria for the No Fly and Selectee lists, "responsibility for maintenance and export of the lists was transferred to the TSC. Prior to this time, TSA maintained the No Fly and Selectee lists."[42] Responding to a draft of this report, TSA Acting Administrator Gale Rossides acknowledged to the Inspector General that "[n]ominations are processed and adjudicated by the TSC with support from TSA."[43] The Inspector

General's graphic representation of this understanding visually depicts TSA's delegation of authority to the TSC (a rendering without color or graphics is made in figure 8).[44]

It is clear that ownership of the No Fly List belongs to TSC, which composes the list, periodically revises it, and maintains a base of expertise (not to mention authority delegated from TSA itself) to resolve problems raised by the list.

What Are the Standards?

Under what standard, then, does the TSC determine who should be included on the No Fly List? According to Mr. Healy,

> The no-fly and selectee lists are unique among TSDB subsets in that they are the only subsets within the terrorist watchlist that have their own substantive minimum derogatory criteria requirements, which are considerably more stringent than the reasonable suspicion standard required for inclusion in TSDB itself.[45]

This statement must be read carefully. It conflates standards (an evaluative test of evidence) with criteria (the evidence itself). In doing so, it creates the misperception that a higher burden is required to add a name to the No Fly List and Selectee List than is used to evaluate nominations to the TSDB. The statement does *not* say that the reasonable suspicion standard is not used to evaluate nominations to these lists. In fact, it doesn't really say anything at all.

The criteria for inclusion in the TSDB are "at least a partial name (e.g., given name, surname, or both) and at least one additional piece of identifying information (e.g., date of birth)," and some "evidence of a nexus to terrorism."[46] Saying that the "substantive minimum derogatory criteria" for the No Fly List and the Selectee List are "considerably more stringent" than criteria for inclusion on the TSDB is meaningful. But saying that the criteria are more stringent than the reasonable suspicion standard makes no sense. It is saying that the evidence required to make a decision is more stringent than the standard for evaluating evidence, a comparison of two different things.

The derogatory information that must pass that standard for a successful nomination to the TSDB is fairly minimal. In 2007, only some "evidence of a nexus to terrorism" was required. Any substantive minimum derogatory criteria requirements for the No Fly List would likely be higher than that modest requirement for a successful nomination to the TSDB. The specif-

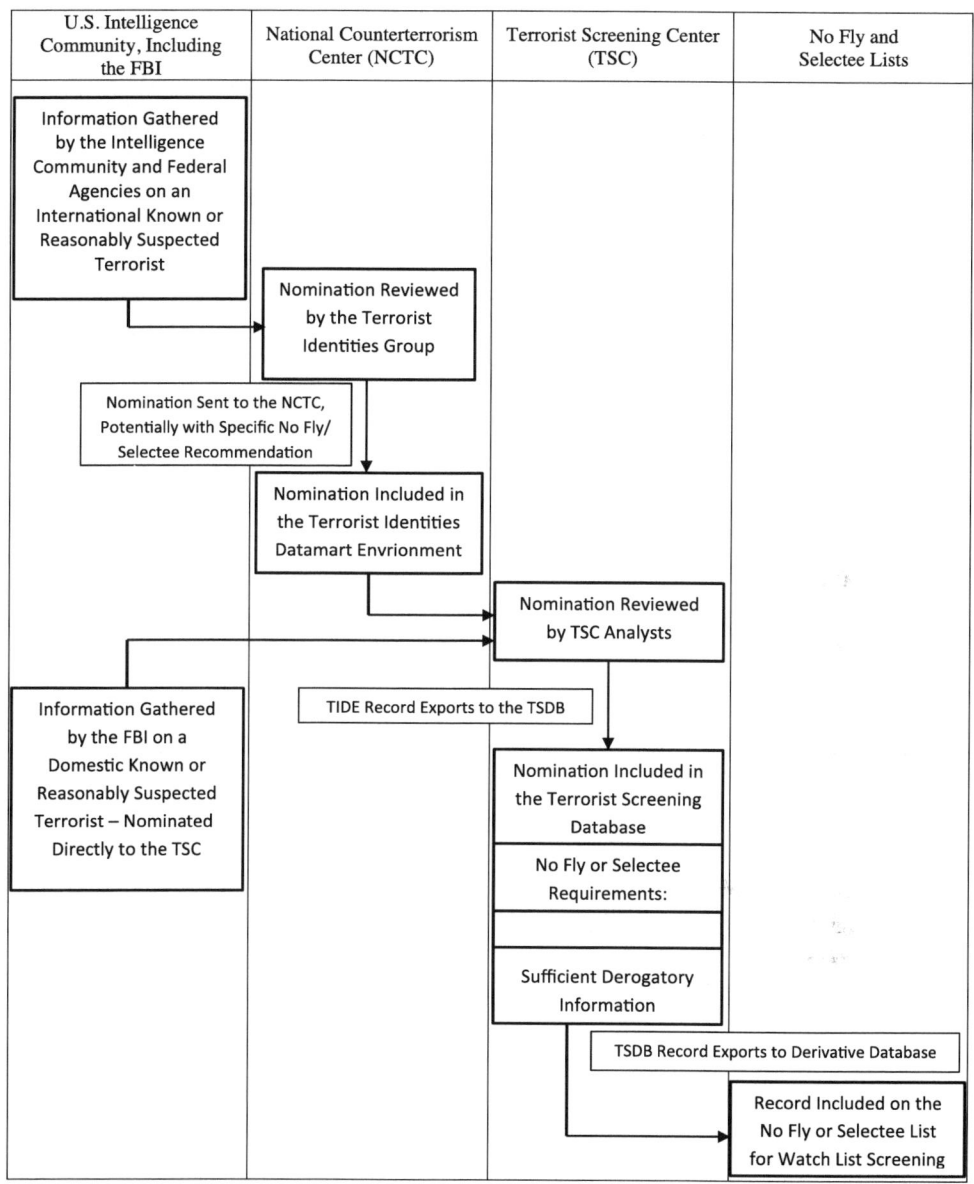

Fig. 8. The DHS View of the No Fly List Nomination Process. (Data from OIG analysis.)

ics are, of course, classified. These criteria were established by the Deputies' Committee of the Homeland Security Council based on the recommendations of a working group in October 2004, then revised in July 2006, and revised again in 2008.[47] In July 2010, the TSC released a new guidance document that made changes to definitions and wording for at least one of the criteria for inclusion on the No Fly List.[48]

But whatever the substantive minimum criteria might be, derogatory information still needs to be evaluated to determine whether the criteria are in fact met. So the question remains: what standard does a TSC analyst use to conclude that a successful nomination to the TSDB is also sufficient to meet the "more stringent" criteria to include someone on the No Fly List? Should the analyst be certain that the information is true beyond a reasonable doubt? Convinced that the available evidence about this individual is more likely than not to meet these criteria, and thus pose a threat to civil aviation or national security sufficient to justify placement on the No Fly List? Or perhaps the analyst should merely be able to articulate facts adequate to form the basis for a reasonable suspicion that the criteria are met?

The policy implications of such a question may be more important than establishing the particular "substantive minimum derogatory criteria requirements" themselves. Counterterrorism is a piecemeal game of putting together fragmentary information, assessing the shards, and trying to see in the mosaic that they produce a clearer picture of the threat. Suppose that one of the "substantive minimum derogatory criteria" were that there be evidence that a person has the technical ability to threaten an aircraft's security, *for example,* that the person is a bomb maker. That requirement is only the first step. What evidence satisfies that criterion? How much should the analyst trust the information that comes across his screen? Is it enough to show the requisite ability? Is the source reliable? Adjusting the standard for evaluating information affects the outcome of the decision. And the shift can be enormous: from the beyond-a-reasonable-doubt level of confidence that a jury must possess to render a guilty verdict to a mere hunch.

Both the hunch and the jury's standard have been disavowed by the TSC as too extreme.[49] It is widely accepted that beyond-a-reasonable-doubt certainty for watchlisting is far too high. And Timothy Healy has made clear that more than a hunch is necessary even to get past the TSDB nomination process. But that still leaves a broad middle ground of options from which to choose a standard. What should the supervisor tell the analyst who asks, "Is this fragment of information enough?"

High-level individuals familiar with the process found it quite difficult to speak about the problem in a way that did not reveal classified information.

One person attempted to explain by saying that the analyst would look at the totality of the circumstances to determine whether the criteria were satisfied. But by what standard would that totality be judged? Was it sufficient merely to be reasonably suspicious that the totality of the circumstances satisfied the criteria, or more certain of it? After much discussion, others suggested that part of the difficulty in answering the question lay in their inability to reveal the criteria being evaluated. It could be said, one person concluded, that the analyst must *at least* have a reasonable suspicion that the criteria were met, but the process of decision making is hard to reduce to the traditional legal standards familiar to lawyers.

"At least" is a pointless modifier. Setting a floor sets the standard. The answer thus turns out to be the same as before: the low hurdle of the reasonable suspicion standard.

How could this be? The State Department ultimately lost its legal battles to use the reasonable basis standard (*i.e.,* Mrs. Shipley's judgment) unconstrained by judicial review to control travel. But that loss was because the "reasonable basis" standard, if met, resulted in a concrete injury: denial or loss of a passport. The TSC perhaps recognized that its two-tiered system of watchlisting had the unexpected benefit of shielding the TSDB from that objection.[50] No objection could be lodged to the lawful collection of information that the government believes important to decide questions of national security. And when the TSC perceives a reasonable basis to accept a nomination to the TSDB, no *immediate* injury results from that determination. The decision is simply to add the name to the consolidated pool of "known or suspected terrorists" from which downstream watchlists may be derived and distributed to other government agents. On the other hand, the No Fly List *does* result in a concrete injury (the denial of the use of commercial air transportation). Therefore, the TSC needed new legal arguments for what was essentially the old legal standard. Where did their legal basis for this standard come from?

The differences between Secretary Acheson's expression of the reasonable basis standard and Director Healy's description, above, may be attributable to a Supreme Court decision handed down in the intervening years. The standard the TSC uses is derived from the Supreme Court's opinion in *Terry v. Ohio,*[51] which upheld the power of police to briefly detain, question, and frisk an individual on grounds less than probable cause: the police officer "must be able to point to specific and articulable facts which, taken together with rational inferences from those facts, reasonably warrant that intrusion."[52]

When it came to the consolidated watchlist from which the No Fly List is derived, the working group was well aware that the *Terry* case concerned the use of the "reasonable suspicion" standard by law enforcement officials in a criminal investigative context. Some concern was expressed about applying this standard in the intelligence context. Participants therefore were careful to use the *Terry* case only as a starting point for discussion. Thus, the working group did not concern itself with the focus in the *Terry* case on officer safety, or the time limits placed on the limited detention permitted by this standard. It was not the intention of the working group to adopt the *Terry* standard as such, but to use the case only as a starting point for guidance in defining the phrase "reasonable suspicion." This is reflected in the name adopted for the standard ultimately adopted by the working group: the "Reasonable Suspicion Standard," not the "*Terry* standard" known to specialists in criminal procedure.[53]

Whatever the label, and however stringent the substantive criteria, the standard is a low one. The result is a five-step decision-making process. A name will be added to the No Fly List if affirmative steps are taken at each point in the following process:

1. A nomination is submitted to the TSC from the NCTC or the FBI for inclusion in the consolidated watchlist (the TSDB);
2. The TSC confirms that the nomination contains the minimum biographical information in the correct formats;
3. If the minimum biographical information criteria are met, the TSC analyst determines whether reasonable suspicion based on articulable facts exists to conclude that the individual is a "known or suspected terrorist," that is, there is "evidence of a nexus to terrorism," as those phrases are specially defined;
4. If there is such reasonable suspicion, the nomination is successful. An unclassified but law enforcement sensitive record is entered into the consolidated watchlist (the TSDB);
5. That record is now assessed for inclusion in "downstream" watchlists. To determine whether the nomination should also be included in the No Fly List, the analyst must have at least a reasonable suspicion based on articulable facts that the more stringent substantive minimum derogatory information required to show that the individual is a threat to "civil aviation or national security" exists. Close cases may be assisted by TSA detailees to the TSC, but the final decision is made by the TSC.

Of course, legal standards mean little if they are not applied. As Mrs. Shipley ably demonstrated, departing from standards is especially easy when the exercise of discretion is unchecked by outsiders. That is why the Supreme Court premised its "*Terry* stop" standard on "the more detached, neutral scrutiny of a judge" that would follow.[54] Capable officials tend to have little difficulty justifying departures, too. As the TSC started up in 2004, overinclusion was justified as the natural effect of gradually starting up a new office and creating a consolidated list out of disparate sources. When Justice Department auditors criticized continued problems of overinclusion in 2005, then TSC Director Donna Bucella suggested to them that an even lower standard might be the norm: "She informed us that, to err on the side of caution, individuals with any degree of a terrorism nexus were included in the TSDB, as long as minimum [identifying] criteria was [*sic*] met."[55]

Not everything is the same as in Mrs. Shipley's day; some things are worse in the digital age. First is the steady expansion of the No Fly List. As the history of the passport reveals, and Mrs. Shipley's reign confirmed, there exists constant and omnipresent pressure for expansion of systems of travel control. The No Fly List is no exception. Second, although Mrs. Shipley was a hero to some and a tyrant to others, at least her office was the *identifiable* source of a traveler's frustrations. Eventually, courts forced open her closed system of travel controls. As the redress process makes clear, the operative force behind the No Fly List—the TSC—has been carefully shielded from judicial scrutiny by hiding its decision making behind a remnant of the old FAA power to issue security directives. These problems are examined in the following sections.

2. Expanding the Mission

Dean Acheson offered a statistical defense of Mrs. Shipley's war on Communism. At the peak of her power, the Secretary of State took a sampling of her work: in a universe of 325,000 passports issued between July 1951 and June 1952, only 95 passports were recalled and another 95 requests for passports denied, either because of membership in a subversive organization or because of evidence of some other subversive intent by the passport holder.[56] In other words, criticism of her program was much ado about nothing.

Timothy Healy, the Director of the Terrorist Screening Center, took a similar approach to the defense of his program. In testimony to the Senate Homeland Security and Government Affairs Committee in early December 2009, he emphasized the small number of Americans on the list: "Most of the individuals on the Terrorist Watchlist are not U.S. citizens, but are terrorists living and operating overseas. The Terrorist Watchlist is made up of approximately 400,000 people. . . . [T]he 'No Fly' list is a very small subset of the Terrorist Watchlist currently containing approximately 3,400 people, of those, approximately 170 are U.S. persons."[57]

Of course, numbers without context are meaningless. A timeline of the No Fly List's growth helps one assess a number that will continue to grow. On September 11, 2001, the FAA's Security Directives identified only about a dozen individuals to be denied transport because they posed a "direct and credible threat to aviation security."[58] In the aftermath of the attacks, that number changed daily. By November 2001, it had grown to 400 names.[59] By mid-December, the now divided No Fly and Selectee lists contained 594 names and 365 names respectively.[60] Others gave more extreme estimates, not always accurately. According to a former vice president for security at United Airlines, within a week of September 11, the No Fly List had grown to over 1,800 names.[61] In comparison with these other sources, this number appears too high. But this testimony and other statements in the press gave the impression that the No Fly list was out of control, expanding daily and seemingly without limit. It is more accurate to say that in its early days the No Fly List more closely resembled an accordion, expanding and contracting as the FBI pursued its investigation.

By the middle of the decade, audits of the existing list and a tightening of criteria for inclusion on it had pared down the numbers. In July 2006, the No Fly List contained 71,872 records, which an internal review reduced to 34,230 records by February 2007.[62] (Because some of those records could—and likely did—refer to the same individual identified in different entries, the number of discrete persons on the list was still lower, but not publicly disclosed.) As of September 30, 2009, the number of *people* on the No Fly List was 3,403, of which 171 were U.S. persons.[63]

But just over a year after Umar Farouk Abdulmutallab attempted to explode a bomb on board Northwest Airlines Flight 253 on Christmas Day 2009, TSC Director Timothy Healy told National Public Radio that the No Fly List had grown. In a January 2011 radio interview, Director Healy said that the No Fly List contained the names of about 10,000 people, and that the number of "U.S. citizens on the no-fly list is even much smaller, between 500 and 1,000." In other words, between September 2009 and January 2011, the number of people on the list had increased almost threefold and the number of American citizens on the list could have increased by as much as a factor of six.[64] In February 2012, an unnamed counterterrorism official told CNN that the No Fly List had doubled in the last year, to 21,000 people.[65] Note, too, that the number has grown even as the categories for measurement have narrowed from the broader "U.S. persons" (which includes permanent resident aliens) to U.S. citizens.

It is unsurprising that the No Fly List should have grown, and grown so rapidly. First, the starting point was zero or near zero—no such list had existed before 9/11, and the FAA's Security Directives contained just a handful of names. Second, the TSDB from which the No Fly List was created was itself growing at an extraordinary rate of speed. In the four years between April 2004 and April 2007, the number of records in the TSDB quadrupled to over 724,000.[66] The influx of more and more records to evaluate naturally led TSC analysts to find more and more cases that fit their changing criteria for inclusion in the No Fly List.

From Aviation Security . . .

It was hard to resist the urge to do more with watchlists then their original purpose required, especially when watchlists were *capable* of doing so much more. If the post-9/11 goal was to push the border outward—to check people and things long before they ever arrived at the airport—watchlists like APIS or TIPOFF fit that new thinking perfectly. The process could begin even before a ticket was purchased, a visa granted, or a customs checkpoint reached, and the government's power to act on information it gathered about the traveler could be ratcheted up at any number of decision points.

In the aftermath of September 11, the FAA's old Security Directives were out of sync with this new thinking and operated quite differently than APIS or TIPOFF. To be effective, the FAA's directives required the speedy compliance of private airlines; APIS and TIPOFF were entirely government-controlled lists that required no private party cooperation to operate successfully. Security Directives were a last line of defense, responding to specific and credible intelligence of impending threats to security that had evaded regular law enforcement; APIS and TIPOFF had a more passive orientation, accumulating data routinely accessed as a regular response to visa applicants and border crossers.

These nuances were not well received by members of the 9/11 Commission. When the FAA's Claudio Manno responded to questions about the FAA's failure to use the State Department's TIPOFF system, which contained more than 60,000 names, by asserting that the airlines would have been unable to handle such a large list of names, Commissioner John Lehman responded with anger: "But they sure had no trouble handling their frequent flyer lists—I mean that's ridiculous."[67] That these lists were composed for different purposes, based on different standards, and not computer-searchable other than by proper name, did not hold the commissioners' interest. Sure enough, the report that the Commission released in July 2004 contained a recommendation that TSA should not limit itself to the narrow confines of the existing No Fly List, but rather "utilize the larger set of watchlists maintained by the federal government."[68] Expansion was in the air.

The commissioners had been in no mood to observe government officials blaming each other for hoarding intelligence, or exchanging accusations with airline officials about the proper cost-benefit balance. Information sharing to prevent the next terrorist attack was the singular focus of the Commission's attention. Commissioner Timothy Roemer was livid:

> Your list, according to what you just said, or what our staff has told me, is 12 people. So there's a difference of 60,988 names, a difference of 60,988 names between what's been accumulated at the State Department as dangerous people, shouldn't be flying, and what you have with your 12 people. Now, I can't understand why there are not more efforts in liaison activities to reach out to State Department and start to bring some of those names over and prevent those people from flying.[69]

Claudio Manno sought to explain that Security Directives were limited to those individuals about whom there was "specific and credible information that they posed a threat." Furthermore, Manno emphasized that "it was simply very difficult to get clearance from the [Intelligence] Community in cases where there wasn't a direct connection to civil aviation for them to get the release information. We had to justify that in each case. Now, did we do it? Did we go in and say we want all 61,000 of these names? No, that was not—we didn't do that. We focused on the information, again, that was specific to aviation at the time."[70]

As noted above, that restraint did not last long. The State Department's TIPOFF list and the FBI's VGTOF list were among the first to be dumped into the new No Fly List. Nevertheless, although the number of people on what became the No Fly List skyrocketed after September 11, Claudio Manno, the man initially in charge of it, remained adamant about the limited purpose of the No Fly List: "[T]he benchmark for credibility must be set sufficiently high to ensure that only individuals who present a danger to U.S. aircraft or aviation assets are prohibited from travel."[71]

But that standard was immediately undercut by transferring de facto authority to the FBI to dictate its contents. As Stewart Verdery, former Assistant Secretary for Policy and Planning in the DHS Border and Transportation Security Directorate observed: "Essentially the theory after 9/11 was, we are not going to let that happen to us again, . . . any plausible problem [person] is going in. And then, for every name you throw in you're creating lots of problems for other people who have similar names. And there were all these cases of the FBI throwing in Russian criminals from the fifties and IRA people from the seventies, not to mention you have the current crop of problematic persons."[72] Richard Falkenrath, who as the Deputy Homeland Security Advisor sought to impose coherence and order on the system by creating the TSC, himself admits to the overpowering temptation this new tool presented: "All I know is, at the White House we would routinely just shout out this person has got to be no-flied. And, you know, we expected it to happen."[73]

Even if Manno's exhortation to remain focused on threats "specific to aviation" reflected a strong desire at the FAA, that feeling was not shared by an intelligence community awakened to the potential power of Security Directives transformed into a No Fly List. And even if FBIHQ could have been persuaded to come around to the FAA's way of thinking, FBI agents in the field enjoyed an extraordinary autonomy. The description of a former assistant INS commissioner about that agency's decentralization might apply even more to the relationship of FBI field offices to headquarters: "The mountains are high and the emperor is far away."[74] The power of such a list was too great a temptation for agents who had been told that preventing another terrorist attack was their number one priority.

Indeed, as noted above, Congress had subtly expanded the contours of the No Fly List when it created the TSA in November 2001. The TSA now had the power to require air carriers "to use information from government agencies to identify individuals on passenger lists who may be a threat to civil aviation or national security" and, if so identified, "prevent the individual from boarding an aircraft."[75] A whole new world of opportunity was packed into that new, small disjunctive clause "or national security," which had never before been part of the FAA's mission.

The Security Directives—previously so undervalued by an intelligence community that could be stingy with the intelligence it shared—had grown quite popular as mechanisms to distribute the No Fly and Selectee lists.[76] In addition to the FBI, the CIA and other agencies sent TSA requests to add names to the lists. In December 2001, when the No Fly and Selectee lists were created under those names, the TSA still tried to emphasize two primary guidelines for use of the lists: (1) "Does the individual present a threat to civil aviation?" and (2) "Is there sufficient unclassified biographical data to ensure proper identification?"[77] In other words, use of SDs was still limited to individuals who "presented a specific known or suspected threat to aviation."[78]

But the genie was out of the bottle. Increasingly, limiting these lists to a "threat to civil aviation" seemed inconsistent with the broader post-9/11 mandate and therefore subject to question. In a TSA PowerPoint briefing to congressional staff on November 12, 2002, the TSA identified a new issue: "Difficulty in determining who poses a threat to aviation and why."[79] The preparation of "criteria for placement of individuals on the lists" was identified as a next step. This would be an odd slide to show congressional staff if the No Fly List were still believed to play the same role that Security Directives did before September 11. The fact is, nobody believed that it should anymore.

. . . to National Security

In his testimony to the Senate Homeland Security Committee in March 2010, TSC Director Healy described the steps in this progressive expansion of the scope of the No Fly List:

> Following the creation of the TSC in 2003, the Homeland Security Council Deputies Committee established the initial terrorist screening nomination criteria for the no-fly and selectee lists in October 2004. At that time, the no-fly list consisted of substantive derogatory criteria that focused attention on individuals intending to commit acts of terrorism against civil aviation or the domestic homeland. Over time, that initial criteria proved to be too restrictive. Consequently, in February 2008, the Homeland Security Council Deputies Committee approved additional criteria that served to broaden the scope of terrorists eligible for the no-fly list. In other words, the criteria to place individuals on the no-fly list has broadened to make the no-fly list more inclusive to respond to additional terrorism threats.[80]

Now, the No Fly List prevents the travel of "known or suspected terrorist[s]" who "present a threat to civil aviation or national security."[81] Both of these elements have expanded far beyond the original objective of ensuring the security of commercial aircraft. It is difficult to give credence to the assertion that the list is "not for use as [a] law enforcement or intelligence-gathering tool[]."[82] Indeed, in an FBI component entirely the creation of the Executive Branch, what save executive discretion establishes this limitation?

Consider the first part of the equation, the determination that a person is a "known or suspected terrorist." The publicly released definition of this phrase is sufficiently broad to include those who are or have been "engaged in conduct constituting, in preparation for, in aid of, or related to" terrorism.[83] The most recent published references to the watchlisting guidance used by the TSC define a *known* terrorist as "an individual who has been convicted of, currently charged with, or under indictment for a crime related to terrorism in a U.S. or foreign court of competent jurisdiction."[84] A *suspected* terrorist is "an individual who is reasonably suspected to be, or have been, engaged in conduct constituting, in preparation for, in aid of, or related to terrorism and terrorist activities based on an articulable and reasonable suspicion."[85]

At first glance, terrorism might seem a word that needs no definition; as U.S. Supreme Court Justice Potter Stewart once wrote (and later regretted writing) of hard-core pornography: "I know it when I see it."[86] But the term is not consistently defined in federal law: Congress defined the term quite broadly in requiring the State Department to deliver annual reports, but more rigorously in the contexts of terrorism prosecutions, and with even more detail for purposes of regulating immigration and naturalization.[87] Depending on the chosen definition, the associates of a suspected terrorist may be chosen from a series of broad concentric circles.

The choice of definition sets the parameters for exercising powers circumscribed by the term—what is a terrorist and what does it mean to be associated with one? Judge Joyce Hens Green famously illustrated this definitional power by asking a Justice Department lawyer whether a "little old lady from Switzerland" could be detained as an enemy combatant for unwittingly contributing to a faux charity that used her money to finance Al-Qaeda terrorists (the lawyer, Brian Boyle, unhappily conceded that the Government could do so in theory but would refrain in practice).[88] Unlike the self-restraint on its prosecutorial discretion exercised by the Justice Department, the TSA preferred to err in the opposite direction: *associates* was a broad term that could include spouses, children, relatives, and others with mere acquaintance to the "known or suspected terrorist." The result, compounded by the limitations of a name-based list, was that little old ladies, as well as infants, the deceased, and other unlikely terrorists and their associates routinely made it on to the early lists. Remember Cat Stevens—both the singer and the former Senator's wife?

The disjunctive clause separating "civil aviation *or* national security" is another broad source of expanding power. The No Fly List is not a system limited to protecting the physical security of commercial airlines. A person who presents no known threat to civil aviation, but who is considered a threat to broader national security interests, is a candidate for the No Fly List. In fact, Congress ordered that anyone ever detained at Guantánamo Bay automatically be added to the No Fly List without evaluation under any other criteria.[89] The nature of the No Fly List makes its limitation an exercise in self-policing. And, like the pressures operating on Mrs. Shipley, those who compile and manage the No Fly List operate under constant pressure to expand its coverage.

How far could "or national security" extend? Could the key financier or strategic mastermind of a terrorist organization be considered a sufficient threat to national security (although not necessarily a threat to civil aviation)? High-level officials criticized this hypothetical as an overly broad reading of the phrase "national security." The phrase, they said, is meant to include only actual physical threats of death or destruction that would be facilitated by travel on board an aircraft. Thus, a terrorist intending to blow up a building in a city to which he seeks to travel by plane would fit this description and therefore be subject to the No Fly List. Financiers and strategic masterminds were not sufficiently immediate threats to national security as that term was understood in this context.

But what legal authority placed such a constraint on the term "national security"? Where did the limitations of immediacy, and actual physical threats come from? There is no legal document *requiring* this interpretation. It is a limit placed only by implementation guidance found in various policy documents vetted nowhere outside the Executive Branch and susceptible to no outside constraint.

But even these limitations seem breachable. Consider, for example, the September 2004 unscheduled landing in Bangor, Maine, of the London-to-Washington United Airlines flight that carried Yusuf Islam, the folk singer formerly known as Cat Stevens. In a break with protocol, DHS Secretary Tom Ridge confirmed that the musician was on the No Fly List (while distancing his department from any blame for the action by noting its passive receipt of intelligence for use in the No Fly List). "Celebrity or unknown," he said, "our job is to act on information that others have given us. And in this instance, there was some relationship between the name and the terrorists' activity with this individual's name being on that no-fly list, and appropriate action was taken."[90] According to DHS spokesman Brian Doyle, his boarding had been a mistake because the federal government had information that "further heightens concern" about him.[91]

Was Cat Stevens placed on the No Fly List because he was "a threat to civil aviation"? Not in the FAA's original meaning of that term. There was no concern that he was a bomber or a hijacker, or scouting out security and aircraft details for a future attempt by someone else. If he were suspected of such an intent, then the decision to allow him to fly from Boston to Washington, where he then caught a second flight to return to London, would seem to have been particularly improvident.[92] The previous May, he had meetings about his philanthropic interests with President Bush's White House Office of Faith-Based and Community Initiatives.[93]

How about a threat to "national security"? That was the reason given by DHS spokesman Dennis Murphy for his detention upon arrival in Maine.[94] Another federal official speaking with a promise of anonymity told CBS News that he was suspected of making donations to Hamas and Omar Abdel-Rahman, the "blind sheikh" convicted for his part in the 1993 World Trade Center bombing.[95] If suspicions about his donations were the true cause of his watchlisting, that would fit the working definition of someone whose conduct (giving money) was "in aid of" or "related to" terrorism. Both the "blind sheikh" and Hamas are serious threats to national security. DHS spokesman Brian Doyle: "Why is he on the watch lists? Because of his activities that could be potentially linked to terrorism."[96] Financiers and masterminds.

Criteria agreed by a multiagency memorandum of understanding are supposed to limit the inclusion of individuals to only those who fit agreed profiles. But these minimum criteria are not only self-imposed, they are subject to override. According to then TSC Deputy Director for Operations Christopher Piehota, TSC personnel screen nominations to be sure that each nomination "is supported by the minimum substantive derogatory criteria for inclusion in the TSDB, *with limited exceptions*, as well as the additional derogatory requirements for the No Fly and Selectee lists."[97] In fact, Deputy Director Piehota acknowledged that even the *Terry* stop standard for nominations is not an absolute requirement for inclusion: "*Generally*, nominations to the TSDB are based on whether there is reasonable suspicion to believe that a person is a known or suspected terrorist."[98] The exceptions that the Deputy Director implied were left unstated, but it is not a stretch to presume that they reserve authority to summarily add names to the list based on the perceived urgency of an operational need.

An example of how easy it was to succumb to pressure to make such exceptions is suggested by a recounting of "Terrorism Tuesdays" in the Bush administration. According to Michael Jackson, the chief operating officer of the Department of Homeland Security from 2005 through 2007, "we used to have what we called Terrorism Tuesday when Chertoff was secretary. So on every Tuesday morning after the President's foreign intelligence briefing [composed of the President, the Vice President, the National Security Advisor, the DNI, the President's CIA briefer, and the Chief of Staff], the session would be expanded and added to that would be the Attorney General, the Secretary of Homeland Security, the FBI Director, Fran Townsend, acting as a national security advisor."[99] Jackson remembers the sessions he attended in Secretary Chertoff's place:

> So I frequently went through this session and you'd read a certain thing and at a certain point the President or somebody in the room would look up and they would look over to the FBI Director and say, or the AG or somebody, and say "And this guy's on the watchlist, right?" . . . The first time I saw that it was like, well, we're going to do that but we haven't done that. Well, that goes along. You know, there's only so many times you can get beat up by the President of the United States and asked this question, where you know when you come in, when you've got a case where there's a significant concern enough to where you're briefing the President of the United States, that you say: "and we've already got the guy on the watchlist."[100]

How did it feel to get "beat up" by President Bush? "You know, because he just looks at you like, are you stupid? . . . But then he would rightfully ask, 'Is he on the watchlist?' And it was just not acceptable to say no if you thought that he was seriously enough a problem to be in there briefing POTUS about it."[101]

Could such a feeling trickle down to influence the level of people who weren't important enough to brief the President, but who were briefing those that were? Did Michael Jackson ever give that same look and ask those same questions? By way of example, Jackson turned the conversation to the case of the Ismail family, the focus of chapter 2:

> So when you asked the question is it plausible for an SAC to put somebody on the list, if the SAC was running a major investigation and that investigation looked pretty dicey, it doesn't seem at all unlikely to me that at some point the SAC says to somebody, you know, put them on the watch list. Does that mean that he sat down at his e-mail and filled out a form and sent it in? No, you know, shit, for all I know maybe he did.[102]

In other words, while legal standards and objective criteria were all well and good, when the right people determined that someone needed to be put on the watchlist, it happened. And not just for the safety of air travel: "I did care that if we thought that there was some significant trouble that you could make sure that you foreclosed the possibility that that could turn into an airplane bombing. *Or that they were just going to willy-nilly come here and disappear into the country, which goes to the second half of your question about protecting the airplane or national security.*"[103]

This expansion is absolutely natural. Why wouldn't the men and women tasked with tracking dangerous terrorists and national security threats, every day, month after month and year after year, want to expand the use of this watchlisting tool? To acknowledge this pressure, this intense focus on preventing another terrorist attack, is not to question their professionalism. It is simply to ask if, given such pressures, those in whose hands this powerful watchlist has been placed should also be left to police themselves about its use.

As it turns out, the temptation has proven to be too much.

Secure Flight

The expansion of "mission creep" could take other forms beyond an ever broadening definition of the criteria for watchlisting. It was perhaps inevitable that TSA would eventually displace the airlines in enforcing Security Directives. Originally, the airlines were expected to implement the No Fly List themselves, just as they had complied with Security Directives in the past. This proved disastrous and led to the conclusion that prescreening against the watchlist should be considered an "inherently governmental function."[104] Distributing lists to airlines compromised the security of the lists and injected too much variability into their use. Airline personnel occasionally informed passengers (rightly or wrongly) that they were watchlisted, notwithstanding the instruction that all lists should be treated as sensitive security information (SSI).[105]

To eliminate these problems, and to decrease the number of false-positive matches with the No Fly List caused by the similarity between watchlisted names and unsuspected travelers, the TSA created the "Secure Flight" prescreening system.[106] Congress gave the green light for this shift to greater government control in the Intelligence Reform and Terrorism Prevention Act of 2004.[107] Importantly, however, Congress shifted to TSA only the *ministerial* task to perform "the passenger prescreening function of comparing passenger information to the automatic selectee and no fly lists and utilize all appropriate records in the consolidated and integrated terrorist watchlist maintained by the Federal Government in performing that function."[108]

Congress did nothing to shift the *discretionary* power to decide whose names should appear on those lists. That power remained uniquely lodged in the TSC. In fact, in its own final rule implementing the limited power Congress gave it, the TSA explained that "TSA defines 'watch list' for purposes of the Secure Flight program as the No Fly List and Selectee List components of the Terrorist Screening Database maintained by the Terrorist Screening Center."[109]

This is how Secure Flight works today. TSA now obtains an electronic record of the full name, date of birth, and gender of every passenger at the time a ticket is purchased.[110] That data is then compared to the relevant watchlists, including the No Fly List; TSA sends watchlist "hits" to the TSC for final adjudication.[111] Airlines must submit this data at least seventy-two hours before the scheduled departure; last-minute ticket purchases made within that time period must be submitted immediately.[112] TSA presents Secure Flight as a service to the traveling public (like Mrs. Shipley's passports), providing security while expediting the processing of false positives. Figure 9 shows how TSA presents the system in graphical form (a full-color figure appears on the website).[113]

Having identified prescreening as an "inherently governmental" function, Secure Flight seems the natural next step. But the graphic reveals its power. To use a commercial aircraft to travel within, out of, or into the United States, an individual must now (1) purchase a ticket from an airline, and then (2) seek permission from the U.S. Government to use it.[114]

As this graphic implies, Secure Flight has other advantages beyond decreasing false positives. Secure Flight could provide flight information to TSA well in advance of departure, thus "pushing back" the border, especially on international flights. Naturally, earlier access to data encouraged greater use of it. As the Inspector General for the Department of Homeland Security observed, "with the Secure Flight program, in cases where certain yet-to-be-defined security considerations exist, TSA could screen against the federal government's entire consolidated terrorist watch list for particular flights or routes."[115] In other words, Secure Flight worked a trifecta: prescreening earlier, with a bigger watchlist, based on security considerations that were open to redefinition.

Remarkably, if almost certainly unintentionally, this Secure Flight system is little more than a computerized version of Mrs. Shipley's "red card" system, which she used to flag suspect passport applicants: "Red cards list identifying information, such as the date and place of birth, to keep the innocent from being tagged with a guilty record through similarity of names. Each card carries a code to a full file. The file contains all available information—whether the person concerned is a Communist, a dope addict, a criminal,

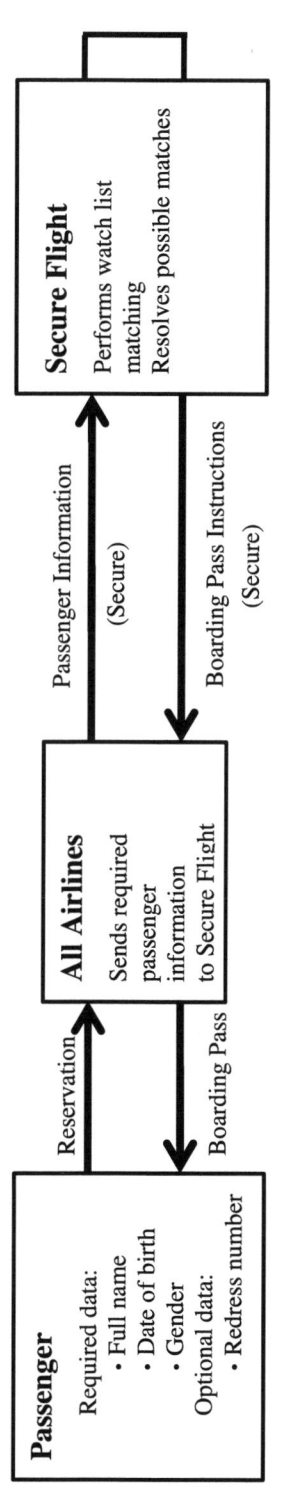

Fig. 9. TSA Graphical Representation of the Secure Flight Program

or just has views that might embarrass policy makers if he expressed them in a foreign land."[116] But the result is just the same: as in Mrs. Shipley's day, a traveler is only allowed to proceed on his itinerary once the state has satisfied itself that he should be allowed to go.

3. Shrinking Responsibility: The Redress Shell Game

In *The Closing of the American Border*, Edward Alden summarized the early policy thinking that went into the creation of a new border agency, Customs and Border Protection: "What it added up to was a faith in the government's ability to use technology and intelligence to sort the bad from the good."[117] The very same attitude animated thinking about the use of terrorist watchlists under the control of the Terrorist Screening Center and utilized by the TSA. But what happens when a would-be traveler complains that unseen government officials got it wrong? From whom should the thwarted traveler seek a remedy? This section analyzes the failure to adopt a recommendation of the 9/11 Commission that went hand in hand with its encouragement of greater watchlisting: "If the power is granted, there must be adequate guidelines and oversight to properly confine its use."[118]

Among the 9/11 Commission's criticisms was the charge that responsibility and accountability in counterterrorism efforts were too "diffuse."[119] The TSC was one response to that criticism. Ironically, consolidating intelligence sharing and watchlisting in the TSC concentrates information inside the Government, but in a way that thwarts outside attempts to hold accountable the actual officials in charge. Digitizing Mrs. Shipley disperses her ghost throughout the machine. She is omnipresent but untouchable.

Those who created this system view this intangibility as an asset, not a liability. DHS Deputy Secretary Michael Jackson highlighted the need "to execute an interagency mission that required an unusual degree of coordination and accommodation in how you manage that institution."[120] He was not concerned that such a system could confuse the lines of delegated authority to the point that it becomes hard to distinguish TSA orders from TSC recommendations, or vice versa.[121] Senior officials present at the creation of DHS, TSA, and TSC praise the synergies, fluidity, and responsiveness that they built into this new interagency system. The checks and balances that traditionally constrain zealous government officials from exceeding their mandates were not part of this picture. Like the redress process itself, this was an afterthought. As Jackson recalled, in the early days "It was chaos. And so they were happy just to have a No Fly List, . . . so some [innocent] guy turns up on the No Fly List, and it's a problem. We'll deal with that problem when it comes up."[122] Admiral James Loy, the second administrator of the TSA, concurred. The formal and institutional checks on discretion within this new security directive-driven system were "TBD. That's where it was in those days. To Be Determined."[123]

This attitude of afterthought for dealing with that problem "when it comes up" illustrates the singular focus of the officials who first created the No Fly List and then began to establish the structures to give it permanence. In light of the unknown dangers and fears of another terrorist attack, Jackson continued, "I think it was considered to be a relatively acceptable trade-off that [for] some people who had duplicate names that triggered them as a selectee, . . . we would work through a process of building a system that you would have a redress capability to give your number in and then get, tell you how to get around it."[124]

But this attitude, initially justified by the desperate circumstances after 9/11, never went away. Instead, it permeated later thinking. There was no perceived need for an external authority, let alone a *judicial* authority, to determine when to interfere with a citizen's travel. Discussing a threat perceived in August 2007, Jackson summarized his view of the relationship between the No Fly List and the redress process:

> I think that erring on the side of caution to put people on the list in the heat of the circumstances is what happens and it's right. And then, over time, . . . maybe that person's going to end up as, not a no fly, but likely would be, say, a selectee. But depending upon the nature of it, it could be a no fly. And it might be three months or four months before everything got settled out and they go back and they say okay, it's all right, now let me look at this and we don't need this person here on the list. It might be six months, I don't know, I don't know the answer. But it's not an unreasonable inconvenience to impose upon certain parties. What would be unreasonable is if there's not a way to ultimately evaluate one of those cases and obtain redress if it has languished there too long. So that's what the whole redress process is about. So I think that it's fair and it's true to say that nominating agencies are given quite a bit of latitude to put somebody, to err on the side of caution. But that they are instructed to have a culture at the watchlist-operating level to compel routine reexamination of the nominations and to see what happens with those.[125]

In other words, say the creators of the lists, trust us to police ourselves, to develop the proper "culture" among our closed ranks to get the balance right. But don't interfere with our work by imposing outside scrutiny of our decisions.[126]

The problem is that the keepers of the watchlists, from the heights of policymaking to the operational trenches, are poorly placed to exercise such self-restraint. The culture that will develop is one that naturally will diminish the importance of individual liberties in the light of perceived threats to the nation. It is easy to understand how the daily onslaught of intelligence briefings that present risks and threats and dangers could produce such an attitude. The binder that Vice Admiral John Redd perused each dawn as director of the NCTC was four inches thick.[127] This binder, one of many such binders reviewed each morning by senior government officials responsible for national security, was filled with an ever-changing "threat matrix" of as many as "sixty or seventy potential terrorist threats against the United States."[128] Those who receive it report "a profound impact on one's thinking—it's hard to ever see the world in the same way after witnessing the worst that humans can imagine doing to others. It hangs over you all day and each night."[129]

There are two problems with the view that the officials in charge of the No Fly List should be left unconstrained by outsiders, that they should be trusted to develop the proper culture within their ranks to make prudent choices about when and how much to infringe the freedom of movement of their fellow citizens. The first problem is bias from within. The second is pressure from without.

To suggest bias is not to suggest malice. It is simply the natural result of the day-to-day experience of a keeper of the watchlist, especially those at the higher levels of government. Michael Jackson's experience as a senior trusted advisor provides insight into how that worldview is shaped. Jackson described his morning routine during the two years that he was the chief operating officer for the Department of Homeland Security. It was a routine, he said, similar to that experienced by his counterparts at the NCTC, FBI, NSC, Defense Department, and other top positions in the country's homeland security apparatus:

> I was a Secret Service protectee. So every morning, 6:30, the car's out there, the armored guy and the guy in the front seat with the gun to jump in front of a bad guy for you. That's a pretty humbling position to be in, to be a Secret Service protectee. But they show up and the first thing you get is the list of the overnight horribles. And

you start tracking them. And you've got maybe a 100 names and incidents that you're trying to make sure that you can remember to say this thing, this thing, how'd this work out, what is this going on? It is a massively sobering responsibility to wake up and to have to deal with the terrorist threats that the country faces every day. And I'm just saying, ask yourself a prudential question. Would you rather those people have the authority to err on the side of caution, or do you want to have the ACLU beat them on the head every time they put somebody's name on the list? I say err on the side of caution, but combine that with a real and prudent commitment for continuous review of the list, let the things wash out over time and then be dealt with appropriately. And that seems to me where the prudential balance is.[130]

Naturally enough, therefore, the cases that were of most concern in the beginning were those that could ignite a political firestorm or a public relations debacle that would undermine the independence from judicial oversight upon which the keepers of the watchlists—like Mrs. Shipley—depended. Ironically, therefore, the development of the redress system was not catalyzed by the travails of the innocent but ordinary traveler. Rather, the cases that attracted attention were those that could fall into the category of the "T. Kennedy" problem.[131]

When, in 2004, Senator Ted Kennedy found himself stopped several times at Logan Airport, the story naturally received nationwide attention. Such attention was hardly desirable as policymakers and operations specialists worked hard to build a system that was both reliable and accurate and perceived by the public to be so, too. As the travel stories of Larry Musarra, Jaber Ismail, and others recounted in chapters 1 and 2 demonstrate, requests by ordinary travelers for help with watchlisting snafus rarely caught the attention of TSA or DHS officials on their own. What did? Michael Jackson described the pressures on his office:

> So you get the press on your case, you get a congressman on your case, you get another cabinet member on your case, you get the White House on your case, you get DHS on the case or you get FBI on the case. The punch line is, in this system, there are multiple entry points for people to look at an alleged complaint here, or a complaint or alleged injustice, and to have other people come in, get enough information to say, I'm not going to second-guess that. . . . And sometimes I'd look into it, or have somebody look into it, and I'd call back and

say, you were right and we've taken care of that and here's the number, we'd called them, it's done. In other cases, I would just call back and say, I can't do anything about this. It wasn't because I didn't look into it. It's just that I saw enough stuff there that I said I'm not putting my name on the record to give this person a get-out-of-jail-free card in terms of the watchlist.[132]

This, then, is where the second problem emerged: pressure. This problem affects both high-level political officials and those career officials whose work is on the day-to-day operational level. The "Are-you-stupid?" look that President Bush could give his advisors on "Terrorism Tuesdays" was neither the sole prerogative of the President's to convey nor limited to the Oval Office or the Situation Room. The officials who briefed the President returned to their departments and agencies and were equally capable of giving such looks to their subordinates.

It should be noted that Jackson strongly objects to this suggestion of defensive groupthink. In our conversation, he repeatedly emphasized the importance of developing an institutional culture that encouraged periodic reviews and empowered participants to second-guess authority or received wisdom. Of course, the secrecy of the process prevents any outside evaluation of it. But it is not hard to see how this trickle-down effect shapes institutional culture, too. Whether the political appointee responding to a congressional inquiry, or the analyst making a tough judgment call, the pressures to reach the same conclusion were equally present: "I'm not putting my name on the record to give this person a get-out-of-jail-free card in terms of the watchlist."

Down the Rabbit Hole

What if different agencies in the watchlisting process disagreed about whether to add someone to the No Fly List, each agency taking a strong position? Some former officials could not recall a single instance when officials at TSA and TSC were in strong disagreement about whether to watchlist someone, while others thought such conflicts happened routinely.[133] Hypothetically, disagreement in those sorts of cases could rise to the higher-deputy levels of authority within the agencies.

How does this translate into an actual response to the ordinary would-be traveler, the average citizen whose government has secretly decided the parameters for his acceptable movement? Return now to the hypothetical that introduced this book and prepare for a journey down the rabbit hole:

Imagine waiting in Hong Kong International Airport for the final leg of a long journey home to the United States. You are traveling with your family. Everyone is tired. When you reach the front of a long line at the ticket counter, the agent looks nervous: "I'm sorry, but I cannot print your boarding pass. Your name appears on a United States terrorism watchlist."

How do you get back home?

The employee of the commercial airline who denies the traveler a boarding pass at its check-in counter is the first dead end. When the airline's computer flags a traveler, the ticketing agent will contact the TSA and perhaps the TSC through its 24/7 telephone hotline.[134] As the traveler waits, the TSC will determine the accuracy of the suspected match and likely consult with TSA and the agency or agencies that originally supplied the derogatory information that landed the traveler on the watchlist. Then the TSC and TSA will tell the airline's agent what to do. Regardless of the outcome, he or she will have no more knowledge than the traveler receives. The airlines' employees are merely the messengers.

The traveler might reasonably decide to seek redress from the agency in charge of composing the list, the TSC. After all, it is the TSC that accepts nominations to the No Fly List, manages the criteria for approving them (and makes exceptions to them), and coordinates the government's response to the inquiry from the airline ticketing counter. According to the Inspector General of the Department of Homeland Security, TSA's parent agency, "TSC quality assurance measures ensure that the correct individuals are on the appropriate watch lists."[135] As then Deputy Director for TSC Operations explained in late 2010 to a federal judge: "[W]hen a traveler's inquiry may appear to concern data in the TSDB, the matter is referred to the TSC Redress Unit, which assigns the matter to a TSC redress analyst for research."[136]

These statements make clear that the TSC is where the action is. The TSC, however, "does not accept redress inquiries directly from the public, nor does it respond directly to redress inquiries."[137] Nor will the TSC identify the agency or component of the federal government that was the source for the derogatory information that resulted in the nomination in the first place, let alone what the content of that information is. A Freedom of Information Act request either to the TSC or to the TSA would fail because of national security and law enforcement exemptions to the general requirement of disclosure.[138] In fact, the TSC will not even disclose where it is located when it makes its decisions.

If the TSC is hard to access, how about those who implement its decisions? Confusingly enough, the traveler is now confronted by a surfeit of choices. There is both a DHS Office for Civil Rights and Civil Liberties and a TSA Office of Civil Rights and Liberties. Where should a traveler begin?

The former second-in-command at DHS, Michael Jackson, was dismissive of the DHS Office for Civil Rights and Civil Liberties, an advice-giving office that "doesn't have a line responsibility for anything at DHS." In fact, in the most sensitive cases, that office would not even be allowed a seat at the table. Jackson chose to recount a particularly terrifying episode during his tenure to illustrate that point and underscore what role he felt should be accorded to institutional checks and balances.[139]

> So the Office of Civil Rights? Pffft [*makes a dismissive gesture*]. At that point, this is where I'm talking about, when you think about your legal issues, you've got [to] ask yourself, what are the people responsible for running the government going to say about stuff like this? They don't care. I mean, if we have ten names on that list or twenty-five names on that list that ultimately get washed out, but you don't know if one of them [. . .]? Here are some guys who we know, we've seen the pictures, we know what's going on. They're about to get on the planes with this. They are looking at flight times, I mean it was a dead-serious no-kidding, no-shit, going-to-blow-up American airplanes plot. And so, in that environment, that's what I'm saying, you have to understand is, people don't care if there's a little bit of temporary addition to the watchlist while you sort it out. And maybe it's at such a level that routine parts of government aren't going to be able to have access to the full reason why someone was added on.[140]

Such an attitude is completely understandable from a former recipient of a daily list of threats to national security. What honorable and competent official (and Michael Jackson is widely regarded in respected circles as both) would not feel enormous pressure to prevent a perceived threat to American national security with every available means possible? Who would choose to err on the side of liberty over security? But the answer is the same as before: Trust us.

How about the TSA Office of Civil Rights and Liberties? The TSA office describes its "compliance mission" to be to "conduct inquiries and respond to complaints of unlawful discriminatory treatment from the traveling public about TSA's security screening programs and activities," and its "policy mission" to be to "provide civil rights and liberties guidance in the review of TSA's existing and proposed policies and programs."[141] A careful read of its website, however, reveals that it only accepts complaints from travelers alleging mistreatment by a TSA employee based on unconstitutional discrimination. Since the source of the problem is the decision to add the traveler's name to a watchlist, and that decision making is neither made by TSA employees nor revealed to the traveler, this is a dead end.

Instead, the "single point of contact for all traveler screening issues" is the DHS Traveler Redress Inquiry Program, DHS TRIP.[142] DHS TRIP has no corporeal form to visit (like Mrs. Shipley's Winder Building). It exists only in the ether of the Internet, through which the traveler may complete an online form at the DHS website.[143] That web page does not indicate who will review the inquiry, by what standards, or even which agency will make the relevant decision.

Although DHS TRIP is the only avenue for redress, neither DHS nor TSA will examine the complaint beyond the need to ascertain that the complaint is based on a positive match to the No Fly List. As TSC Director Timothy Healy told Congress, "the complaint is reviewed by the agency that received it, and referred to the TSC Redress Unit after it has been determined that there is a connection to the Terrorist Watchlist."[144] In court filings, the Justice Department has argued that the TSC—not the DHS, TSA, or any other agency—is in charge: "The TSC Redress Unit makes a determination as to whether any adjustment in the individual's status, including modification or removal, is required and informs DHS TRIP accordingly; DHS TRIP, in conjunction with TSA OSTR [Office of Transportation Security Redress], subsequently sends a determination letter to the complainant" as required under law.[145] More concretely, as Director Healy's deputy informed a federal judge in a declaration submitted in response to litigation:

> After reviewing the available information and considering any recommendation from the nominating agency, the TSC Redress Unit will make a determination on whether the record should remain in the TSDB, or have its TSDB status modified or removed, unless the legal authority to make such a determination resides, in whole or in part, with another government agency. In such cases, TSC will only prepare a recommendation for the decision-making agency and will implement any determination once made. When changes to a record's status are warranted, the TSC will ensure such corrections are made, since the TSC remains the final arbiter of whether terrorist identifiers are removed from the TSDB. The TSC will also verify that such modifications or removals carry over to the various screening systems that receive TSDB data (*e.g.,* the Selectee and No Fly Lists).[146]

TSC—and no other agency—will "make a determination" about the disputed record. Unless, that is, some other government agency has the "legal authority . . . in whole or in part," to make that determination. But, even when that is the case, TSC "remains the final arbiter" over removing or changing records in the TSDB and the No Fly List.

But once the traveler's inquiry has been referred to the TSC (as it must if there is a match with the No Fly List) who actually decides what to do, TSC or TSA, DHS, or some other agency? Director Healy told Congress, "Upon the conclusion of our [TSC] review, we advise DHS TRIP representatives of the outcome so that they can directly respond to the complainant."[147] That TSC review is completed by working "with the nominating or originating agency to determine if the complainant's watchlisted status should be modified."[148] As if this circular flowchart were not a confusing enough, the Office of Transportation Security Redress in the TSA "acts as DHS's lead agent managing DHS TRIP."[149]

Supposing the long-suffering traveler perseveres, and completes the DHS TRIP complaint online. The end result is a "final agency decision" letter that obscures the various roles of this alphabet soup of agencies just as it evades any clear statement of the decision.[150] Read the DHS TRIP letter sent in October 2008 to Erich Scherfen, whose travel story was explored in chapter 1.[151] The operative language is identical to that found in the letter reprinted in chapter 2 that Jaber Ismail received in August 2006.

Despite its Orwellian language, the form letter spit out of the TSA system is considered final agency action. This is despite the Government's description of its content as indicating "either that Plaintiffs are on the No Fly or Selectee List, and thus subject to travel restrictions and/or enhanced screening with consequent travel delays, or not included on the No Fly or Selectee List. In either event, the letters reflect the fact that a final determination has been made that fixes some legal relationship."[152]

Some legal relationship, indeed. But with whom? About what? The problem, of course, is that the determination letter is impenetrable. It is impossible to decipher what final agency action has been taken, if any, and by whom. What legal relationship has been fixed? What should the traveler do next? DHS TRIP is the impermeable shield that protects the TSC in its glorious isolation. The traveler will discover this fact if, frustrated and having exhausted this administrative remedy, he decides to file a civil action for injunctive relief against the agency.

Whom should the traveler name as the defendant in that suit? The logical choice is the TSC. If the traveler has been placed on the No Fly List, it was the TSC that made the decision and only it has the power to remove a name

U.S. Department of Homeland Security
Traveler Redress Inquiry Program (TRIP)
601 South 12th Street, TSA-901
Arlington, VA 22202-4220

October 15, 2008

Mr. Erich Michael Scherfen

Control Number:

Dear Mr. Scherfen:

Thank you for submitting your Traveler Inquiry Form and identity documentation to the Department of Homeland Security (DHS) Traveler Redress Inquiry Program (TRIP).

In response to your inquiry concerning travel delays at the airline ticket counter or airport security checkpoint, we conducted a review of any applicable records in consultation with other Federal agencies, as appropriate. Where it was determined that a correction to records was warranted, these records were modified to address any delay or denial of boarding that you may have experienced as a result of the Transportation Security Administration's watch list screening process. This determination constitutes our final agency decision, which is reviewable by the United States Court of Appeals under 49 U.S.C. § 46110.

DHS cannot ensure your travel will always be delay-free as this redress process does not affect other standard screening procedures in place at the security checkpoint. For example, an individual may be selected for additional screening in order to resolve a walk-through metal detector alarm, because of random selection, or based on certain non-identity factors reflected in reservation information. Additionally, this process may not eliminate the need to go to the ticket counter in order to obtain a boarding pass. For instance, an airline might still require a brief period of time to comply with identity verification requirements prior to issuing a boarding pass.

Based on our analysis of those persons who have applied for redress through DHS TRIP, more than 99 percent are not on a Federal watch list. DHS and the airlines have developed solutions to reduce inconvenience and facilitate remote check-in. Before your next flight, contact the designated office of the airline in advance to inquire about its procedures for collecting your full name and date of birth. The airline will likely be able to store your information or enroll you in its frequent flyer program, which may enable you to print your boarding pass at a kiosk or online.

Concerning the difficulties you have experienced clearing inspection at a U.S. port of entry, we have completed our review of this matter.

We assure you that it is not the intent of DHS to subject the traveling public to unwarranted scrutiny. The traveling public is entitled to, and is accorded, the utmost courtesy and facilitation we can offer

www.dhs.gov/trip

Fig. 10. DHS Letter to Erich Scherfen

Mr. Erich Michael Scherfen
October 15, 2008
Page 2

within the limits of our law enforcement responsibilities. Regrettably, the results of our efforts cannot always be as you might hope.

Please understand that in order to detect those international travelers involved in illicit activities, we must, at times, unfortunately inconvenience law-abiding travelers. We are especially aware of how those selected for inspection may perceive the inspection process as upsetting, uncomfortable, inconvenient, and stressful. That is why we try to emphasize to our officers on a nation-wide basis the need to perform their duties with the highest levels of courtesy and professionalism.

While DHS cannot guarantee complete freedom from intensive inspections, whether the inspections are random or specific, we can strive for a better understanding of our mutual needs. DHS must rely upon the professional judgment of individual inspections officers to determine the extent of examination necessary and to do their best to differentiate between travelers who are of interest to DHS, and those who are not.

Although we can neither confirm nor deny that DHS has records or information that prompted this inspection, if DHS has determined based on your correspondence that there is a need to make changes or corrections to any such record or information, should it exist, I can assure you such changes or corrections have been made.

We regret any inconvenience or unpleasantness you may have experienced during your airline check-in or recent travel into a U.S. port of entry. We hope that your future encounters with DHS will be of a more pleasant nature. To contact DHS TRIP, send an e-mail to TRIP@dhs.gov, or write to the following address:

DHS Traveler Redress Inquiry Program (TRIP)
601 South 12th Street, TSA-901
Arlington, VA 22202-4220

Sincerely,

Jim Kennedy
Traveler Redress Inquiry Program

Control Number:

Fig. 10. DHS (*continued*)

from the watchlist. But if the TSC is named as the defendant, the Justice Department attorneys tasked to respond to the lawsuit will argue that the TSC is the wrong party. The TSA must be named because it retains final authority to determine redress appeals, even though as a practical matter those determinations, too, are made by the TSC.[153] This is because the TSA adopts the TSC's No Fly List in the form of a Security Directive, the old power it acquired from the FAA to deny boarding to dangerous, but ticketed, passengers.[154] This is further reflected in a memorandum of understanding on redress procedures signed by the TSC, TSA, and other agencies in 2007. The relevant sections of that memorandum indicate that TSC "will make a determination . . . unless the legal authority to make such a determination resides, in whole or in part, with another agency."[155] If that is the case, TSC "will only prepare a recommendation" to that agency. On this basis rests the argument that the decision making of the TSC and TSA is "inextricably intertwined" concerning redress appeals.

That entwinement argument is a crucial step because it is the hook for an argument about which court may hear these legal claims, and even what information that court may be entitled to review. The Justice Department has argued that federal law requires that jurisdiction to hear any lawsuit filed concerning the No Fly List rest not in the ordinary federal trial courts but only in a federal court of appeal.[156] That shift means that the routine processes of discovery, through which evidence is obtained by each side to present their respective cases, do not apply.[157] Instead, the decision-making record of the relevant agency is the basis for any appellate review under principles of administrative law. On at least one occasion, the Justice Department has even argued not only that jurisdiction may only be had in an appellate court, but that an administrative record is not even required for the jurisdiction-shifting statute to apply.[158]

The origin of the jurisdiction-shifting provision of law, found in section 46110 of Title 49 of the United States Code, goes back to the 1958 statute that created the Federal Aviation Administration, long before the No Fly List or even its security-directive predecessors were even conceived.[159] In the standard rule-making context for which this departure from the norm was conceived, it made sense to allocate judicial review in the first instance to an appellate court for cases that were largely disputes filed by airlines and pilots about regulations concerning industry safety standards, licenses, certificates, and other matters. In the typical case complaining about an FAA rule or decision, the facts that trial courts ordinarily evaluate would not come from live witnesses and outside exhibits. Logically, the case should be heard by an appellate court because the "facts" on which the decision was based had already been gathered in the form of the administrative record of the agency's challenged decision making. It was the evaluation of the agency's decision based on the compiled record that a court was tasked to evaluate—in a way, a sort of appellate review.

But in the case of the No Fly List, whose administrative record would be lodged with the court? The whole point of watchlisting is to do it secretly. As Chief Judge Alex Kozinski of the U.S. Court of Appeal for the Ninth Circuit asked in *Ibrahim v. DHS* (the first of two important cases on this issue in which the Ninth Circuit would rule), "Just how would an appellate court review the agency's decision to put a particular name on the list? There was no hearing before an administrative law judge; there was no notice-and-comment procedure. For all we know, there is no administrative record of any sort for us to review. So if any court is going to review the government's decision to put [a] name on the No-Fly List, it makes sense that it be a court with the ability to take evidence."[160]

The Government's argument has persuaded several federal trial courts that they lack jurisdiction to hear claims about the No Fly List.[161] But Chief Judge Kozinski, writing for the Ninth Circuit in the *Ibrahim* case, rejected the assertion that any relevant decision-making was "inextricably intertwined." TSC compiled the list and resolved interagency disputes about its composition. Once that task was done, its customer, TSA, was sent the product for use on the front lines. A complaint about composition, the court said, was distinct from one about applying the list via a TSA Security Directive:

> The district court determined, based on undisputed facts, that an agency called the Terrorist Screening Center "actually compiles the list of names ultimately placed on the No-Fly List." And the Terrorist Screening Center isn't part of the Transportation Security Administration or any other agency named in section 46110; it is part of the Federal Bureau of Investigation, as the government concedes. Because putting Ibrahim's name on the No-Fly List was an "order" of an agency not named in section 46110, the district court retains jurisdiction to review that agency's order under the APA.[162]

Nevertheless, the Justice Department has routinely argued that the TSA and DHS are indispensable parties to any lawsuit.[163] The determination letters, after all, are mailed from TSA and DHS. For example, the Justice Department argued in a November 2010 filing:

> As explained above, TSA is responsible for identifying travelers who pose a threat to national security, preventing those individuals from

boarding an aircraft, and for redress. *See* 49 U.S.C. §§ 114(h)(3), 114(f) (1)–(4), 44903. TSA and DHS are responsible for providing redress to travelers who complain that they have been delayed or denied boarding due to wrongful placement on a government watchlist.[164]

This is a partially true statement, but not responsive to the issue. TSA is not responsible for "identifying" threatening travelers; it is responsible for instructing the airlines to prevent the boarding of passengers that the TSC No Fly List has identified for them. The cited sections of § 114(f) grant TSA powers to "receive, assess, and distribute intelligence information related to transportation security; assess threats to transportation; develop policies, strategies, and plans for dealing with threats to transportation security; make other plans related to transportation security, including coordinating countermeasures with appropriate departments, agencies, and instrumentalities of the United States Government."[165] Congress described these powers to receive intelligence from other agencies and make policies based on it quite differently than it defined the core functions identified in the previous subsection, to "be responsible for day-to-day Federal security screening operations," like airport security checkpoints.[166] Indeed, the strongest powers referenced by the Justice Department—"identifying" and "preventing" the boarding of individuals who threaten airline or passenger safety—are actually statutory powers to establish policies and procedures to accomplish those ends "in consultation with appropriate Federal agencies and air carriers," not grants of exclusive, decision-making authority.[167] In fact, Congress specifically required the Secretary of the Department of Homeland Security (not the Assistant Secretary for TSA) to collaborate with the TSC on No Fly List issues.[168] When Congress sought to give the TSA exclusive power, it knew how to do that, and markedly did not do so with regard to the No Fly List.[169] In this case, Congress instructed the TSA to utilize records controlled by another agency.[170]

Congress ordered the TSA to establish "a timely and fair process for individuals identified as a threat . . . to appeal to the Transportation Security Administration the determination and correct any erroneous information."[171] The process created in response to that mandate—DHS TRIP—is administered through the TSA: it is from TSA's Office of Transportation Security Redress (TSA OTSR) that the traveler will receive the letter announcing the final determination. But the *decision making* itself—as distinguished from the letter-drafting to report that result—is done by the TSC. As Deputy Director Piehota explained, "After the TSC Redress Unit completes its review of the matter, DHS TRIP is notified of the recommendation so DHS

TRIP may send a determination letter to the traveler."[172] The word "recommendation" is a euphemism; as Piehota notes in the previous paragraph of his declaration, this "recommendation" comes from the "final arbiter" over these lists, the TSC.[173] Figure 11 shows the TSC's perception of the process, in a flowchart it supplied to the Justice Department's Inspector General (a full-color version appears in the IG's report).

As the flowchart indicates, the TSC Redress Office "reviews related watchlist record(s) and resolves complaint."[174] The TSC then revises the watchlist and instructs the screening agency—the TSA in the case of the No Fly List—to respond to the complainant. Based on its audit and review of the governing documents, the Justice Department's Inspector General expressed no doubt as to the chain of command:

> If, as a result of a redress review, the TSC recommends a change to the watchlist record or status (for either a positive match or misidentification referral), the Redress MOU and the TSC Redress SOP both require that the TSC discuss its findings with the nominating agencies. *While the nominating agencies may provide input, the TSC has the ultimate authority to resolve all terrorist watchlist redress matters.* Finally, the TSC Redress Office ensures that the necessary changes are made to watchlist records before closing its review and alerting the frontline screening agency of its resolution. The TSC does not respond to the complainant. Rather, the TSC coordinates with the frontline screening agency, which should submit a formal reply to the complainant.[175]

As the DOJ Inspector General noted, the TSC is completely insulated from the complainant. It is not possible for an individual to file a redress complaint directly with the TSC, and the TSC will not respond to such complaints.

While it is true that the vehicle for distributing the No Fly List is a Security Directive that only the TSA has legal authority to issue, control over the real substantive matter at issue—the content of the No Fly List—belongs to the TSC analysts and officials who assess the TSDB entries and decide whether the criteria for inclusion in the No Fly List are met. And with enough agencies represented in the process—the agency that originated the derogatory information, the TSC that organized it, and the TSA that used it—decision making can begin to look like a dissenter's veto. As Richard Falkenrath described the issue: "[T]hese sorts of decisions, one dissenter can usually block it. Affirmative action by government is done on the ba-

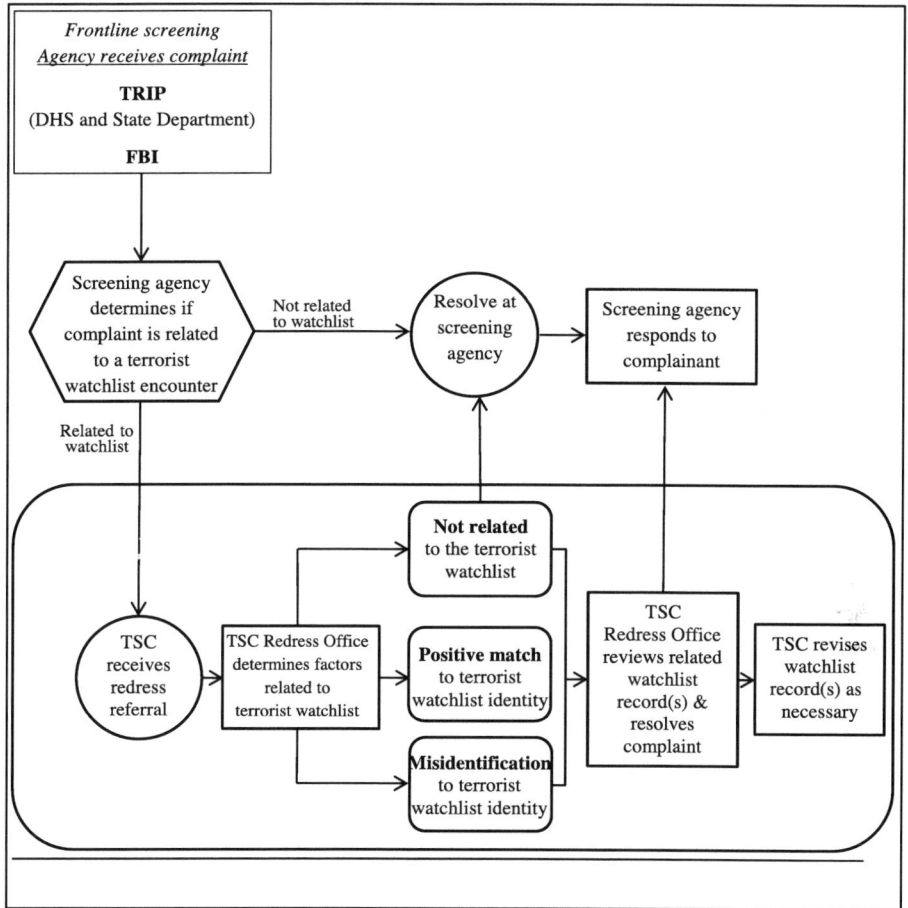

Fig. 11. TSC Flowchart of Terrorist Watchlist Redress Process. (Courtesy the Terrorist Screening Center.)

sis of consensus, which is bad if you are [seeking] redress. Any one agency rep[resentative] can just show up and say, 'Yeah, we don't think so.'"[176]

Just as this book was going to press, the U.S. Court of Appeals for the Ninth Circuit issued its second groundbreaking opinion rejecting the Government's entwinement theory. Some of the plaintiffs' allegations in the case for which the opinion was rendered, *Latif v. Holder*, were described in chapter 1. Judge Richard Tallman, writing for himself and his colleagues, Chief Judge Alex Kozinski and Judge A. Wallace Tashima, refused to allow the Government to use the division of labors it had created between the TSC and the TSA to evade the jurisdiction of the district courts. The court found that Ayman Latif and his fellow plaintiffs had alleged both a substantive challenge to the composition of the No Fly List and a procedural challenge to the redress process. As to the substantive challenge, the TSC was the proper defendant and the district court was the proper court: "Because TSC actually compiles the list of names ultimately placed on the list, § 46110 does not strip the district court of federal question jurisdiction over substantive challenges to the inclusion of one's name on the List."[177]

As to the procedural component, Judge Tallman wrote, the district court had correctly determined that the TSA was a necessary party (and therefore did not abuse its discretion) but erred in concluding that § 46110 made TSA's joinder as a defendant infeasible. The key, again, was in rejecting the Government's division of authority between the TSC and TSA as a means of evading review. In that way, the opinion has an elegant irony to it: the very jurisdictional move that the Government had used to skip up to the court of appeals landed the Government right back in the trial-level district court on the grounds that the appellate court lacked jurisdiction under the same statute to render an appropriate remedy.[178] Concluding the opinion, Judge Tallman observed:

> At oral argument, the government was stymied by what we considered a relatively straightforward question: what should United States citizens and legal permanent residents do if they believe they have been wrongly included on the No Fly List? In *Ibrahim I*, we held that district courts have original jurisdiction over travelers' substantive challenges to inclusion on the List. Today, we take another step toward providing an answer. We hold that the district court also has original jurisdiction over Plaintiffs' claim that the government failed to afford them an adequate opportunity to contest their apparent inclusion on the List. We leave it to the district court to determine whether to require joinder of TSA on remand.[179]

This ambiguity about the source of a traveler's woes did not afflict the traveler in Mrs. Shipley's day. Because the passport was a tangible document in the possession of the traveler, it was immediately clear whether travel was permitted. Even when the Passport Division occasionally dragged its heels in acting on an application, the traveler knew that no travel was permitted without a passport. You either possessed one or you did not.

Today that certainty is gone. No amount of unimpeded travel in the past is an assurance that a trip will be permitted in the future. No notice is given until the moment a boarding pass is sought for imminent travel. Even then, the denial of a boarding pass is not certain evidence that the traveler has been watchlisted. This means that judicial review of the determination is much more difficult to obtain.

If the traveler sues the TSC for compiling the No Fly List, the Department of Justice will argue that the list has no effect unless a *different* agency, the TSA, uses it to deny boarding. But if the traveler sues the TSA for using the No Fly List, the Department of Justice will argue that the source of the injury is not in the application of the list by TSA, but in the compilation of the list itself, by TSC. Sue both, but prepare oneself for a battle over the proper judicial forum to hear the case. If the Government wins that argument, the evidence offered for the court to consider, if any, will be provided by the Government in the form of an administrative record, part or all of which the plaintiff may not even be permitted to see.[180] The rationale for this secret evidence is the same one that was offered, and rejected, in Mrs. Shipley's day.

Just as in Mrs. Shipley's day, these procedures are designed to shield the real decision maker from outside oversight and control. Promises to respect civil liberties mean little if the guardian against their infringement is the same set of unsupervised officials against whom the complaint of infringement is lodged. As Congressman John Dingell long ago explained, before anyone had ever heard of a No Fly List, "I'll let you write the substance . . . you let me write the procedure, and I'll screw you every time."[181] DHS and TSA officials like to boast that DHS TRIP provides travelers "one-stop shopping" for redress. In fact, for citizens whose right to travel has been infringed by the No Fly List, the TSA is one shop stopping access to the real decision makers.

IV · *Principle*

CHAPTER EIGHT

Civis Americanus Sum

The Constitution sets forth a variety of fundamental rights, most prominently in the first eight amendments in the Bill of Rights. Over time, rights beyond these enumerated protections have also been found in the Constitution. Though not identified as clearly in the text as the fundamental rights to free speech or religious expression in the First Amendment, or the right to a speedy and public trial in the Sixth Amendment, these individual liberties are considered just as important in our society. These include both rights easy to specify and rights more abstractly conceived, from the right to vote to the right to privacy. These unenumerated, fundamental rights have most often been held to be guaranteed by the substantive protections of the Due Process Clauses of the Fifth and Fourteenth Amendments.[1]

Due process of law is, of course, available to all persons in the United States. The fundamental right to travel that I defend may well be protected in that way, too. This book stakes no position whether a right to travel could or should be found in those clauses. There is no need to search for it there, because a more straightforward basis exists: citizenship. Citizens of a democratic republic have a different relationship to their state than the subjects of a monarchy or a dictatorship. Whatever else American citizenship may mean, at the very least it means the fundamental right to travel about the country freely, to leave it, and to return home again. As Jaber Ismail and his father learned, this was not an understanding of citizenship shared by the FBI agents that barred their return.

Of course, no constitutional right held by an individual sets an absolute boundary to state power. "The Constitution," the Supreme Court has repeatedly warned, "is not a suicide pact." (Interestingly enough, the Court has used this phrase in both a travel case and a citizenship case.)[2] Individual rights may be infringed by the state, and even the most fundamental rights are no exception. Wherever they be found, the modifier "fundamental" is meant to indicate their special status in law. To infringe a fundamental right, as the name implies, is to take a dramatic action of great significance. Therefore, only the most compelling government interests have been found by the courts to warrant such infringement. Even if such an interest is identified, fundamental rights are considered to be so central to our American concept of liberty that the Constitution tolerates only the least restriction of the right that is necessary to secure that compelling government interest.

The right to travel in, out of, and about the country should be viewed as an intrinsic part of what it means to be a citizen of this democratic and distinctively American republic. It should be held to be a fundamental right. Our courts have already found domestic travel to be such a right, although for reasons other than citizenship. This chapter therefore emphasizes foreign travel and begins by setting forth the textual and historical premises for my argument, based predominantly on the Citizenship Clause of the Fourteenth Amendment. First, to be a citizen is to be something different than a subject. Second, the Citizenship Clause grants to American citizens certain rights that flow from that distinction. Because international travel cannot reasonably be claimed to have been foremost in the mind of Representative John Bingham and the Framers of the Fourteenth Amendment, the chapter next explains why such an interpretation is not too great a weight for the Citizenship Clause to bear.

1. Citizens, Not Subjects

The meaning of citizenship in the United States was initially somewhat elusive.[3] Notwithstanding that ambiguity, the Constitution makes frequent references to "a Citizen of the United States." United States citizenship is a requirement for election to federal offices.[4] Naturalization, the power to create citizens, is the plenary and exclusive power of Congress.[5] Citizens must be counted every ten years.[6] When voting, citizens of the United States possess special protections against racial, sexual, and (upon reaching majority) age discrimination that extend beyond any protection otherwise provided to "persons" by the Equal Protection Clause of the Fourteenth Amendment.[7] Nor may citizens be subjected to any poll or other tax as a condition for voting for federal officials.[8]

The text of the Constitution provides some clues to what it means to be a citizen beyond these formal categories.[9] Most importantly, the Constitution distinguishes between citizens and subjects. Both the original Section 2 of Article III and the Eleventh Amendment expressly make the distinction between citizens and subjects of foreign states. Records and commentaries on the main body of the Constitution offer no guidance as to the reason for the distinction.[10] Farrand's *Records of the Federal Convention of 1787* show that the phrase "citizens or subjects" in Article III, section 2, evolved over several weeks from the more generic category of "foreigners."[11] Why does the Constitution make such a careful distinction?

That the Founding Fathers wished to make clear that a citizen is *not* a subject should come as no surprise. The Constitution recognizes a fact of eighteenth-century life. Two radically different types of civic creatures roamed the earth: subjects of royal sovereigns—some beneficent monarchs, others despotic czars—and citizens of self-governing republics. Of the latter type, there were only two at the time: the United States and France after 1789.[12] The nationals of both countries bought the change in nomenclature at the high price of revolution. But it was a change that mattered deeply to the citizens of the United States and the *citoyens* of the First French Republic.[13] Chief Justice Earl Warren described citizenship as "the right to have rights."[14] And as Justice Antonin Scalia noted with regard to the constitutional right of citizens, but not foreigners, to seek a writ of habeas corpus to contest their imprisonment outside the United States, "[t]he common-law writ, as received into the law of the new constitutional Republic, took on such changes as were demanded by a system in which rule is derived from the consent of the governed, *and in which citizens (not 'subjects') are afforded defined protections against the Government.*"[15]

The Constitution was conceived, after all, in the crucible of a struggle against injustices felt by colonial *subjects* of George III. Antimonarchical sentiment was constitutionally embedded: "No Title of Nobility shall be granted by the United States."[16] The feeling is so strong that this is one of the few noneconomic prohibitions placed on the states, following repetitiously after the same restriction on federal legislative power.[17] As a nation, we are constitutionally suspicious of officeholders who would accept any "present, Emolument, Office, or Title," from any foreign state, but especially from any king or prince, categories of grant-givers given special attention in the text.[18] Although the Guaranty Clause of Article IV has since been held to be nonjusticiable,[19] a "republican form of government" was guaranteed to every state and defined at the time of the Founding against its despised alternative: monarchies and aristocracies.[20]

The constitutional distinction between citizens and subjects, with an institutional aversion against the latter, is the starting point for my argument that a right to travel should be based on the Citizenship Clause. Travel, especially foreign travel, was a request originally understood to be directed to the monarch for permission before the subject could depart the realm. Likewise, those who live under dictatorships in nondemocratic regimes suffer considerable restrictions on their travel. The citizen of a country founded on republican *and* democratic principles, however, might well be expected to enjoy the fruits of that status.

The Fourteenth Amendment, however, offers little more guidance than other references to citizenship in the Constitution. Section 1 in general, and the Citizenship Clause in particular, were "the subject of relatively little debate in Congress."[21] The Citizenship Clause has rarely been interpreted by the Supreme Court.[22] The text makes only two straightforward declarations.[23] First, national citizenship is obtained by birthplace or naturalization of a person subject to U.S. jurisdiction. Second, state citizenship is a function of national citizenship. Because the *casus belli* for the Civil War were domestic concerns, the Reconstruction Amendments reflect those issues. Thus, the catalyst for the Citizenship Clause was to overturn the infamous Supreme Court decision *Dred Scott v. Sandford*.[24]

What does it mean to be a citizen of the United States? Section 1 of the Fourteenth Amendment implies that citizens of the United States may possess "privileges or immunities" that cannot be abridged by the states. Since *The Slaughter-House Cases,* however, these have been severely limited. Suppose that there were no Privileges or Immunities Clause at all. Surely the Citizenship Clause would have meant something more than merely to overturn *Dred Scott*.[25]

Every clause in the Constitution is understood to have meaning.[26] Thus, it is reasonable to expect a difference between whatever privileges or immunities of citizenship Congress might establish (and that no state shall thereafter abridge) and a core concept of what citizenship *is* on its own terms. Thus, reliance on the Citizenship Clause does not depend on how broadly or narrowly the Privileges or Immunities Clause is interpreted. For whatever benefits specific constitutional clauses (or Congress by statute) might bestow as special privileges or immunities of citizenship, at an irreducible minimum citizenship is something different from the status of a royal subject or a feudal serf or a slave.[27]

This approach to parsing the clauses of the Fourteenth Amendment is consistent with the political and legal philosophy of its drafters. As Daniel Farber and John Muench explain, the Framers of the Fourteenth Amendment held a theory of government that "was something of a compromise between natural law and legal positivism."[28] The Framers "envisioned a body of inherent human rights protected by a social contract."[29] *That* view was reified as citizenship and protected by the Citizenship Clause. The Framers also recognized the power of legislatures to raise this baseline with their positivist enactments.[30] *That* sentiment could be expressed by positive laws expanding or abridging the privileges or immunities of that citizenship (in the absence of proscription by either a supreme legislature or an inalienable natural right).[31]

Exactly what those natural rights included, or not, is the source of endless debate among historians. But as Senator Lyman Trumbull of Illinois argued in a major speech opposing President Johnson's veto of what would become the Civil Rights Act of 1866: "The right of American citizenship means something."[32] Drawing from Blackstone and Chancellor Kent, he insisted on the fundamental understanding of citizenship as a receptacle of "inalienable rights, belonging to every citizen of the United States, as such, no matter where he may be. . . . American citizenship would be little worth if it did not carry protection with it."[33] (By no strange coincidence, Senator Trumbull introduced a new bill just a few months after defeating Johnson's veto, entitled "An Act Relating to the granting of passports." The bill limited the issue of passports "only to citizens of the United States.")[34]

Valuable contemporaneous understanding of what this citizenship "meant" is found in the debates over what became the Civil Rights Act of 1875.[35] This law was entitled "An act to protect all citizens in their civil and legal rights," and was defended on citizenship grounds, since the statute presented what would become known as the "state action" problem.[36] Thus, among the reasons that Senator Howe of Wisconsin stated to support the bill was that "it will shield from wanton indignity that great franchise in which we all have a common and priceless estate, American citizenship."[37] His remarks were immediately followed by those of Senator Alcorn of Mississippi. Notwithstanding a past as a slave-owner and a brief turn as a Confederate general, Alcorn vigorously defended the Fourteenth Amendment. His defense of the 1875 act included a link between citizenship and a right to travel:

> Very well, the citizen has a right then to come here—to travel. That implies his right to free travel. . . . Are we told that it would be unconstitutional for Congress to interpose and say that he may travel, being a citizen of the United States, precisely as other people travel? If he cannot travel precisely as other people travel, where does the distinction stop? Under our theory of government, if the right of travel is guaranteed, where can you make the distinction?[38]

The conclusion that emerges from these sources is that citizenship in a republic is a status different from that of a subject of a monarchy or even citizenship in an autocracy. It is a status that conveys rights that stand on their own bottom. That is, citizenship is an independent source of a core of rights beyond those "privileges and immunities" of citizenship that a legislature might additionally enact. This was the understanding of the Framers of the Fourteenth Amendment, at least some of whom even went so far as to include a right to travel among those inherent rights of the citizen of a free republic.

From these starting premises comes my argument that American citizenship is an independent and sufficient source for the fundamental right to travel. The citizen whose travel is not treasonous, nor the source of imminent danger to others, is a free agent. Unless a court restricts his movement in conformity with the law (*e.g.,* as a condition of bail in a criminal case), he is free to travel as he pleases. The extent to which the state can prevent the traveler from thwarting its policy goals should be limited by the necessity to do so to achieve a compelling government interest. In other words, because the state would violate a fundamental right to achieve its ends, the strictest judicial scrutiny must be applied to the state's actions. Because the citizen is not a subject, the state cannot prohibit travel "not in the interests" of the state, for it generally lacks a compelling interest in requiring citizens to promote its interests through their travels.

This is a new constitutional argument, to be sure, but not too much weight for the Citizen Clause to bear. Commenting on the strain placed on the Due Process Clause of the Fourteenth Amendment by arguments for incorporating various rights found in the first eight amendments, Professor Charles Black observed that such a burden need not necessarily fall only or always on the same text. The conclusion that some such federal protection is as essential to "a scheme of ordered liberty" (to use Justice Cardozo's famous phrase)[39] in state as well as federal government "could seemingly be derived quite as well from the relations of citizenship as from the phrase 'due process of law.'"[40] As Professor Black argued in his structural interpretation:

> Can it be that the man who is positively declared to be a citizen of the United States and of the state wherein he resides does not enjoy, by virtue of standing in that relationship, the right to live under a "scheme of ordered liberty"? That would seem to be the least possible domestic implication of the conferral of citizenship, unless one is prepared to say that all that relationship implies is the privilege of writing "citizen" after your name. If the due process clause only gets us, in

some fields of its application, as far as a "scheme of ordered liberty," surely it would seem, in such fields, to get us no further than would a quite warrantable inference from the status of citizenship.[41]

My textual argument resonates with Professor Black's structural argument. It seems clear to me that Black's structural argument is sound both as a matter of history and as a matter of logic. But I think it is not just the structure of the Constitution that permits such an inference from the Citizenship Clause. I think there is a strong textual argument that to be a citizen is to be endowed with certain rights that a serf, a monarchical subject, or the resident in an autocracy does not possess.

The most recent case concerning travel and the Fourteenth Amendment, *Saenz v. Roe*, provides additional support for my argument, even though *Saenz* concerned only the right to interstate travel. During oral argument, Solicitor General Waxman asserted that "interstate migration" was "both a right of national citizenship and a structural feature of the national union."[42] In other words, the U.S. Government argued that interstate travel was a right integral to the meaning of national citizenship separate and apart from the structural requirements of open internal borders in a federal union. My argument makes the same definitional point about what it means to be a citizen.

2. American Citizenship and Freedom of Movement

The meaning I attribute to the citizenship defined so formalistically in Section 1 of the Fourteenth Amendment accords with long-held understandings of that term. That is not to contend that the meaning of citizenship is settled.[43] Many have debated the "subjective dimension" of citizenship, asking what criteria ought to define membership in the polity, or how citizenship should affect the establishment of "the good polity."[44]

To argue that a free citizen in a republic has a fundamental right to travel does not require an opinion about who should be a citizen.[45] Nor does it require opinions about how "good citizens" are created, what their responsibilities to the state ought to be, or how they should create the "good polity" through various forms of self-restraint, loyalty, or participation. My purpose is much more limited. When it comes to travel, I argue that the state cannot favor some citizens with full access to common carriers, while withholding such an essential means of travel from others based on secret assessments of their perceived threat to the security of their fellow citizens or country. To parcel out the ability to travel in such a manner is to infringe this fundamental right of free movement. This argument is explored further in evaluating the practical effect of the No Fly List later in this chapter.

In addition, I argue that the state cannot treat its citizens as if they were agents to further national policies, including policies concerning the nation's security. The state does not stand in such a relationship to the citizen. That is, although the republic can obviously prohibit the citizen from criminal acts, it cannot command allegiance to the foreign policies that its leaders have deemed to be wisest or best.[46] Whatever else it may include or mean, at the very least, to be a citizen of a democratic republic such as the United States must mean that one is not to be treated as the subject of an undemocratic monarchy.

Democracy

Freedom of movement broadly defined has long been accepted as a fundamental component of citizenship in a representative democracy.[47] Its restriction is "in conflict with the essential elements of a democracy—the freedom of the citizen to gather information and to associate with whomever he wants."[48] To borrow the title of one of the classics of American political science, Albert O. Hirschman's *Exit, Voice, and Loyalty* concisely states the choices long considered the right of a citizen in a democratic republic. The options are interdependent, and there may be an optimal but elusive balance to them, but a totalitarian regime is the clearest example of how the destruction of one option (*e.g.,* exit) can make dangerous the election of another (*e.g.,* voice) and lead to the worst source of coerced loyalty, fear.[49]

The right to travel has been viewed as a right of free citizens since the Age of Athens, when Plato reports on the last days of Socrates. Contemplating the choice between certain death and escape from his (unjust) conviction and sentence, Socrates reflects on what the Laws would say to him were he to flee. In so doing, he notes a principle of ancient Athens:

> [W]e openly proclaim this principle, that any Athenian, on attaining to manhood and seeing for himself the political organization of the state and us its laws, is permitted, if he is not satisfied with us, to take his property and go away wherever he likes. If any of you chooses to go to one of our colonies, supposing that he should not be satisfied with us and the state, or to emigrate to any other country, not one of us laws hinders or prevents him from going away wherever he likes, without any loss of property.[50]

More specifically, freedom of movement has been recognized as intrinsic to the concept of human liberty that grounds American citizenship, one of the most sought-after intangible possessions on the planet. Justice Douglas considered freedom of movement "at home and abroad" to be the very essence of our free society, setting us apart. Like the right of assembly and the right of association, it often makes other activities meaningful—knowing, studying, arguing, exploring, conversing, observing, and even thinking. Once the right to travel is curtailed, other rights suffer, just as when curfew or home detention is placed on a person.[51]

So long as the citizen's actions are not treasonous, immediately dangerous, or contrary to some obligation made to the state (*e.g.,* bail or parole in the criminal context, or military conscription, or contractual conditions of government employment), a citizen's travel is not something under the state's control. Consider if the right in question were not one of travel but speech. Whether a citizen may publicly advocate war when the nation is at peace, or participate in a nonviolent peace protest when the nation is at war, or associate with foreigners to persuade them of the merits of peace or war, are all hypotheticals easily answered today in the affirmative.[52] There is no such thing as seditious libel in our democratic republic.[53] That is because the state is presumed to lack the power to demand conformity between its citizens' preferences and the policy preferences of their elected government.[54]

A more extreme example than loss of a citizen's right to travel abroad may be useful to illustrate this point. If a citizen is such a threat to national security that he should be forbidden from traveling as other citizens do, why not simply banish him altogether? It was once believed that Congress had the power to deprive an American of citizenship for conduct "contrary to the interests of his own government."[55] In *Perez v. Brownell*, that conduct was voting in a foreign election. The Court first noted how the growth in international travel had jeopardized the effective conduct of foreign relations:

> Experience amply attests that in this day of extensive international travel, rapid communication and widespread use of propaganda, the activities of the citizens of one nation when in another country can easily cause serious embarrassments to the government of their own country as well as to their fellow citizens. . . . The citizen may by his action unwittingly promote or encourage a course of conduct contrary to the interests of his own government[.][56]

The Court held that involuntary expatriation was within the implied foreign affairs powers of Congress. The decision, however, did not last long before it was explicitly overruled in *Afroyim v. Rusk*.[57] Afroyim had engaged in the same conduct as Perez: he voted in a foreign election. (Interestingly enough, Beys Afroyim filed suit after discovering his expatriation the hard way: he unsuccessfully applied for a passport.)[58] But the Court held that both the Citizenship Clause and "[t]he very nature of our free government" prohibited involuntary expatriation.[59]

Trop v. Dulles was decided the same day as *Perez*, but *Trop* reached the opposite conclusion.[60] It relied not on Congress's implied foreign affairs power (as the Court did to uphold the expatriation at issue in *Perez*) but on the much stronger, and explicit, war power. Congress had enacted a statute that subjected army deserters to involuntary expatriation. Albert Trop was an unruly private in the U.S. Army who in 1944 was convicted and dishonorably discharged for the crime of desertion (which in Trop's case amounted to less than a day wandering with a friend in the Moroccan desert before returning to his base). Trop filed his case after an unsuccessful passport application, which (just like Beys Afroyim) revealed that he had been stripped of his citizenship for his wartime desertion.[61] The Court invalidated the law, holding that even if the death penalty may be imposed on a deserter, loss of citizenship was a penalty "more primitive than torture" and in violation of the Eighth Amendment.[62] "Citizenship is not a license that expires upon misbehavior," Chief Justice Warren wrote in his opinion,

> The duties of citizenship are numerous, and the discharge of many of these obligations is essential to the security and well-being of the Nation. . . . But citizenship is not lost every time a duty of citizenship is shirked. And the deprivation of citizenship is not a weapon that the Government may use to express its displeasure at a citizen's conduct, however reprehensible that conduct may be.[63]

Return now to the right to travel. What is the effect of expatriation, but to force upon an individual a condition of statelessness "deplored in the international community of democracies"?[64] It is (as in the case of Jaber and Muhammad Ismail) to lock the erstwhile citizen out of the United States. Here the criminal case against William Worthy is instructive. Worthy willfully violated a statute that made it a crime to enter or depart the United States without a valid passport.[65] He was charged with entering the United States without a valid passport, his passport renewal having been rejected after he refused to give his commitment to abide by various travel restrictions on it.[66] The court of appeals distinguished the crime of a citizen unlawfully *departing* from the United States (a crime with which Worthy was not charged) from the crime of a citizen unlawfully *entering* the United States.⁶⁷ The court reasoned that although the citizen can refrain from violating a departure prohibition and "continue to exercise all of the rights and privileges of citizenship," the citizen cannot constitutionally "be required to choose between banishment or expatriation on the one hand or crossing the border on the other hand, being faced with criminal punishment and the loss of some of the rights and privileges of citizenship as a felon."⁶⁸ The court reversed the judgment and sentence of the district court, concluding that "it is inherent in the concept of citizenship that the citizen, when absent from the country to which he owes allegiance, has a right to return, again to set foot on its soil."⁶⁹

By distinguishing between entry and departure, the appellate court failed to accord the full complement of travel rights inherent in citizenship. A citizen *does not* "continue to exercise all of the rights and privileges of citizenship" if the state conditions departure on possession of a valid passport but then refuses to issue one to the citizen wishing to leave. Indeed, it is hard to imagine what value a right to return could have absent an equally unabridged right to exit. Consideration of the opposite travel sequence clarifies the point: other than those cases in which the citizen seeks to cut all ties to home, *i.e.*, expatriation, the right to depart is empty without the assurance of an equally unabridged right to return. Exit and entry are almost always two sides of the same coin.

Afroyim did not reach, and *Trop* did not require, a judgment whether travel could be regulated in the interests of avoiding an embarrassment, or worse, to the nation's foreign affairs due to a rogue citizen's conduct abroad. But in *Haig v. Agee*, discussed in chapter 3, the Court held that citizen Agee's conduct abroad was so destructive of national security as to warrant passport revocation.⁷⁰ During oral argument in Agee's case, Solicitor General McCree was asked whether passport revocation had prejudiced Agee's ability to return to the United States. The unlikelihood that Agee would wish to return immediately occurred to the questioner. But what result if he did? The response was telling, and not one normally associated with the government of a democratic republic that lacked (as was the case for Philip Agee) a criminal statute that covered Agee's actions. Replied General McCree: "He would not get out again."⁷¹

That is the crude effect of passport revocation, or placement on a No Fly List, or simply an order to prevent travel. The Ismails were locked out, but they could just as easily have been forced to *remain in* the country, unable to leave for perceived greener fields abroad. The citizen who draws the ire of the state is locked within the confines of the state's borders, where the citizen can do no harm to the state's perceived interests abroad. That was precisely the goal of Mrs. Shipley's passport office in numerous cases.

The premise that the citizen's actions must always advance the state's interests is more typically associated with nondemocratic, nonrepublican regimes.[72] Thus, what citizenship should be construed to mean in a democratic constitutional republic may most easily be discerned by comparison to what it is not: a subject in a monarchy or some other form of autocracy.[73] Only democracies can truly be said to have citizens.[74] As William Allen explained: "The original British constitution wisely denominated all other political relationships as the relations between subjects and sovereigns—subjects, precisely because the persons comprehended in the description owe a loyalty and belong to their states in a condition of subjection (relations not based on consent) rather than command."[75] For this negative case, I find support in history.

History

Travel restriction was once considered symptomatic of medieval times, when "a subject was prohibited from leaving the Realm without leave of the Crown, since to do so would deprive the King of the subject's military or other feudal services."[76] To deprive a citizen of the right to travel abroad because the state's interest is perceived to outweigh this liberty interest is, except in truly compelling circumstances, to change the citizen into a subject. This is a change that the Citizenship Clause forbids the state to make.

The history of the right to travel illustrates its emergence as a fundamental right of free citizens. This is a history on which American constitutional law draws. More recently, the history of American foreign policy, especially in the early days of the republic (when the rights of its citizens were challenged) and in the Short Twentieth Century (when American foreign policy sought to highlight the distinction between the freedom of the American citizen and the unfreedom of the Soviet citizen), illustrates the continued vitality of that idea.

Magna Carta was the first serious attempt to alter such a feudal relationship. It makes reference to the rights of foreign merchants who, in peacetime, could "enter or leave England unharmed and without fear, and may stay or travel within it, by land or water, for purposes of trade, free from all illegal exactions, in accordance with ancient and lawful customs."[77] Likewise, it anticipates that "any man" may "leave and return to our kingdom unharmed and without fear, by land or water, preserving his allegiance to us, except in time of war, for some short period, for the common benefit of the realm."[78] Restrictions on the comings and goings of subjects were viewed as statutory exceptions to this common-law rule.[79] Thus, in Sir Matthew Hale's *Commentary on Fitzherbert's New Natura Brevium*, the "Writ de Securitate inveniend' quod se non divertat ad partes exteras, sine Licentia Regis"[80] is described as an exception to the common law, by which

> every Man may go out of the Realm to Merchandise, or on Pilgrimage, or for what other Cause he pleaseth, without the King's Leave; and he shall not be punished for so doing; but because that every Man is of Right for to defend the King and his Realm, therefore the King as his Pleasure by his Writ may command a Man that he go not beyond the Seas, or out of the Realm, without License; and if he do the Contrary, he shall be punished for disobeying the King's Command.[81]

Such a feudalistic notion of the individual as a mere subject obliged to do service to the sovereign was "obsolete by the time of Blackstone."[82] Likewise, the writ *Ne exeat Regno* (*i.e.,* "let him not leave the kingdom") a surviving derivative of the earlier writ *de Securitate*, is admitted "to have been unknown to the ancient Common Law, which, in the freedom of its spirit, allowed every man to depart the Realm at his own pleasure."[83]

As Kurt Lash notes, "One of the greatest sources of friction between Britain and the American colonies" was the perception of the colonists that they were not accorded full rights as the King's good subjects under the laws of England.[84] The Revolution secured such rights under new sovereigns: the states now tasked to maintain their unity in diversity. A right to free travel was central to their evolving notions of what citizenship meant in their emerging federal system:

> Prior to the adoption of the Federal Constitution, however, it was not at all clear what privileges or immunities they could expect when traveling to, or through, other states. It seemed inappropriate to establish "visitation" rights by treaty—such an approach would create friction with nonparticipating states and it would have the effect of treating the sojourning citizen as if he were an alien from a foreign country, a status that would deprive the traveler of a number of rights commonly enjoyed by citizens, including the right of entrance and the right to own and dispose of real property.[85]

The result was Article IV of the Articles of Confederation, which expressly provided for a right to travel: "the people of each State shall have free ingress and regress to and from any other State," a right that seemed so obvious and essential to the Framers of the Constitution, the very structure of which manifested the necessity of open borders, that this language was omitted without any recorded debate. Even without it, the concept of comity that the new Article IV of the Constitution promoted would be meaningless without the right of citizens to travel throughout the Union.

Defense of the right to international travel was "a dominant theme" of American foreign policy in the first century of the Republic.[86] The source of this policy was twofold. First, the young nation sought to protect Americans seeking to travel abroad.[87] No less important to a nation built by immigrants, was protection of the rights of naturalized citizens who occasionally left American shores. A perpetual concern of the United States in its first century was the tendency of European states to assert claims to the indefeasible allegiance of former subjects who became naturalized U.S. citizens (and therefore claims to their property and military service).[88] Congress in 1868 declared that "the right of expatriation is a natural and inherent right of all people, indispensable to the enjoyment of the rights of life, liberty, and the pursuit of happiness."[89] As such, Congress announced the policy of the United States to provide at least an unfettered right to one-way travel: no officer of the United States could encumber the right to renounce attachments to one country in place of another.[90]

Freedom of movement has been enshrined in the founding documents of the United Nations[91] and identified in numerous international human rights treaties.[92] During the Cold War, the restrictions placed on the travel (internal and external) of Soviet and Warsaw Pact citizens were routinely held forth as sufficient evidence of unfreedom in those countries.[93] As Justice Douglas observed in 1964:

> Free movement by the citizen is of course as dangerous to a tyrant as free expression of ideas or the right of assembly and it is therefore controlled in most countries in the interests of security. That is why riding boxcars carries extreme penalties in Communist lands. That is why the ticketing of people and the use of identification papers are routine matters under totalitarian regimes, yet abhorrent in the United States.[94]

In response to emigration restrictions, Congress passed the so-called Jackson-Vanik Amendment to penalize the Soviet Union and other countries by denying "most favored nation" trading status until emigration taxes, restrictions on travel documents, and other impediments to the freedom to leave the country were lifted.[95] Likewise, the Helsinki Final Act (through which the United States and others sought, inter alia, to put pressure on Soviet and Eastern Bloc restrictions on travel) expresses the intent of its signers "to facilitate wider travel by their citizens," "gradually to simplify and to administer flexibly the procedures for exit and entry," and "to ease regulations concerning movement of citizens from the other participating States in their territory, with due regard to security requirements."[96]

WHAT WOULD BE THE EFFECT on national security if a citizen's right to travel could only be abridged by the least restrictive means necessary to achieve a compelling government purpose, *i.e.,* if citizenship provides the fundamental right to travel within, leave, and return to one's country? National security and foreign affairs are generally held to be compelling government interests.

The judicial branch is sometimes reluctant to scrutinize the conduct of foreign affairs by the political branches. But not all assertions that national security is behind an official decision are the same; they are often fact-dependent, and susceptible to judicial analysis. The Court has not shirked its duty to reconcile the exercise of national security or foreign affairs powers by the political branches with their effect on the fundamental rights of citizens.[97] Evaluating restriction of a fundamental right of citizenship is in keeping with this tradition.

Strict scrutiny would not keep the state from preventing the travel of one who is "participating in illegal conduct, trying to escape the toils of the law, promoting passport frauds, or otherwise engaging in conduct which would violate the laws of the United States."[98] These have long been grounds for travel restriction in the United States and they are unchanged by the standard of review. Nor does citizenship bear on assessing the clearly compelling nature of such traditional government objectives. Note, however, how this power differs from the power of a No Fly List. A state that would prevent its citizen from traveling for these reasons would do so through a judicial process, most likely a criminal trial. Supporters of the No Fly List, however, wish to stop travel *without* the burden of proving that a "known or suspected terrorist" has committed a crime or otherwise violated a state or federal law. The difference between these approaches is the difference between identifying bad acts and bad people. In our democratic republic, more is needed to restrain the freedom of citizens than a government official's conviction—however sincerely held—that someone is bad or will behave badly in the future. The rights of citizenship are not so fragile as to crumble on the secret say-so of a state official.

Likewise, the prevention of epidemics through the spread of infectious disease, a growing concern in a globalized world, would surely be considered a compelling government interest that also has nothing to do with citizenship. It is hard to imagine that quarantine regulations and customs controls would not pass constitutional muster fairly easily under this higher standard. The case of Andrew Speaker, for example, led to calls for tighter restrictions on both departures and arrivals of all persons (including citizens) in the United States. Speaker was thought to be highly contagious with an especially dangerous strain of tuberculosis (although this later proved to be untrue). The Centers for Disease Control sought to prevent his return from Europe, and urged that his name be placed on the No Fly List when Speaker disregarded requests not to travel.[99] After several hours, "a conference of lawyers" from the Justice Department, DHS, TSA, "and possibly others" had his name entered onto the list.[100]

That the No Fly List should have been used when Speaker was clearly not a "known or suspected terrorist" is revealing. So much for the internal checks, self-policing, and culture of restraint that its keepers offer as evidence that none should tamper with their discretion. These were all cast away to do what was immediately desired, though not within the framework established to limit use of the watchlist. Ironically, it wasn't even necessary to scramble to use the secret systems of the No Fly List. Had no such list existed, an FAA Security Directive of the pre-9/11 kind would have been adequate to prevent this "specific and credible threat" to civil aviation—a reasonable definition of a passenger in close quarters inside a pressurized cabin who is believed to be highly contagious with a drug-resistant strain of tuberculosis. But the No Fly List did exist, and naturally led other government agencies to seek to expand its use to cover their own urgent need.[101] When your tool is a hammer, more and more problems begin to look like nails.

Similarly, Philip Agee's passport would still be revocable under my approach to citizenship, so long as the determination was made on the particularized grounds of his extremely dangerous conduct (now a crime),[102] not on the grounds that his travel could be restricted because under the "sponsorship" of the state. Again, it is worth noting the public nature of these valid state actions to stop a citizen's travel. They stand in distinction to the secret criteria that a No Fly List would use to stop a person whom the experts at the Terrorist Screening Center have satisfied themselves to be sufficiently dangerous to lose that right to citizenship at their command.

But these are easy cases. They are, in a sense, the run-of-the-mill concerns of a state in times of peace—flight from crime, spread of disease, conduct that is actually and imminently dangerous—and they are all susceptible to action that does not require any secretly composed list or closed proceedings to administer. Harder cases present themselves in times of war or national emergency, when even the citizen of a democratic republic may be obliged to take a much more direct role (and personal stake) in the nation's foreign policy.

By their nature, these are fact-intensive inquiries. Compulsory military service is the most obvious example of what might be called an "easy" harder case. Could the citizen whose attempt to evade conscription by flight across the border successfully claim that his fundamental right to travel abroad had been unconstitutionally infringed? In a time of declared war, conscription (and prohibitions on its evasion) would seem to be the least restrictive means to achieve a very compelling government interest—military victory. That conclusion might change. Has the draft continued long after peace has been declared?[103] Is conscription riddled with exemptions and exceptions?

Likewise, "area restrictions" would present harder cases under the closer scrutiny that I advocate. In time of war, the exclusion of citizens from the theater of military operations would seem to be the least restrictive means of achieving the compelling government interest of achieving victory on the battlefield. But could such exclusion include accredited journalists? Citizen employees of organizations like the Red Cross or the United Nations? Or consider a peacetime economic embargo on nations in official disrepute, such as apartheid South Africa or Communist Cuba. This also presents a tougher case, but one that would not necessarily fall prey to a strict scrutiny "fatal in fact."

Compare, for example, two cases regarding travel restrictions to Cuba. In *Zemel v. Rusk*, the Supreme Court upheld a State Department policy to grant exceptions to a general ban on travel to Cuba (prior to the embargo) to "persons whose travel may be regarded as being in the best interests of the United States, such as newsmen or businessmen with previously established business interests."[104] Shortly after the Cuban Missile Crisis, Louis Zemel sought an exemption simply to satisfy his curiosity.[105] The Court upheld the ban and the denial of Zemel's requested exemption as part of "foreign policy considerations affecting all citizens."[106] The *Rusk* Court was persuaded that the risk of damage to American foreign policy from an international incident caused by a bumbling American tourist was grave enough to uphold the Executive Branch's decision.[107]

Roughly twenty years later, in *Regan v. Wald*, the Court upheld a comprehensive economic embargo on Cuba.[108] American policymakers prohibited most American travel there on the grounds that infusions of hard currency from travelers would weaken the embargo's intended effect on the Cuban government. The travel ban was based on a general policy that made no distinction between travelers based on their political views or conduct in Cuba; dollars would weaken the embargo regardless of who spent them. The Court sustained the Executive Branch's decision "to curtail the flow of hard currency to Cuba—currency that could then be used in support of Cuban adventurism—by restricting travel."[109]

Strict scrutiny of the fundamental right to travel would overrule *Rusk* but sustain *Regan*. *Rusk* confuses the difference between a citizen and a subject in a way that *Regan* does not. The individual citizen is not an extension of the state's foreign policy, even if that fact makes policymaking more difficult and unpredictable. The fear of adverse foreign policy implications expressed in *Rusk* is no different than the fear that once justified expatriation to penalize a citizen's vote in a foreign election: "The citizen may by his action unwittingly promote or encourage a course of conduct contrary to the interests of his own government; moreover, the people or government of the foreign country may regard his action to be the action of his government, or at least as a reflection if not an expression of its policy."[110]

This is undoubtedly true. But the Supreme Court ultimately (and rightly) held that such fear was no ground for such a sanction. What is more, the risk of international incident does not compel the conclusion that citizens may only travel when the risk is acceptable to a select coterie of state officials. The republic cannot use its citizens as a monarch or a dictator would use his subjects. They are not instruments of foreign policy. That a citizen's travel is "not in the interests of the United States," therefore, is not, standing alone, a constitutional ground on which to restrict the citizen's travel.

Still, some might see an anomaly. A citizen who knowingly provides material support to a foreign terrorist organization like Hamas can be prosecuted for a federal crime and imprisoned for fifteen years to life.[111] This is so even if the support is for a lawful and nonviolent purpose, like buying supplies for a Hamas-run orphanage, and even if the citizen had no interest in supporting Hamas's illegal terrorist activities.[112] The reason, in part, is because such support "frees up other resources within the organization that may be put to violent ends."[113] Few would disagree.

What if the citizen, known to harbor sympathies for this terrorist group, expressed his intent to go to Gaza to join them? Could he be stopped from flying there to do so? Under the standards by which the watchlists operate, such an individual might very well qualify as "appropriately suspected to be . . . engaged in conduct . . . in aid of, or related to terrorism" and thus subject to inclusion in the Terrorist Screening Database.[114] From there, it is not hard to imagine the additional criteria needed to establish that the citizen is a "threat . . . to national security," and therefore added to the No Fly List. If the United States could prohibit this citizen from sending Hamas aid, even convict him of *conspiring* to do so, why shouldn't it prevent him from traveling to Gaza, perhaps with the same end in mind?

The difference is both procedural and substantive. First, consider the difference between prosecuting this citizen for a crime and so obstructing his travel as to effectively prohibit it. The criminal statute provides all citizens with a list of foreign organizations—notice to all, in other words, that aiding such groups is prohibited. This looks very much like the economic embargo upheld in *Regan v. Wald*. It has nothing to do with the individual and therefore makes no distinctions between citizens. Those who object to this national foreign policy decision are free to lobby, protest, campaign, and exercise all of their power to change that policy through the political process.

The No Fly List, on the other hand, functions in precisely the opposite way. It gives *no* notice at all. It is organized to target the individual, based on individual assessments—secretly made and closely held—that *this* citizen should be singled out for a constraint on his liberty. Exceptions can be made, of course, at the discretion of the keepers of the lists, but they are in nearly all cases insulated and removed from public policymaking by many layers of anonymity and bureaucracy. This is much closer to the world of *Zemel v. Rusk*. As noted above and in chapter 3, *Rusk's* travel ban to Cuba was riddled with ways for an official to exempt preferred individuals.

Consider another procedural difference. The citizen accused of providing material support to a foreign terrorist organization enjoys all of the protections of criminal process. One would expect no less given the heavy fines and imprisonment in which such conduct, if proven, could result. It would be unthinkable to hold that—on grounds of national security—this citizen should be deprived of liberty without trial, or tainted with the charge of supporting terrorism but denied the right to face his accusers or confront their evidence. The No Fly List, on the other hand, is premised on just this limitless power of secret executive decision-making. If *someone* (or, perhaps worse, some *office*) concludes that its unpublished criteria are met by evidence unseen by anyone else, that citizen becomes a citizen of the second class—like Bulgakov's sturgeon of the second freshness[115]—one no longer trusted to travel by aircraft.

The substantive difference goes to the core of our understanding of the state's power. Our law has generally required an act as well as an intention before the state could deprive one of liberty.[116] Our criminal law demands both an *actus reus* and *mens rea*. Our First Amendment doctrine revolts at the censorship of a prior government restraint on speech or the press, with a heavy evidentiary burden on the government to overcome this presumption.[117] Likewise, when it comes to its citizens (at the very least), the state's officials cannot decide for themselves, in secret councils and with privileged dossiers, who is not to be trusted to travel. Such authority reduces to the power to establish categories of citizens whose exercise of their right to travel is subject to infinite gradation. If this citizen is not to be trusted to travel to Gaza, may he go to Egypt? Anywhere? If he is classified as a "known or suspected terrorist" who presents a threat to "civil aviation or national security," why should he be allowed to travel by passenger ship or freighter? Or at all?

This is the hazard of what the eminent legal scholar Harry Kalven called the "security calculus," and why it is so crucial that such reckoning against a citizen's rights be subject to protection by an office other than that which makes the initial computation:

> Carried to its logical extreme, the security calculus would lead to exile, to the total removal of the suspect individual from the society—to a merging, that is, of the partial sanction with that of the total sanction. If he is not reliable enough to work in a defense plant or teach school or work for the state or be a member of the bar, is there *any* position within the society where he can be trusted? Since the inexorable tendency of the calculus is to resolve doubts in favor of security and against the individual and since there will always be some doubts, the answer will be that no, there are no places within the society where the risk of his presence need be endured.[118]

Surely no one, not even the watchlisters, would go to such an extreme. But that is precisely the point: it is not their call to make. To quote Justice Jackson, "Such power either has no beginning or it has no end."[119]

CONSIDER, FINALLY, THE EFFECT of this textually based fundamental rights analysis on the operation of the No Fly List to prevent citizens from traveling at home and abroad. Because much about the No Fly List is classified or sensitive security information, one must speculate about the criteria for its compilation. But it is clear that the No Fly List is intended to prevent travel based on some assessment of the individual's future dangerousness. (Were the danger not future but immediate, such as a particular traveler's threat to a particular aircraft, then a wide variety of security measures could be engaged to thwart a crime.)

The No Fly List has the effect of arresting travel in both a literal and metaphorical sense. Travel stops, and it does so because the citizen is either locked in the United States (and can't get out) or locked out of the country (and can't get in). Analogy to an enormous jail is not too extreme; indeed, commentators on Mrs. Shipley's reign were drawn to the same image to illustrate their criticisms.[120] Examining the passport cases in his magisterial posthumous work, *A Worthy Tradition*, Harry Kalven, Jr. noted the superficial similarities: "We may profitably pause for a moment to reflect on the extension of the security calculus logic to passports. On the surface there is the intriguing point that here, in sharp contrast to deportation, the tactic is to *lock* the 'unreliable' person within the community and to make it impossible for him to get out."[121] Louis Jaffe made the same observation: "Nearly every passport denial has been a decision to keep the citizen here within the high walled fortress where he can be isolated, neutralized, kept, let us say, to his accustomed and observable routines of malefaction."[122]

Thus, Paul Robeson was "locked in" when the State Department issued a "stop notice" at all U.S. ports to prevent his international travel.[123] Simultaneously, FBI Director J. Edgar Hoover "sent out an 'urgent' teletype ordering FBI agents to locate Robeson's whereabouts."[124] Immigration and customs officials were ordered "to endeavor to prevent his departure from the U.S."[125] Almost two years later, Robeson still lived under this house arrest. To give a concert originally planned for Vancouver, Canada, he was forced to stand on the back of a flatbed truck pulled up to the edge of the U.S.-Canada border, with his audience standing in Canada.[126]

The Ismails were essentially "locked out" of the United States, first by order of Special Agent Parenti of the FBI, and then by addition of their names to the No Fly List. The No Fly List, like the passport controls of Mrs. Shipley's era, can be used as well for exile as for a form of national house arrest. Professor Kalven ultimately concluded that making secret security criteria the basis for issuing passports was more about "symbolic considerations" than about an "exquisite security calculus" (an assertion that the government files used to justify these security considerations do not always seem to support). He also noted the perfidious effect on citizenship: "this logic leads to an insanely corrosive division of the community of citizens into two groups: those who are loyal and those who are suspect, those for whom the government will vouch and those for whom it will not."[127]

The jail analogy is apropos for another reason. With the sole exception of the need for serious curtailment of liberty in time of war, Justice Douglas considered there to be "no way to keep a citizen from traveling within or without the country, unless there is power to detain him" as a convicted criminal or if there were probable cause to issue an arrest warrant under the Fourth Amendment.[128] Whether the result is de facto statelessness or nationwide house arrest, the denial of the right to travel begins to resemble regulatory detention on grounds of perceived future dangerousness. The constitutionality of indefinite detention on grounds of future dangerousness is determined by the same standard that I advance for the No Fly List: strict scrutiny.[129] The effective detention on grounds of future dangerousness that is the result of placement on the No Fly List cannot pass that test.

The seminal case on future dangerousness in the criminal context is *U.S. v. Salerno*. Although *Salerno* concerned the indefinite pretrial detention of an organized crime boss, oral argument began with a hypothetical about terrorism. Then Solicitor General Charles Fried introduced his case by imagining a "member of a terrorist organization [who] has been indicted for blowing up an airliner for political reasons, and there is clear and persuasive evidence that he will do so again if not confined."[130] Even in that circumstance, the government argued, the terrorist could not be detained, only placed under surveillance, to prevent a second crime.[131]

This introduction produced the first question from Justice Scalia, who sought to complicate this terrorism hypothetical to test the breadth of the government's position. What if, Justice Scalia asked, the terrorist "isn't arrested for a past offense yet; he has just gone around saying, I am going to blow up an airline."[132] (Such a person would seem a strong candidate for placement on the No Fly List.) General Fried reassured Justice Scalia that unless the detention was "ancillary to . . . the normal working of the criminal process," with all of the defendant's rights and state's burdens squarely in place, detention of the terrorist on grounds of future dangerousness would be impermissible.[133]

In the context of criminal procedure, preventive detention for future dangerousness has only been upheld after the demonstration of a compelling government interest and the narrow tailoring of the detention to be the least restrictive means possible of achieving that interest.[134] This strict scrutiny was applied even though the Court declined to hold that liberty from such pretrial detention was a fundamental right.[135] Justice Souter, dissenting on the merits in *Demore v. Kim*, described the "simple distillate" of the Court's case law:

> Due process calls for an individual determination before someone is locked away. In none of the cases cited did we ever suggest that the government could avoid the Due Process Clause . . . by selecting a class of people for confinement on a categorical basis and denying members of that class any chance to dispute the necessity of putting

them away. The cases, of course, would mean nothing if citizens and comparable residents could be shorn of due process by this sort of categorical sleight of hand. Without any "full-blown adversary hearing" before detention, or heightened burden of proof, or other procedures to show the government's interest in committing an individual, procedural rights would amount to nothing but mechanisms for testing group membership.[136]

None of these requirements were met in the case of the Ismails. Nor is it easy to see how they could have been met without destroying the essential value of a No Fly List, which requires secrecy concerning the method of its composition. If the Ismails were added to the No Fly List to explore concerns about their future dangerousness, and it is hard to imagine an alternative reason, this restriction on their travel could not pass strict scrutiny. What compelling government interest was served by demands that they submit to an FBI polygraph test and interrogation in Pakistan as a precondition to returning to California? Is it reasonable to conclude that two Americans abandoned by the FBI for weeks at a time while waiting in Islamabad and ignored upon their eventual return to the United States were reasonably believed at the time to be "threats to civil aviation or national security"? Even if they were, was conditioning their return upon compliance with the orders of the FBI—in effect, denying them the right to return home in a manner unquestionably unconstitutional had it taken place in the United States—the least restrictive means of achieving any compelling government interest?

Some might be tempted to dismiss the Ismails as a rogue case, a bad example. What about other American citizens on the No Fly List? Suppose that all would agree that a particular citizen was reasonably suspected on the basis of articulable facts of being a terrorist. And suppose that what government officials knew about this person would meet almost anyone's criteria for substantive derogatory information that he was a threat to civil aviation or national security. Shouldn't the state notify a commercial airline of the impending travel of such a person and try to prevent him from boarding the plane? Wouldn't you want to know that such a person is flying in the seat next to yours?

The question must be answered in the context in which the No Fly List is used. Government officials frequently describe the No Fly List as part of a multilayered security strategy, "only one component of a larger security cycle that protects the commercial aviation system."[137] The other layers and components of this system range from other watchlists run by other agencies to onboard federal air marshals, to screening systems as old as the police pat-down and as new as full-body backscatter X-ray imaging machines. According to the TSA, "Each one of these layers alone is capable of stopping a terrorist attack. In combination their security value is multiplied, creating a much stronger, formidable system."[138] The TSA graphically depicted the role that the No Fly List plays in context and in full color on the TSA website (see figure 12).

The question, then, does not present a choice between action and inaction. Nor does it present a choice between knowledge and ignorance. The *only* questions presented—if one accepts that a citizen has the fundamental right to travel that this book describes—are (1) whether the No Fly List infringes this right and, if so, (2) whether it is the least restrictive means of achieving a compelling government interest.

The first question has already been answered in chapter 3. To suggest that depriving a citizen of the ability to travel by plane (or ship, as there also exists a maritime version of the No Fly List) works no injury on the right to travel is preposterous. Yet this is the argument of proponents of the No Fly List from TSC Director Timothy Healy down to the TSA officers on the front lines of airport security checkpoints. Airplanes are to travel today what e-mail and telephones are to communication. No one would accept the claim that a summary decision of a federal official could deprive a citizen of such devices on the grounds that the official believed—even to a certainty—that the citizen was a known terrorist who would endanger others by their use. The Constitution forbids such a manner of action. Nevertheless, the government defense of the No Fly List rests on the premise that so long as one mode of transportation is left unprohibited—however implausible or difficult it might be to use with any frequency—the right to travel remains uninfringed. In its latest defense of the list against American citizens whose activities abroad aroused enough government suspicion of them to result in the addition of their names to the No Fly List, the Justice Department submitted the affidavit of one of its paralegals reporting on her Internet research on travel from Europe to the United States by cargo ship and freighter—one-way voyages that could take more than two weeks.[139] It is an old trick to find an alternative that is theoretically plausible but practically unavailing. Justice Jackson once responded in disgust to a government claim that an alien indefinitely detained on Ellis Island without any judicial process was free to travel to any country that would admit him, when the refusal of the United States to do so had worked a domino effect of fear that resulted in refusals everywhere else. "It overworks legal fiction to say that one is free in law when by the commonest of common sense he is bound. Despite the

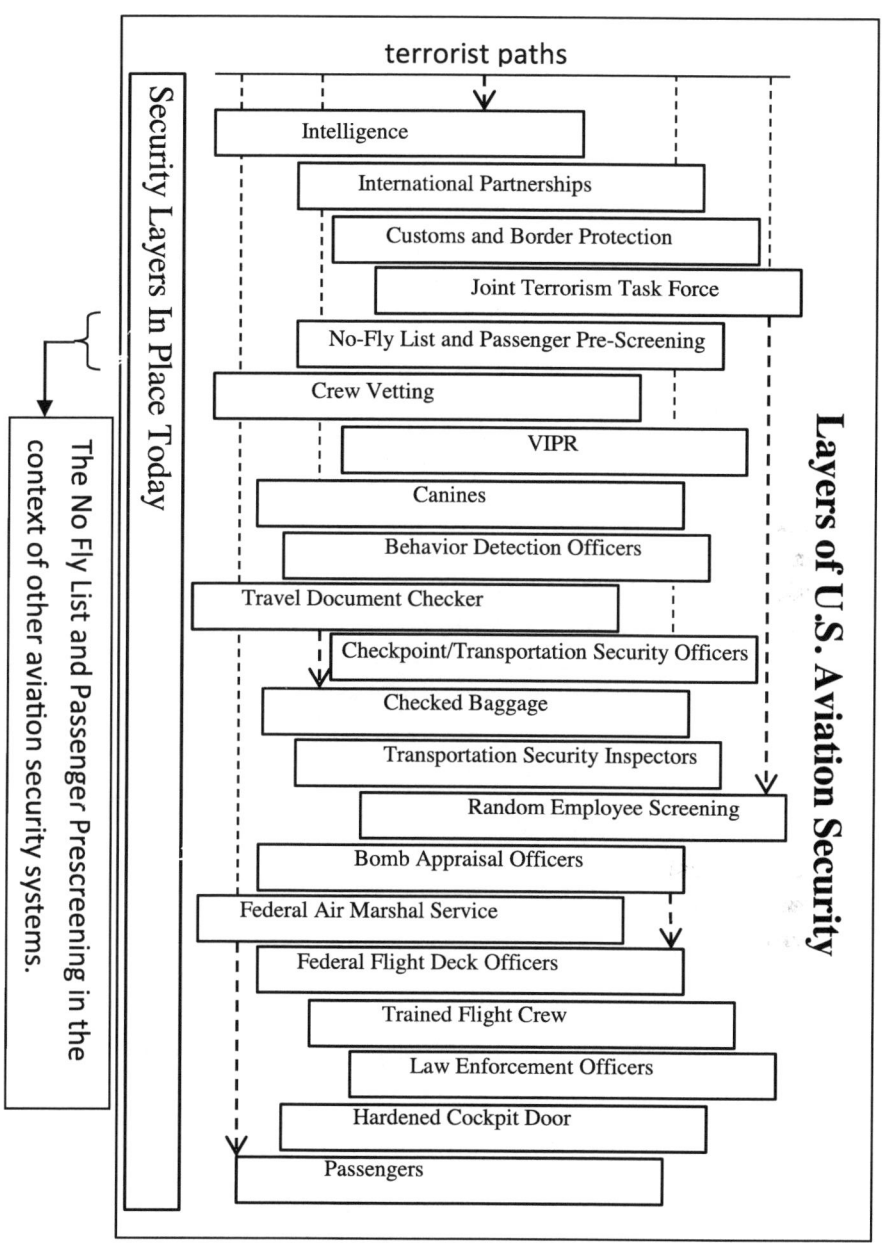

Fig. 12. TSA—Layers of U.S. Aviation Security

impeccable legal logic of the Government's argument on this point, it leads to an artificial and unreal conclusion."[140]

The claim is also short-lived, for it depends on the availability of other modes of transportation. But why should there not be lists to prohibit travel on those systems, too? There is no logical reason why such lists should be confined to just one mode of transport. Transcontinental railway systems, public buses, commuter trains—these are all susceptible to attacks by known or suspected terrorists. Why should the government hesitate to prohibit travel by train if a TSC analyst possessed a reasonable suspicion based on articulable facts that a person posed a threat to rail transportation? Union Station is within sight of Capitol Hill. Grand Central Terminal is in the heart of Manhattan.

If, then, the No Fly List does infringe the right to enter or leave the country, is its use nevertheless one that would pass the strict scrutiny of a court? Consider whether American citizen Yahya Wehelie's fundamental right to return to the United States suffered only the least restriction necessary to achieve a compelling government interest.

Yahya Wehelie was born in Fairfax, Virginia, a suburb just outside of Washington, D.C.[141] When his parents, Somali immigrants, felt that their twenty-something son was adrift, they sent him to study in Sana, the capital of Yemen in East Africa.[142] On May 5, 2010, after eighteen months in Yemen, Yahya and his younger brother Yusuf sought to return home to Virginia.[143] But when they tried to change planes in Cairo, Egyptian police stopped them.[144] They were denied permission to board their New York–bound flight and sent to the U.S. Embassy for an explanation, where they were told they would have to wait for the arrival of FBI agents from Washington.[145] Yusuf was questioned by the FBI and then handed over to Egyptian police, who kept him chained to a wall and blindfolded for three days before he was permitted to fly to the United States.[146]

Yahya was not so lucky. He was told that he was on the No Fly List.[147] When Yahya begged to be allowed to return home, even if handcuffed and accompanied by federal air marshals, he was turned down. Said Yahya: "The lady told me that Columbus sailed the ocean blue a long time ago when there were no planes."[148] The air-travel ban extended to any flight that would enter U.S. or Canadian airspace.[149] News accounts did not reveal whether Yahya's name was also on the maritime equivalent of the No Fly List, barring him from any travel at all.

If Yahya had fallen into bad company in the United States—run-ins with the law for marijuana possession and reckless driving had led his parents to send him away to study in the first place—Yahya's judgment in making friends was particularly poor in Yemen.[150] It may have been his casual acquaintance with another expat American, Sharif Mobley, that heightened the FBI's suspicions.[151] Mobley was later accused of membership in Al-Qaeda, in whose service he was thought to have killed a Yemeni guard.[152]

Was Wehelie a "suspected terrorist"? If his acquaintance with Mobley was accurately reported, he certainly satisfied the broad definition of that term used by the TSC: "an individual who is reasonably suspected to be, or have been, engaged in conduct constituting, in preparation for, in aid of, or related to terrorism and terrorist activities based on an articulable and reasonable suspicion."[153] Even failing sufficient information to label him a suspected terrorist, his acquaintance with Mobley suggested he fit within the TSC's associates project.[154] Was Wehelie a threat to civil aviation? That would seem unlikely if his wish to be handcuffed and accompanied by air marshals were to have been granted. Was Wehelie a threat to national security? It is impossible to speculate based on published accounts. But even if he were, was the constitutional result to keep him in limbo in Cairo?

American officials seized his passport and issued him one with a special notation: "valid only for return to the United States before Sept. 12, 2010."[155] Six weeks, ten FBI interrogations, and one polygraph test later, he was still sitting in Cairo, waiting.[156] His diet consisted of fast food purchased with coupons provided by the U.S. Embassy.[157] Then, without any public explanation, Wehelie was permitted to fly home, arriving back in his native Virginia on July 17.[158] More than two months had passed. According to Fox News, Wehelie was told that his passport would not be renewed until he paid the U.S. Government $1,500 to cover his hotel bill in Cairo.[159]

The fast food, apparently, was complimentary.

CHAPTER NINE

What Is to Be Done?

> Where discretion is absolute, man has always suffered. At times it has been his property that has been invaded; at times, his privacy; at times, his liberty of movement; at times, his freedom of thought; at times, his life. Absolute discretion is a ruthless master. It is more destructive of freedom than any of man's other inventions.
>
> —Justice William O. Douglas[1]

"What is to be done" asks both what is likely to be done next with the No Fly List as well as what should be done to stop its expansion. Terrorist watchlists have no natural stopping point. There is no intrinsic reason why anyone should create a list of people too dangerous to fly and not a list of people too dangerous to buy a gun, or transport hazardous materials, or anything else. The logic of making lists of people suspected of future danger presupposes no limit to their use. But such logic is upside down and unfamiliar to our traditions. It is our tradition—and our law—that a government official's firm belief that someone is dangerous is not enough to restrict that person's freedom to do what is otherwise lawful. That person possesses the same rights as those fortunate enough not to have fallen under government suspicion. Ordinarily, that official's belief in such future danger must be evaluated by a neutral magistrate when the state wants to restrict someone's freedom to move from place to place. This book recommends return to that traditional view of the relationship between the state and the individual.

"What is to be done" could also be read another way. One might ask what is to be done, not by the state, but by enemies of the United States. What is to be done *to us by them?* And what should be done to stop that threat? Terrorism is likely to continue for the foreseeable future; it may become even more threatening on an even more frightening scale. There are very good reasons for making watchlists and using them to find, track, and stop terrorists. No reasonable policymaker would choose to remain willfully ignorant about such people and their reasons for seeking access to guns, chemicals, or airplanes—technologies that can promote liberty and progress as much as destroy them. Surely it is not prudent to neuter the government agencies tasked with this investigative purpose. But beyond the *collecting* and *sharing* of information—crucial tasks of counterterrorism that can lawfully be done and should be done—what limit should be placed on how that information is routinely used? Where should those limits come from?

Those limits are found in the Constitution. The No Fly List breaches those limits by violating the fundamental right to travel. As one legal scholar and counsel in the earliest cases opposing the No Fly List and its premises described the problem: "Some people are treated differently than others, implicating equality. Some people are forbidden to engage in otherwise lawful behavior, implicating freedom. The possibility of official error and oppression is magnified, implicating fairness."[2]

Depending on the civic identity of the traveler and her itinerary, the Citizenship Clause, the Due Process Clause, and often their combination prohibit use of the No Fly List, as presently conceived, as a counterterrorism tool. Within the United States, all those whose travel the No Fly List arrests are victims of a constitutional violation of their right to due process of law. Citizens possess an additional constitutional guarantee. Ordinarily, the state cannot stop a citizen of the United States from leaving the country or returning home on the ground that the government dislikes the traveler or suspects her motive for travel.[3] Our constitutional principles reject such a relationship between state and citizen. So long as the citizen's actions are not treasonous, immediately dangerous, or contrary to some lawful obligation made to the state, a citizen's travel (like a citizen's speech) does not require the consent of the sovereign.

It is no answer to suggest that Secure Flight—the program by which the Federal Government grants permission to the airline to print a traveler's boarding pass after vetting a purchased ticket against the No Fly List—arrests the travel of only a few, or merely obstructs one mode of transportation. The Government is not licensed to violate the Constitution so long as it keeps the numbers down.[4] Nor is the violation obscured by the suggestion that the businessman or student or parent who needs to cross an ocean or continent may take a boat or some other conveyance more common to past centuries than to our own times.

The United States will not bar entry to a citizen who manages to reach our borders. But after attempting to strand the citizen abroad, this seems so insincere an assurance that one would hardly think it worthy of answer. Nevertheless, the Government's agents, in the field and in the courtroom, routinely advance such a claim.[5] In any event, the promise is illusory, for there exists a maritime watchlist, too. And why shouldn't there be, under the logic of watchlists? A cruise liner or an oil tanker may be just as tempting a target for terrorists as a commercial aircraft. The premise that the state must approve the citizen's travel is uncontainable. It is also the hallmark of regimes to which we would shudder to compare our own democratic republic.

In a system of checks and balances defined by the interplay between three coequal branches of government, the No Fly List first arouses suspicion by the nature of its origins. It is entirely a creature of the Executive Branch. It was created by a series of White House policy directives and interagency memorandums. No regulations have been promulgated to govern it. Secrecy protects the specific criteria used to add names to the list. In any event, these criteria are binding only until the officials who have agreed among themselves to use them for guidance decide to change their minds. Analysts use these criteria to evaluate "derogatory information" (jargon for the intelligence they receive, whether it is evidence from firsthand surveillance or thirdhand gossip). This, too, is classified. The No Fly List is then composed by unnamed officials in an undisclosed location. No role is imagined for the judicial branch. After initial interest in Secure Flight, the legislative branch has responded with no more than gentle prodding at the occasional congressional hearing.[6]

When legal challenges have been raised against the No Fly List, the Government has responded with evasion and denial. Evasion takes the form of avoiding or contesting the jurisdiction of courts to scrutinize this executive action. Sometimes this evasion of judicial review is accomplished (as in Erich Scherfen's case) by last-minute action to moot a live controversy by removing the plaintiff's name from a watchlist on the eve of a judicial decision that could go the wrong way. Sometimes this is done by contesting the jurisdiction of the court to proceed at all.[7] Denial takes the form of any number of arguments: denial that a right to travel exists; if it exists that it has been infringed; if it has been infringed that the infringement is substantial enough to merit judicial attention; and, if the last redoubt has been reached, that existing administrative remedies are sufficient to accord the exhausted litigant what little process she is due.

True, the Terrorist Screening Center and the Department of Homeland Security have constructed their own "redress" process. But the process is one that takes place entirely behind closed doors, an inner sanctum to which the individual seeking redress is uninvited. Each attempt to pry those doors open through litigation has failed. But when one of those attempts succeeds, as it will, what should the judge in charge of that case anticipate that she will see? Nothing more than her predecessors on the bench saw fifty or more years earlier: "In short, several officials gather[ed] secretly behind closed doors, perus[ing] secret intelligence reports and purport[ing] to arrive at a fair judgment affecting not only the citizen's right to travel but also his reputation and possibly his livelihood and financial well-being."[8]

Our judge might order the keepers of the No Fly List to open themselves up to more and greater process. This order will be resisted: the watchlisters insist that the workability of the No Fly List depends on the state's ability to make its watchlisting decisions in a manner that forecloses any public scrutiny or judicial review. What should that judge imagine the dénouement will resemble? A sound prediction of the end game is found in the story told in chapter 5, of the last foot-dragging winters of the Passport Office's power. For, like the Passport Office under Mrs. Shipley's reign, there is no process that could be applied to the No Fly List envisioned by its creators that would not destroy the foundation on which it rests: total secrecy as to the nature of the evidence considered, the criteria used to consider it, and the result of that consideration.

The evolution of the passport from a convenience to a license (examined in chapter 4), and the story of how control of that license was so recently abused (found in chapter 5), teaches that there are limits to the Government's power to regulate the comings and goings of its citizens. The administrative process must be open and fair, and not so onerous or treacherous a path to follow that one concludes that its actual purpose is to impede inquiry and defeat safeguards, not facilitate them. During the Cold War, the state sought to deny the fundamental right of citizens to enter and leave the country. When the courts finally demanded that the State Department establish a review and appeal process to protect individual travelers from mistake or abuse in the exercise of its passport power, the maze of obstacles and restrictions that the Department imposed on this court-ordered reform revealed how indefensibly subjective and arbitrary its decision making really was. Those days are not recalled with any pride today.

Mrs. Shipley's successors were unable to retain the unbounded discretion she exercised so powerfully. When her office's power was rolled back by Supreme Court decisions that opened the way to judicial oversight, the passport ceased to be the useful tool of national security that it had been when passports could be withheld or restricted from those whose travel was "not in the interests of the United States." In other words, the United States lost the power to use the passport to restrict its citizens in the way that a visa restricts the movement of foreigners.

Mrs. Shipley's ghost inhabits the secret machinery of the No Fly List. Her authority has been diffused among intelligence analysts in multiple agencies who now engage watchlists of people deemed too dangerous to travel. This diffusion of authority reduces responsibility. Although judicial review is now theoretically possible, as of this writing none has been completed. The agency action to be evaluated is not only shielded by the traditional deference accorded to national security and the secret processes by which that government interest is secured, it is further hidden from view by separating authority over the compilation of the watchlists (which resides in the TSC) from the "customer" agencies that use them (such as the TSA). When this combines with the anonymity and diffusion of decision making across the multiple agencies and their databases that control the original sources of intelligence, the practical effect is hard to distinguish from the results in Mrs. Shipley's day. If anything, it is worse.

The No Fly List's utility as one of many layers of security used to protect civil aviation from terrorist attacks does not salvage the premise on which it rests, so destructive to our most basic American values and sense of individual liberty. That premise is that the state may decide which citizens it will permit to enter and leave, and which may travel freely while within the country's borders. Today air travel is no longer the province of the elite. It is a source of mass transportation used by millions of Americans every day. The power to create such a No Fly List is the power to destroy businesses and private interests that rely on twenty-first-century transportation. This power itself depends on twenty-first-century technology. But only the digital technique is new. It is Mrs. Shipley's ghost in this machine.

Some will criticize this analogy with the past.[9] The threat then just wasn't as great as it is now. The stakes today are much higher. The No Fly List is needed to keep out dangerous foreigners and to keep dangerous Americans grounded.[10] The nuclear threat from a Soviet superpower is different from the risk of nuclear attack from terrorist groups with "no scruples about employing any weapon or tactic," as one national intelligence estimate described one threat. The travel restriction of a few Communist rabble-rousers is nothing compared to the dangers of terrorists who would take advantage of the nation's "virtually unpatrolled borders." Detection, deterrence, and control are essential given the higher stakes of today. Just consider the scenario posed in a recently unclassified FBI memo: "[A] saboteur could easily pose as a Mexican 'wetback' and get into the country without detection, presumably carrying an atomic weapon in his luggage." Mrs. Shipley never had to worry about suitcase nukes.

Actually, she did. The quotations in the paragraph above are taken from a CIA report in 1951, a *New York Times* report in 1953, and an FBI memo of the same year.[11]

Never mind, some might continue. The historical comparison is a mistake precisely because the U.S. Government overreacted to the threat of Communist subversion. These government reports and news stories are evidence of how, as Benno Schmidt memorably phrased it, the United States suffered a "loss of national composure in dealing with radical dissent in the 50's and beyond."[12] The Red Scare was a false scare, as it turned out, but the threat of terrorism—as proven on September 11, 2001—is terrifyingly real. There is no comparison to be made between such false hysteria and our present desperate times, calling for desperate measures.

This criticism is profoundly misguided. Aside from diminishing the gravity of a threat that kept the hands of the doomsday clock of the *Bulletin of the Atomic Scientists* within minutes of midnight (signifying nuclear Armageddon), it ignores the most crucial point of all. What drives government action is its *perception* of reality, not reality itself. Time will tell whether our republic faced a graver threat from terrorism at the start of this century than it did during the Cold War. But no more time is needed to evaluate how government officials acted, then and now, based on their perception of threats. If the arguments in this book are persuasive, it is because citizenship has a value that is not pegged to rise and fall with the variable dangers of the daily threat matrix.

The relatively small number of people on the No Fly List seems to some of its defenders a reasonable price to pay for more aviation security. Others point to the much larger number of non-Americans subjected to the list. Those defenders should take cold comfort in such facts. As Edward Alden observed of border controls: "[T]he biggest reason that objections regarding privacy did not derail the technocrats' plans is that the schemes were aimed mostly at foreigners."[13] David Cole has documented the trajectory of counterterrorism measures that are aimed at foreigners: inevitably they boomerang to affect American citizens as well.[14] The No Fly List began because of attacks by foreign terrorists on September 11, 2001. Government officials, frantic to prevent further attacks, turned first to the TIPOFF database that had been constructed by the State Department to deny visas to suspected terrorists. As the Congressional Research Service summarized this progression:

> In the past, terrorism-related watch lists were used principally for purposes of screening noncitizens applying for visas abroad at consular offices and at the border when applying for admission at international ports of entry. Today, . . . state and local law enforcement officers are

able to screen persons stopped for routine traffic violations against terrorist TSDB lookout records.[15]

On its current trajectory, there is no reason to believe that the No Fly List will not grow in size and broaden in use. Name-based watchlists will give way to biometric watchlists, that is, those based on fingerprints, iris scans, and the like. Just as a global passport system was built once states realized the power that passports gave them over their citizens, a global regime of shared watchlists will become permanent fixtures of modern life. In 2007, the European Union announced its plans to require passenger data from aircraft incoming from the United States, just as American officials demanded it from Europe.[16] The United States has shared the fruits of its watchlisting with other countries, which have mimicked the U.S. watchlisting approach or set up their own systems. As of January 2011, the TSC had signed information-sharing agreements (so-called "HSPD-6 Agreements") with twenty-two countries to provide information about their nationals traveling to the United States.[17] Just as with the global system of passports, watchlists have become global tools of government. And, someday, it may be the case that a global No Fly List emerges, similar to the global asset forfeiture lists that are now approved by the Sanctions Committee of the United Nations Security Council and shared by many countries.[18]

Such watchlists have no natural subject-matter stopping points. Other modes of transportation are susceptible to terrorist attack. Different professions present avenues for the intrepid terrorist who would seek access to hazardous materials, water supplies, energy generation, even pharmaceuticals or the nation's food supply. Many of these fields require government licensing. Shouldn't we know who is in charge of water reservoirs, nuclear generators, or nationally distributed processed foods? As Richard Falkenrath, one of the creators of the Terrorist Screening Center, remarked: "it's a very difficult spot to create tools and then as a matter of policy preference, electively exclude certain categories of offenses from the scope of those tools. It was hard for law enforcement to do that."[19]

The premises behind these lists, and the secret processes necessary to run them, are all the same. The subject of the No Fly List is a historical accident due to the choice of weapons terrorists made on September 11. The concept is a fill-in-the-blank: the No _____ List is coming soon. Unless, that is, the old Shipleyian premises that support these new digital marvels are rejected. We should learn from history. The unchecked power that such lists require has no place within the system of checks and balances that our Constitution places on executive action, even action at the height of perceived national peril.

So what is to be done in place of the No Fly List that we have now? There is nothing wrong with the U.S. Government seeking to identify threats to the nation. A statute authorizing the state to collect the names found in commercial flight manifests does not per se violate the Citizenship Clause for the same reason that statutes allowing for the collection of lots of information are considered permissible. Indeed, the *watching* utility of watchlists may be more valuable to the important work of national security intelligence than actually denying some suspected malefactor a boarding pass, which may have the undesired effect of alerting the individual or his network that someone is on to them. It is how the information is *used* that turns a useful watchlist into an odious blacklist.[20]

Is the state, aware of a potential threat on a plane, to be rendered impotent to deal with that threat? Not at all. As the DHS diagram in figure 12 indicates, the No Fly List is just one shell in a multilayered matryoshka doll of security measures. As none other than Kip Hawley, the TSA administrator under whom Secure Flight was conceived, explained: "Under Secure Flight, and enabled by checkpoint technology that links boarding passes and passenger identification to its information systems, TSA can customize security such as place an Air Marshal behind and next to a specific passenger of concern or allow quicker screening of lower risk passengers. The possibilities are so tantalizing from a security perspective that great care and discipline must be sustained to respect the privacy and civil rights protections, which if breeched, could shut down the program."[21]

And if an individual, having successfully run the gauntlet of all of those security layers, remained a "specific and credible" threat to a particular aircraft or flight path, the law since 1961 has exempted the airlines from their duties of transport as common carriers.[22] The case law is full of judicial opinions upholding the right of a plane's captain to refuse transport on the basis of his or her judgment that such transport "might be inimical to safety of flight." That power is strengthened, not weakened, by the provision of information to the captain by the state's intelligence services. Of course, the No Fly List is no longer limited to threats to aviation; you may be added to the List for reasons of national security unrelated to air travel. Such decisions the watchlisters wish to keep for themselves, and they do not wish to have their judgments challenged or subject to review.

But there the limitations begin. The state's officials cannot arrogate for themselves the authority to decide who may travel as a free citizen without meaningful review of their judgments. It is no longer true that the No Fly List is merely a sophisticated tool for implementing these long-standing and carefully circumscribed exceptions to the common carrier's duty, exceptions imbedded in regulations drafted decades before September 11, when the horrors of that day had yet to be imagined. The right to travel is effectively denied when an FBI agent wishes to prevent travel to coerce a citizen to submit to a polygraph test overseas—Jaber Ismail. Or because suspicions have been raised about the citizen's foreign contacts—Yahya Wehelie. Or because unnamed analysts, shielded from outside review of their evaluations by the assertion of national security, conclude that someone is suspected in some secret and unspecified way of being a threat to also unspecified national security interests.

When confronted with the criticism that their power is too broad to be so unchecked, the keepers of these lists—from Mrs. Shipley to Director Healy—have always answered in the same way: trust us. Those officials cannot be allowed to decide—also in the name of national security—which citizens may travel when, and where, and how. That is how a closed autocracy, not a democratic republic, interacts with its citizens.

There is no constitutional case to be made against security restrictions on travel that are lawfully and equally imposed on all by an open and democratic process and subject to the check of judicial review. Restrictions on travel that result from economic embargoes or quarantines are good examples. There may even be a place for exceptional cases of executive action to prevent specific and identifiable threats to the traveling public, for which only *ex post* review by a neutral judicial body is possible. But having identified its concerns, the state's agents are not then free to select, on their own say so, who is a citizen with the freedom to travel and who is a citizen of a lesser order. Our system does not contemplate such absolute power, even in the name of national security. The judicial branch has a greater role to play, whether *ex ante* or *ex post*, than the watchlisters have allowed and scholars have advanced a variety of possible approaches.[23] The judicial role should not be diminished by fears of terrorism. Federal judges have demonstrated that they can exercise their authority with an awareness both of the responsibilities and the limitations of their office.[24] The bedrock principle of separation of powers, as much as the individual's right to travel, demands access to courts with meaningful powers of review. "The fragmentation of power produced by the structure of our Government is central to liberty, and when we destroy it, we place liberty at peril."[25]

THE 9/11 COMMISSION observed that "[f]or terrorists, travel documents are as important as weapons."[26] In that vein, obtaining and using documents—like weapons—is a high-risk venture: "Terrorists must travel clandestinely to meet, train, plan, case targets, and gain access to attack. To them, international travel presents great danger, because they must surface to pass through regulated channels, present themselves to border security officials, or attempt to circumvent inspection points."[27] The 9/11 Commission therefore made the following recommendation:

> Targeting travel is at least as powerful a weapon against terrorists as targeting their money. The United States should combine terrorist travel intelligence, operations, and law enforcement in a strategy to intercept terrorists, find terrorist travel facilitators, and constrain terrorist mobility.[28]

The 9/11 Commission also recommended the expansion of intelligence collection concerning terrorist travel and, in particular, the use of integrated terrorist watchlists in order to constrain terrorist travel, which it recommended "should become a vital part of counterterrorism strategy."[29] To this end, the Commission included among its recommendations the use of biometric screening systems (to detect fraudulent travel documents) and expansion of the No Fly and Selectee lists.[30] One can imagine a system that would improve the odds of detecting visa fraud and catching those who would attempt to flee rather than face justice. The No Fly List goes far beyond such security improvements.

The tool has come to define the mission. The steady expansion of the No Fly List, both in its absolute size and in the scope of its mission, has transformed it into something one hopes was beyond the imagination of the 9/11 commissioners. The No Fly List was originally conceived as a last line of defense to protect the physical safety of an aircraft from a specific and imminent threat that might somehow evade every other security safeguard. Now it is a frontline measure, vetting travelers and granting the state's permission to travel as a matter of routine. Its purpose has expanded from protecting civil aviation to combating general threats to national security. One suspects that its utility as an investigative tool and pressure tactic has proven to be irresistible. Jaber Ismail certainly felt that power.

The mission of counterterrorism is one of undeniable importance. Intelligence, perseverance, and ingenuity must be brought to bear on the task. But this particular tool, the No Fly List, though wielded by well-meaning hands, has worked an insidious encroachment on the defining principle of American self-government: the relationship between the state and its citizens.

"What's the point of being a citizen?" Usama Ismail asked in despair as he watched his father and brother struggle to return home. The answer to his question should not come from Mrs. Shipley's ghost.

Notes

Acknowledgments

1. Randal C. Archibold, Wait Ends for Father and Son Exiled by F.B.I. Terror Inquiry, N.Y. TIMES, Oct. 2, 2006, at A10.
2. International Travel and the Constitution, 56 UCLA L. REV. 271–350 (2008).
3. The Extraordinary Mrs. Shipley: How the United States Controlled International Travel before the Age of Terrorism, 43 CONN. L. REV. 819–88 (2011).

Introduction

1. Olmstead v. United States, 277 U.S. 438, 572–73 (1928) (Brandeis, J., dissenting).
2. Author's interview with Timothy J. Healy, Dec. 4, 2009, FBI Headquarters.
3. Prepared Statement of Richard A. Falkenrath, Deputy Commissioner for Counterterrorism, New York City Police Department, before the Committee on Homeland Security and Government Affairs, U.S. Senate, Sept. 12, 2006, at 22.
4. Author's interview with Michael P. Jackson, Arlington, Virginia, Mar. 14, 2011 (Author: "What keeps [watchlists] cabined in to air travel? Jackson: Nothing. It shouldn't be. It shouldn't be restricted to air travel").
5. Memorandum for the Record, 9/11 Commission interview with Claudio Manno, Oct. 1, 2003, at 6 & 8. Author's interview with Claudio Manno, Acting Assistant Administrator for Security and Hazardous Materials, FAA, Washington, D.C., October 20, 2009. Memorandum for the Record, 9/11 Commission interview with Lee Longmire, Oct. 28, 2003, at 5 & 6. Longmire had held operational and policy posts at FAA since 1980. When interviewed, he was Assistant Administrator for Operations Policy at TSA.
6. Statement of Timothy J. Healy, Director, Terrorist Screening Center, Testimony before the Senate Homeland Security and Governmental Affairs Committee, Dec. 9, 2009 (emphasis added).
7. Jamie Tarabay, *The No-Fly List: FBI Says It's Smaller Than You Think*, NATIONAL PUBLIC RADIO (Jan. 26, 2011), http://www.npr.org/2011/01/26/133187841/the-no-fly-list-fbi-says-its-smaller-than-you-think.
8. Eileen Sullivan, *AP Exclusive: US No-Fly list doubles in 1 year*, ASSOCIATED PRESS,

Feb. 2, 2012, available at: http://news.findlaw.com/apnews/e4d8073c24804c96b 889d05eb4a12942. The AP story reveals a common problem with news reports about terrorist watchlists: conflation of statistics about names (which could include aliases and multiple spellings of a name for a single person) and statistics about individual people.

9. U.S. DEPARTMENT OF JUSTICE OFFICE OF THE INSPECTOR GENERAL, A REVIEW OF THE FBI'S INVESTIGATIONS OF CERTAIN DOMESTIC ADVOCACY GROUPS 188 (Sept. 2010) ("This practice did not violate the broad definitions of domestic terrorism in federal law, the Attorney General's Guidelines, and FBI policies. However, this practice relied upon potential crimes that may not commonly be considered as "terrorism" (such as trespassing or vandalism) and that could alternatively have been classified differently. . . . [P]ersons who are subjects of domestic terrorism investigations are normally placed on watchlists, and their travels and interactions with law enforcement may be tracked.").

10. JACK GOLDSMITH, THE TERROR PRESIDENCY: LAW AND JUDGMENT INSIDE THE BUSH ADMINISTRATION 71–72 (2007).

11. Helen Jung, Case of Tigard man, grounded by no-fly list, offers glimpse into secretive airport security screening, THE OREGONIAN, Apr. 13, 2012, at A1. Available at: http://blog.oregonlive.com/travel_impact/print.html?entry=/2012/04/case_of_tigard_man_grounded_by.html.

12. Publ. L. No. 108-458, § 4012(a), 118 Stat. 3638, 3714–18 (2004) (codified at 49 U.S.C. § 44903(j)(2)(C)). *See also* Advance Electronic Transmission of Passenger and Crew Member Manifests for Commercial Aircraft and Vessels, 72 FED. REG. 48,320 (Aug. 23, 2007) (codified Feb. 19, 2008, at 19 C.F.R. pts. 4 and 122).

13. GOVERNMENT ACCOUNTABILITY OFFICE, AVIATION SECURITY: TSA HAS COMPLETED KEY ACTIVITIES ASSOCIATED WITH IMPLEMENTING SECURE FLIGHT, BUT ADDITIONAL ACTIONS ARE NEEDED TO MITIGATE RISKS (GAO-09-292) 4 (May 2009).

14. DHS Press Release, *DHS Achieves Major Aviation Security Milestone One Month Ahead of Schedule,* Nov. 30, 2010 (http://www.dhs.gov/ynews/releases/pr_1291142559247.shtm).

15. In fact, the USA PATRIOT Act prohibits states from issuing such a "hazmat" license to anyone unless the federal government determines that the individual does not pose a security risk. Uniting and Strengthening America by Providing Appropriate Tools Required to Intercept and Obstruct Terrorism (USA PATRIOT ACT) Act of 2001, Pub. L. No. 107–56, § 1012, 115 Stat. 272 (Oct. 26, 2001) (codified at 49 U.S.C. § 5103a). As a result, the Transportation Security Administration (TSA)—the federal agency that uses the No Fly List—also runs the Hazardous Materials Endorsement Threat Assessment Program. That program evaluates applicants according to a variety of reasonable criteria based on identifiable conduct and public records: criminal record, immigration status, mental health, etc. But it also tests the application against secret evidence that only the government sees and by which anonymous analysts may conclude that the individual poses "a threat to national security, to transportation security, or of terrorism." The TSA obtains that evidence by searching terrorist watchlists and related databases. 49 C.F.R. § 1572.107. The TSA will not release to the applicant any classified information and "reserves the right not to disclose any other information or material not warranting disclosure." The appeals process is found at 49 C.F.R. § 1515.

16. Unclassified PowerPoint presentation supplied by Trent Duffy, TSC Public Af-

fairs, e-mail to author, April 20, 2010. On file with the author. The slide shown to congressional staff was SSI, Sensitive Security Information.

17. Haig v. Agee, 453 U.S. 280, 309 (1981).

18. Briehl v. Dulles, 248 F.2d 561, 572 (D.C. Cir. 1957), *rev'd on other grounds sub nom.* Kent v. Dulles, 357 U.S. 116 (1958).

19. Ironically, this phrase appears in a travel case, *Haig v. Agee*, 453 U.S. 280, 309–10 (1981), which cited its use in a citizenship case, *Kennedy v. Mendoza-Martinez*, 372 U.S. 144, 160 (1963). Justice Jackson coined it in dissent in *Terminiello v. Chicago*, 337 U.S. 1, 37 (1949) ("There is danger that, if the Court does not temper its doctrinaire logic with a little practical wisdom, it will convert the constitutional Bill of Rights into a suicide pact.").

20. DAVID COLE, ENEMY ALIENS: DOUBLE STANDARDS AND CONSTITUTIONAL FREEDOMS IN THE WAR ON TERRORISM (2003).

21. Wm. J. Krouse, *Terrorist Identification, Screening, and Tracking Under Homeland Security Presidential Directive 6*, CRS REPORT FOR CONGRESS (RL32366) 26 (2004); EDWARD ALDEN, THE CLOSING OF THE AMERICAN BORDER: TERRORISM, IMMIGRATION, AND SECURITY SINCE 9/11 162 (2009).

22. U.S. DEPARTMENT OF JUSTICE OFFICE OF THE INSPECTOR GENERAL, THE FEDERAL BUREAU OF INVESTIGATION'S TERRORIST WATCHLIST NOMINATION PRACTICES I n. 40 (Audit Report 09-25, May 2009). This is a TSC estimate as of September 9, 2008.

23. Ruth Bielaski Shipley, by Don Menn CS/R, 59-SO-288, # 1730-3, NARA.

24. Author's interview with Stewart A. Baker, Washington, D.C., July 22, 2009.

25. Author's interview with Randy Beardsworth, Washington, D.C., Mar. 11, 2010.

26. Author's Interview with McGregor Scott, Sacramento, California, May 28, 2010.

27. Author's interview with Timothy J. Healy, *supra* note 2.

28. Author's interview with Michael P. Jackson, *supra* note 4. Dr. Jackson criticized this analogy as creating "a caricature of a petty tyrant that has taken over a process that should have complex fail-safe switches that you can use to correct injustices. And so I think by comparing the current process to that, there's no Mrs. Shipley, there's no one person, and there's a hell of a lot of process that has learned from the McCarthy era that is embedded in the whole system that we designed to try to manage the risk that we have in this era."

Chapter 1

1. WILLIAM FAULKNER, REQUIEM FOR A NUN 92 (Act. I, Sc. III) (1950).

2. Amended Complaint, filed Mar. 20, 1952, ¶ 3, and Answer to Amended Complaint, filed Apr. 21, 1952 (admitting truth of ¶ 3). With the exception of the court's opinion, all documents cited in this case were obtained from the U.S. National Archives and Records Administration. *See* Anne Bauer v. Dean Acheson, Civil No. 743-52 (D.D.C. 1952), Records Group 21, Stack Area 16W3, Row 17, Compartment 05, Shelf 04, Box 1132, National Archives Building, Washington, D.C.

3. Woman Sues for Passport, WASH. POST, Feb. 19, 1952, at B7.

4. Airgram 3614 from Secretary of State Acheson to American Embassy, Paris, May 23, 1951, true copy attached to Defendant's Memorandum of Points and Authorities in Support of Motion for Summary Judgment, filed Apr. 21, 1952.

5. Am. Compl. at ¶ 6, and Answer to Am. Compl. (admitting truth of ¶ 6), *supra* note 2.

6. Am. Compl. at ¶ 9, and Answer to Am. Compl. (admitting truth of ¶ 9), *supra* note 2.

7. Telegram 5936 from Ambassador Dunn, American Embassy, Paris, to Secretary of State Acheson, Mar. 28, 1952, true copy attached to Defendant's Memorandum of Points and Authorities in Support of Motion for Summary Judgment (filed Apr. 21, 1952).

8. Plaintiff's Points and Authorities in Support of Motion for Preliminary Injunction, filed Feb. 18, 1952, at 2.

9. Am. Compl. at ¶¶ 13 & 14, *supra* note 2. The United States never revealed the basis of its suspicion. Evidence that it existed is only available on the basis of a government lawyer's error. In its Answer, the United States gave a stock reply, stating that the Secretary of State had "no knowledge or information sufficient to enable him to form a belief as to the truth" of those assertions. Answer to Am. Compl. About two months later, the United States sought to amend its answer, now flatly denying, without explanation, plaintiff's assertions about her loyalty and activities. Motion for Leave to File Amendment to Answer, filed June 23, 1952. It is hard not to form the conclusion that the reason for the government's amendment is that the United States *did* have knowledge or information sufficient to form a belief as to the truth of Anne's asserted loyalty and activities.

10. Memorandum of Points and Authorities in Support of Motion to Dismiss, filed Mar. 10, 1952, at 4.

11. *Id.*, at 7.

12. *Id.*, at 4.

13. Memorandum of Points and Authorities in Support of Motion for Summary Judgment, filed Apr. 21, 1952, at 2.

14. Memorandum of Points and Authorities in Support of Motion to Dismiss, filed Mar. 10, 1952, at 4.

15. Memorandum of Points and Authorities in Support of Motion for Summary Judgment, filed Apr. 21, 1952, at 4.

16. Bauer v. Acheson, 106 F.Supp. 445, 451 (D.D.C. 1952).

17. Bauer v. Acheson, 106 F.Supp. 445, 452–53 (D.D.C. 1952).

18. Alfred Friendly, Appeals Procedure Planned in Cases of Passport Denial, WASH. POST, Aug. 5, 1952, at 6. The Board was established on August 28, 1952. Section 51.139, 17 FED. REG. 8013 (Sept. 4, 1952). Its rules were finally promulgated in January 1954. 19 FED. REG. 161–62 (Jan. 9, 1954).

19. Section 51.163, 19 FED. REG. 162 (Jan. 9, 1954) ("The Passport file and any other pertinent Government files shall be considered as part of the evidence in each case without testimony or other formality as to admissibility. Such files may not be examined by the applicant, except the applicant may examine his application or any paper which he has submitted in connection with his application or appeal.").

20. Leonard B. Boudin, The Right to Travel: A Significant Victory, 181 THE NATION 95, 96 (July 30, 1955); Alan Rogers, Passports and Politics: The Courts and the Cold War, 47 THE HISTORIAN 497, 502 (Aug. 1985).

21. Complaint, filed Aug. 19, 2008, at ¶¶ 22–32, and Praecipe, filed Aug. 20, 2008, at 3 (Memo from Mary C. Finnigan, Vice President, Administration, Colgan Air, to Eric [sic] Scherfen), Scherfen v. Department of Homeland Security, 3:CV-08-1554,

2010 WL 456784 (M.D. Pa. Feb. 2, 2010); Mike McIntire, Ensnared by Error on Growing U.S. Watch List, With No Way Out, N.Y. TIMES, Apr. 7, 2010, at A1.

22. Compl. at ¶ 41, *supra* note 21.

23. Praecipe, *supra* note 21.

24. Compl., at ¶¶ 46–53, *supra* note 21.

25. Compl., at ¶¶ 63–64, *supra* note 21.

26. Plaintiff's Motion for Voluntary Withdrawal of Motion for Expedited Preliminary Injunction, available at Docket #17 (Sept. 2, 2008) in Scherfen v. Dep't of Homeland Security, 3: CV-08-1554 (M.D. Pa. Feb. 2, 2010). Defendants concurred in this withdrawal.

27. Letter dated October 15, 2008, from Jim Kennedy, DHS Traveler Redress Inquiry Program, to Erich Scherfen, *available at* Docket # 33, Defendants' Motion to Stay or, in the Alternative, for Extension of Time, Jan. 2, 2009, *in* Scherfen v. Department of Homeland Security, 3:CV-08–1554 (M.D. Pa. Feb. 2, 2010).

28. Memorandum in Support of Defendants' Motion to Dismiss, or, in the alternative, for Summary Judgment, filed Jan. 30, 2009, at 29, Scherfen v. Department of Homeland Security, 3:CV-08-1554. The government defendants made several other arguments, both jurisdictional and on the merits, that are discussed in chapter 7.

29. *Id.*, at 29.

30. *Id.*, at 29 n. 6.

31. Scherfen v. Department of Homeland Security, 3:CV-08-1554, 2010 WL 456784, at *4 & *8, n.5 (M.D. Pa. Feb. 2, 2010).

32. *Id.*, at *8 (internal citation omitted).

33. A.J. Gordon, U.S. Cancels Robeson's Passport After He Refuses to Surrender It, N.Y. TIMES, Aug. 4, 1950, at 1.

34. MARTIN BAUML DUBERMAN, PAUL ROBESON 389 (1989).

35. *Id.*

36. Robeson v. Acheson, 198 F.2d 985 (D.C. Cir. 1952).

37. Leon Hurwitz, Judicial Control Over Passport Policy, 20 CLEV. ST. L. REV. 271, 274 (1971) (citing Brief for Appellee, p. 20. Robeson v. Acheson, 198 F.2d 985 (D.C. Cir. 1952)).

38. Robeson Exit Barred, N.Y. TIMES, Feb. 1, 1952, at 14.

39. DUBERMAN, *supra* note 34, at 399–400.

40. Canadians Hear Robeson, N.Y. TIMES, May 19, 1952, at 12.

41. Robeson v. Dulles, 235 F.2d 810, 811 (1956), *cert. denied* 352 U.S. 895 (1956).

42. E-mail from Cori Sieger to Chad Wolf, Dec, 2, 2002, 2:48 PM (ACLU FOIA Release A1-019). Note the misspelling of the watchlisted person's name in this e-mail between TSA officials.

43. Associated Press, *Military retiree on FBI list. Not Cleared to Fly: Larry Musarra doesn't know why his name shows up*, Sept. 16, 2002.

44. Internal Memorandum to Tom Blank from [REDACTED] dated December 23, 2002 (ACLU FOIA Release A1-022); Letter from Willie J. Gripper, Jr., Director, Civil Aviation Security Operations, TSA, to Congresswoman Louise Slaughter, dated July 18, 2002 (ACLU FOIA Release A1-023).

45. Alan Gathright, No-Fly Blacklist Snares Political Activists, SAN FRAN. CHRON., Sept. 28, 2002. This article was included in an ACLU FOIA Release (ACLU FOIA Release B4-257-259). The names of the sender and recipient of the e-mail in which it was copied were redacted by the FBI.

46. E-mail from Chad Wolf to Cori Sieger, December 8, 2002, 1:15PM (ACLU FOIA Release A1-041).

47. *Id.*

48. Sara Kehaulani Goo, Sen. Kennedy Flagged by No-Fly List, WASH. POST, Aug. 20, 2004, at A01. It is unclear whether Kennedy was actually on the No Fly List or another watchlist, the Selectee List, which results in heightened security procedures for identified travelers. CBS News, *Ted Kennedy's Airport Adventure,* Aug. 19, 2004.

49. Sen. Kennedy Flagged by No-Fly List, *supra* note 48.

50. *Id.*; *see also* CBS News, *Ted Kennedy's Airport Adventure, supra* note 48.

51. ABC News, *Cat Stevens 'In the Dark' Over No-Fly List,* Oct. 1, 2004. A spokesman for United Airlines contested the implicit shifting of blame from DHS to the airline, confirming the confusion that was inherent in requiring private airlines to vet government watchlists. ABC News, *Cat Stevens deported amid terrorism fears,* Sept. 23, 2004 (Jeff Green, United Airlines spokesman: "All I can say is that we followed all of our procedures and we came up with nothing. To suggest that the blame lies on a United employee is incorrect and unfair.").

52. Sally B. Donnelly, You Say Yusuf, I Say Youssouf . . . , TIME MAGAZINE, Sept. 25, 2004. This explanation corresponds to the singer's description of his encounter with FBI agents: "[T]hey kept on repeating that question actually and saying, 'Are you sure you don't spell it Y-O-U-S?'" ABC News, *Cat Stevens 'In the Dark' Over No-Fly List, supra* note 51.

53. *The Transportation Security Administration's Aviation Passenger Prescreening Programs: Secure Flight and Registered Traveler,* Hearing before the Senate Committee on Commerce, Science, and Transportation, 109th Cong., 2d Sess., 36 (Feb. 9, 2006).

54. Docket # 41, Joint Statement of Stipulated Facts, Latif v. Holder, Case 3:10-cv-00750-BR (D. Ore. Nov. 17, 2010) at ¶ 6 ("When a traveler files an inquiry with DHS TRIP on-line or by electronic mail, the system automatically provides the traveler a Redress Control Number to help monitor the progress of the inquiry").

55. The most obvious of these procedures, called "Secure Flight," requires that travelers provide their full names, date of birth, and gender when purchasing an airplane ticket. This information is used to dispatch the most obvious false positives.

56. As was the case with Erich Scherfen, it took the threat of the plaintiffs' motion for a preliminary injunction to obtain return to the United States for those plaintiffs trapped overseas by the No Fly List. On the eve of the hearing to decide the motion, "[a]s a result of the parties' efforts, the PI Plaintiffs who wished to return to the U.S. did so, and Plaintiffs then withdrew their Motion for a Preliminary Injunction." Docket # 44, Defendants' Memorandum of Law in Support of Motion to Dismiss or for Summary Judgment, Latif v. Holder, Case 3:10-cv-00750-BR, (D. Ore. Nov. 17, 2010), at 15.

57. Docket # 15, First Amended Complaint, Latif v. Holder, Case 3:10-cv-00750-BR, (D. Ore. Aug. 5, 2010).

58. *Id.*, at ¶¶ 44–48, 54–56, 60.

59. *Id.*, at ¶¶ 57–58, 69.

60. *Id.*, at ¶ 64.

61. *Id.,* at ¶ 8, 77, 80. The last of the trio of veterans was Ibraheim (Abe) Y. Mashal, a former U.S. Marine. The complaint alleges that he "resides with his wife and three children in St. Charles, Illinois and works as a traveling dog trainer. He was recently

unable to travel from Chicago to Spokane, Washington, where he was scheduled to provide dog training services to a client, because Defendants barred him from boarding commercial flights to or from the United States or over U.S. airspace." *Id.*, at ¶ 17. The complaint alleges that Mashal, like other plaintiffs, was asked to become an FBI informant in exchange for having his name removed from the No Fly List. *Id.*, at ¶ 287. These claims are substantially repeated, though in abbreviated form, in the Second Amended Complaint, *infra* note 66.

62. *Id.*, at 83–84, 87.
63. *Id.*, at ¶ 90.
64. *Id.*, at ¶ 8, 92–93.
65. *Id.*, at ¶ 11.
66. It should be noted that the ACLU later filed a second amended complaint in which these allegations are substantially repeated but in abbreviated and less detailed form. Docket # 64, Second Amended Complaint, Latif v. Holder, Case 3:10-cv-00750-BR, (D. Ore. Feb. 4, 2011). The plaintiffs' filing does not appear to have been driven by any doubt about the truth of their previous allegations, but rather resulted from the court's preference for brevity and precision. At an early hearing, the court narrowed the issues before it and invited the plaintiffs to file a new complaint that "plainly and concisely sets forth the jurisdictional and elemental bases of Plaintiffs' claims" in light of recent case law. Document # 69, Opinion and Order, Latif v. Holder, Case 3:10-cv-00750-BR, at 5 (D. Ore. May 3, 2011; *see also* Docket #63, Transcript of Proceedings, Jan. 21, 2011, at pages 4–5, 58–63.). As with all complaints, the unproven nature of the allegations should temper their evaluation. But these changes may simply reflect a reaction to the defendants' late decisions to allow the travel of some of the plaintiffs in an attempt to moot their claims. Cf. *supra* note 54, and Docket # 65, Defendants' Supplemental Memorandum in Support of their Motion to Dismiss Plaintiffs' Complaint Pursuant to Federal Rule of Civil Procedure 19(b), Latif v. Holder, Case 3:10-cv-00750-BR, (D. Ore. Feb. 18, 2011) ("Now that Plaintiffs' moot claims of 'banishment' are no longer included in the Complaint, it is clear that their remaining claims are a challenge to the redress procedures in place for persons who have been delayed or prohibited from boarding a commercial aircraft as a result of their alleged inclusion on the No Fly list.").

67. Document # 69, Opinion and Order, Latif v. Holder, Case 3:10-cv-00750-BR, at 5 (D. Ore. May 3, 2011). This theory is examined in detail in chapter 7.

68. Consider the allegations made about the experience of Stephen Persaud, who was kept from returning to California from the Virgin Islands with his pregnant wife and toddler son by the airline's refusal to issue him a boarding pass. The complaint alleges that FBI agents separated Persaud from his family and questioned him "about his overseas travels, including his time teaching English in Puntland, the area of northeastern Somalia, in 2006. During this questioning, Agent Hernandez informed Mr. Persaud that he was on the No Fly List. Agent Hernandez stated, 'We know you were in Somalia. We'd like to know where, why, and what parts you visited.'" Docket # 15, First Amended Complaint, Latif v. Holder, Case 3:10-cv-00750-BR (D. Ore. Aug. 5, 2010), at ¶ 330. When Persaud booked passage on a cruise ship to Puerto Rico in an effort to return home, the complaint alleges, "Agent Hernandez boarded the ship while it was docked. Mr. Persaud was surprised to see Agent Hernandez and asked why he was following him onto a ship. The agent told Mr. Persaud that his name would re-

main on the No Fly List and that this was a 'symptom of a greater problem' that would be resolved only if Mr. Persaud cooperated with the FBI." *Id.* at ¶ 338. The complaint alleges that Agent Hernandez told Persaud, "Agent Hernandez stated, "There is no judicial process for getting off the No Fly List. The only way to get off the list is to talk to us." *Id.*, at ¶ 339. Agent Hernandez is alleged to have dogged Persaud as the latter made his way back to California by boat and train over the course of the next ten days, urging him to become an FBI informant. *Id.*, at ¶¶ 340–41. These claims are substantially repeated, though in abbreviated form, in the Second Amended Complaint, *supra* note 66.

69. Canceled Passport, WASH. POST, May 13, 1952, at 10.

70. *Id.*

71. Pres. Procl. 2914, Dec. 16, 1950, 15 FED. REG. 9029 (Dec. 19, 1950); Pub. L. 82-450, July 3, 1952, 66 Stat. 330.

72. "Passport Dodge" of Reds Disclosed, N.Y. TIMES, Feb. 8, 1952, at 14.

73. Conference Proceedings of the 2002 Tenth Circuit Judicial Conference, Life After 9/11: Issues Affecting the Courts and the Nation, 51 U. KAN. L. REV. 219, 226 (2003).

74. U.S. v. Dennis, 183 F.2d 201, 212 (2d Cir. 1950).

75. Dennis v. United States, 341 U.S. 494 (1951) (internal citations omitted).

76. Court Basis Cited in Passport Policy, N.Y. TIMES, May 25, 1952, at 29.

77. Sec. 2(1), Subversive Activities Control Act of 1950, Act of Sept. 23, 1950, 64 Stat. 987, 993, codified at 50 U.S.C. 285 (1950).

78. Linus Pauling, My Efforts to Obtain a Passport, 8 BULL. OF THE ATOMIC SCIENTISTS 253 (Oct. 1952). The denial preceded Pauling's Nobel Prizes in Chemistry (1954) and Peace (1962). Dr. Pauling described his efforts to obtain a passport on this and subsequent occasions in a 1977 interview for the PBS television program *NOVA*. See Audio tape: Passport problems, Dep't of Special Collections, The Valley Library, Oregon State University (http://osulibrary.orst.edu/specialcollections/coll/pauling/dna/audio/nova4.html).

79. *Id.* at 254, 256.

80. MARTIN GOTTFRIED, ARTHUR MILLER: HIS LIFE AND WORK 236 (2003). *See also* ENOCH BRATER, ARTHUR MILLER: A PLAYWRIGHT'S LIFE AND WORKS 66–67 (2005). When the Belgian audience exclaimed, "Author, author!" on opening night, it was the American ambassador who appeared onstage. *Id.*; *see also* Playwright Arthur Miller Refused Visa For a Visit to Brussels to See His Play, N.Y. TIMES, Mar. 31, 1954, at 16.

81. Allen Drury, Arthur Miller Admits Helping Communist-Front Groups in '40's, N.Y. TIMES, June 22, 1956, at 1. The link between application and testimony may have been quite direct. Martin Gottfried argues that Miller's application "provided HUAC with an excuse to summon him to hearings. These were designed just for him and a few select others on 'The Unauthorized Use of United States Passports." Gottfried, *supra* note 80, at 286.

82. *Investigation of the Unauthorized Use of United States Passports—Part 4: Hearings before the H. Committee on Un-American Activities,* 84th Cong., 4655–91(1956). Miller's conviction was later unanimously reversed on procedural grounds. U.S. v. Miller, 152 F.Supp. 781, 783 (1957), *judgment rev'd en banc,* 259 F.2d 187 (D.C. Cir. 1958).

83. Eugene Gressman, The Undue Process of Passports, 127 NEW REPUBLIC 13, 14 (Sept. 8, 1952).

Chapter 2

1. Author's interview with Jeff Hood, former reporter for the *Stockton Record*, Lodi, Calif., May 27, 2010 (hereinafter "Hood interview").

2. Ralph Lea and Christi Kennedy, Grape Festival Grew out of Community Spirit, LODI NEWS-SENTINEL, Sept. 16, 2004.

3. *FBI: Al Qaeda Plot Possibly Uncovered*, CNN, June 9, 2005, posted: 5:21 AM EDT (0921 GMT) (http://www.cnn.com/2005/US/06/08/terror.probe/).

4. *Id.*

5. *See Frontline: The Enemy Within*, PBS, Oct. 10, 2006 (transcript at http://www.pbs.org/wgbh/pages/frontline/enemywithin/etc/script.html).

6. Daniel Pipes, Right of Return, JERUSALEM POST, Sept. 6, 2006, at 14; Press release, ACLU of N. California, Statements from Jaber Ismail and Muhammad Ismail, Oct. 2, 2006, http://www.aclunc.org/news/press_releases/statements_from_jaber_ismail_and_muhammad_ismail.shtml. Jeff Hood, Hayats' Relatives Return Home after Five Months: Men Stuck Abroad When Names Turned Up on Fed's No-Fly List, THE RECORD (STOCKTON, CALIF.), Oct. 3, 2006.

7. Author's interview with Muhammad Ismail, Usama Ismail, Jaber Ismail, and Julia Harumi Mass, Cesar Chavez Public Library, Stockton, Calif., May 29, 2010 (hereinafter "Ismail/Mass interview").

8. Letter from Julia Harumi Mass, Staff Attorney, ACLU of N. California, to Office of Civil Rights & Civil Liberties, Dep't of Homeland Sec., Aug. 9, 2006, at 1 (hereinafter ACLU Complaint).

9. Ismail/Mass interview, *supra* note 7.

10. ACLU Complaint, *supra* note 8, at 1–2; Barclay Crawford, Terror-Linked Pakistanis Bounced From Airport, S. CHINA MORNING POST, Sept. 3, 2006, at 4. Ismail/Mass interview, *supra* note 7.

11. ACLU Complaint *supra* note 8, at 1.

12. *Id.*

13. Stella Richardson, U.S. Citizens Allowed to Return Home after ACLU Files Complaint, 70 ACLUNEWS 1 (Fall 2006).

14. *Id.*

15. Ismail/Mass interview, *supra* note 7.

16. Jeff Hood, Two Lodi Men Stuck in Pakistan: Family Relation to Hayats Keeps Pair Exiled Until They Talk to FBI, THE RECORD (STOCKTON, CALIF.), Aug. 29, 2006; Demian Bulwa, Lodi: Men OKd to Return to U.S. From Pakistan, S.F. CHRON., Sept. 13, 2006, at B5. Telephone interview with Julia Harumi Mass, Staff Attorney, ACLU of N. California (July 2, 2007) (hereinafter "Mass interview"); Ismail/Mass interview, *supra* note 7.

17. ACLU complaint, *supra* note 8 at 2; Crawford, *supra* note 10, at 4.

18. Ismail/Mass interview, *supra* note 7.

19. *Id.*

20. ACLU Complaint, *supra* note 8, at 2.

21. *Id.*; Ismail/Mass interview, *supra* note 7.

22. Ismail/Mass interview, *supra* note 7. According to Mass's notes, taken in August 2006, the tickets cost 53,000 Pakistani rupees each, then roughly USD $885 a ticket.

23. Ismail/Mass interview, *supra* note 7.

24. *Id.*

25. Ismail/Mass interview, *supra* note 7 (from notes taken by Julia Harumi Mass in August 2006).

26. Mass interview, *supra* note 16.

27. Ismail/Mass interview, *supra* note 7.

28. Jeff Hood, Hayats' Relatives Return Home after Five Months: Men Stuck Abroad When Names Turned Up on Fed's No-Fly List, THE RECORD (STOCKTON, CALIF.), Oct. 3, 2006. Mass interview, *supra* note 16. Ismail/Mass interview, *supra* note 7. Mr. Parenti declined multiple written requests to interview him. See *infra* note 31.

29. Mass interview, *supra* note 16.

30. Hood, *supra* note 16. Mass interview, *supra* note 16. Ismail/Mass interview, *supra* note 7.

31. TSC Director Timothy Healy strongly disputed this account. In written comments to a law review article by the author that reported Mass's description of her conversation with SAC Parenti, Healy wrote by hand in the margin "tough to believe any FBI would say this.—No true, can't do don't have the authority." (Annotated copy of International Travel and the Constitution, 56 UCLA L. REV. 271, 278 (2008) (on file with the author).) Repeated requests to interview SAC Parenti or submit written questions to him were denied separately by both Mr. Parenti and FBIHQ. See Letter from Drew S. Parenti, Special Agent-in-Charge, FBI Sacramento Field Office (July 12, 2007); *see also* e-mail exchange with Drew S. Parenti, May 20, 2010 (ending with "For the sake of the accuracy of my own work, I only want to corroborate whether you did tell Ms. Mass that you were behind the request." Mr. Parenti did not reply.); *see also* e-mail exchanges with Susan T. McKee, Public Affairs Specialist, Office of Public Affairs, FBIHQ (Mar. 19, 2010). All communications are on file with the author.

32. Statement of U.S. Attorney McGregor W. Scott, posted: 4:03 PM PDT June 8, 2005, at http://www.foxreno.com/news/4586401/detail.html.

33. Author's interview with McGregor W. Scott, May 28, 2010, Sacramento, Calif.

34. See *Frontline*, *supra* note 5.

35. See *Frontline: Interview with Drew Parenti*, PBS, Oct. 5, 2006, http://www.pbs.org/wgbh/pages/frontline/enemywithin/lodi/response.html; Press Release, Dep't of Justice, Hamid Hayat Convicted of Terrorism Charges, Apr. 25, 2006; Press Release, FBI National Press Office, Director Mueller Appoints Drew S. Parenti to Head the FBI's Sacramento Division, June 3, 2005 ("Mr. Parenti is expected to report to Sacramento on June 20, 2005").

36. Second Superseding Indictment, U.S. v. Hayat, No. 2:05-CR-00240-GEB (E.D. Cal. Jan. 26, 2006).

37. Hood interview, *supra* note 1; KTVU.com, Son Guilty on All Counts; Mistrial For Father, KTVU NEWS, Apr. 26, 2006, http://www.ktvu.com/print/8989205/detail.html; Amy Waldman, Prophetic Justice, THE ATLANTIC MONTHLY, Oct. 2006; *Frontline*, *supra* note 5.

38. Minutes for proceedings held before Magistrate Judge Peter A. Nowinski, U.S. v. Hayat, No. 2:05-CR-00240-GEB (E.D. Cal. June 7, 2005).

39. Statement of U.S. Attorney McGregor W. Scott, Posted: 4:03 PM PDT June 8, 2005, at http://www.foxreno.com/news/4586401/detail.html; *FBI: Al Qaeda Plot Possibly Uncovered*, CNN, Thursday, June 9, 2005, Posted 5:21 AM EDT (0921 GMT) (http://www.cnn.com/2005/US/06/08/terror.probe/).

40. The charges alleged violations of 18 U.S.C. § 2339A and § 1001. Second Superseding Indictment, *supra* note 36.

41. Second Superseding Indictment, *supra* note 36, at Count 1(A)(7).

42. Verdict, U.S. v. Hayat, No. 2:05-CR-00240-GEB (E.D. Cal. Apr. 25, 2006). Carolyn Marshall, 24-Year Term for Californian in Terrorism Training Case, N.Y. TIMES, Sept. 11, 2007, at A20.

43. Minutes for proceedings held before Judge Garland E. Burrell Jr., U.S. v. Hayat, No. 2:05-CR-00240-GEB (E.D. Cal. Apr. 25, 2006). Umer Hayat later pled guilty to a one-count information alleging a false statement to a customs official that he was returning to the United States carrying less than $10,000. See Information, U.S. v. Hayat, No. 2:05-CR-00240-GEB (E.D. Cal. May 31, 2006). He was sentenced to time served, fined $3,600, and ordered to pay a $100 special assessment. *See* Minutes for proceedings held before Judge Garland E. Burrell Jr., U.S. v. Hayat, No. 2:05-CR-00240-GEB (E.D. Cal. Aug. 25, 2006).

44. Minutes for proceedings held before Judge Garland E. Burrell Jr., U.S. v. Hayat, et al., No. 2:05-0240 (E.D. Cal. Apr. 21, 2006). Randal C. Archibold, Wait Ends for Father and Son Exiled by F.B.I. Terror Inquiry, N.Y. TIMES, Oct. 2, 2006, at A10; Crawford, *supra* note 10.

45. ACLU Complaint, *supra* note 8, at 2; Richard Gonzales, *U.S. Government Blocks Citizens' Return Home*, NPR Morning Edition, NPR, Sept. 12, 2006 (transcript available on Westlaw at 2006 WLNR 22951510 and audio file available at: http://www.npr.org/templates/story/story.php?storyId=6059911) (Jaber Ismail: "[The FBI Agent at the American embassy in Islamabad] told me the reason that why we're on the no-fly list and the reason was that in the emergency contact number, we wrote our uncle's name, you know, Umer Hayat"); Crawford, *supra* note 10.

46. KTVU.com, *Son Guilty On All Counts; Mistrial For Father*, *supra* note 37. Archibold, *supra* note 44.

47. Bulwa, *supra* note 16, at B5.

48. Demian Bulwa, 2 Lodi Residents Refused Entry Back Into U.S., S.F. CHRON., Aug. 26, 2006, at A1. Beyond his confessions, which Hayat's attorneys claimed were coerced and misleading, the government presented no evidence of his own or anyone else's attendance at any camps. Randal C. Archibold, U.S. Blocks Men's Return to California from Pakistan, N.Y. TIMES, Aug. 29, 2006, at A17; Archibold, *supra* note 44; Amy Waldman, Prophetic Justice, THE ATLANTIC MONTHLY, Oct. 2006. At least one source alleges that Hayat later changed his story. *See* Pipes, *supra* note 6.

49. Scott interview, *supra* note 33.

50. Hood interview, *supra* note 1.

51. *Id.*

52. Ismail/Mass interview, *supra* note 7.

53. Scott interview, *supra* note 33.

54. Ismail/Mass interview, *supra* note 7.

55. Hood, Two Lodi Men Stuck in Pakiston, *supra* note 16; Ismail/Mass interview, *supra* note 7.

56. ACLU Complaint, *supra* note 8, at 1.

57. *Id.*, at 2.

58. *Id.*, at 3.

59. Gonzales, *supra* note 45.

60. Archibold, *supra* note 44, at A10.

61. Bulwa, *supra* note 48, at A1. Scott interview, *supra* note 33.

62. Bulwa, *supra* note 48, at A1; Archibold, *supra* note 44, at A17; Bulwa, *supra* note 16, at B5. According to Mr. Scott, this quotation is accurate. *See* Letter from McGregor W. Scott, United States Attorney, Eastern District of California, Sept. 24, 2007 (on file with author) ("I did in fact say what he quoted me as saying: '[T]hey've been given the chance to meet with the FBI over there and answer a few questions, and they've declined to do that'"). Scott explained: "This was a random press inquiry to which I gave an answer which was based on information provided to me by the FBI in a cursory briefing." *Id.*

63. One former government official considered it wrong to identify this relatively low-level staff member of the DHS Office for Civil Rights and Civil Liberties. Since she was not responsible for any policy decision, this person argued, she should remain anonymous in executing the decisions of others.

I reject this "only-following-orders" approach to state action and identify all known participants in this case. Doing so promotes factual accuracy and allows others to check my research. Dividing government between senior officials and lower-level employees who should be protected from public view (despite professional qualifications, experience, or expertise) also strikes me as a paternalistic approach to office management.

But most importantly, this inclination toward anonymity is itself a telling admission. I describe how the redress process actually appeared to work to someone who tried to use it. It is not the fault of the Ismails or their lawyer if government agencies elect to create a system in which someone stranded overseas is only given access to low-level employees who lack knowledge or authority to answer basic questions (addressed to them with considerable urgency). To demand anonymity for the low-level messenger, while denying access to the higher-level decision makers, is to encourage unaccountability for both.

64. Mass interview, *supra* note 16. Ismail/mass interview, *supra* note 7.

65. *Id.*

66. Ismail/Mass interview, *supra* note 7.

67. Mass interview, *supra* note 16.

68. For discussion regarding identities of government employees, see *supra* note 63.

69. Mass interview, *supra* note 16.

70. *Id.*

71. *Id.*

72. This letter is an example of a common type of government communication known as a "Glomar response." The Hughes Glomar Explorer was a large research vessel secretly used by the CIA in an attempt to recover a sunken Soviet submarine. In response to a journalist's Freedom of Information Act request concerning the episode, the CIA replied that "involvement by the U.S. Government in the activities which are the subject matter of your request can neither be confirmed nor denied." This was upheld as a legitimate response, in theory, by the United States Court of Appeals for the District of Columbia Circuit in Phillippi v. CIA, 546 F.2d 1009 (D.C. Cir. 1976), which nevertheless reversed the District Court's judgment for the CIA and remanded the case due to a procedural flaw in the development of the public record. The use of such a response in the context of the No Fly List is critically analyzed in chapter 7.

73. Ismail/Mass interview, *supra* note 7. Scott interview, *supra* note 33.

74. Letter from Timothy J. Keefer, Deputy Officer and Acting Chief Counsel, Office for Civil Rights and Civil Liberties, DHS, to Julia Harumi Mass, Staff Attorney, ACLU (Sept. 8, 2006) (on file with author).

75. On the face of the facts presented above, it would appear that the Ismails had a colorable claim for monetary damages for a variety of constitutional torts that would be governed under Bivens v. Six Unknown Named Agents of Federal Bureau of Narcotics, 403 U.S. 388 (1971). If the action were filed in the U.S. District Court for the Eastern District of California, the statute of limitations for such a claim would have run, at the latest, sometime in late May or June 2008, two years after the time when the Ismails knew or had reason to know of their constitutional injury (i.e., when FBI agents in Pakistan placed unconstitutional conditions on their return home). *See* Pesnell v. Arsenault, 490 F.3d 1158, 1163 & 1163, n. 3 (9th Cir. 2007) (forum law sets statute of limitations for *Bivens* claim); Cal. Civ. Proc. Code § 335.1 (two-year statute of limitations); Western Center For Journalism v. Cederquist, 235 F.3d 1153, 1156 (9th Cir. 2000) ("A Bivens claim accrues when the plaintiff knows or has reason to know of the injury").

The Ismails did not file a civil suit against Special Agent Parenti or other federal officials. Why? There may be many reasons why the Ismails declined to file suit, but several possible explanations stand out. First, it is not unreasonable to speculate that the Ismails may have negotiated a settlement agreement with the relevant federal officials or agencies. A second explanation, however, might be that the Ismails were so traumatized by the episode (which followed the federal prosecution of two of their relatives on terrorism-related charges), that they harbored fears of retaliation for filing such a lawsuit. Regardless of the objective reasonableness of such a fear, it is not unreasonable to speculate that concerns about future travel might work a chilling effect on those who have suffered such an injury in the past.

Alternatively, the Ismails may not wish to pursue litigation that could expose them to greater scrutiny. As TSC Director Timothy Healy observed in handwritten annotations to my law review article briefly describing these events: "Maybe it wasn't true! . . . A third stands out: their version of the facts were [*sic*] inaccurate. A fourth—maybe the terrorist connections are accurate." *See supra* note 31. Director Healy has access to the Government's reasons for the action it took against the Ismails. Thus, his comment is either based on information he declines to share or it traduces the Ismails' decision not to litigate. Regardless, it is unfair to impugn the family by drawing inferences solely from their decision not to elect to incur the expenses and trauma attendant to nearly all civil litigation.

76. Bulwa, *supra* note 16, at B5.

77. *Id.*

78. Archibold, *supra* note 44, at A10.

79. Press Release, ACLU of N. California, *Statement from Jaber Ismail,* Oct. 2, 2006, http://www.aclunc.org/news/press_releases/statements_from_jaber_ismail_and_muhammad_ismail.shtml; *see also* CNN Newsroom, *Inside the Madrassa* (television broadcast, Sept. 12, 2006), http://transcripts.cnn.com/TRANSCRIPTS/0609/12/cnr.04.html) ("Because they said I have to do a lie detector test and I was thinking like, you know, I was born in the United States. Why do I have to take a lie detector test to enter my own country.").

80. Ismail/Mass interview, supra note 7.

81. Edited transcript of interview conducted July 24, 2006, for Frontline: The Enemy Within, PBS, Oct. 10, 2006 (transcript at http://www.pbs.org/wgbh/pages/frontline/enemywithin/interviews/scott.html).

82. Scott interview, *supra* note 33.

83. *Id.*

84. DEPARTMENT OF HOMELAND SECURITY OFFICE OF THE INSPECTOR GENERAL, ROLE OF THE NO FLY AND SELECTEE LISTS IN SECURING COMMERCIAL AVIATION 11 (July 2009).

85. JACK GOLDSMITH, THE TERROR PRESIDENCY: LAW AND JUDGMENT INSIDE THE BUSH ADMINISTRATION 74 (2007). Kip Hawley, the fourth administrator of the TSA from 2005 to 2009, describes how his first experience with threat intelligence "scared the hell out of me" and left him with the feeling that "I had been dumped into a sea swarming with sharks. I wanted everyone around me to have the same fire to their feet and twist in their gut." KIP HAWLEY AND NATHAN MEANS, PERMANENT EMERGENCY: INSIDE THE TSA AND THE FIGHT FOR THE FUTURE OF AMERICAN SECURITY 124, 130 (2012).

86. Author's interview with Randy Beardsworth, Mar. 11, 2010, Washington, D.C.

87. Author's interview with Michael P. Jackson, Mar. 14, 2011, Arlington, VA.

88. *Id.*

89. *Id.*

Chapter 3

1. U.S. DEP'T OF COMMERCE, INT'L TRADE ADMIN., OFFICE OF TRAVEL & TOURISM INDUS., PRELIMINARY U.S. CITIZEN AIR TRAFFIC TO OVERSEAS REGIONS, CANADA & MEXICO 2006 1 (2007).

2. Passengers, All Carriers—All Airports, U.S. Department of Transportation Bureau of Transportation Statistics, at http://www.transtats.bts.gov/Data_Elements.aspx?Data=1.

3. U.S. Census Bureau, 2010 population estimate for Philadelphia, Pa. (1,526,006 people), at http://quickfacts.census.gov/qfd/states/42/4260000.html.

4. Arts. of Confed., Art. IV, § 1.

5. 4 THE RECORDS OF THE FEDERAL CONVENTION OF 1787 121 (Max Farrand, ed. 1937) (indexing references to what became Art. IV, § 2, in the Records, none of which provide substantive guidance). Joseph Story's *Commentaries* shed no light on the change and, in fact, omit the passage "free ingress and regress to and from any other State." *See* JOSEPH STORY, 2 COMMENTARIES ON THE CONSTITUTION OF THE UNITED STATES § 1805 (1851). Akhil Reed Amar suggests that this language was "pruned away" as "excess and confusing verbiage." AKHIL REED AMAR, AMERICA'S CONSTITUTION: A BIOGRAPHY 251 (2005).

6. *See, e.g.*, Passport Denied: State Department Practice and Due Process, 3 STAN. L. REV. 312, 315 (1951) ("The framers of the Constitution did not intend to include international travel as specifically within the term 'liberty'").

7. *See, e.g.*, Thomas Jefferson, A Bill Declaring Who Shall be Deemed Citizens of This Commonwealth, May 1779 (Intending "to preserve to the citizens of this commonwealth, that natural right, which all men have of relinquishing the country, in which birth, or other accident may have thrown them, and, seeking subsistence and happiness wheresoever they may be able, or may hope to find them" and declaring that defined inhabitants of the Confederation "shall have free egress, and regress, to and

from" the Commonwealth of Virginia), *reprinted in* 4 THE FOUNDERS' CONSTITUTION 488 (Philip B. Kurland and Ralph Lerner, eds. 1987).

8. "He has endeavoured to prevent the population of these States; for that purpose obstructing the Laws for Naturalization of Foreigners; refusing to pass others to encourage their migrations hither, and raising the conditions of new Appropriations of Lands." The Declaration of Independence para. 9 (U.S. 1776). *See also* ROGERS M. SMITH, CIVIC IDEALS 53–54 (1997) ("The colonists were ordered to remain east of a Proclamation Line drawn along the crest of the Alleghenies. This restriction, culminating a long history of British restraints on colonial expansionism, was fiercely denounced by the colonists.").

9. *See, e.g.,* ZECHARIAH CHAFEE, JR. THREE HUMAN RIGHTS IN THE CONSTITUTION 163–67, 176–81 (1956); The Liberties of the Massachusets Collonie in New England (1641), Art. 17 ("Every man of or within this Jurisdiction shall have free libertie, notwithstanding any Civill power to remove both himselfe, and his familie at their pleasure out of the same, provided there be no legall impediment to the contrarie."), http://history.hanover.edu/texts/masslib.html#ms; Pennsylvania Constitution of 1776, Declaration of Rights, Art. XV ("That all men have a natural inherent right to emigrate from one state to another that will receive them, or to form a new state in vacant countries, or in such countries as they can purchase, whenever they think that thereby they may promote their own happiness.") reprinted in 5 THE FEDERAL AND STATE CONSTITUTIONS, COLONIAL CHARTERS, AND OTHER ORGANIC LAWS OF THE STATES, TERRITORIES, AND COLONIES NOW OR HERETOFORE FORMING THE UNITED STATES OF AMERICA 3084 (Francis Newton Thorpe, ed. 1909); Constitution of Vermont, July 8, 1777, Art. XVII ("That all people have a natural and inherent right to emigrate from one State to another, that will receive them, or to form a new State in vacant countries, or in such countries as they can purchase, whenever they think that thereby they can promote their own happiness.") and Constitution of Vermont, July 4, 1786, Art. XXI (same), http://www.yale.edu/lawweb/avalon/states/vt01.htm.

10. *See, e.g.,* Chafee, *supra* note 9, at 185–87; Amar, *supra* note 5, at 251 ("Not only were such rights sheltered by Article IV's more general formulation, but they also found further refuge in the Constitution's overall structure of sister states formed into a more perfect union, and in the negative implications of the Article I interstate-commerce clause: Congress, not states, would generally regulate who and what could cross state lines."). *See also* Saenz v. Roe, 526 U.S. 489, 501 (1999) ("The right of 'free ingress and regress to and from' neighboring States, which was expressly mentioned in the text of the Articles of Confederation, may simply have been 'conceived from the beginning to be a necessary concomitant of the stronger Union the Constitution created'.") (footnote and citation omitted); U.S. v. Guest, 383 U.S. 745, 764 (1966) (Harlan, J., concurring in part and dissenting in part) ("This right to 'free ingress and regress' was eliminated from the draft of the Constitution without discussion even though the main objective of the Convention was to create a stronger union. It has been assumed that the clause was dropped because it was so obviously an essential part of our federal structure that it was necessarily subsumed under more general clauses of the Constitution."); New York v. O'Neill, 359 U.S. 1, 12 (1959) (Douglas, J., dissenting) (citing Chafee to argue that "the failure to make specific provision for this right in the Constitution must have been on the assumption that it was already included. For it is impossible to think that a right so deeply cherished in the Colonies was rejected outright.").

11. *See* The Federalist Papers, No. 84 (Hamilton).

12. Right of Expatriation, 9 Op. Att'y Gen. 356 (1859) ("Here, in the United States, the thought of giving it up cannot be entertained for a moment. Upon that principle this country was populated. We owe to it our existence as a nation. Ever since our independence we have upheld and maintained it by every form of words and acts. We have constantly promised full and complete protection to all persons who should come here and seek it by renouncing their natural allegiance and transferring their fealty to us. We stand pledged to it in the face of the whole world."); *see also* Charles E. Wyzanski, Jr., Freedom to Travel, ATLANTIC MONTHLY 66, 67 (Oct. 4, 1952) ("freedom of travel was in the nineteenth century a dominant theme in our foreign policy"); Alan G. James, Expatriation in the United States: Precept and Practice Today and Yesterday, 27 SAN DIEGO L. REV. 853, 862 (1990) ("[I]n the first three-quarters of a century of the Republic a central concern of the Department of State was protection of naturalized American citizens abroad against claims of the state of their nativity to their services as soldiers or seamen.").

13. These arguments were originally formulated in an article, from which I draw heavily. *See* Jeffrey Kahn, International Travel and the Constitution, 56 UCLA L. REV. 271 (2008).

14. For example, the Ninth Circuit Court of Appeal has declared the literally true statement that "the Constitution does not guarantee the right to travel by any particular form of transportation." Gilmore v. Gonzales, 435 F.3d 1125, 1136 (9th Cir. 2006).

15. Attorney General of New York v. Soto-Lopez, 476 U.S. 898, 901–2 (1986). *See also, e.g.,* Shapiro v. Thompson, 394 U.S. 618, 630 (1969) (observing without explaining that "[w]e have no occasion to ascribe the source of this right to travel interstate to a particular constitutional provision," before identifying four possible sources for rights to interstate and foreign travel).

16. LAURENCE TRIBE, AMERICAN CONSTITUTIONAL LAW 1252, 1336–38 (3rd ed., 2000).

17. Corfield v. Coryell, 6 Fed. Cas. 546, 551–52 (C.C.E.D. Pa. 1823).

18. *Id.*

19. *See, e.g.,* Paul v. Virginia, 75 U.S. (8 Wall.) 168, 180 (1868) ("[I]t gives them the right of free ingress into other States, and egress from them;"); Ward v. Maryland, 79 U.S. 418, 430 (1870) ("[T]he [Privileges and Immunities] clause plainly and unmistakably secures and protects the right of a citizen of one State to pass into any other State of the Union.").

20. *See, e.g.,* Lemmon v. People, 20 N.Y. 562, 607 (1860). Justice Denio observed that this clause "was inserted substantially as it stood in the Articles of Confederation," *id.* at 608, glossing over the deletion of the travel-related language to assert that "any law which should attempt to deny [citizens] free ingress or egress would be void." *Id.* at 610. This gloss is particularly odd given that Justice Denio observes later in his opinion that the exception of "paupers and vagabonds" from the provision of citizenship in Article IV of the Articles of Confederation "was omitted in the corresponding provision of the Constitution." *Id.* at 611.

21. The Slaughter-House Cases, 83 U.S. 36, 75 (1872).

22. Justice Miller, citing *Corfield*, explained that "[i]n the article of the Confederation we have some of these specifically mentioned, and enough perhaps to give some general idea of the class of civil rights meant by the phrase." *Id.*

23. *Id.* at 77.

24. *Id.*

25. *Slaughter-House*, 83 U.S. at 79. For *Crandall,* see *infra* text at notes 38–48.

26. *Id.* at 75. Justice Bradley ascribed to the natural rights view espoused by Justice Washington in *Corfield,* and quoted that case in the process of noting Justice Miller's error: "It is pertinent to observe that both the clause of the Constitution referred to, and Justice Washington in his comment on it, speak of the privileges and immunities of citizens *in* a State; not of citizens *of* a State. It is the privileges and immunities of citizens, that is, of citizens as such, that are to be accorded to citizens of other States when they are found in any State. . . ." *Id.* at 117–18 (emphasis in original). *See also* Tribe, *supra* note 16, at 1306, on the effect, intended or not, of this misquotation.

27. *Slaughter-House*, 83 U.S. at 78–79.

28. Smith v. Turner *and* Norris v. Boston (*The Passenger Cases*), 48 (7 How.) U.S. 283 (1849). The New York tax was assessed at a variable rate on all hands aboard foreign and domestic vessels. *Smith,* 48 U.S. at 283–84. Only the provision concerning foreign passengers was at issue. *Id.* at 298. The Massachusetts tax was limited to alien passengers. *Norris,* 48 U.S. at 286.

29. *Id.* at 405 (McLean, J.), 444–45 (Catron, J.), and 460–61 (Grier, J.).

30. *Id.* at 462 ("Commerce, as defined by this court, means something more than traffic,—*it is intercourse . . .*") (Grier, J., citing *Gibbons v. Ogden,* 22 U.S. (9 Wheat.) 1, 72 (1824)) (emphasis in original).

31. Edwards v. California, 314 U.S. 160, 173 (1941).

32. *Id.* at 174.

33. *Id.* at 172.

34. U.S. v. Guest, 383 U.S. 745, 757 (1966).

35. *See, e.g.,* Paul v. Virginia, 75 U.S. 168, 180 (1869); Blake v. McClung, 172 U.S. 239, 256–57 (1898); U.S. v. Guest, 383 U.S. 745, 767 (1966) (Harlan, J., dissenting in part).

36. *The Passenger Cases,* 48 (7 How.) U.S. 283, 492 (1849) (Taney, C.J., dissenting).

37. *Id.*

38. Crandall v. Nevada, 73 U.S. 35 (1867).

39. *Crandall,* 73 U.S. at 48–49.

40. *Id.,* at 41, 43–44. Professor Charles Black, in a famous series of lectures at Louisiana State University in 1968, observed that Justice Miller's majority opinion in *Crandall* implies that the Court only considered those textual arguments because counsel in the case "assumed that the decision had to go on the interpretation" of one textual provision or another. CHARLES L. BLACK, JR. STRUCTURE AND RELATIONSHIP IN CONSTITUTIONAL LAW 16 (1969). "But we do not concede," Justice Miller wrote for seven members of the Court, "that the question before us is to be determined by the two clauses of the Constitution which we have been examining." *Id.* (quoting *Crandall v. Nevada*).

41. *Crandall,* 73 U.S. at 44.

42. Dissenting in *United States v. Guest,* 383 U.S. 745, 765 (1966), Justice Harlan noted how Justice Miller had "found a correlative right of the citizen" to unimpeded interstate travel, only as "[a]ccompanying this need of the Federal Government." *But see* Twining v. New Jersey, 211 U.S. 78, 97 (1908) (citing *Crandall v. Nevada* for the proposition that "among the rights and privileges of national citizenship recognized by this court are the right to pass freely from state to state").

43. *Crandall*, 73 U.S. at 44.
44. *Id.* ("But if the government has these rights on her own account, the citizen also has correlative rights.").
45. *Id.* at 47. Professor Black perceived that the holding was based on "a reciprocal relation between the national government which might have need for its citizens to travel, and their right to travel." *See* Black, *supra* note 40, at 27.
46. *Crandall*, 73 U.S. at 44.
47. *Id.* at 44–45.
48. *Id.* at 44. Explicit reference was made to the Civil War and a counterfactual asked whether the Union would have survived in the face of border states like Tennessee subjecting federal troop trains to a similar capitation tax. *Id.*
49. Nevertheless, Justice Douglas, concurring in *Edwards v. California* seventy-four years later, interpreted Justice Miller's language to support his view that the right to travel was a right of national citizenship protected by the Fourteenth Amendment. Justice Douglas preferred to interpret the language of contingency that infused Miller's analysis as "merely in illustration" of the dangers of allowing states to infringe this right, rather than as sources for the right itself. After all, Douglas argued, there was "not a shred of evidence in the record" that any passengers conveyed by Crandall sought to engage in any such political acts or missions of state. *Edwards*, 314 U.S. at 178. Justice Douglas thus argued that when the Fourteenth Amendment was adopted a year after *Crandall*, it had already been "squarely and authoritatively settled that the right to move freely from State to State was a right of *national* citizenship." *Id.* at 179. But this is error, possible only by ignoring the steady and heavy emphasis throughout Justice Miller's opinion on the derivative justifications for the right to travel.
50. *The Slaughter-House Cases*, 83 U.S. 36, 79 (1872).
51. *Id.*
52. *Corfield v. Coryell*, 6 Fed. Cas. 546, 551–52 (C.C.E.D. Pa. 1823).
53. 83 U.S. 36 at 76.
54. 83 U.S. at 112.
55. 83 U.S. at 117.
56. The Privileges or Immunities Clause states that "No State shall make or enforce any law which shall abridge the privileges or immunities of citizens of the United States."
57. *Edwards*, 314 U.S. at 177 (Douglas, J., concurring). Eighteen years after *Edwards*, Justice Douglas would find his own international travel obstructed by the State Department. This episode is noted in chapter 5. *See also* Black, *supra* note 40, at 28–29 ("I should prefer to think of Edwards' right to travel, and of his brother-in-law's right to bring him into the state, as a consequence of his being one of the people in a unitary nation, to which, because of its nationhood, internal barriers to travel are unthinkable, rather than pretending that I have performed a warranted inference from a clause empowering Congress to regulate commerce among the several states.").
58. 314 U.S. at 183.
59. *See, e.g., Oregon v. Mitchell*, 400 U.S. 112, 285 (1970) (Stewart, J., concurring in part and dissenting in part, joined by Burger, C.J., and Blackmun, J.) ("Freedom to travel from State to State—freedom to enter and abide in any State in the Union—is a privilege of United States citizenship."); *see also Bell v. Maryland*, 378 U.S. 226, 293 n.10 (1964) (Goldberg, J., concurring, joined by Warren, C.J., and Douglas, J.).

60. Saenz v. Roe, 526 U.S. 489 (1999).
61. *Id.* at 492.
62. *Id.* at 493, 495.
63. *See* Green v. Anderson, 811 F.Supp. 516 (E.D. Cal.,1993) (citing case law on durational residency requirements to invalidate program) *and* Roe v. Anderson, 134 F.3d 1400 (9th Cir. 1998).
64. *Saenz*, 526 U.S. at 501.
65. *Id.*
66. *Id.* at 502–3.
67. *Id.* at 503 (Privileges or Immunities Clause) and 506 & 507 (Citizenship Clause).
68. Title IV of the federal statute at issue, the Personal Responsibility and Work Opportunity Reconciliation Act of 1996, Pub. L. 104–93, 110 Stat. 2105, tightened restrictions on welfare and other benefits for noncitizens.
69. *Saenz*, 526 U.S. at 506, 505.
70. *Id.*, at 507–8.
71. It should be noted here that ambiguity about the constitutional source of the right to travel did not prevent, and may have facilitated, constitutional protection under the fundamental interests branch of equal protection analysis. Since such cases are not concerned with *where* the right is found, they are of little value to the analysis presented above. The typical case concerned durational residency requirements for state benefits. *See* Shapiro v. Thompson, *supra* note 15, at 630 ("We have no occasion to ascribe the source of this right to travel interstate to a particular constitutional provision."); Mem'l Hosp. v. Maricopa County, 415 U.S. 250, 254 (1974) (noting that the "right of interstate travel has repeatedly been recognized as a basic constitutional freedom" without seeking its constitutional source); Zobel v. Williams, 457 U.S. 55, 66 (1982) (Brennan, J., concurring) ("frequent attempts to assign the right to travel some textual source in the Constitution seem to me to have proved both inconclusive and unnecessary."); Attorney General of New York v. Soto-Lopez, 476 U.S. 898, 902 (1986) (applying equal protection analysis to residency requirement while conceding that "we have not felt impelled to locate this right [to travel] definitively in any particular constitutional provision.").

Likewise, the cases on *intra*-state travel also have not tarried long searching for the source of that supposed right as judges grappled with the level of scrutiny to be applied to assess equal protection claims alleging its violation. *See, e.g.,* King v. New Rochelle Municipal Housing Authority, 442 F.2d 646, 648 (2d Cir. 1971) ("Indeed, the Supreme Court specifically refused to ascribe the source of the right to travel to a particular constitutional provision, but relied on 'our constitutional concepts of personal liberty.' It would be meaningless to describe the right to travel between states as a fundamental precept of personal liberty and not to acknowledge a correlative constitutional right to travel within a state.") (internal citations omitted), *and* Ramos v. Town of Vernon, 353 F.3d 171 (2d Cir. 2003) (citing *New Rochelle*), *but see* Dickerson v. City of Gretna, No. 05-6667, 2007 WL 1098787 at *3 (E.D. La. 2007) (declining to find fundamental right to intrastate travel, citing controlling Fifth Circuit precedent, and therefore dismissing travel-based cause of action by putative class of plaintiffs alleging unconstitutional interference with their attempted flight from New Orleans through Gretna following Hurricane Katrina), *leave to appeal from interlocutory order denied,* No. 07-19 (5th Cir. June 4, 2007).

72. Shapiro v. Thompson, *supra* note 15, at 642–43 (emphasis in original; citations and footnotes excluded).

73. *Id.* at 643.

74. *Soto-Lopez*, 476 U.S. at 903. The "classification" prong might initially seem to fit the No Fly List—at its core, a system of classifying people. However, in the context of the case, the reference is to the line of fundamental interests equal protection cases that evaluate residency requirements. *See supra* note 71. It is that classification that is meant in *Soto-Lopez* and which would trigger heightened scrutiny.

75. Tutor-Saliba v. City of Hailey, 452 F.3d 1055, 1062 (9th Cir. 2006); Town of Southold v. Town of East Hampton, 477 F.3d 38, 54 (2nd Cir. 2007) ("[T]ravelers do not have a constitutional right to the most convenient form of travel, and minor restrictions on travel simply do not amount to the denial of a fundamental right."); Duncan v. Cone, No. 00-5705, 2000 WL 1828089, at *2 (6th Cir. 2000); Miller v. Reed, 176 F.3d 1202, 1205 (9th Cir. 1999); Dixon v. Love, 431 U.S. 105 (1977); Monarch Travel Servs., Inc. v. Associated Cultural Clubs, Inc., 466 F.2d 552, 554 (9th Cir. 1972).

76. *Miller, supra* note 75, at 1206.

77. City of Houston v. FAA, 679 F.2d 1184, 1198 (5th Cir. 1982) (upholding 1000-mile perimeter rule for non-stop flights to National Airport against a challenge by the City of Houston and American Airlines).

78. *Miller,* at 1205, and *Tutor-Saliba,* at 1062 (both relying on *Monarch Travel,* 466 F.2d at 554), *supra* note 75.

79. Bureau of Transportation Statistics, September 2010 Airline Traffic Data, available at http://www.bts.gov/press_releases/2010/bts058_10/html/bts058_10.html.

80. Bureau of Transportation Statistics, Findings from the National Household Travel Survey 1 (October 2003), available at http://www.bts.gov/publications/america_on_the_go/us_business_travel/pdf/entire.pdf.

81. *Miller, supra* note 75, at 1205.

82. *Tutor-Saliba,* 452 F.3d at 1059.

83. *Dixon,* 431 U.S. at 110–11 & 113.

84. *Town of Southold,* 477 F.3d at 44.

85. *City of Houston v. FAA,* 679 F.2d at 1188.

86. *See, e.g.,* Defendants' Memorandum of Law in Support of Motion to Dismiss or Summary Judgment, Latif v. Holder, Case No. 3:10-cv-00750-BR, at 25–27 (D. Ore. Nov. 17, 2010).

87. Kent v. Dulles, 357 U.S. 116, 126 (1958).

88. *See, e.g.,* Haig v. Agee, 453 U.S. 280, 306 (1981) ("The Court has made it plain that the *freedom* to travel outside the United States must be distinguished from the *right* to travel within the United States.") (emphasis in original); *and* Califano v. Aznavorian, 439 U.S. 170, 176 (1978) ("the 'right' of international travel has been considered to be no more than an aspect of the 'liberty' protected by the Due Process Clause of the Fifth Amendment."). In cases such as *Califano,* concerning a statutory entitlement that "does not have nearly so direct an impact on the freedom to travel internationally" as the Court's earlier passport cases involved, the Court expressed its view that legislation would be constitutional unless the limitation on travel were "wholly irrational." *Id.* at 177. This "rational basis" review has sometimes been adopted by the lower courts. *See, e.g.,* Clancy v. Office of Foreign Assets Control, 559 F. 3d 595, 604 (7th Cir. 2009).

89. Justice Scalia made this point in passing with regard to the Dormant Commerce Clause in *Bray v. Alexandria Women's Health Clinic,* 506 U.S. 263, 277 n.7 (1993). Women seeking abortions alleged that abortion opponents conspired to deny them their right to interstate travel. "That right," he noted, "does not derive from the negative Commerce Clause, or else it could be eliminated by Congress."

90. Aptheker v. Sec'y of State, 378 U.S. 500, 518 (1964).

91. *Id.*

92. 2 Stat. 203 (1803).

93. *See* Black, *supra* note 40, at 27. Black observes that this reasoning can easily be extended beyond the rights of citizens to all inhabitants "in a unitary nation" to travel unrestricted by internal barriers. *Id.* at 28–29.

94. 357 U.S. 116 (1958).

95. *Id.* at 126.

96. *Id.* at 125.

97. 66 Stat. 190, 8 U.S.C. § 1185(b). This act, for the first time in American history, required a valid passport for transit across a U.S. border in time of peace. *Kent,* 357 U.S. at 127.

98. 378 U.S. 500 (1964).

99. Pub. L. 81-831, 64 Stat. 993.

100. 378 U.S. at 506.

101. The Court concluded that travel regulations "may not be achieved by means which sweep unnecessarily broadly and thereby invade the area of protected freedoms," in this case First Amendment associational freedoms. *Id.* at 508 and 517.

102. 378 U.S. at 526–27 (Clark, J., dissenting, joined here by Harlan, J.).

103. *Id.*

104. *Id.* at 506 (internal quotations omitted).

105. *Id.* at 511, 512.

106. 44 Stat. 887, 22 U.S.C. § 211a (1958) ("The Secretary of State may grant and issue passports . . . under such rules as the President shall designate and prescribe for and on behalf of the United States. . . .").

107. Zemel v. Rusk, 381 U.S. 1, 7 (1965).

108. *Id.*

109. *Id.* at 13.

110. *Id.* at 8–10.

111. Worthy v. Herter, 270 F.2d 905, 907 (1959). William Worthy's loss in the D.C. Circuit did not immobilize him. His foreign escapades ultimately led to his conviction for violating the Immigration and Nationality Act, which made it a crime, inter alia, to willfully depart or enter the United States without a valid passport. This conviction was overturned by the Fifth Circuit Court of Appeals. *See* Worthy v. United States, 328 F.2d 386 (1964).

112. *Id.* at 910.

113. *Id.*

114. 22 U.S.C. § 1732.

115. *Worthy v. Herter, supra* note 111, at 910 (internal quotations omitted).

116. *Id.* at 911.

117. *Id.* at 913.

118. Briehl v. Dulles, 248 F.2d 561, 572 (D.C. Cir. 1957).

119. Haig v. Agee, 453 U.S. 280, 283–90 (1981).

120. *Haig,* 453 U.S. at 307. The Solicitor General explained that Agee's conduct "may not be punishable, we're not contending that it's punishable here." Transcript of Oral Argument, *Haig,* 453 U.S. 280 (No. 80–83).

121. Agee made good on his threat, publishing lists of hundreds of assertedly CIA personnel. The deaths of several CIA operatives overseas were attributed to Agee's "thinly-veiled invitations to violence." *Haig, supra* note 119, at 285 n. 7.

122. *Id.* at 125; Aptheker v. Sec'y of State, 378 U.S. 500, 505 (1964); Zemel v. Rusk, 381 U.S. 1, 14 (1965).

123. *Zemel,* 381 U.S. at 14.

124. *Id.*

125. *Id.* at 16.

126. *See, e.g.,* Urtetiqui v. D'Arcy, 34 U.S. (9 Pet.) 692, 699 (1835). *But see* Act of February 23, 1803, 2 Stat. 205 (restricting federal agents from knowingly granting a passport or other paper certifying an alien to be a citizen).

127. Dwight D. Eisenhower, Special Message to the Congress on the Need for Additional Passport Control Legislation, July 7, 1958, text available at http://www.presidency.ucsb.edu/ws/index.php?pid=11120&st=passport&st1=control.

128. Act of February 4, 1815, 3 Stat. 195.

129. *Id.*

130. Act of May 22, 1918, 40 Stat. 559.

131. *Id.* at 15.

132. *Zemel,* 381 U.S. at 15.

133. Abu Ali v. Ashcroft, 350 F.Supp.2d 28, 66 (D.D.C. 2004) (holding that the Hostage Act, 22 U.S.C. § 1732, did not create "any duty enforceable by a writ of mandamus"); Redpath v. Kissinger, 415 F.Supp. 566 (1976), *aff'd* 545 F.2d 167 (5th Cir., 1976) (holding that no writ of mandamus could issue under the Hostage Act to require further action by Executive Branch to aid citizen imprisoned in Mexico); U.S. ex rel. Keefe v. Dulles, 222 F.2d 390, 393–94 (1955) (holding that Secretary of State "was not under a legal duty to attempt through diplomatic processes to obtain Keith's release. Quite to the contrary, the commencement of diplomatic negotiations with a foreign power is completely in the discretion of the President and the head of the Department of State, who is his political agent. The Executive is not subject to judicial control or direction in such matters.").

134. 8 U.S.C. § 1101(a)(30) ("The term 'passport' means any travel document issued by competent authority showing the bearer's origin, identity, and nationality if any, which is valid for the admission of the bearer into a foreign country.").

Chapter 4

1. U.S. DEP'T OF STATE (GAILLARD HUNT), THE AMERICAN PASSPORT: ITS HISTORY AND A DIGEST OF LAWS, RULINGS, AND REGULATIONS GOVERNING ITS ISSUANCE BY THE DEPARTMENT OF STATE 77 (1898) (reproducing the first recorded passport issued by the United States to a United States citizen, Francis Maria Barrere, dated July 8, 1796); Graham H. Stuart, Safeguarding the State Through Passport Control, 12 DEP'T ST. BULL. 1066, 1066 (1945).

2. Louis L. Jaffe, The Right to Travel: The Passport Problem, 35 FOREIGN AFF. 17,

17 (Oct. 1956); Kenneth Diplock, Passports and Protection in International Law, 32 TRANSACTIONS OF THE GROTIUS SOCIETY 42 (1947).

3. Hunt, *supra* note 1, at 3–5. *See also* the opinion of the State Department's then Solicitor, W. E. Faison, reprinted, *id.* at 26–31, distinguishing passports under international law ("written permission given by a belligerent to subjects of the enemy whom he allows to travel without special restrictions in the territory belonging to him or under his control") with passports for the sovereign's own citizens in peacetime ("documents of an entirely different nature"), which tracks the description provided in the text above.

4. Hunt, *supra* note 1, at 5. Hunt cites Richard Henry Dana, Jr.'s notes to Henry Wheaton's *Elements of International Law* (1866). Wheaton is better known as a reporter of the U.S. Supreme Court's decisions, 1816–27. Dana was the U.S. Attorney for the District of Massachusetts during the Civil War. See Eugene Wambaugh, Book Review, 51 HARV. L. REV. 942, 945 (1938).

5. Hunt, *supra* note 1, at 3.

6. James Madison's Notes of Debates (Jan. 24, 1783), 19 LETTERS OF DELEGATES TO CONGRESS 608 (Paul H. Smith et al., eds. 1976–2000). The letter describes the work of a committee established by the Continental Congress to resolve a dispute with Pennsylvania. Madison notes that the position of the committee was "that the power of granting passports for the purpose in question [was] inseparable from the general power of war delegated, to Congress, & [was] essential for conducting the war." *Id.* It appears that "the Indian Country" was also considered a zone in which foreigners would require passports (but citizens merely a "license") to reside and trade with Native Americans. See An Ordinance for Regulating the Indian Department, submitted to Congress by Charles Pinckney, James Monroe, and Rufus King, Wednesday, June 28, 1786, in 30 JOURNALS OF THE CONTINENTAL CONGRESS 370 (Worthington C. Ford et al., ed. 1904–1937).

7. This debate is described with rich citation to primary sources in Calvin H. Johnson, The Dubious Enumerated Powers Doctrine, 22 CONST. COMMENT. 25, 40–42 (2005). Professor Johnson also provides citations for several examples of passports granted by the Continental Congress for the movement of people or goods through the war zone. *Id.* at 40 n. 54 & 51 n. 55.

8. Present Passport Restrictions, 1 COMMERCE MONTHLY 12 (Nov. 19, 1919).

9. Hunt, *supra* note 1, at 4. The author notes, without citation or statistics, that passports were required of citizens and foreigners alike to enter or leave the United States during the Civil War.

10. David Riesman, Jr., Legislative Restrictions on Foreign Enlistment and Travel, 40 COLUMBIA L. REV. 793, 815–17 (1940); Reginald Parker, The Right to Go Abroad: To Have and to Hold a Passport, 40 VA. L. REV. 853, 863 (1954); Daniel A. Farber, National Security, the Right to Travel, and the Court, SUP. CT. REV. 263, 265 (1981).

11. Brendan Mullan, The Regulation of International Migration: The US and Western Europe in Historical Comparative Perspective, in REGULATION OF MIGRATION: INTERNATIONAL EXPERIENCES 28 (Anita Böcker, Kees Groenendijk, Tetty Havinga, Paul Minderhoud, eds., 1998) ("Because of the limited state involvement in emigration, the endurance of free travel as a liberal ideal until the first third of the 20th century, and the relative youthfulness of today's nation states, economic considerations have outweighed political considerations in explaining the dynamics of international migration") (citation omitted).

12. Zechariah Chafee, Jr. THREE HUMAN RIGHTS IN THE CONSTITUTION 193 (1956); see also Riesman, *supra* note 10, at 817.

13. Zemel v. Rusk, 381 U.S. 1, 31 (1965) (Goldberg, J., dissenting).

14. FREEDOM TO TRAVEL: REPORT OF THE SPECIAL COMMITTEE TO STUDY PASSPORT PROCEDURES OF THE ASSOCIATION OF THE BAR OF THE CITY OF NEW YORK 5–6 (Fifield Workum, chairman, 1958).

15. Section 23, Act of August 18, 1856, 34 Cong., Ch. 127, 11 Stat. 52, 60–61. The original statute enacted in 1856 states that "the Secretary of State shall be authorized to grant and issue passports, . . ." But the version in the Revised Statutes authorized by Congress in 1873 seems to have incorporated a slight change of wording: "The Secretary of State may grant and issue passports, . . ." Rev. Stat. § 4075 (1878). The commissioners appointed to create for reenactment the Revised Statutes were charged only to "revise, simplify, arrange, and consolidate," Act of June 27, 1866, 39 Cong. Ch. 140, 14 Stat. 74, not to make substantive changes. It is unclear, therefore, what was meant by this change, which has been noted by other scholars. See FREEDOM TO TRAVEL, *supra* note 14, at 6–7.

16. Basic Passports, 32 FORTUNE 123 (Oct. 1945).

17. Act of May 30, 1866, 39 Cong. Ch. 102, 14 Stat. 54.

18. See 13 Op. Atty Gen. 89, 92 (Opinion of Atty Gen. Hoar to Sec'y of State Fish, June 12, 1869) ("I do not understand that the granting of passports from your Department is obligatory in any case, but is only permitted where it is not prohibited by law."); 23 Op. Atty Gen. 509, 511 (Opinion of Atty Gen. Knox to Sec'y of State Hay, Aug. 29, 1901) ("I know of no law which gives to the citizen a right to a passport.").

19. Section 10, Act of February 4, 1815, 13 Cong. Ch. 27, 3 Stat. 195, 199–200 ("[N]o citizen or person usually residing within the United States, shall be permitted to cross the frontier into any of the provinces or territory belonging to the enemy, or of which he may be possessed, without a passport first obtained from the Secretary of State, the Secretary of War, or other officer, civil or military, authorized by the President of the United States to grant the same, or from the governor of a state or territory; . . . and whosoever shall voluntarily offend against any of the prohibitions aforesaid, mentioned in this section, shall be considered guilty of a misdemeanor, and be liable to be fined in any sum not exceeding one thousand dollars, and to imprisonment for any term not exceeding three years."). According to Gaillard Hunt, the U.S. Passport Clerk in 1897, "during the civil war persons traveling between points which were under military occupation by the United States Army were given passports signed by the Secretary of State which really partook of the nature of military passes." Hunt, *supra* note 1, at 8 & 21. Examples are reproduced by Hunt at 50–54.

20. Farber, *supra* note 10, at 265.

21. The term refers to "a coherent historical period," the years 1914–1991. ERIC HOBSBAWM, THE AGE OF EXTREMES: A HISTORY OF THE WORLD, 1914–1991 5 (1994); Farber, *supra* note 10, at 265 ("The Czars are dead, but many of their security measures live on. Passports have become obligatory throughout the free world"); Paul Minderhoud, Regulation of Migration: Introduction, in Böcker et al., *supra* note 11, at 8 ("The shift towards stricter immigration controls in Europe accelerated at the outbreak of war in 1914, as marked by the widespread imposition of passport controls during the first year of conflict. By 1919, systematic immigration regulations and alien control measures were the norm, and the 'open world' of the nineteenth century had come to an end.") (citation omitted); Leo Lucassen, The Great War and the Origins of Mi-

gration Control in Western Europe and the United States (1880–1920), in Böcker, et al., *id.*, at 45 ("Whereas laissez faire ruled during the long nineteenth century, for the movement of capital as well as for people, World War I put an end to this free flow of labour."). Lucassen points to a variety of factors beyond war or the rise of the nation-state to explain this change, but emphasizes the development of the welfare state as a motive to control migration.

22. JOHN TORPEY, THE INVENTION OF THE PASSPORT: SURVEILLANCE, CITIZENSHIP AND THE STATE 111–17 (2000).

23. *Id.*

24. Present Passport Restrictions, *supra* note 8, at 12 ("The United States, however, did not impose restrictions until nearly a year and a half later, when, in consequence of several embarrassing cases of forged passports, the development of an effective system of supervision and regulation became imperative."). The United States declared war in April 1917. The Travel Control Act was passed in May 1918. The President issued orders under the act in August 1918.

25. Act of May 22, 1918, 65 Cong. Ch. 81, 40 Stat. 559.

26. Sec. 1(a) of the act required only that the President's commands be "reasonable."

27. *Id.* at § 2.

28. 65 Proclamation, Aug. 8, 1918, 40 Stat. 1829, 1831.

29. Executive Order No. 2932 (Aug. 8, 1918), reprinted in 12 AMER. J. INT'L L. 331–43 (Oct. 1918).

30. *Id.* at §§ 11, 13, 36–38. Although primary authority was delegated to the Secretary of State, which "control officer" the citizen actually met depended on whether entry or departure was via a seaport (in which case, customs officials of the Department of the Treasury), or land border (in which case, representatives of the Bureau of Immigration of the Department of Labor). *Id.* at § 36.

31. Confidential Instructions, August 8, 1918. Control of Foreign Travel. Issued for the Guidance of Officials Connected with the Administration of the Act of May 22, 1918. (Public No. 154) 6 (1918).

32. *Supra* note 29, at § 36. Upon making that determination, the Control Officer was obliged to telegraph a full report (including a transcript of relevant testimony or information) to the Secretary of State within two days. *Id.*

33. 13 Op. Att'y Gen. 89, 91 (Opinion of Att'y Gen. Hoar to Sec'y of State Fish, June 12, 1869).

34. 23 Op. Att'y Gen. 509, 511 (Opinion of Att'y Gen. Knox to Sec'y of State Hay, Aug. 29, 1901).

35. Riesman, *supra* note 10, at 817.

36. Kathleen McLaughlin, Woman's Place Also in the Office, Finds Chief of the Nation's Passport Division, N.Y. TIMES, Dec. 24, 1939, at 22.

37. *Id.*

38. Present Passport Restrictions, *supra* note 8, at 13.

39. Ezra Pound, The Passport Nuisance, 125 THE NATION 600, 601 (Nov. 30, 1927). Although an influential modernist poet, Pound's support for Italian fascism (not to mention his anti-Semitism) could easily have led an American official in Mrs. Shipley's office to recommend denying him a passport for travel "not in the interests of the United States." At least, had Pound sought one. It was only on the grounds of a suspicious insanity plea that he later avoided conviction for treason. Upon his release

in 1958 he returned to Italy, where he died. Had Mrs. Shipley then been in charge of a Passport Office not yet shorn of its powers under *Kent v. Dulles*, one wonders whether he would have received a passport.

40. Present Passport Restrictions, *supra* note 8, at 13.

41. Joint Congressional Resolution of Mar. 3, 1921, 66 Cong. Ch. 136, 41 Stat. 1359. A subsequent statute, the Act of November 10, 1919, Ch. 104, 41 Stat. 353, contained many provisions similar to the Travel Control Act of 1918 except that its sunset provision was linked to a date certain rather than to the cessation of war. *See* § 5, 41 Stat. 354 (1919) ("[T]his Act . . . shall continue in force and effect until and including the 4th day of March, 1921.").

42. 32 Op. Att'y Gen. 493, 495 (Mar. 30, 1921) ("it is clear that . . . [the act] has been for the present rendered wholly inoperative by the Joint Resolution."). The Attorney General concluded the same for the Act of November 10, 1919. *Id*. at 496 ("[I]t has . . . become defunct by expiration of its period of limitation.").

43. Jaffe, *supra* note 2, at 17.

44. Sec. 1 & 4, Act of July 3, 1926, 69 Cong. Ch. 772, 44 Stat. 887.

45. *Id.*, § 2.

46. Pound, *supra* note 39, at 601.

47. Good News for Summer Travelers, 101 LITERARY DIGEST 12 (June 1, 1929) (reporting positions of these mastheads).

48. McLaughlin, *supra* note 36, at 22.

49. Letter to J. H. Mackey, Bureau of the Budget, from Ira F. Hoyt, July 1, 1931; File 111.28 New York/71; CDF 1930–39; RG 59; NACP. Mr. Hoyt, the Passport Agent in New York, noted that his agency "is used by persons from all over the United States who come to New York to sail, the port from which about 95% of all departures occur." *Id.*

50. McLaughlin, *supra* note 36, at 22.

51. Egidio Reale, The Passport Question, 9 FOREIGN AFF. 506 (1931). The Nansen passport, created largely for Russians stripped of their citizenship by the Soviet regime, was the clearest example of this approach. The Nansen passport facilitated travel and entry into another state without creating a right to return to one's country of origin (ordinarily the passport-issuing country). *Id*. at 507.

52. Riesman, *supra* note 10, at 819–20 (footnotes omitted).

53. E.O. 7856, 3 FED. REG. 799 (Mar. 31, 1938).

54. *Id.*, §§ 2, 14, 37.

55. *Id.*, §§ 32, 33–35, 56, 58–59, 72.

56. *Id.*, § 124.

57. Departmental Order No. 749, Order by the Secretary of State Regarding Passports and Applications for Passports (Mar. 31, 1938). File 111.28/260; CDF 1930–39; RG 59; NACP.

58. *Id.*, Section VII.16.

59. *Id.*, Section VII.25.

60. See Regulations Under Section 9 of the Joint Resolution of Congress Approved May 1, 1937 (Sept. 5, 1939), 4 FED. REG. 3838–39 (1939). These regulations were promulgated by Secretary of State Hull under the authority provided by President Roosevelt's proclamation of the same day concerning export controls on arms and ammunition (4 FED. REG. 3819 (1939)) and a Joint Resolution of Congress approved May 1, 1937 (50

Stat. 121–28 (1937)). The new regulations forbade travel on French, German, Polish, British, Indian, Australian, and New Zealand vessels "on or over the north Atlantic Ocean, east of 30 degrees west and north of 30 degrees north or on or over other waters adjacent to Europe or over the continent of Europe or adjacent islands."

61. 4 FED. REG. 3809 (1939).

62. Regulations Concerning the Validation and Issuance of Passports for Use in European Countries, Departmental Order No. 811 (Sept. 4, 1939), 4 FED. REG. 3892 (1939).

63. Validation for business travel required a letter from one's firm. Travel "for any purpose other than commercial business must satisfy the Department of State that it is imperative that he go, and he must submit satisfactory documentary evidence substantiating his statement concerning the imperativeness of his proposed trip." 4 FED. REG. 3892 (1939). See chapter 5 for the implementation by Mrs. Shipley and others.

64. *Id.* ("Women and children will not be included in passports issued to their husbands or fathers unless the urgent and imperative necessity of accompanying them is conclusively established.").

65. Riesman, *supra* note 10, at 831–832 (footnotes omitted). Riesman reports that restrictions on brides subsequently eased, in a manner of speaking. Brides were allowed to travel "when they have been engaged for a certain length of time, on condition that they will renounce American citizenship on becoming married." *Id.* at 831, n.249.

66. See 22 U.S.C. § 220 (1939) (quoted in the regulation as providing for a fine up to $2000 and five years imprisonment).

67. 4 FED. REG. 3892 (1939).

68. Instruction to the American Consular Officer in Charge, Mexico, from Ruth Shipley, Oct. 11, 1939; File 138 Emergency Program/ 223; CDF 1930–39; RG 59; NACP.

69. Sec. 20, Joint Resolution of Nov. 4, 1939, 76th Cong., Ch. 2, 54 Stat. 4. The full title was "Joint Resolution to preserve the neutrality and the peace of the United States and to secure the safety of its citizens and their interests."

70. NORMAN DAVIES, EUROPE: A HISTORY 910 (1996).

71. Sec. 2(a), Joint Resolution of Nov. 4, 1939, *supra* note 69. Violation of this subsection or relevant regulations was punishable by up to a $50,000 fine and five years imprisonment. *Id.*, § 2(b).

72. Sec. 3(a), Joint Resolution, *supra* note 69. Violation of this subsection by an American vessel was punishable by a similar $50,000 fine/five-year imprisonment. Citizen-passengers were subject to a $10,000/two-year penalty. *Id.*, at § 3(b).

73. Sec. 5(a), Joint Resolution, *supra* note 69.

74. Memorandum—Ruth B. Shipley: Background and Performance, enclosed in Memorandum to the President from Secretary of State John Foster Dulles, Dec. 11, 1953; File 110.4 PD/12-953; CDF 1950–54; RG 59; NACP.

75. *Id.*

76. Act of Oct. 14, 1940, 76 Cong., Ch. 876, 54 Stat. 1137.

77. Naturalized citizens faced a five-year ban on their permanent residence abroad, which was to be monitored by diplomatic and consular officials of the State Department. Violation of the restriction could lead to proceedings to revoke the person's certificate of naturalization and set aside court orders admitting the person to citizenship. Sec. 338(c), Act of Oct. 14, 1940, 76 Cong., Ch. 876, 54 Stat. 1137. Nationals of the United States (which the act defined as both U.S. citizens and those owing permanent

allegiance to the United States) faced a rebuttable presumption of self-expatriation if they remained for more than six months in a country in which they or their parents had once been nationals. *Id.*, § 402. American nationality (whether acquired by birth or naturalization) could also be lost by (*a*) residing for two years in a country of which one was formerly a national or in which nationality would be conferred by such residency by operation of law; (*b*) continuous residence of at least three years in one's country of birth or of which one was formerly a national; or (*c*) continuous residence of at least five years in any foreign state. *Id.*, § 404(a)–(c).

78. Rule on Naturalized Citizens, N.Y. TIMES, Jan. 14, 1952, at 6 ("Mrs. Ruth B. Shipley, head of the Passport Division of the State Department, explained tonight that under the Nationals Act of 1940 naturalized Americans must limit visits to their native lands to three years, and stays in other countries to five years. Over-staying such stays cancels the person's citizenship, and the State Department, in administering this law, has no discretion in the matter."). A "precise record" of foreign residence was required of naturalized citizens seeking passports. Ruth B. Shipley, Passport Office Rolls Up A Record, N.Y. TIMES, June 20, 1954, at X17 ("[I]n the case of naturalized citizens, . . . prolonged foreign residency may, in many cases, endanger citizenship itself.").

79. Act of May 22, 1918, 65 Cong., Ch. 81, 40 Stat. 559.

80. Section 1, Act of June 21, 1941, 77 Cong. Ch. 210, 55 Stat. 252. The penalties for willful violation were reduced from a $10,000 maximum fine or twenty years imprisonment, or both, in the 1918 act, to a $5,000 maximum fine and up to five years imprisonment, or both. *Id.* at § 2. The reduction does not appear to have been a reflection on the gravity of the offense. As Mrs. Shipley noted in a letter to be read out in the House as part of the Department's lobbying for the amendment, "It has not been deemed desirable to retain the severe penalities prescribed by the act of May 22, 1918, since the experience has shown that severe penalties too frequently influence both courts and juries in favor of defendants and result in the miscarriage of justice." 87 CONG. REC. 5048 (June 11, 1941). As with the 1918 act, restrictions on aliens were not so carefully policed by Congress. The President could restrict their departure and entry "whenever there exists a state of war between, or among, two or more states, and the President shall find that the interests of the United States require" such restrictions.

81. Proclamation: Control of persons entering and leaving the United States (No. 2523), 6 FED. REG. 5821 (Nov. 18, 1941).

82. *Id.*

83. Departmental Order (No. 1003), 6 FED. REG. 6069 (Nov. 28, 1941) (codified at 22 C.F.R. pt. 58 (1941 Supp.)). Regulations of aliens leaving or entering the United States were promulgated first, on November 22, 1941, with the concurrence of Attorney General Francis Biddle. 6 FED. REG. 5927, 5927–34 (Nov. 22, 1941) (codified at 22 C.F.R. pt. 58 (1941 Supp.)).

84. Departmental Order (No. 1003), *supra* note 83, at § 58.1.

85. *Id.* (codified at 22 C.F.R. §§ 58.3 & 58.6 (1941 Supp.)); see also § 2(g), Joint Resolution of November 4, 1939 (The Neutrality Act), 76 Cong., Ch. 2, 54 Stat. 4.

86. Departmental Order (No. 1003), *supra* note 83, at § 58.8.

87. *Id.*, at § 58.2.

88. Exec. Order 8820, 6 FED. REG. 3421 (July 15, 1941) (codified at 22 C.F.R. § 121.2(c) (1941 Supp.)).

89. Departmental Order (No. 1003), *supra* note 83, at § 58.7.

90. *Id.*, at § 58.10.

91. Memorandum—Ruth B. Shipley: Background and Performance, *supra* note 74.

92. *Id.*

93. Memorandum to Assistant Secretary of State G. Howland Shaw from Ruth Shipley, Jan. 14, 1943; File 111.28/279; CDF 1940–44; RG 59; NACP. Mrs. Shipley arranged for her deputy, John Scanlan, to travel to Mexico to "temper any possible feeling that the regulations will tend to discriminate against persons intending to cross the Mexican border and favor those intending to cross the Canadian border," which was not so regulated. *Id.*

94. Departmental Order No. 1207, Card of Identification for use by a Person who claims to be a Citizen of the United States when Travelling Between Points in Continental United States and Points in Mexico and Conditions Under Which Issued (Oct. 23, 1943); File 111.017/700; CDF 1940–44; RG 59; NACP.

95. George Orwell, As I Please 24, TRIBUNE, May 12, 1944, reprinted in GEORGE ORWELL, ESSAYS 598 (John Carey, ed. 2002).

96. Andre Visson, Ruth Shipley—The State Department's Watchdog, 59 READER'S DIGEST 73 (Oct. 1951) (condensed and reprinted from INDEPENDENT WOMAN (Aug. 1951)).

97. Passports No Longer Valid for Bulgaria or Hungary, 22 U.S. DEP'T OF STATE BULL. 399 (Mar. 13, 1950). Permission to travel to Hungary was taken away on December 20, 1949, on those grounds. *Id.* On May 1, 1951, permission was restored but without any official stated reason. Removing Prohibition Against Travel in Hungary, 24 U.S. DEP'T OF STATE BULL. 770 (May 14, 1951).

98. Briehl v. Dulles, 2248 F.2d 561, 572 (D.C. Cir. 1957) (en banc), *rev'd on other grounds sub nom.* Kent v. Dulles, 357 U.S. 116 (1958).

99. Internal Security Act of 1950, Pub. L. No. 81-831, 64 Stat. 987. The Emergency Detention Act of 1950, 64 Stat. 1019, authorized (for the duration of a presidentially proclaimed "internal security emergency") the preventive detention on grounds of future dangerousness of any person "as to whom there is a reasonable ground to believe that such person probably will engage in, or probably will conspire with others to engage in, acts of espionage or sabotage." *Id.*, § 104(a). The emergency detention envisioned by that act was circumscribed by numerous limitations, including a probable-cause warrant requirement, a multilevel administrative review process, and, ultimately, access via habeas to an Article III court. Unlike its sister act, travel restriction short of complete detention was not a primary focus of the act. However, if on the basis of additional information submitted by the detainee, the Attorney General concluded that such a reasonable ground of belief no longer existed, then the Attorney General could order the detainee's release or "apply to such detainee such lesser restrictions in movement and activity as the Attorney General shall determine will serve the purposes of this title." *Id.*, § 104(e).

The Emergency Detention Act was revoked by the Non-Detention Act, Pub. L. 92–128, 85 Stat. 347 (Sept. 25, 1971), codified at 18 U.S.C. § 4001(a) (2009).

100. Sec. 2(1), Subversive Activities Control Act of 1950, 64 Stat. 987, 993 (Sept. 23, 1950), codified at 50 U.S.C. § 285 (1950).

101. *Id.*, § 2(2) & (10).

102. *Id.*, § 7.

103. *Id.*, § 6. The statute required knowledge of the registration or final order to register.

104. *Id.*, § 15(c).

105. *Id.*, § 2(8).

106. *Id.*, § 2(9).

107. Act of June 27, 1952 (the McCarran Act), § 215(a), 66 Stat. 190, codified at 8 U.S.C. § 1185 (emphasis added).

108. *Id.*

109. "Except as otherwise provided by the President and subject to such limitations and exceptions as the President may authorize and prescribe, it shall be unlawful for any citizen of the United States to depart from or enter, or attempt to depart from or enter, the United States unless he bears a valid passport." Act of Oct. 7, 1978, Pub. L. 95–426, § 707(b), 92 Stat. 992, 993, codified at 8 U.S.C. § 1185(b). Congress also struck out all penalties for violating the control. *Id.* at § 707(d).

110. Farber, *supra* note 10, at 263.

111. Aptheker v. Sec'y of State, 378 U.S. 500, 507 (1964) ("[t]he denial of a passport . . . is a severe restriction upon, and in effect a prohibition against, world-wide foreign travel.").

Chapter 5

1. Kathleen McLaughlin, Woman's Place Also in the Office, Finds Chief of the Nation's Passport Division, N.Y. TIMES, Dec. 24, 1939, at 22; Passport Chief to End Career, N.Y. TIMES, Feb. 25, 1955, at 15; Joseph A. Wytrwal, Lincoln's Friend: Captain A. Bielaski, 14 POLISH AMERICAN STUDIES 65 (1957); Letter from Frank Brooks Bielaski to Oscar Bielaski, Esq., dated May 5, 1958 (on file with the author). The Bielaski family had government service in its blood. Ruth's older brother, Alexander Bruce Bielaski, led the Federal Bureau of Investigation from 1912 to 1919. Bruce Bielaski, Justice Aide, Dies, N.Y. TIMES, Feb. 20, 1964, at 29. A younger brother, Frank Brooks Bielaski, was an aide to the OSS, the agency that became the CIA. Frank Bielaski, O.S.S. Aide, Dead, N.Y. TIMES, Apr. 6, 1961. An uncle, Oscar Bielaski, was a major league baseball player. Henry L. Gaidis, Lithuanian FBI Connection, BRIDGES: LITHUANIAN AMERICAN NEWS JOURNAL 6 (Nov. 2009); see also http://polishsportshof.com/inductees/baseball/oscar-bielaski/. I am grateful to Ms. Nancy Bielaski for pointing me to several of these sources.

2. McLaughlin, *supra* note 1, at 22. Carson C. Hathaway, Woman to Head Passport Bureau, N.Y. TIMES, May 20, 1928, at 111.

3. Passport Chief to End Career, *supra* note 1. The *Times* reported that "[t]he custom then required that women quit work when they were married."

4. Citation to Accompany the Award of the Medal for Merit to Mrs. Ruth Bielaski Shipley, for Exceptionally Meritorious Conduct in the Performance of Outstanding Services to the United States During the War Emergency, attached to Memorandum to the President from John Foster Dulles, dated Dec. 11, 1953; File 110.4-PD/12-953 CS/MC; CDF 1950–54; RG 59; NACP.

5. Hathaway, *supra* note 2. It may be that Mrs. Shipley focused on a State Department career as a result of her husband's death in 1919, the same year she became Adee's special assistant. Andre Visson, Ruth Shipley—The State Department's Watchdog,

59 READER'S DIGEST 73, 74 (Oct. 1951) (condensed and reprinted from INDEPENDENT WOMAN (Aug. 1951)).

6. Woman Passport Chief, N.Y. TIMES, Apr. 19, 1928, at p. 27.

7. Mildred Adams, The Women Who Man Our Ship of State, N.Y. TIMES, Oct. 13, 1929, at SM5. The appointment was "based upon merit and experience." GRAHAM H. STUART, THE DEPARTMENT OF STATE: A HISTORY OF ITS ORGANIZATION, PROCEDURE, AND PERSONNEL 288 (1949).

8. Stuart, *supra* note 7, at 288.

9. Ruth B. Shipley and John Foster Dulles, by Herbert J. Meyle, 59-SO-288, # 7331, NARA.

10. Adams, *supra* note 7.

11. Hathaway, *supra* note 2; Adams, *supra* note 7.

12. *Id.* Even gray-eyed Athena would have raised an eyebrow at the muse who inspired this Homeric description. As it turned out, she had more in common with white-armed Hera, though at times she appeared more powerful than both goddesses combined.

13. Letter from Congressman D. Lane Powers to Secretary of State Cordell Hull, Sept. 7, 1933; File 112/1166; CDF 1930–39; RG 59; NACP. Secretary Hull thanked the Congressman without correcting his error identifying Mrs. Shipley. Copy of Letter from Secretary of State Cordell Hull to Congressman D. Lane Powers, Sept. 12, 1933; File 112/1166; CDF 1930–39; RG 59; NACP. The mistake was common. See, e.g., Stanley I. Stuber, Can Christians Obtain Passports? 49 CHRISTIAN CENTURY 1102 (1932) (referring to the Chief of the passport division, "Mr. R.B. Shipley").

14. Mrs. Shipley's professional achievements were not confined to the Passport Division. In early 1930, Acting Secretary of State Cotton named her as a delegate to the International Conference for the Codification of International Law held at The Hague that spring. Copy of Letter from Acting Secretary of State Cotton to R. B. Shipley, Feb. 27, 1930; File 504.418 A 2/173; CDF 1930–39; RG 59; NACP. Mrs. Shipley was the only female delegate from the United States. Final Act, Conference for the Codification of International Law Held at The Hague in March–April, 1930, 24 AMER. J. INT'L L. No. 3, Supplement: Official Documents (Jul. 1930), p. 170. Although her work to resolve conflicts in nationality laws did not result in substantial reform or codification (like much of the rest of the products of the conference), her efforts were hailed within the Department and in academic circles. Secretary of State Henry L. Stimson singled out her work at the conference in a letter of appreciation he sent her on his last full day in office. Copy of letter from Secretary of State Stimson to R. B. Shipley, Mar. 3, 1933; File 111.28/232A; CDF 1930–39; RG 59; NACP. The distinguished American lawyer and scholar James Brown Scott singled Mrs. Shipley out for praise in an editorial comment on the work on nationality done at the conference. James Brown Scott, Editorial Comment, 24 AMER. J. INT'L L. 556, 557 (Jul. 1930).

In spring 1953, Mrs. Shipley was designated to serve as "Chairman [*sic*] of the Department of State Loyalty Security Appeals Board." Letter to Mrs. Shipley from Acting Secretary Walter B. Smith, May 13, 1953; File 110.4-LSB/5-1353; CDF 1950–54; RG 59; NACP. The Board was the penultimate step (before the Secretary himself) to termination of a State Department employee found to constitute a security risk.

15. Present Passport Restrictions, 1 COMMERCE MONTHLY 12 (Nov. 19, 1919).

16. McLaughlin, *supra* note 1.

17. French Strother, Fighting Germany's Spies: The Inside Story of the Passport Frauds and the First Glimpse of Werner Horn, 35 WORLD'S WORK 513, 514 (1919).

18. Letter from Acting Secretary of State Joseph C. Grew to F. J. Bailey, Chairman of the Personnel Classification Board, Aug. 12, 1924; File 112/720a; CDF 1910–29; RG 59; NACP.

19. *Id.*

20. Letter from Acting Secretary of State Joseph C. Grew to F. J. Bailey, *supra* note 18.

21. Note from "ECW" stating "This appeal was granted" attached to letter from Acting Secretary of State Joseph C. Grew to F. J. Bailey, *supra* note 18.

22. Hathaway, *supra* note 2.

23. Memorandum from R. B. Shipley to the Solicitor's Office, Department of State, Aug. 16, 1930; File 111.28/214; CDF 1930–39; RG 59; NACP.

24. In the Field of Travel, N.Y. TIMES, Feb. 1, 1948, at X15.

25. Enclosure to copy of letter from Division of Research and Publication Assistant Chief E. Wilder Spaulding to Fletcher Cooper, Dec. 11, 1933; File 112/1171½; CDF 1930–39; RG 59; NACP. Miss Hanna, who remained Chief of the Office of Coordination and Review, earned $600 less than Mrs. Shipley's $5,600 base salary. This meant that by the end of 1933, Mrs. Shipley was the highest paid woman in the State Department.

26. Memorandum by R. B. Shipley, Dec. 1, 1933; File 111.28/233½; CDF 1930–39; RG 59; NACP.

27. *Id.* This was accomplished, Mrs. Shipley complained, despite a 12 percent reduction in her staff from an average personnel of 78.8 in fiscal year 1932 to 66 in fiscal year 1933. For inflation adjustment, see http://www.dollartimes.com/calculators/inflation.htm.

28. Copy of memorandum from R. B. Shipley to Assistant Secretary of State Wilber J. Carr, Jan. 22, 1932; File 111.28 Los Angeles/5; CDF 1930–39; RG 59; NACP. In locations lacking a passport agency, applications could be executed by clerks of federal or state courts that had naturalization authority. Letter to James A. Davis from R. B. Shipley, Sept. 28, 1937; File 111.28/255; CDF 1930–39; RG 59; NACP.

29. Copy of memorandum from R. B. Shipley to Assistant Secretary of State Wilber J. Carr, Jan. 22, 1932; File 111.28 Los Angeles/5; CDF 1930–39; RG 59; NACP; *see also* Attachment to internal memorandum to W. J. Carr from R. B. Shipley, Feb. 23, 1937; File 111.28 Los Angeles/37; CDF 1930–39; RG 59; NACP.

30. Consider a battle she won against an assistant secretary at the Labor Department. The overmatched assistant secretary used concern about passport fraud as an excuse to write to Secretary of State Henry Stimson requesting that passport agents be obliged to seek certificates of naturalization (for a fee payable to the Labor Department) in connection with passport applications, rather than rely on clerks of court (who often doubled as passport agents and therefore were under the influence of Mrs. Shipley) who could check court records regarding naturalization themselves. Letter from Assistant Secretary of Labor Robe Carl White to Secretary of State Henry L. Stimson, Nov. 9, 1931; File 111.28/221; CDF 1930–39; RG 59; NACP. Mrs. Shipley saw "no possibility of fraud" and deftly parried the bureaucratic move. "I should like not to tie our hands in this matter and yet have no wish to antagonize Labor," she wrote to her lieutenant, John Scanlan. She proposed answering Labor "that passport agents will

be requested to communicate with the commissioners of naturalization in the cities where they are stationed when they wish information contained in the local records regarding naturalization. We can then continue as we have done with the clerks of courts who are acting as our agents in passport matters and who are, as well, the custodian of court records regarding naturalization." Memorandum to John Scanlan from R. B. Shipley, Dec. 13, 1931, attached to Letter from Assistant Secretary of Labor Robe Carl White to Secretary of State Henry L. Stimson, Nov. 9, 1931; File 111.28/221; CDF 1930–39; RG 59; NACP.

31. Internal note exchange between R. B. Shipley and Herbert C. Hengstler, Aug. 11, 1931, attached to letter from R. A. Proctor, Passport Agent, Chicago, to R. B. Shipley, Aug. 6, 1931; File 111.28 Chicago/29; CDF 1930–39; RG 59; NACP. Mr. Proctor wrote in response to a letter from Mrs. Shipley earlier that month to describe the pictures of foreign cruise ships that had hung in the reception room at the Chicago Passport Agency and inform her that they had been taken down.

32. *See, e.g.,* Letter to Secretary of State Cordell Hull from D. P. Aub, Washington, D.C. District Manager, American Express Co., Aug. 8, 1934; File 111.28/235; CDF 1930–39; RG 59; NACP (commending Mrs. Shipley and her office and, no doubt, hoping to stay in her good graces). *See also* Memorandum from the Assistant Secretary, Dec. 8, 1937; File 113/777; CDF 1930–39; RG 59; NACP (reporting testimony of Assistant Secretary George Messersmith before a subcommittee of the House Appropriations Committee, praising Mrs. Shipley for her work preparing new codes concerning passport and citizenship laws).

33. Letter to Captain George T. Summerlin, Chief of Protocol, U.S. Department of State, from Ruth B. Shipley, Dec. 10, 1937; File 811.0011 Roosevelt Family/170; CDF 1930–39; RG 59; NACP. Mrs. Roosevelt was unable to attend. Letter to Captain George T. Summerlin from Mrs. J. M. Helm, Secretary to Mrs. Roosevelt, Dec. 31, 1937; File 811.001 Roosevelt Family/172 H/HC; CDF 1930–39; RG 59; NACP.

34. Bielaski is Held, Companion Freed, N.Y. TIMES, June 27, 1922, at 1.

35. Bielaski Company Loses, N.Y. TIMES, July 18, 1922, at 7.

36. Bielaski is Held, Companion Freed; *supra* note 34; A. Bruce Bielaski Kidnapped in Mexico and Held for $10,000, N.Y. TIMES, June 26, 1922, at 1.

37. Bielaski Lays Seizure to Amateur Bandits, N.Y. TIMES, June 30, 1922, at 3.

38. Obregon to Deport a Group of Radicals; Acts to Clear the Region Where Bielaski Was Captured of Foreign Reds, N.Y. TIMES, June 28, 1922, at 22. President Obregon was reported to have traveled to Cuernavaca to personally oversee the investigation.

39. Bielaski Escapes, Pays No Ransom; Flees Barefoot, Falls Over Cliff, Swims River, Safe in Mexico City, N.Y. TIMES, June 29, 1922, at 1.

40. Bielaski's Arrest Reported Ordered, N.Y. TIMES, July 6, 1922 at 1. As arrests go, this one was fairly comfortable; Mr. and Mrs. Bielaski lived in a local hotel or as guests of the American chargé d'affaires and it may be that Mexican legal procedures were misreported by the American press. Bielaski to See It Out, N.Y. TIMES, July 29, 1922, at 12; Bielaski is Cleared by Mexican Court, N.Y. TIMES, Aug. 13, 1922, at 21. The chauffeur, on the other hand, remained lodged in a Mexican provincial jail. Bielaski Is Under Guard, N.Y. TIMES, Aug. 3, 1922, at 20. Bielaski himself later made light of the situation and disputed some newspaper accounts of his detention. Bielaski Explains Charges, N.Y. TIMES, Aug. 22, 1922, at 23.

41. Obregon in Morelos, Sifts Bielaski Case, N.Y. TIMES, July 15, 1922, at 3.
42. Intervenes for Bielaski, N.Y. TIMES, Aug. 12, 1922, at 6.
43. Bielaski is Cleared by Mexican Court, *supra* note 40.
44. Bielaski Reaches Texas, N.Y. TIMES, Aug. 20, 1922, at 2.
45. There seems to have been some friendship between Ruth Shipley's mentor, Alvey Adee, and her brother. Years earlier, Adee had given Bielaski "a small, pearl-handled revolver . . . insisting that Bielaski carry it" for safety's sake given his livelihood. Bielaski a Fighter, but Quiet about It, N.Y. TIMES, June 30, 1922, at 3.
46. It also may have triggered other kidnappings. While Bielaski was still in captivity, a rebel Mexican General Gorozave seized an oil company and forty Americans near Tampico. Secretary of State Charles Evans Hughes called the seizure an "outrage" and demanded "vigorous" measures in a telegram to the American vice consul at Tampico. 40 Americans held by Tampico Rebels; Bielaski not Freed, N.Y. TIMES, June 28, 1922, at 1.
47. Briehl v. Dulles, 2248 F.2d 561, 572 (D.C. Cir. 1957) (en banc), *rev'd on other grounds sub nom.* Kent v. Dulles, 357 U.S. 116 (1958). Speculation filled the American and Mexican press about both the Bielaski affair and the Tampico "outrage," sometimes labeling them hoaxes and speculating about intrigues and special interests seeking to disrupt Mexican-American relations. Mexican Press Tries to Discredit Bielaski, N.Y. TIMES, July 1, 1922, at 3; Drop Bielaski Accusation, N.Y. TIMES, July 2, 1922, at 10.
48. Despatch No. 1569 from American Consul General C. F. Deichman to the Secretary of State, Aug. 9, 1929; File 032 Austin, C.J./1; CDF 1910–29; RG 59; NACP.
49. Id.
50. Indeed, no rules were promulgated for the brief 1926 Passport Act until 1938. See Exec. Order 7856, 3 FED. REG. 681 (Apr. 2, 1938). The 1926 Act, 44 Stat. 887, repealed the preceding statute, § 4075 of the Revised Statutes, leaving the United States without any rules to implement the new statute for twelve years.
51. File copy of dispatch from R. B. Shipley to the American Consul General, Valparaiso, Chile, Sept. 13, 1929; File 032 Austin, C.J./4; CDF 1910–29; RG 59; NACP. A handwritten note from "R.S." dated September 11 and appended to the file copy of this dispatch states: "I think this is as far as we should go in the matter and it should safeguard any unsuspecting victims."
52. Letter from Ira F. Hoyt, Passport Agent, New York City, to R. B. Shipley, Sept. 16, 1929; File 032 Austin, C.J./8; CDF 1910–29; RG 59; NACP.
53. File Copy of Letter to R. C. Bannerman, Chief Special Agent, Department of State, New York City, from R. B. Shipley, Sept. 11, 1929; File 032 Austin, C.J./2; CDF 1910–29; RG 59; NACP. File Copy of Letter to Ira Hoyt, Passport Agent, New York City, from R. B. Shipley, Sept. 11, 1929; File 032 Austin, C.J./3; CDF 1910–29; RG 59; NACP.
54. Letter to R. C. Bannerman, Chief Special Agent, Department of State, New York City, from R. Burr, Special Agent in Charge, Sept. 18, 1929; File 032 Austin, C.J./6; CDF 1910–29; RG 59; NACP. This letter reported a reply from Austin himself, which gave assurances that "no tour with a ballet company or any other group will take place for the time being" due to unspecified unsatisfactory conditions in Latin America, and that any future venture would only be considered if producers in those countries were willing to "furnish a bond and deposit the money" in an American bank. In other words, exactly what the Consul General had suggested.

55. Letter to Secretary of State Hull from Judge Martin DeVries, July 14, 1938; File 111.28 Los Angeles/39; CDF 1930–39; RG 59; NACP.

56. Copy of Letter to Judge DeVries from R. B. Shipley, July 22, 1938; File 111.28 Los Angeles/40; CDF 1930–39; RG 59: NACP. This was not entirely true. Mrs. Shipley had known for years that the Los Angeles office drew "many complaints from our best people . . . [The deputy clerk] does not have the time to be as courteous as he would like to be." Letter to R. B. Shipley from W. A. Newcome, Passport Agent, San Francisco, Feb. 18, 1931; File 111.28 Los Angeles/24; CDF 1930–39; RG 59; NACP. In another letter to Mrs. Shipley, Newcome confessed that "Los Angeles has always had exceedingly unsatisfactory facilities for making applications for passports. I refer to the inadequate office space and inadequate staff to properly handle applications in a business-like, courteous and efficient manner. From the complaints which have reached me from transportation people and applicants, the situation in this regard has been most unsatisfactory. Such people would relish being served by trained and courteous passport workers and in offices adapted to their needs." Letter to R. B. Shipley from W. A. Newcome, Feb. 16, 1931; File 111.28 Los Angeles/23; CDF 1930–39; RG 59; NACP.

57. Copy of letter to R. S. Zimmerman, Clerk, U.S. District Court, Los Angeles, from R. B. Shipley, July 22, 1938; File 111.28 Los Angeles/41; CDF 1930–1939; RG 59; NACP.

58. Letter to Secretary of State Stimson from S. Stanwood Menken, July 23, 1930; File 111.28 New York/63; CDF 1930–39; RG 59; NACP.

59. Letter to S. Stanwood Menken from R. B. Shipley, August 2, 1930; File 111.28 New York/63; CDF 1930–39; RG 59; NACP.

60. *Id.*

61. Letter to J. H. Mackey, Bureau of the Budget, from Ira F. Hoyt, July 1, 1931; File 111.28 New York/71; CDF 1930–39; RG 59; NACP.

62. That is not to say that these regulations could not be put to such purpose, as demonstrated by the conviction of Earl Browder, head of the Communist Party of the United States (CPUSA) from 1934 to 1945 and, by some scholarly accounts, a spymaster without equal for the Soviet Union. James G. Ryan, Socialist Triumph as a Family Value: Earl Browder and Soviet Espionage, 1 AMERICAN COMMUNIST HISTORY 125, 126 (2002). Browder had obtained passports in the past under various aliases but a charge of fraudulent procurement was time-barred. Browder was therefore tried and convicted of using the fraudulently obtained passport. Browder unsuccessfully challenged the statutory interpretation of "use" since his conviction was for using his passport to prove his citizenship upon reentry to the United States, a use that was permitted but not required under the passport law at that time and therefore not the kind of use the statute was intended to reach. Browder v. United States, 312 U.S. 335 (1941). This was seen by some as the equivalent of convicting Al Capone for tax evasion. Purge by Passport, 150 THE NATION 117 (Feb. 3, 1940).

63. Memorandum to File by R. B. Shipley, July 13, 1936; File 111.28/247; CDF 1930–39; RG 59; NACP.

64. See U.S. v. Schwimmer, 279 U.S. 644 (1929); U.S. v. Macintosh, 283 U.S. 605 (1931); U.S. v. Bland, 283 U.S. 636 (1931). The interpretation upheld in these cases was overturned in Girouard v. U.S., 328 U.S. 61 (1946).

65. Stuber, *supra* note 13.

66. *Id.* at 1102. It may be that Mrs. Shipley was not going out on much of a limb in this case. According to this periodical, her decision was defended by Assistant Secretary of State Wilbur Carr against an attack by H. Ralph Burton, a rising star in official Washington. Carr is reported to have responded to Burton by noting that the oath for a passport is not fixed by law, as was the case for the oath required for naturalization. *Id.*

67. *Id.* at 1101.

68. As in World War I, American passports were subject to fraud. *See, e.g.*, Herbert Solow, Stalin's American Passport Mill, 47 AMER. MERCURY 302, 303 (July 1939) ("In spy lingo passports are 'boots,' and American boots are especially valuable. The fact that we have a polyglot population makes it possible for spies of almost any nationality to pass as Americans throughout the world without exciting suspicion. The United States, with mild competition from Canada, is therefore bootmaker to international spydom.").

69. Memorandum to J. P. Moffat and J. J. Scanlan from G. S. Messersmith, Aug. 28, 1939; File 138 Emergency Program/9; CDF 1930–39; RG 59; NACP. Messersmith warned in particular of "many thousands of persons in Europe, particularly in Poland and in the states of Southeastern Europe, who have a tenuous claim to American citizenship. . . . It is, I believe, not going too far to say that the great majority of those who will be applying for passports are persons who have not been carrying out any of the responsibilities of citizenship in this country, have had no intention of doing so and who would only be endeavoring to come to this country for purely selfish reasons." *Id.* Expecting that the "presumption of expatriation" would ultimately be raised against these desperate people, Messersmith expressed his view that the United States "would not be particularly concerned in making available transportation facilities for them." *Id.*

70. Memorandum to J. P. Moffat and J. J. Scanlan from G. S. Messersmith, Aug. 28, 1939; File 138 Emergency Program/9; CDF 1930–39; RG 59; NACP.

71. Memorandum—Ruth B. Shipley: Background and Performance, enclosed in Memorandum to the President from Secretary of State John Foster Dulles, Dec. 11, 1953; File 110.4 PD/12-953; CDF 1950–54; RG 59; NACP.

72. McLaughlin, *supra* note 1.

73. *Id.*

74. Memorandum to American Diplomatic and Consular Officers in Europe from Assistant Secretary of State G. S. Messersmith, Oct. 6, 1939; File 138/4085 A; CDF 1930–39; RG 59; NACP. Memorandum to American Diplomatic and Consular Officers except in Europe from Assistant Secretary of State G. S. Messersmith, Nov. 30, 1939; File 120.3/523B; CDF 1930–39; RG 59; NACP.

75. In a telegram reply to inquiries from the U.S. Embassy in Sweden (which appears to have been signed by Secretary Hull and initialed by Ruth Shipley), the American Consul in Stockholm was told, "Diplomatic and special passports must be limited and may be validated for travel in European countries where reasonably required for official purposes. They should, however, conform in this latter respect to general practice with respect other passports." Telegram from Department of State to American Consul in Stockholm, Dec. 8, 1939; File 138 Emergency Program/404 MM; Passport Office Decimal File 1910–1949; RG 59; NACP. Mrs. Shipley sent a similar reply to inquiries from the American Consul in Mexico concerning border crossings by government officials. Instruction to American Consular Officer in Charge, Mexico,

D.F., Mexico, from Ruth B. Shipley, Oct. 11, 1939 ("[Y]ou should advise all officers and employees who have diplomatic or special passports that they should surrender such documents to the immigration authorities upon their arrival in this country and that, when communicating with this Department regarding the return of such documents, they should furnish complete information regarding their proposed travel. The Department assumes that officers and employees of the Consulates along the border, who reside in the United States and cross the border daily to their offices, do not need to exhibit their passports as evidence of citizenship and identification."); File 138 Emergency Program/223; Passport Office Decimal File 1910–1949; RG 59; NACP.

76. Telegram to Secretary of State Hull from Ambassador Kennedy, Sept. 14, 1939; File 138 Emergency Program/98; Passport Office Decimal File 1910–1949; RG 59; NACP.

77. Telegram to American Embassy London from Secretary of State Hull, Sept. 15, 1939; File 138 Emergency Program/98; Passport Office Decimal File 1910–1949; RG 59; NACP.

78. Telegram to Secretary Hull from Dr. Harry Gilbert, Sept. 13, 1939; File 138 Emergency Program/77 MM; Passport Office Decimal File 1910–1949; RG 59; NACP.

79. Letter to Dr. Harry Gilbert from Ruth Shipley, Sept. 14, 1939; File 138 Emergency Program/77 MM; Passport Office Decimal File 1910–1949; RG 59; NACP.

80. Memorandum to George Messersmith from Ruth Shipley, Nov. 22, 1939; File 138 E.P./364; Passport Office Decimal File 1910–1949; RG 59; NACP.

81. McLaughlin, *supra* note 1.

82. Memorandum to Ruth Shipley from George S. Messersmith, Assistant Secretary of State, Nov. 21, 1939; File 138 E.P./364 LS; Passport Office Decimal File 1910–1949; RG 59; NACP.

83. Confidential Cable to American Consul in Calcutta from Secretary of State Hull, Nov. 27, 1939; File 138 Emergency Program/368 MM; CDF 1930–39; RG 59; NACP.

84. Representative Sol Bloom (D-NY), Chairman of the House Foreign Affairs Committee, could think of no better way to introduce the bill to amend the Travel Control Act of 1918 than by reading into the record a letter from Mrs. Shipley encouraging the enactment of legislation "providing for the centralization of control over the entry into and departure from the United States of persons of all classes [of citizenship and alienage]." 87 CONG. REC. 5048 (June 11, 1941).

85. Memorandum—Ruth B. Shipley: Background and Performance, *supra* note 71.

86. State Department Order # 1118 from Secretary of State Hull, Dec. 17, 1942; File 111.28/279 (cross-reference file note); CDF 1940–44; RG 59; NACP. A State Department reorganization at the end of 1943 created the Office of Controls, which was composed of Mrs. Shipley's Passport Division as well as the Visa Division, Special War Problems Division, and Division of Foreign Activity Correlation. This appeared to reflect recognition for what these units did, rather than to shift any power away from Mrs. Shipley. State Department Order # 1218: Organization of the Department of State, Jan. 15, 1944; File 111.017/711; CDF 1940–44; RG 59; NACP.

87. Travel Order No. 4-2575 to Mrs. Ruth B. Shipley from Assistant Secretary G. Howland Shaw, Mar. 10, 1944; File 111.661/IC; CDF 1940–44; RG 59; NACP.

88. U.S. Polish Groups Protest to Hull, N.Y. TIMES, May 6, 1944, at 7.

89. President Clarifies Priest's Passport, N.Y. TIMES, May 10, 1944, at 7. *Newsweek*

later reported that the President had been less than candid: "Last month Premier Stalin sent a personal letter to President Roosevelt requesting that passports for a visit to Russia be issued to Father Orlemanski and Prof. Oscar Lange of the University of Chicago. . . . After lengthy discussions within the State Department and with the White House, it was finally agreed to grant Stalin's request but to inform him at the same time that should any publicity be given to the visit by the Russians, the American Government would be forced to declare that the men involved were acting in a private capacity and were in no way connected with the government." Father Orlemanski: The Inside Story, NEWSWEEK 30 (May 22, 1944).

90. *Id.*

91. Office Memorandum from Mr. Nidiffer, Division of Departmental Personnel, to Robert Ward, Acting Chief, Division of Departmental Personnel, dated Dec. 22, 1944; File FW 111.661/11-2344 CS/V; CDF 1940–44; RG 59; NACP.

92. Office Memorandum from Mr. Nidiffer, Division of Departmental Personnel, to Robert Ward, Acting Chief, Division of Departmental Personnel, dated Dec. 22, 1944; File FW 111.661/11-2344 CS/V; CDF 1940–44; RG 59; NACP.

93. Office Memorandum from Passport Division to Division of Administrative Management re: "Increase in Long Distance Telephone Calls," dated Nov. 23, 1944; File 111.661/11-2344; CDF 1940–44; RG 59; NACP.

94. This figure is calculated using the Consumer Price Index and an average annual inflation rate. *See* http://dollartimes.com/calculators/inflation.htm.

95. Department of State Record and Certification of Long Distance Calls Made, Passport Division, Aug. 11–Sept. 10, 1944, attached to Office Memorandum from Passport Division to Division of Administrative Management re: "Increase in Long Distance Telephone Calls," dated Nov. 23, 1944; File 111.661/11-2344; CDF 1940–44; RG 59; NACP.

96. LEONARD MOSLEY, DULLES: A BIOGRAPHY OF ELEANOR, ALLEN, AND JOHN FOSTER DULLES AND THEIR FAMILY NETWORK 205 (1978).

97. *Id.*

98. *Id.*

99. Harold B. Hinton, Guardian of American Passports, N.Y. TIMES, Apr. 27, 1941, at SM21.

100. In the Field of Travel, N.Y. TIMES, Feb. 1, 1948, at X15.

101. George H. Copeland, Passport Demand is Growing, N.Y. TIMES, Oct. 14, 1945, at X8.

102. Passport Curbs Will Stay a While, N.Y. TIMES, Aug. 25, 1945, at 11. The article reported some exceptions for hardship cases.

103. MARTIN BAUML DUBERMAN, PAUL ROBESON 388 (1989).

104. Robeson Loses Passport Suit, N.Y. TIMES, Apr. 13, 1951, at 12. Comment, Passport Refusals for Political Reasons: Constitutional Issues & Judicial Review, 61 YALE L.J. 171, 177 (1952).

105. Hurwitz, Judicial Control Over Passport Policy, 20 CLEV. ST. L. REV. 271, 274 (1971). That explanation was in response to Robeson's lawsuit to obtain a new passport. Duberman, *supra* note 103, at 389. The complaint was dismissed. See Robeson v. Acheson, 198 F.2d 985 (1952). Professor Alan Rogers attributes a very similar quotation to Mrs. Shipley herself. Alan Rogers, Passports and Politics: The Courts and the Cold

War, 47 THE HISTORIAN 497, 499 (Aug. 1985) ("Shipley told Robeson that when he spoke against colonialism, he was 'meddling in matters within the exclusive jurisdiction of the secretary of state'").

106. Case of Paul Robeson—Why Some Americans Can't Get Passports, 39 U.S. NEWS & WORLD REP. 79–80 (Aug. 26, 1955) (reprinting extracts from oral argument before the U.S. District Court for the District of Columbia at an Aug. 16, 1955, hearing on Robeson's motion seeking injunctive relief in the form of an order compelling issuance of a passport).

107. Dr. Pauling described his efforts to obtain a passport on this and subsequent occasions in a 1977 interview for the PBS television program *NOVA*. See Audio tape: Passport problems, Dep't of Special Collections, The Valley Library, Oregon State University (available at Linus Pauling and the Race for DNA: A Documentary History website, http://osulibrary.orst.edu/specialcollections/coll/pauling/dna/audio/nova4.html).

108. Linus Pauling, My Efforts to Obtain a Passport, 8 BULL. OF THE ATOMIC SCIENTISTS 253 (Oct. 1952). The denial preceded Pauling's Nobel Prizes in Chemistry (1954) and Peace (1962).

109. *Id.* at 254, 256.

110. Richard L. Strout, Win a Prize—Get a Passport, 133 NEW REPUBLIC 11, 12 (Nov. 28, 1955).

111. *Id.* at 13.

112. *Id.*

113. MARTIN GOTTFRIED, ARTHUR MILLER: HIS LIFE AND WORK 236 (2003); see also ENOCH BRATER, ARTHUR MILLER: A PLAYWRIGHT'S LIFE AND WORKS 66–67 (2005).

114. *Id.*; see also Playwright Arthur Miller Refused Visa for a Visit to Brussels to See His Play, N.Y. TIMES, Mar. 31, 1954, at 16.

115. Allen Drury, Arthur Miller Admits Helping Communist-Front Groups in '40's, N.Y. TIMES, June 22, 1956, at 1. The link between application and testimony may have been quite direct. Martin Gottfried argues that Miller's application "provided HUAC with an excuse to summon him to hearings. These were designed just for him and a few select others on 'The Unauthorized Use of United States Passports.'" Gottfried, *supra* note 113, at 286.

116. Investigation of the Unauthorized Use of United States Passports—Part 4: Hearings before the H. Committee on Un-American Activities, 84th Cong., 4655–91 (1956). Miller's conviction was later unanimously reversed on procedural grounds. U.S. v. Miller, 152 F.Supp. 781, 783 (1957), *judgment rev'd en banc*, 259 F.2d 187 (D.C. Cir. 1958).

117. Presbytery Discusses Passport Denial, 60 CHRISTIAN CENTURY 869 (1952).

118. His efforts are recounted in detail in his memoir, MARTIN D. KAMEN, RADIANT SCIENCE, DARK POLITICS: A MEMOIR OF THE NUCLEAR AGE (1985).

119. *Scoundrel Time* must be treated with caution as a historical source, if not some suspicion. Joseph Rauh, her lawyer when she was subpoenaed to appear before the HUAC, noted, at least with regard to her testimony, that "her account in *Scoundrel Times* [sic] is not the way it happened." WILLIAM WRIGHT, LILLIAN HELLMAN: THE IMAGE, THE WOMAN 248 (1986). On the other hand, Carl Rollyson and Robert P. Newman, two respected Hellman scholars, use this source in recounting her meeting

with Shipley. CARL ROLLYSON, LILLIAN HELLMAN: HER LEGEND AND HER LEGACY 342–44 (1988); ROBERT P. NEWMAN, THE COLD WAR ROMANCE OF LILLIAN HELLMAN AND JOHN MELBY 236 (1989). Both of them nevertheless are quite aware of the problem that, as William Wright observed, even where the truth of the matter has been verified elsewhere, her retelling should be suspected for "the hand of a dramatist at work." Wright, *supra*, at 253.

120. LILLIAN HELLMAN, SCOUNDREL TIME 79 (1976).

121. *Id.* at 80–82. The letter was written, and notarized, and expressed her continued willingness to barter her rights to freely speak and associate in exchange for a passport. Newman, *supra* note 119, at 237–39.

122. *Id.* at 82. Though colorfully descriptive, this is hardly explanatory. It may simply be that Mrs. Shipley discounted the FBI's derogatory information. Rollyson, *supra* note 119, at 343. It probably did not hurt that among Hellman's close friends were a number of Mrs. Shipley's colleagues and superiors at the State Department, including Loy Henderson, Christian Herter, and Averell Harriman. Newman, *supra* note 119, at 16 (cited approvingly by Rollyson, *supra*, at 220).

123. Rollyson, *supra* note 119, at 216; Newman, *supra* note 114, at 1 & 14.

124. Rollyson, *supra* note 119, at 217.

125. *Id.* at 271–72; Newman, *supra* note 119, at 127.

126. Rollyson, *supra* note 119, at 312–13. Newman, *supra* note 119, 160–62, reprints the letter in which Hellman pleadingly offers "proof of my loyalty" and begs for a passport because "I need to earn the money."

127. Dennis v. United States, 341 U.S. 494 (1951).

128. Newman, *supra* note 119, at 329.

129. *Id.*, at 236, 255–56. Much of the problem was due to the investigation of Hellman's onetime lover and longtime confidante, John Melby, by a State Department loyalty board that ultimately led him to be fired for his affair with Hellman. The passport Mrs. Shipley promised within days took almost a month. Mrs. Shipley wrote a carefully worded "memorandum for file" to justify her action, just in case: "The time given Miss Hellman for the consideration of this work was very limited and the file was out of our hands too long for me to consult SY [Security] before granting the extension if she was not to lose her contract." *Id.* at 256.

130. Letter to Sen. John L. McClellan from Assistant Sec'y of State Wm. B. Macomber, Jr. dated August 21, 1959; File 110.4-PPT/6-859; CDF 1955–59; RG 59; NACP.

131. Memorandum—Ruth B. Shipley: Background and Performance, *supra* note 71. The memo refers to a case brought against American Communists under the Smith Act, which made it unlawful to knowingly teach the duty of violently overthrowing the U.S. government. The case was tried by Judge Harold Medina and the defendants were convicted of engaging in a conspiracy to advocate such views. The convictions were ultimately affirmed by the Supreme Court in Dennis v. United States, 341 U.S. 494 (1951).

132. George H. Copeland, Passport Demand is Growing, N.Y. TIMES, Oct. 14, 1945, at X8.

133. Outgoing Airgram to Certain American Diplomatic and Consular Officers from Sec'y of State Acheson, Aug. 16, 1950; File 110.4-PD/8-1650; CDF 1950–54; RG 59; NACP.

134. Visson, *supra* note 5.

135. Memorandum—Ruth B. Shipley: Background and Performance, *supra* note 71.

136. *Id.*

137. Memorandum to Undersecretary of State for Administration Donald B. Lourie from Assistant Secretary for Congressional Relations Thruston B. Morton dated April 9, 1953; File 110.4 PD/4-953; CDF 1950–54; RG 59; NACP.

138. Personal Letter to Sec'y of State Dulles from Congressman John McCormack dated Dec. 28, 1954; File 110.4-PD/1-455 CS/S; CDF 1950–54; RG 59; NACP (original letter at File 110.4-PD/12-2854 CS/S; CDF 1955–59; RG 59; NACP.). Rep. McCormack, the Democratic Whip, wrote: "All I can say, Mr. Secretary, is that during my many years in Washington I have contacted Mrs. Shipley on many occasions. She is one of the most courteous ladies I have ever talked to, and she is one of the most cooperative Government officials I have ever contacted during my service in the Congress."

139. Congressman McCormack's personal letter was sent to forward a copy of a letter that Secretary Dulles had already received, from a friend of the congressman, Lawrence Valenstein, the President of Grey Advertising in New York City. That letter seems truly to have been penned out of love, not fear. It begins by asking the Secretary to "[p]ermit me to tell you a beautiful Thanksgiving Day story" in which Mrs. Shipley played the starring role in clearing bureaucratic hurdles to issue travel documents for a doctor to reach a sick relative in the Philippines. "One day, I hope to be able to say hello to Mrs. Shipley. I just want to say, 'Thank you.' She probably is not even interested in the mildest form of appreciation. She was commanded by her inner fine instincts." Copy of Letter to Sec'y Dulles from Lawrence Valenstein, dated Dec. 1, 1954; File 110.4-PD/12-154; CDF 1950–54; RG 59; NACP.

140. Answer to Attack on Passport Operations, 26 DEP'T OF STATE BULL. 110, 111 (1952) (emphasis added).

141. Graham H. Stuart, Safeguarding the State Through Passport Control, 12 DEP'T OF STATE BULL. 1066, 1067 (1945).

142. Memorandum to Jack B. Tate, Deputy Legal Advisor, from Mr. Yingling, July 24, 1951; File 110.4 PD/7-2451; CDF 1950–54; RG 59; NACP. See also Zemel v. Rusk, 381 U.S. 1, 8 (1965).

143. § 2, Act of July 3, 1926, 69 Cong. Ch. 772, 44 Stat. 887. See also Stuart, *supra* note 141, at 1069. Short time limits were a further control "to channelize the travel of persons proceedings abroad and to review their cases at regular intervals." *Id.*

144. Stuart, *supra* note 141, at 1069 (describing wartime restrictions on passports "for use to specific countries through which the bearer would travel en route to his ultimate destination.").

145. Exec. Order 7856, 3 FED. REG. 681, 687 (Mar. 31, 1938).

146. Part XIV of Exec. Order 7856, 3 FED. REG. 681, 687 (Mar. 31, 1938) codified in 22 C.F.R. § 51.75 (1949) cited by Yingling in memorandum to Jack B Tate, Deputy Legal Advisor, July 24, 1951; File 110.4 PD/7-2451; CDF 1950–54; RG 59; NACP.

147. Procedure for Travel in Iron Curtain Countries, 26 U.S. DEP'T OF STATE BULL. 736 (May 12, 1952).

148. Visson, *supra* note 5 ("In addition to issuing or renewing passports—a record of 299,665 in 1950—she has under her jurisdiction some 430,000 Americans residing abroad").

149. Letter to Under Sec'y Herbert Hoover, Jr., from Dr. H. Truman Gordon, dated Oct. 20, 1954; File 110.4-PD/10-2054 CS/W; CDF 1950–54; RG 59; NACP (emphasis in original).

150. Office Memorandum to Director Walter K. Scott, Executive Secretariat, from Mrs. Shipley, dated Oct. 26, 1954; File 110.4-PD/10-2054 CS/W; CDF 1950–54; RG 59; NACP.

151. Memorandum to Jack B. Tate from Mr. Yingling, July 24, 1951, *supra* note 142.

152. *Id.*

153. Sec. 6, 64 Stat. 987, 50 U.S.C. § 285 (1950). The act required knowledge of registration or a final order to register as an element of the offense.

154. Eugene Gressman, Have You the Right to Travel Abroad? 127 NEW REPUBLIC 14 (Sept. 15, 1952).

155. New Passport Regulations Issued, 27 U.S. DEP'T OF STATE BULL. 417–18 (Sept. 15, 1952) (reprinting text of new regulations codified at 22 C.F.R. §§ 51.135–143).

156. 17 FED. REG. 8013 (Sept. 4, 1952) (codified at 22 C.F.R. § 51.137 (1957)).

157. *Id.* at § 51.139.

158. *Id.*

159. *Id.* at § 51.141(a).

160. *Id.* at § 51.135.

161. 19 FED. REG. 162 (Jan. 9, 1954) (codified at 22 C.F.R. § 51.163 (1957)). The Board "shall take into consideration the inability of the applicant to meet information of which he has not been advised, specifically or in detail, or to attack the creditability of confidential informants." 22 C.F.R. § 51.170 (1957).

162. 17 FED. REG. 8013 (Sept. 4, 1952) (codified at 22 C.F.R. § 51.141(b) (1957)).

163. *Id.* at § 51.142.

164. Leonard B. Boudin, The Right to Travel: A Significant Victory, 181 THE NATION 95, 96 (July 30, 1955).

165. H. W. Erksine, You Don't Go If She Says No, 132 COLLIERS 62, 63 (July 11, 1953).

166. *Id.* (nine-month mark); Boudin, *supra* note 164 (reporting personal communication from Mrs. Shipley averring to no appeals at the ten-month mark). Roughly eighteen months later, a total of twenty-two appeals had been filed (out of twenty-eight passport refusals since Jan. 19, 1954). Paul J. C. Friedlander, 'Due Process' for Passports, N.Y. TIMES, July 3, 1955, at X13. By mid-1957, twenty cases had been accepted and heard by the Board, including Otto Nathan's case (*see infra*), which was handled *ex parte* at the request of the Secretary. Memorandum to John M. Raymond, Deputy Legal Advisor, from John W. Sipes, June 19, 1957; File 110.4-PPT/6-1957; CDF 1955–59; RG 59; NACP.

167. 17 FED. REG. 8013 (Sept. 4, 1952) (codified at 22 C.F.R. § 51.136 (1957)). ("[N]o passport . . . shall be issued to persons as to whom there is reason to believe, on the balance of all the evidence, that they are going abroad to engage in activities while abroad which would violate the laws of the United States, or which if carried on in the United States would violate such laws designed to protect the security of the United States.").

168. 21 FED. REG. 336 (Jan. 18, 1956) ((codified at 22 C.F.R. § 51.136 (1957)).

169. *Id.*

170. Eugene Gressman, The Undue Process of Passports, 127 NEW REPUBLIC 13, 15 (Sept. 8, 1952).

171. *Id.* at 14.

172. Bauer v. Acheson, 106 F.Supp. 445 (D.D.C. 1952). Since the court was otherwise quite deferential to the executive's asserted power to withhold passports from those "whose activities abroad might be in conflict with its foreign policy", *id.* at 452, it

may be that the State Department preferred to accommodate the relatively modest procedural concerns of the court (which the court felt could be addressed "under the existing statute and regulations"), since the Department did not appeal the court's judgment.

173. Louis L. Jaffe, The Right to Travel: The Passport Problem, 35 FOREIGN AFF. 17, 18 (Oct. 1956).

174. Charles E. Wyzanski, Jr. Freedom to Travel, ATLANTIC MONTHLY 66, 67 (Oct. 4, 1952).

175. Passport Chief to End Career, N.Y. TIMES, Feb. 25, 1955, at 15. It appears that Mrs. Shipley may have stepped down because she reached the mandatory retirement age. Obituary, Ruth B. Shipley, Ex-Passport Head, N.Y. TIMES, Nov. 5, 1966, at 29. On the other hand, an article published weeks before her retirement stated that "Secretary of State Dulles in a letter dated March 14 urged her to stay on." Passport Head Named, N.Y. TIMES, Apr. 1, 1955, at 8. Characteristically, "Mrs. Shipley refused to change her mind." *Id.*

176. Passport Chief to End Career, N.Y. TIMES, Feb. 25, 1955, at 15. Characteristically, Mrs. Shipley intended to pick her heir: "Yes, my successor has been chosen—by me. We have a good ship. Don't you think that after twenty-eight years I should know what's needed?" *Id.* As it turned out, however, her successor came from outside the Passport Division: Frances G. Knight of the Bureau of Inspection, Security and Consular Affairs. *Id.* A few weeks after her departure, Mrs. Shipley claimed that she had chosen Miss Knight. Mrs. Shipley Cited by Anti-Red Group, N.Y. TIMES, May 11, 1955, at 22.

177. Passport Chief to End Career, N.Y. TIMES, Feb. 25, 1955, at 15.

178. Letter to John Foster Dulles, Sec'y of State, from Fifield Workum, Chairman, Special Committee to Study Passport Procedures of the Association of the Bar of the City of New York, May 17, 1957; File 110.4 PPT/5-1757; CDF 1955–59; RG 59; NACP. The findings and recommendations of this distinguished committee (the membership of which included Adrian S. Fisher, former legal advisor to the Secretary of State) presented a damning indictment of the principles and practices that characterized Mrs. Shipley's era. FREEDOM TO TRAVEL: REPORT OF THE SPECIAL COMMITTEE TO STUDY PASSPORT PROCEDURES OF THE ASSOCIATION OF THE BAR OF THE CITY OF NEW YORK (1958).

179. Nathan v. Dulles, 129 F.Supp. 951, 952 (1955).

180. *Id.*

181. *Id.*

182. 129 F.Supp. 950 (1955).

183. *Id.* at 951; see also Reginald Parker, The Right to Go Abroad: To Have and to Hold a Passport, 40 VA. L. REV. 853, 859 (1954).

184. Dulles v. Nathan, 225 F.2d 29, 30 (D.C. Cir. 1955).

185. *Id.*

186. *Id.*

187. *Id.* at 30–31.

188. *Id.* at 31.

189. *Id.*

190. Shachtman v. Dulles, 225 F.2d 938 (D.C. Cir. 1955). For an analysis of the effect of this ruling on the Attorney General's Subversives List, see Robert Justin Goldstein,

Getting "Delisted": The Independent Socialist League's [Ultimately] Successful Challenge to the "Attorney General's List of Subversive Activities," 1948–1958, 52 AMER. J. OF LEGAL HISTORY 143, 165–68 (Apr. 2012).

191. Letter to Senator Theodore Green, Chairman, Senate Foreign Relations Committee, from Assistant Secretary of State Robert Murphy, May 22, 1957; File 110.4 PPT/5-2257; CDF 1955–59; RG 59; NACP. Although this file copy was cleared for release by the initials of five relevant office heads, it is unclear whether it was ultimately sent to Senator Green.

192. Boudin v. Dulles, 136 F.Supp. 218, 222 (D.D.C. 1955).

193. *Id.* at 221.

194. Boudin v. Dulles, 235 F.2d 532, 536 (D.C. Cir. 1956). The same conclusion was reached, citing *Boudin,* a few months later: Dayton v. Dulles, 237 F.2d 43 (D.C. Cir. 1956).

195. Letter to Senator Theodore Green, Chairman, Senate Foreign Relations Committee, from Assistant Secretary of State Robert Murphy, May 22, 1957, *supra* note 191.

196. Case of Paul Robeson—Why Some Americans Can't Get Passports, 39 U.S. NEWS & WORLD REP. 79, 80 (Aug. 26, 1955).

197. DONALD J. KEMPER, DECADE OF FEAR: SENATOR HENNINGS AND CIVIL LIBERTIES 119–20, 159–64 (1965).

198. Loy Henderson, Deputy Under Secretary for Administration, described the danger in a memorandum to the Acting Secretary: "It is quite possible that when a name is given the Committee will call the person named before it in order to request that he explain why he took the decision. This person will then have the difficulty of disclosing the records or of refusing to answer questions put to him. . . . The precedent which would be established in naming the persons responsible for making decisions could have far-reaching consequences. . . . This is so important that I hope we can take a new look at the matter before Mr. McLeod commits himself too far today." Confidential Memo for the Acting Sec'y from Loy Henderson, Nov. 16, 1955; File 110.4 PPT/11-1655 CS/HHH; CDF 1955–59; RG 59; NACP. A note dated the same day and pinned to the memo carried the scent of relief about it: "Mr. McLeod's office reports the hearings are over on the Hill; that Mr. McLeod was not asked any pertinent questions, and the hearing went very smoothly." *Id.*

199. 357 U.S. 116 (1958).

200. *Id.* at 119. Although, as the Court noted, the Subversive Activity Control Board created by the Internal Security Act of 1950 had the power to prohibit members of registered organizations from applying for passports, the Board had not issued any such final orders to organizations requiring registration at the relevant time in the Kent case. See Comments on S. 2095, p. 6, attached to letter to Senator John L. McClellan from Assistant Sec'y of State William B. Macomber, Jr. dated August 21, 1959; File 110.4-PPT/6-859; CDF 1955–59; RG 59; NACP (noting "no organization is registered or has been finally ordered to register by the Subversive Activities Control Board.").

201. 357 U.S. at 128.

202. *Id.*

203. *Id.* at 129.

204. Comments on S. 2095, p. 3, attached to letter to Senator John L. McClellan from Assistant Sec'y of State William B. Macomber, Jr. dated Aug. 21, 1959; File 110.4-PPT/6-859; CDF 1955–59; RG 59; NACP.

205. *Id.*

206. Comments on S. 2095, p. 5, *supra* note 200. These comments noted with favor the (then) recent D.C. Circuit opinion *Worthy v. Herter* that upheld this power.

207. Dayton v. Dulles, 357 U.S. 144, 145 (1958).

208. Although Mrs. Shipley would not provide specifics, she informed Dayton's lawyer that "the determining factor in the case was Mr. Dayton's association with persons suspected of being part of the Rosenberg espionage ring and his alleged presence at an apartment in New York which was allegedly used for microfilming material obtained for the use of a foreign government" five years prior to his application. *Id.* at 146–47.

209. Aptheker v. Secretary of State, 378 U.S. 500 (1964) (holding Section 6 of the Subversive Activities Control Act to be a facially unconstitutional infringement on the right to travel by criminalizing the application for, or use of, a passport by a member of a registered Communist organization). But see Worthy v. Herter, 270 F.2d 905, 907 (D.C. Cir. 1959) (upholding area restrictions on, and ultimate denial of, journalist's passport); Zemel v. Rusk, 381 U.S. 1 (1965) (upholding blanket area restriction on travel to Cuba); Regan v. Wald, 468 U.S. 222 (1984) (upholding Treasury regulations restricting travel to Cuba in support of an economic embargo); Haig v. Agee, 453 U.S. 280 (1981) (upholding revocation of rogue former CIA agent's passport without hearing).

210. Indeed, President Eisenhower sent an urgent message to Congress in the aftermath of *Kent v. Dulles* conceding, "Any limitations on the right to travel can only be tolerated in terms of overriding requirements of our national security, and must be subject to substantive and procedural guarantees." Dwight D. Eisenhower, Special Message to the Congress on the Need for Additional Passport Control Legislation (July 7, 1958), available at http://www.presidency.ucsb.edu/ws/index.php?pid=11120&st=passport&st1=control.

211. Letter from William O. Douglas to Robert Daniel Murphy, Dep. Sec'y of State (June 19, 1959), reprinted in THE DOUGLAS LETTERS: SELECTIONS FROM THE PRIVATE PAPERS OF JUSTICE WILLIAM O. DOUGLAS 270–71 (Melvin I. Urofsky, ed., 1987).

Chapter 6

1. ARTHUR KOESTLER, THE GHOST IN THE MACHINE 325–26 (1976).

2. DEPARTMENT OF STATE HISTORICAL DIVISION, THE DEPARTMENT OF STATE, 1930–1955: EXPANDING FUNCTIONS AND RESPONSIBILITIES 53 (January 1955).

3. That is not to say that the idea was necessarily a surprise. The FAA's Civil Aviation Security intelligence office, NORAD, and even a self-actualized Justice Department trial attorney, analyzed the operational and legal implications of a suicide hijacking, although unsystematically, episodically, and incompletely. FINAL REPORT OF THE NATIONAL COMMISSION ON TERRORIST ATTACKS UPON THE UNITED STATES 345–47 (2004) [hereafter "9/11 Commission Report"]. Generally, the leadership of the FAA's security and intelligence offices did not consider suicide hijacking to be a credible threat before September 11. Memorandum for the Record, 9/11 Commission interview with Rear Admiral Cathal "Irish" Flynn USN (ret), Sept. 9, 2003, at 5.

4. Staff of H.R. Subcomm. on Inter-American Affairs, Comm. on Foreign Affairs, 90th Cong., Report pursuant to H. Res. 179 on Air Piracy in the Caribbean Area 1 n.a (Comm. Print 1968) [hereafter "H. Rep. on Air Piracy"].

5. Alona E. Evans, Aircraft Hijacking: Its Cause and Cure, 63 AMER. J. INT'L L. 695, 696 (1969). BLACK'S LAW DICTIONARY 798 (9th ed., 2009).

6. 49 U.S.C. § 46502(a)(1)(A) (defining aircraft piracy to mean "seizing or exercising control of an aircraft in the special aircraft jurisdiction of the United States by force, violence, threat of force or violence, or any form of intimidation, and with wrongful intent").

7. Gary N. Horlick, The Developing Law of Air Hijacking, 12 HARV. INT'L L. J. 33, 65 (1971).

8. BLACK'S LAW DICTIONARY *supra* note 5, at 948.

9. H. Rep. on Air Piracy, *supra* note 4, at 1 & 9. THERESA L. KRAUS, THE FEDERAL AVIATION ADMINISTRATION: A HISTORICAL PERSPECTIVE 1903–2008 15 (2008).

10. Statement of Elmer E. Jones, Jr., Vice President of Public Affairs, National Airlines, Inc., Before the Subcommittee on Inter-American Affairs, of the House Committee on Foreign Affairs, Oct. 1, 1968, *reprinted in* H. Rep. on Air Piracy, *supra* note 4, at 19. There is a discrepancy between the seven passengers that Jones states to have been victims, the number (6) provided by the State Department in an appendix to the report, and the number (8) given by Horlick, *supra* note 7.

11. *Id.*

12. Bearden v. United States, 320 F.2d 99, 101 (5th Cir. 1963); *see also* Crime: The Skywayman, TIME 14 (Aug. 11, 1961).

13. *Bearden*, 320 F.2d at 100–101.

14. *Id.* at 103 ("The jury could have found that appellant himself was transported, rather than doing the transporting himself. The jury should have been instructed that in order for appellant to have 'transported' the plane and passengers he must have been in actual control or command of the aircraft and that the acts of the crew were not of their own volition but done at his direction") (footnote omitted).

15. Bearden v. U.S., 403 F.2d 782, 783 (5th Cir. 1968). H. Rep. on Air Piracy, *supra* note 4, at 4.

16. Kraus, *supra* note 9, at 15. Armed border guards began flying on select flights in August 1961. Attorney General Robert F. Kennedy swore the first "sky marshals" into service in March 1962. *Id.* at 16. These special U.S. deputy marshals flew when requested by the airlines. Special training for a much larger force trained by the Bureau of Customs and assigned to FAA followed a spate of hijackings in Europe in fall 1970. President Nixon announced the measure on September 11, 1970. *Id.* At 41–42.

17. Evans, *supra* note 5, at 697. The fifty-first hijacking was to Syria. *Id.* More than half of these were in 1969. *Id.* at 698. At this time, the United States had no air traffic to Cuba and permitted only limited air travel from Cuba, so-called "Freedom Flights" twice daily to Miami for Cuban refugees. H. Rep. on Air Piracy, *supra* note 4, at 3; Cuba: End of the Freedom Flights, TIME 36 (Sept. 13, 1971).

18. H. Rep. on Air Piracy, *supra* note 4, at 13. The second most frequent citizenship was Cuban, with sixteen individuals. *See also* Evans, *supra* note 5, at 700.

19. John E. Stephen, "Going South"—Air Piracy and Unlawful Interference with Air Commerce, 4 INT'L LAWYER 433 (Apr. 1970); *see also* Kraus, *supra* note 9, at 39 (noting eight U.S. commercial aircraft were hijacked to Cuba in January 1969 and a total of fourteen hijackings occurred between January and March 1969).

20. Richard Witkin, Armed U.S. Guards Reported Ordered on Flights Abroad, N.Y. TIMES, Sept. 11, 1970, at 1. *See also* Kraus, *supra* note 9, at 41–42.

21. Evans, *supra* note 5, at 701–2; Horlick, *supra* note 7, at 39–42.
22. Francis Wellington Dahl, On Voyage, BOSTON HERALD TRAVELER, Sept. 23, 1968, at 30. Reprinted with permission of the *Boston Herald*.
23. Pub. L. No. 87–197, § 1, 75 Stat. 466 (Sept. 5, 1961) (amending Federal Aviation Act of 1958). This amendment also made it a crime, for the first time, to carry a concealed weapon on board a commercial aircraft. *Id*. Aircraft piracy was defined as "any seizure or exercise of control, by force or violence or threat of force or violence and with wrongful intent, of an aircraft in flight in air commerce." Note that scienter required no political or other motive. In fact, the State Department expressed its preference *against* labeling air hijacking a political offense out of concern for the difficulties this would create for international extradition, which tended to exempt individuals seeking political asylum:

> In our extradition treaties—and this is true for treaties of other countries as well—we traditionally have not accepted an obligation to return fugitives accused of common crimes whom we determined to be fleeing from political persecution. We have taken a hard look at this traditional policy in the light of the increasing danger to innocent persons from hijacking of commercial aircraft, and of the importance of an effective deterrent; and we have concluded that the hijacker of a commercial aircraft carrying passengers for hire should be returned regardless of any claim that he was fleeing political persecution. Our [proposed] protocol would provide, however, that he could be tried and punished only for the aircraft hijacking, not for any other offense. Under United States law, a hijacker faces a minimum penalty of 20 years; but obviously the penalty alone is no deterrent if the hijacker thinks he can avoid return for trial by persuading a foreign government to refuse to return him on the ground that he is really fleeing from political oppression. We do not propose to change in any way our general policy on political asylum; but we think the risks involved in the hijacking of commercial aircraft are great enough so that neither we nor others should treat hijackers—whatever their motivation—as simple political offenders.

Testimony of Frank E. Loy, Dep'y Asst. Sec'y for Transportation and Telecommunications, before the House Committee on Interstate and Foreign Commerce, Feb. 5, 1969, *reprinted in* 60 DEP'T OF STATE BULL. 212, 213 (1969); *see also* Horlick, *supra* note 7, at 45–51.
24. Pub. L. No. 87–197, § 4, 75 Stat. 466 (Sept. 5, 1961) as codified in 49 U.S.C. § 1511 (1964).
25. H. Rep. on Air Piracy, *supra* note 4, at 4.
26. On March 17, 1970, an Eastern airlines copilot became the first American killed in a domestic hijacking, dying from gunshot wounds, but not before wounding the hijacker with the hijacker's own gun. Kraus, *supra* note 9, at 40. The passenger, Howard L. Franks, died during a hijacking on a TWA flight about to depart from Chicago to New York. Hijacker Is Seized at Kennedy After Man Is Killed in Chicago, N.Y. TIMES, June 12, 1971, at 1; Darien Consultant Shot on Plane Is First to Die in U.S. Hijacking, N.Y. TIMES, June 13, 1971; Kraus, *supra* note 9, at 42.
27. On September 9, 1949, J. Albert Guay secreted a bomb in the luggage of his wife, killing her (his purpose) and twenty-two others aboard a Quebec Airways flight.

Canada Hangs Air-Crash Killer, N.Y. TIMES, Jan. 12, 1951, at 7; Canadian to Die for Part in Causing Plane Disaster, N.Y. TIMES, Dec. 14, 1950, at 20.

On November 1, 1955, John Gilbert Graham used dynamite to kill his mother (his purpose) and forty-three others aboard a United Airlines flight over Colorado. Civil Aeronautics Board, Accident Investigation Report No. 1-143: United Air Lines, Inc., Douglas DC-6B, N 37559, Near Longmont, Colorado, November 1, 1955 (May 14, 1956); Graham Executed; Killed 44 on Plane, N.Y. TIMES, Jan. 12, 1957, at 11.

On July 25, 1957, a passenger was ejected from a Western Airlines flight over California when he apparently detonated dynamite in the lavatory, but the plane landed safely. Civil Aeronautics Board, Aircraft Accident Report No. 1-065: Western Air Lines, Inc., Convair 240–1, N 8406H, Near Daggett, California, July 25, 1957 (Jan. 9, 1958); Passenger Insured for $125,000 Mysteriously Blasted from Airliner, N.Y. TIMES, July 26, 1957, at 1.

On November 16, 1959, forty-two people were killed aboard a National Airlines flight over the Gulf of Mexico that some investigators believed was lost due to a bomb placed as part of an insurance-collection scheme. Civil Aeronautics Board, Aircraft Accident Report No. 1-071: National Airlines, Inc., Douglas DC-7B, N 4891C, in the Gulf of Mexico, November 16, 1959 (June 14, 1962); Theory on Wreck in Gulf Suggests a Substituted Passenger and Bomb, N.Y. TIMES, Jan. 17, 1960, at 1.

On January 6, 1960, a National Airlines flight was destroyed over North Carolina by dynamite under a passenger seat, with the loss of thirty-four lives. The investigation was inconclusive, but suspicion rested on a lawyer believed to have committed suicide. Civil Aeronautics Board, Aircraft Accident Report No. 1-002: National Airlines, Inc., Douglas DC-6B, N 8225H, Near Bolivia, North Carolina, January 6, 1960 (July 29, 1960); C. P. Trussell, Senator Says Bomb Caused Airliner Crash Fatal to 34, N.Y. TIMES, Jan. 15, 1960 at 1.

On May 22, 1962, forty-five people were killed when a bomb hidden in a lavatory destroyed a Continental Airlines flight over Missouri. Civil Aeronautics Board, Aircraft Accident Report No. 1-003: Continental Air Lines, Inc., Boeing 707-124, N 70775, Near Unionville, Missouri, May 22, 1962 (Aug. 1, 1962). The media speculated that a passenger committed suicide to avoid a pending criminal prosecution and collect life insurance for his wife. Fatal Air Crash Ruled Bomb Plot, N.Y. TIMES, Aug. 2, 1962, at 52.

An American Airlines flight in 1967 and a Continental Airlines flight in 1968 landed safely after midair explosions above Colorado with no loss of life. REPORT OF THE PRESIDENT'S COMMISSION ON AVIATION SECURITY AND TERRORISM 160–61 (1990) (hereafter "President's Commission").

28. Horlick, *supra* note 7, at 51–52 ("The most heavy-handed system is to check passengers and luggage for weapons. If such an examination is thorough enough to be effective, however, airlines fear that it might prove annoying to customers, and further complicate and delay the boarding process as well. Moreover, personal search raises the specter of constitutional problems.") (citations omitted); *see also* Evans, *supra* note 5, at 703 ("Given the congestion which obtains at take-off of most flights, routine search of passengers and baggage would produce an intolerable situation unless it could be managed speedily and with a minimum of inconvenience to all concerned.").

29. Graham later protested his innocence. Guilt Now Denied in Airliner Blast, N.Y. TIMES, Nov. 19, 1955, at 40.

30. Richard Witkin, Airlines Seek Foolproof System to Thwart Sabotage of Planes, N.Y. TIMES, Nov. 15, 1955, at 28.

31. PRESIDENT'S COMMISSION, *supra* note 27, at 50.

32. *Id.*, at 50–51.

33. *Id.*, at 52. The report incorrectly cites the provision as 39 U.S.C. § 3263. The correct provision was 39 U.S.C. § 3623(d), promulgated as part of the Postal Reorganization Act, Pub. L. 91-375, Aug. 12, 1970, 84 Stat. 719, 761: "The Postal Service shall maintain one or more classes of mail for the transmission of letters sealed against inspection. The rate for each such class shall be uniform throughout the United States, its territories, and possessions. One such class shall provide for the most expeditious handling and transportation afforded mail matter by the Postal Service. No letter of such a class of domestic origin shall be opened except under authority of a search warrant authorized by law, or by an officer or employee of the Postal Service for the sole purpose of determining an address at which the letter can be delivered, or pursuant to the authorization of the addressee." This section was repealed in 2006, § 201(b), Pub. L. 109-435, Dec. 20, 2006, 120 Stat. 3205.

34. Evans, *supra* note 5, at 703–4; Horlick, *supra* note 7, at 52.

35. Horlick, *supra* note 7, at 52 n. 103.

36. Evans, *supra* note 5, at 703–4.

37. Kraus, *supra* note 9, at 43.

38. *See* §§ 315(a) & 1111, Pub. L. 93-366, Aug. 5, 1974, 88 Stat. 415. The requirement had previously been enforced by an emergency FAA rule issued in December 1972. Kraus, *supra* note 9, at 44.

39. According to the President's Commission on Aviation Security and Terrorism, convened in the wake of the Pan Am 103 tragedy, other catalysts included the hijacking of Egyptair 648 in November 1985, and the terrorist attack that December on the Rome and Vienna airports. PRESIDENT'S COMMISSION, *supra* note 27, at 74.

40. William E. Smith, Terror Aboard Flight 847, TIME, Jun. 24, 1985, pp. 18–26.

41. PRESIDENT'S COMMISSION, *supra* note 27, at 28; Foreign Airport Security Act (Title V, Part B, of the International Security and Development Cooperation Act of 1985), Pub. L. 99–83, Aug. 8, 1985, 99 Stat 190.

42. Sec. 551(g)(1)-(2), Foreign Airport Security Act, *supra* note 41 (as codified at 49 U.S.C. App. 1515(g), as currently amended and found at 49 U.S.C. 44907(e)(1)–(2)). The determination is made by the Secretary of Transportation with the approval of the Secretary of State.

43. Author's interview with Claudio Manno, Acting Assistant Administrator for Security & Hazardous Materials, Federal Aviation Administration, Oct. 20, 2009, Washington, D.C. (hereafter "Manno, author interview, Oct. 20, 2009"); PRESIDENT'S COMMISSION, *supra* note 27, at 74–75.

44. Memorandum for the Record, 9/11 Commission interview with Claudio Manno, Oct. 1, 2003, at 1 (hereafter "Manno, 9/11 Commission interview").

45. Manno, author interview, Oct. 20, 2009, *supra* note 43. Manno was one of a group of five that started this office. He came from Air Force OSI (counterintelligence).

46. Manno, author interview, Oct. 20, 2009, *supra* note 43; PRESIDENT'S COMMISSION, *supra* note 27, at 78 ("In the FAA model, threat exists only when a person or entity has both the capability to carry out a particular type of attack and the intention

to do so. Either of these factors, standing alone, does not constitute a credible threat. The model used by FAA is widely accepted and used by the majority of U.S. intelligence and law enforcement community agencies").

47. Manno, author interview, Oct. 20, 2009, *supra* note 43.

48. Author's interview with Claudio Manno, Mar. 14, 2011, Washington, D.C. (hereafter "Manno, author interview, Mar. 14, 2011"). Prior to 1986, it appears that SBs were sent by mail, although this finding by the President's Commission on Aviation Security and Terrorism does not comport with Manno's recollection. PRESIDENT'S COMMISSION, *supra* note 27, at 78.

49. Manno, author interview, Oct. 20, 2009, *supra* note 43; PRESIDENT'S COMMISSION, *supra* note 27, at 74.

50. PRESIDENT'S COMMISSION, *supra* note 27, at 14–40 ("The FAA's view of the nature of the threat to domestic flights has not changed for almost two decades. . . . FAA makes clear that it views the terrorism problem as restricted to the international arena. FAA has said that at domestic airports, efforts will continue to focus on the hijacking threat, while research and development will emphasize improved passenger and baggage screening equipment"). This was disputed by Claudio Manno, who cited a number of information circulars issued by the FAA prior to the Pan Am 103 disaster referencing domestic threats. Manno, author interview, Mar. 14, 2011, *supra* note 48.

51. PRESIDENT'S COMMISSION, *supra* note 27, at 14–15.

52. *Id.*, at 6.

53. *Id.*, at 69.

54. *Id.*, at i. In fact, the head of the FAA's Office of Civil Aviation Security himself described the FAA as a "reactive agency." *Id.*, at 53.

55. Manno, author interview, Mar. 14, 2011, *supra* note 48.

56. Memorandum for the Record, Manno, 9/11 Commission interview, supra note 44, at 2.

57. *Id. See also* Nancy Jean Strantz, Aviation Security and Pan Am Flight 103: What Have We Learned? 56 J. AIR L. & COM. 413, 468 (1990).

58. Manno, author interview, Oct. 20, 2009, *supra* note 43; Manno, author interview, Mar. 14, 2011, *supra* note 48.

59. PRESIDENT'S COMMISSION, *supra* note 27, at 78–79.

60. Memorandum for the Record, Manno, 9/11 Commission interview, *supra* note 44, at 6 & 8; Manno, author interview, Oct. 20, 2009, *supra* note 43; Memorandum for the Record, 9/11 Commission interview with Lee Longmire, Oct. 28, 2003, at 5 & 6. Longmire had held operational and policy posts at FAA since 1980. At the time of the interview, he was Assistant Administrator for Operations Policy at TSA.

61. Manno, author interview, Oct. 20, 2009, *supra* note 43.

62. *Id.*

63. *Id.*

64. PRESIDENT'S COMMISSION, *supra* note 27, at 78–79.

65. Memorandum for the Record, 9/11 Commission interview with Rear Admiral Cathal "Irish" Flynn USN (ret), Sept. 9, 2003, at 5. Admiral Flynn was Associate Administrator of Civil Aviation Security (ACS 1) at FAA from 1993 to 2000. Memorandum for the Record, 9/11 Commission interview with John Steven Hawley, Oct. 8, 2003, at 5. Hawley served as a liaison to the State Department for both the FAA and TSA. Memorandum for the Record, 9/11 Commission interview with Lynne Osmus,

Oct. 3, 2003, at 2. Osmus served in a variety of security and administrative positions in FAA since 1979.

66. Testimony of Gerard Arpey, CEO of American Airlines, Seventh Public Hearing of the National Commission on Terrorist Attacks upon the United States, Jan. 27, 2004, at 80 (placing responsibility for threat assessment on federal officials and limiting airline responsibility to "implementing the security procedures that are given to us by the federal government") and 88 (describing post-9/11 lawsuits brought by the Department of Transportation against American Airlines for crew member decisions to refuse transport to passengers they deemed suspicious). Testimony of Edmond Soliday, Former Vice President, United Airlines, Seventh Public Hearing of the National Commission on Terrorist Attacks upon the United States, Jan. 27, 2004, at 82 ("[M]ost recently after 9/11, 38 of our captains denied boarding to people they thought were a threat. Those people filed complaints with the DOT, we were sued, and we were asked not to do it again. . . . We were reminded quite frequently that unless they posed an immediate threat we were disobeying the common carrier rules.").

67. Seventh Public Hearing of the National Commission on Terrorist Attacks upon the United States, Jan. 27, 2004, at 39–42 (testimony of Cathal "Irish" Flynn and Claudio Manno). Memorandum for the Record, 9/11 Commission interview with Rear Admiral Cathal "Irish" Flynn USN (ret), Sept. 9, 2003, at 2–4 (describing the attitudes of both FBI and CIA top officials as "condescending" toward FAA requests for intelligence and his belief that information flows to FAA from these agencies was inadequate); Memorandum for the Record, 9/11 Commission interview with Bruce Butterworth, Sept. 29, 2003, at 8–9 (describing a "take what you can get" relationship between FAA and the FBI). Butterworth served as director for security policy and planning (1991–95) and director of security operations (1995–2000) at the FAA. Memorandum for the Record, 9/11 Commission interview with John Steven Hawley, Oct. 8, 2003, at 2–3 (describing CIA and FBI resistance to intelligence sharing with FAA). Memorandum for the Record, 9/11 Commission interview with Lynne Osmus, Oct. 3, 2003, at 3 (noting that "FBI and other members of the IC did not fully recognize the need for FAA to have the information they wanted."). Memorandum for the Record, 9/11 Commission interview with James Padgett, Oct. 7, 2003, at 2 (noting frustrations with FBI intelligence sharing). Padgett served in a variety of intelligence and security positions at FAA starting in 1990.

68. 9/11 COMMISSION REPORT, *supra* note 3, at 476 n. 54.

69. Manno, author interview, Mar. 14, 2011, *supra* note 48. A more common use of SDs is illustrated by a terrifying precursor to the 9/11 attacks. The "Bojinka" plot, conceived in the mid-1990s by Ramzi Yousef and Khalid Sheikh Mohammed, aimed to destroy twelve U.S. air carriers in a span of forty-eight hours as they flew over the Pacific Ocean. 9/11 COMMISSION REPORT, *supra* note 3, at 147 & 489 n. 8 (2004). Among the responses once the plot was uncovered was the issuance of SDs requiring a variety of new security measures not already required by the overseas security plans of commercial airlines, all of which responded to the new modus operandi that the Bojinka plot uncovered . Manno, author interview, Mar. 14, 2011, *supra* note 48; Kraus, *supra* note 9, at 102.

70. Pub. L. No. 87-197, § 4, 75 Stat. 466 (Sept. 5, 1961). This provision, previously codified at 49 App. U.S.C. § 1511, is now found in slightly revised form at 49 U.S.C. § 44902.

71. 9/11 Commission Report, *supra* note 3, at 80 (2004); Memorandum for the Record, 9/11 Commission interview with Doris Meissner, Nov. 25, 2003, at 8.

72. *Three 9/11 Hijackers: Identification, Watchlisting, and Tracking,* Staff Statement No. 2, National Commission on Terrorist Attacks upon the United States; Written Statement of Mary A. Ryan to the National Commission on Terrorist Attacks upon the United States January 26, 2004, Seventh Public Hearing of the National Commission on Terrorist Attacks Upon the United States; THOMAS R. ELDRIDGE, ET AL. 9/11 AND TERRORIST TRAVEL: STAFF REPORT OF THE NATIONAL COMMISSION ON TERRORIST ATTACKS UPON THE UNITED STATES 79 (2004).

73. William J. Krouse, Terrorist Identification, Screening, and Tracking Under Homeland Security Presidential Directive 6, CRS REPORT FOR CONGRESS (RL32366) 26 (Apr. 21, 2004).

74. EDWARD ALDEN, THE CLOSING OF THE AMERICAN BORDER 163 (2008). The Intelligence Community was concerned about the risk that its sources and methods could be revealed.

75. Memorandum for the Record, 9/11 Commission interview with Doris Meissner, Nov. 25, 2003, at 8.

76. Alden, *supra* note 74, at 161.

77. Eldridge, *supra* note 72, at 78.

78. *Id.* at 80 ("In 2001, the CIA provided 1,527 source documents to TIPOFF; the State Department, 2,013; the INS, 173. The FBI, during this same year, provided 63 documents to TIPOFF—fewer than were obtained from the public media, and about the same number as were provided by the Australian Intelligence Agency (52).").

79. Bart Elias, William Krouse, and Ed Rappaport, Homeland Security: Air Passenger Prescreening and Counterterrorism, CRS REPORT FOR CONGRESS (RL 32802) 5 (Mar. 4, 2005).

80. Alden, *supra* note 74, at 28–30.

81. Written Statement of Doris Meissner to the National Commission on Terrorist Attacks upon the United States, January 26, 2004, Seventh Public Hearing of the National Commission on Terrorist Attacks upon the United States.

82. Alden, *supra* note 74, at 30–31.

83. 9/11 COMMISSION REPORT, *supra* note 3, at 83. In a memorandum dated October 16, 2002, Claudio Manno wrote that "On September 11, 2001, only three of these SDs were in effect, with a total of 16 names of individuals that air carriers were prohibited from transporting." Internal TSA Memorandum on "TSA Watchlists" dated Oct. 16, 2002, from Claudio Manno, Acting Associate Under Secretary for Transportation Security Intelligence, to Associate Under Secretary for Security Regulation and Policy (ACLU FOIA Release, A1–010). See *infra* at note 106 for a description of the ACLU Freedom of Information Act litigation that produced this document. Claudio Manno was not aware of any individual listed on an SD who had contested denial to board, or even showed up for a flight for which an SD had been issued—by that point, such individuals weren't flying. Manno, author interview, Mar. 14, 2011, *supra* note 48.

84. Author's interview with Admiral James M. Loy, U.S.C.G. (ret.), Mar. 16, 2011, Washington, D.C.

85. 9/11 COMMISSION REPORT, *supra* note 3, at 85 & 457 n.91. This statistic depends on the definition of the word *hijack*. On December 7, 1987, a disgruntled former employee, David Burke, used his unrelinquished employee credentials to board Pacific Southwest Airlines Flight 1771 bound from Los Angeles to San Francisco. Armed with a .44 caliber pistol, he caused the plane to crash into a California hillside, killing

all forty-three persons on board. NTSB Brief of Accident File No. 1750 (NTSB ID: DCA88MA008) Adopted 01/04/1989; Richard Witkin, Threatening Note is Found at Site of Fatal Jet Crash, N.Y. TIMES, Dec. 11, 1987. This sort of suicide-hijacking, however, was typically not classified as hijacking by security officials. This one was classified by the NTSB as "sabotage . . . intentional . . . passenger."

86. Memorandum for the Record, Manno, 9/11 Commission interview, *supra* note 44, at 4.

87. *Id.,* at 8.

88. Alden, *supra* note 74, at 98.

89. Commissioner Bob Kerrey also exhibited flashes of anger that day: "The FAA can't just say as they've done, they've given us five or six pages of rebuttal to the Joint Committee saying we didn't know, we didn't know, we didn't know, we didn't know, we didn't know. It's like you know how many times can you say we didn't know before somebody says, Jesus, you should have?" Seventh Public Hearing of the National Commission on Terrorist Attacks upon the United States, Jan. 27, 2004, at 84.

90. Eldridge, *supra* note 72, at 78.

91. Testimony of Rear Admiral Cathal "Irish" Flynn USN (ret), Seventh Public Hearing of the National Commission on Terrorist Attacks upon the United States, Jan. 27, 2004, at 29.

92. Author's interview with Michael P. Jackson, Mar. 14, 2011, Arlington, Virginia.

93. 147 CONG. REC. S9553, S9554–55 (Sept. 20, 2001) (Message of President George W. Bush). According to the 9/11 Commission, Vice President Cheney recommended establishing this office as a means to coordinate multiple agencies quickly as early as September 14, 2001. 9/11 COMMISSION REPORT, *supra* note 3, at 327 & 555 n. 16. Congress passed a joint resolution authorizing the use of military force on September 18th. Pub. L. No. 107-40, § 2(a), 115 Stat. 224 (Sept. 18, 2001) (codified at 50 U.S.C. § 1541 (Supp. V 2005)).

94. Executive Order 13,228 (Oct. 8, 2001). Homeland Security Presidential Directive 1 (HSPD-1) further detailed the functions of the Council.

95. Pub. L. 107-56, 115 Stat. 272 (Oct. 26, 2001).

96. Alden, *supra* note 74, at 127.

97. Alden, *supra* note 74, at 127–28.

98. Author's interview with Michael P. Jackson, Mar. 14, 2011, Arlington, Virginia.

99. Author's interview with Richard Falkenrath, June 8, 2010, New York City.

100. Pub. L. 107-71, 115 Stat. 597, Nov. 19, 2001.

101. The Homeland Security Act, creating the Department of Homeland Security, was signed into law on November 25, 2002. Homeland Security Act of 2002, Pub. L. 107-296, 116 Stat 2135, Nov. 25, 2002.

102. 49 U.S.C. § 114(h)(3)(A)-(B).

103. Author's interview with Michael P. Jackson, Mar. 14, 2011, Arlington, Virginia ("I was one of two negotiators that the administration sent to negotiate the ATSA bill that created TSA"); author's interview with Richard Falkenrath, June 8, 2010, New York City ("And you know TSA was stood up by Michael Jackson. . . . He was the key guy for standing up TSA. Norm Mineta was secretary but Jackson really drove it."); STEVEN BRILL, AFTER: HOW AMERICA CONFRONTED THE SEPTEMBER 12 ERA 235 (2003).

104. Author's interview with Admiral James M. Loy, Mar. 16, 2011, Washington, D.C.

105. Author's interview with Michael P. Jackson, Mar. 14, 2011, Washington, D.C. ("So when TSA promulgated the Selectee and the No Fly List, it was done through security directives, in essence in that authority, and, so at the end of the day, implementing the No Fly List is a TSA, in my understanding of it is, that it relies upon TSA legal authorities.").

106. Redacted e-mail chain (ACLU FOIA Release B2-128). This document is part of a Freedom of Information Act release obtained by the American Civil Liberties Union as a result of civil litigation, Gordon v. FBI, 390 F.Supp.2d 897 (N.D. Cal. 2004). Most of the documents are available at http://www.aclu.org/national-security/unprecedented-release-government-documents-reveal-confusion-and-absence-policy-imp. The remaining documents were obtained from one of the plaintiffs' attorneys, Thomas R. Burke, a partner at Davis Wright Tremaine LLP. The documents were released as separate attachments: attachment A has two parts and attachment B has four parts. All documents are identified by their original titles and dates and also by the attachment, part, and Bates number.

107. Redacted e-mail chain (ACLU FOIA Release B2-130).

108. Alden, *supra* note 74, at 241.

109. Redacted e-mail chain (ACLU FOIA Release B2-137).

110. Redacted e-mail dated Oct. 11, 2002 (ACLU FOIA Release B2-137); redacted e-mail dated Feb. 5, 2003 ("Here is what I need from you and your UC to place an individual that is believed to be a threat to Civil Aviation Security on the TSA No-Fly list. An EC is probably the best vehicle to do this. . . . All the bio info you can put together on this person. This will need to be at the FOUO (for official use only) level, it goes to the airlines. . . . Once we get this, I will forward this person's name to the TSA for placement on the No Fly list. Once this person is on the list, he will not fly within the US, nor will he be able to fly out of the US or from any airport [redacted]") (ACLU FOIA Release B2-130); redacted e-mail dated Dec. 18, 2002 (same) (ACLU FOIA Release B2-128).

111. Internal TSA Memorandum on "TSA Watchlists" dated Oct. 16, 2002, from Claudio Manno, Acting Associate Under Secretary for Transportation Security Intelligence, to Associate Under Secretary for Security Regulation and Policy (ACLU FOIA Release, A1-010). Kip Hawley, a former administrator of the TSA, asserts without citation that, shortly after September 11, a Security Directive containing approximately twenty-five names taken from an unspecified database became "the first iteration of the now-iconic no-fly list" at the suggestion of a former U.S. Marine Captain Joe Salvator, who had been loaned to the FAA from the Department of Defense and later worked as a TSA intelligence deputy. KIP HAWLEY AND NATHAN MEANS, PERMANENT EMERGENCY: INSIDE THE TSA AND THE FIGHT FOR THE FUTURE OF AMERICAN SECURITY 36 (2012). However, this book contains virtually no references to corroborating sources and is self-admittedly unreliable: "I have simplified certain processes or omitted details, or presented as a single scene a composite of events that occurred over time." Although the author states that he has occasionally "lightly fictionalized an event, detail, or process" in the book, the author does not indicate whether this is an instance of that sort of imaginative recreation. *Id.* at vi. I have not located evidence elsewhere to corroborate this version of events in place of those presented in this chapter.

112. *Id.*

113. Memorandum to all field offices titled "Terrorism Watch List," approved by Pasquale D'Amuro, John S. Pistole, Mark E. Miller, and Arthur Cummings, Oct. 23, 2002 (ACLU FOIA Release A2-124-127).

114. *Id.*

115. E-mail from SSA [redacted] to Arthur M. Cummings, May 28, 2002, 1:43PM (ACLU FOIA release B1-29). My efforts to identify the particular SSA who authored this e-mail were unsuccessful. E-mail correspondence with Susan T. McKee, Public Affairs Specialist, FBI Public Affairs Office, May 24–June 12, 2010 (on file with author).

116. E-mail from SSA [redacted] to [redacted], June 18, 2002, 6:35PM (ACLU FOIA release B5-271).

117. E-mail from SSA [redacted], Civil Aviation Security Program, Domestic Terrorism Counterterrorism Planning Section, Counterterrorism Division, to [redacted], July 22, 2002, 1:48PM (ACLU FOIA release B1-43).

118. Author's interview with Randy Beardsworth, Mar. 11, 2010, Washington, D.C.

119. *Id.*

120. E-mail from SSA [redacted], Civil Aviation Security Program, Special Events Management Unit, Domestic Terrorism Counterterrorism Planning Section, Counterterrorism Division FBI, to [redacted], July 5, 2002, 5:50 PM (ACLU FOIA release B3-168).

121. *Id.*

122. E-mail between SSA [redacted], Counterterrorism Squad, Honolulu, and SSA [redacted] Civil Aviation Security Program, Counterterrorism Division, FBI, Sept. 17, 2002 (ACLU FOIA release B4-255).

123. 9/11 Commission Report, *supra* note 3, at 391 ("Over 90 percent of the nation's $5.3 billion annual investment in the TSA goes to aviation—to fight the last war.").

124. *Id.*, at 273–76.

125. Manno, author interview, Oct. 20, 2009, *supra* note 43.

126. 9/11 Commission Report, *supra* note 3, at 274–75.

127. Director of Central Intelligence George J. Tenet, Testimony Before the Joint Inquiry into Terrorist Attacks Against the United States (Unclassified Version), June 18, 2002.

128. Author interview with Richard Falkenrath, June 8, 2010, New York City.

129. Falkenrath was Special Assistant to the President and Senior Director for Policy and Plans in the Office of Homeland Security from October 2001 to January 2003, after which he became Deputy Assistant to the President and Deputy Homeland Security Advisor until spring 2004. Falkenrath explained that both HSPD-6 and its accompanying Memorandum of Understanding were his idea. "Yeah so this was my clever little thing. It was a package deal where you got HSPD-6 and the MOU and you did them simultaneously," Falkenrath recalled. Such policymaking was only possible, he continued, "because everyone agreed we screwed up and we needed to do something." Author interview with Richard Falkenrath, June 8, 2010, New York City.

130. Indeed, according to Edward Alden, "Congress had envisioned that [DHS] would become an information clearinghouse for protecting the country against terrorist attack." Alden quotes Tom Ridge, the first Secretary of DHS, regarding the decision to place the TTIC within the CIA structure: "The president made it pretty clear where he wanted it. He didn't want it in DHS. End of story." Alden, *supra* note 74, at 230. Similarly, Richard Falkenrath describes his role in locating the TSC within the FBI:

> [T]he one squirrelly bit was who was going to own TSC. And that for all the drafts until the final principals' meeting or deputies' meeting we just bracketed it. We didn't decide it and, cause it could have gone to either DHS or FBI. But DHS, you got at this point, is nine months old. . . . DHS comes in and says, Well, we think we should have this. And the FBI says, Well, we think we should have this. But they were very polite and we weren't like cramming it down. We didn't decide it because I actually think, my point here was look, the statutory construction for both agencies would permit it to go either place, but not really anywhere else. And there was no way it could go to State cause we were talking about law enforcement, screening, I mean this was a lot of different kinds of lists and I said, okay, let's not resolve this here, this first meeting. Well, the two of you agencies go back and lay out your step-by-step proposal about how you'd stand up this entity, time frame, budget costs, whatever, staffing whatever."

Two weeks later, Falkenrath says, FBI came back with a detailed plan, while DHS conceded that the state of their internal development as a new agency was such that they couldn't put together a proposal in time.

> [It] was a huge concession but the momentum of the process was such that they couldn't just say everyone in the government wait for us to get our act together then we'll take it over. There was no room to be turfy because I'd created this kind of environment where we had this huge vulnerability hanging out there, we gotta like have a solution, this could happen again today. . . . FBI came forward with their proposal. No one else had any other proposal. DHS has no choice but to assent to letting it go to FBI. And then at some point I remember in the MOU, it may be in there, there was a provision like in a year we would reevaluate whether it should go to DHS, and that was fine with me. So that was it. And then that was the only open issue. Then the President signed this, it was totally, they sent it in and it came back the next day executed and they signed their MOU.

Interview with Richard Falkenrath, New York City, June 8, 2010.

131. E.O. 13228 (Oct. 8, 2001), 66 FED. REG. 51812 (Oct. 10, 2001). As the 9/11 Commission described the process within the NSC (on which it was based), the National Security Advisor, through the NSC Staff, "developed recommendations for presidential directives, differently labeled by each president. For President Clinton, they were to be Presidential Decision Directives; for President George W. Bush, National Security Policy Directives. These documents and many others requiring approval by the president worked their way through interagency committees usually composed of departmental representatives at the assistant secretary level or just below it. The NSC staff had senior directors who would sit on these interagency committees, often as chair, to facilitate agreement and to represent the wider interests of the national security advisor." 9/11 COMMISSION REPORT, *supra* note 3, at 99–100.

132. 149 CONG. REC. 2033, 2035–36 (Jan. 28, 2003) (Message of Pres. George W. Bush).

133. Following its announcement in President Bush's 2003 State of the Union Message, the TTIC's mission was outlined by Director of Central Intelligence Directive (DCID) 2/4. TERRORIST THREAT INTEGRATION CENTER (TTIC) AND ITS RELATIONSHIP WITH THE DEPARTMENTS OF JUSTICE AND HOMELAND SECURITY: JOINT HEARING BE-

FORE THE COMMITTEE ON THE JUDICIARY AND THE SELECT COMMITTEE ON HOMELAND SECURITY, 108TH CONG. 106 (2004) (Responses to Questions for the Record by John O. Brennan, Dec. 4. 2003). The NCTC was established by Executive Order 13354 (Aug. 27, 2004), 69 FED. REG. 53589 (Sept. 1, 2004), and then given statutory authority under section 1021 of the the Intelligence Reform and Terrorism Prevention Act of 2004, Pub. L. 108-458, 118 Stat. 3672, Dec. 17, 2004 (codified at 50 U.S.C. § 4040).

134. CIA Press Release, Terrorist Threat Integration Center Begins Operations, May 1, 2003, available at https://www.cia.gov/news-information/press-releases-statements/press-release-archive-2003/pr05012003.html.

135. U.S. DEPARTMENT OF JUSTICE OFFICE OF THE INSPECTOR GENERAL, FOLLOW-UP AUDIT OF THE TERRORIST SCREENING CENTER [hereafter OIG 2007 REPORT] iv, n.4 (2007); William J. Krouse, *supra* note 72, at 12; Winston P. Wiley, Chair, Senior Steering Group, *Joint Statement of the Terrorist Threat Integration Center Senior Steering Group,* Hearing on Consolidating Intelligence Analysis: A Review of the President's Proposal to Create a Terrorist Threat Integration Center, U.S. Senate Committee on Homeland Security and Government Affairs, February 26, 2003.

136. TERRORIST THREAT INTEGRATION CENTER (TTIC) AND ITS RELATIONSHIP WITH THE DEPARTMENTS OF JUSTICE AND HOMELAND SECURITY, *supra* note 133, at 99 (Responses to Questions for the Record by John O. Brennan, Dec. 4. 2003).

137. The Intelligence Authorization Act for Fiscal Year 2003, Pub. L. 107-306, § 343, 116 Stat. 2383, 2399 (Nov. 27, 2002), mandated the creation of a Terrorist Identification Classification System, a list to be shared with appropriate government agencies of "individuals who are known or suspected international terrorists, and of organizations that are known or suspected international terrorist organizations."

138. U.S. DEPARTMENT OF JUSTICE OFFICE OF THE INSPECTOR GENERAL, REVIEW OF THE TERRORIST SCREENING CENTER 127 (App. IV) (June 2005) (hereafter OIG 2005 REPORT). This statement was made by the TSC, quoting the language of paragraph 10 of the Memorandum of Understanding that accompanied HSPD-6, in its written response to the OIG draft audit; *see also* Memorandum of Understanding on the Integration and Use of Screening Information to Protect Against Terrorism, § 10, Sept. 16, 2003 (hereafter TSC 2003 MOU).

139. Written Statement of Russell E. Travers, Jan. 26, 2004, Seventh Public Hearing of the National Commission on Terrorist Attacks upon the United States; Krouse, *supra* note 73, at 14; TSC 2003 MOU, *supra* note 138, at § 28. At the time of his testimony, Mr. Travers was a deputy director at TTIC.

140. RONALD KESSLER, THE TERRORIST WATCH: INSIDE THE DESPERATE RACE TO STOP THE NEXT ATTACK 166 (2007) (quoting then Vice Admiral John Scott Redd).

141. TERRORIST THREAT INTEGRATION CENTER (TTIC) AND ITS RELATIONSHIP WITH THE DEPARTMENTS OF JUSTICE AND HOMELAND SECURITY, *supra* note 133, at 123 (Responses to Questions for the Record by John O. Brennan, Dec. 4. 2003).

142. HSPD-6, § 1 (Sept. 16, 2003). See notes 129 and 130 for background on the development of HSPD-6.

143. Author interview with Timothy J. Healy, Director, Terrorist Screening Center, December 4, 2009, Washington, D.C.

144. *Id.*

145. OIG 2005 REPORT, *supra* note 138, at iv.

146. These include Defense, Homeland Security (CIS, Coast Guard, CBP, ICE, Secret Service, and TSA), Justice (FBI, ATF, and DEA), State, Treasury, and private con-

tractors. Unclassified PowerPoint presentation supplied by Trent Duffy, TSC Public Affairs, e-mail to author, April 20, 2010.

147. Krouse, *supra* note 73, at 15.

148. Healy interview, *supra* note 143; *see also* TSC 2003 MOU, *supra* note 138, at § 5.

149. OIG 2005 REPORT, *supra* note 138, at iv.

150. Homeland Security Presidential Directive 11, § 2, August 21, 2008 ("The Terrorist Screening Center (TSC), which was established and is administered by the Attorney General pursuant to HSPD-6, enables Government officials to check individuals against a consolidated Terrorist Screening Center Database.").

151. Healy interview, *supra* note 143.

152. *Id.*

153. OIG 2005 REPORT, *supra* note 138, at 1. OIG 2007 REPORT, *supra* note 135, at 1.

154. OIG 2005 REPORT, *supra* note 138, at 109 (App. IV).

155. HSPD-6, a short and general document, was accompanied by a memorandum of understanding signed by Attorney General John Ashcroft, DHS Secretary Tom Ridge, Secretary of State Colin Powell, and CIA Director George Tenet that provided operational details. *See* TSC 2003 MOU, *supra* note 138; *see also* Travers, *supra* note 139.

156. Krouse, *supra* note 73, at 14.

157. Kessler, *supra* note 140, at 3–4; http://www.nctc.gov/about_us/about_nctc.html (last visited June 15, 2012).

158. Keeping Watch: Inside the Terrorist Screening Center, http://www.fbi.gov/news/stories/2007/august/tsc083107 (accessed on TSC homepage, last visited June 15, 2012).

159. The only exception, carved out by the language concerning U.S. persons, concerned "purely domestic terrorism information," i.e., information concerning U.S. persons that lacked any connection to foreign or international terrorism. Such information remains the purview of the FBI, which independently provides it to the TSC. Travers, *supra* note 139.

160. TSC 2003 MOU, *supra* note 138, at § 13 ("The TTIC identities database will serve, with the exception described in paragraph (10) [concerning purely domestic terrorism information to be supplied by the FBI], as the single source for the Terrorist Screening Center terrorist screening database.").

161. Travers, *supra* note 139. Access to classified information held by the Intelligence Community for entry into TIPOFF by State, and the INS's subsequent access to TIPOFF, was governed by at least one MOU on sharing four unclassified elements: name, date of birth, country of birth, and passport number. Eldridge, *supra* note 72, at 79.

162. U.S. DEPARTMENT OF JUSTICE OFFICE OF THE INSPECTOR GENERAL, THE FEDERAL BUREAU OF INVESTIGATION'S TERRORIST WATCHLIST NOMINATION PRACTICES 28 (May 2009) (hereafter OIG 2009 REPORT).

163. TSC 2003 MOU, *supra* note 138, at § 13. The TSC does not "own" derogatory information in this sense: derogatory information is not included in the TSDB. Derogatory information is typically classified; it is "owned" by the source agency. Therefore, although TSC analysts may (and often do) view derogatory information associated with a TSDB record, only unclassified data elements of an identifying nature are included in the TSDB. This distinction could be described in a metaphorical (but not technical) sense as the difference between accessing derogatory information as if on

the Internet and possessing unclassified biographical information as if on a hard drive. TSC analysts are able to use both derogatory and biographical information, but only the latter is kept within the confines of the TSDB. In this sense, the TSC had merely a usufructuary's right to this information.

164. *Id.*, at 8; OIG 2005 REPORT, *supra* note 138, at 24.
165. OIG 2009 REPORT, *supra* note 162, at vii & 13.
166. Unclassified PowerPoint presentation supplied by Trent Duffy, TSC Public Affairs, e-mail to author, April 20, 2010. The slide shown to congressional staff was SSI, Sensitive Security Information.
167. OIG 2009 REPORT, *supra* note 162, at 5.
168. OIG 2005 REPORT, *supra* note 138, at 91 (App. III).
169. OIG 2005 REPORT, *supra* note 138, at 25.
170. *Id.*, at 12.
171. *Id.*, at viii.
172. HSPD-6, Sept. 16, 2003.
173. OIG 2009 REPORT, *supra* note 162, at 1 n. 40; Timothy J. Healy, Statement before the Senate Homeland Security and Governmental Affairs Committee, Dec. 9, 2009.
174. OIG 2007 REPORT, *supra* note 135, at 3 n.23.
175. Executive Order 13354, § 7(d), 69 FED. REG. 53589, 53591–92 (Aug. 27, 2004). This language almost exactly mirrors the definition of terrorism information made in a preceding memorandum of understanding between the Intelligence Community, Federal Law Enforcement Agencies, and the Department of Homeland Security Concerning Information Sharing, § 2(r), Mar. 4, 2003.
176. OIG 2009 REPORT, *supra* note 162, at 8; OIG 2005 REPORT, *supra* note 138, at 24.
177. OIG 2009 REPORT, *supra* note 162, at 8.
178. Author's interview with Randy Beardsworth, Mar. 11, 2010, Washington, D.C.
179. *Id.*
180. U.S. DEPARTMENT OF JUSTICE OFFICE OF THE INSPECTOR GENERAL, A REVIEW OF THE FBI'S INVESTIGATIONS OF CERTAIN DOMESTIC ADVOCACY GROUPS 27 (Sept. 2010). The OIG quoted from the TSC's response to a 2005 audit: "The Associates Project was developed to identify possible associates of known or suspected terrorists. During their normal course of duties, law enforcement officers, DOS officials and Border Agents encounter known or suspected terrorists in the TSDB from querying their case management systems during an encounter. These encounters provide valuable information which includes who the known or suspected terrorist is with at the time of the encounter. These encounters with possible associates will be documented and provided to the office of origin for appropriate action." OIG 2005 REPORT, *supra* note 138, at 100.
181. OIG 2005 REPORT, *supra* note 138, at 30.
182. OIG 2007 REPORT, *supra* note 135, at vii.

Chapter 7

1. ARTHUR KOESTLER, THE GHOST IN THE MACHINE 202 (1976).
2. Letter from Secretary of State Charles Evans Hughes to H. M. Lord, Director, Bureau of the Budget, Jan. 20, 1925; File 112/721a; CDF 1910–29; RG 59; NACP.

3. H. W. Erksine, You Don't Go If She Says No, 132 COLLIERS 62, 64 (July 11, 1953).

4. Letter to Secretary Acheson from Charles Maylon, former legislative assistant to President Truman, June 20, 1952; File 110.4 PD/6-2052; CDF 1950–54; RG 59; NACP ("Due to extenuating circumstances it was necessary to procure the passport without delay. Mrs. Shipley issued her passport in less than twenty-four hours. That is indeed service to the people").

5. RONALD KESSLER, THE TERRORIST WATCH: INSIDE THE DESPERATE RACE TO STOP THE NEXT ATTACK 168 (2007).

6. See chapter 6, note 158.

7. Harold B. Hinton, Guardian of American Passports, N.Y. TIMES, Apr. 27, 1941.

8. Leaving America is Easy—for Most, 33 U.S. NEWS & WORLD REP. 28, 29 (July 4, 1952).

9. Explanation of Passport Procedures: Press Conference Remarks by Secretary Acheson, 27 U.S. DEP'T OF STATE BULL. 40, 41 (July 7, 1952).

10. Statement of Timothy J. Healy, Director, Terrorist Screening Center, Testimony before the Senate Homeland Security and Governmental Affairs Committee, Dec. 9, 2009 (hereafter "Healy 2009 Testimony"); *see also* author interview with Timothy J. Healy, Director, and Jacqueline F. Brown, General Counsel, Terrorist Screening Center, FBI Headquarters, Washington, D.C., Dec. 4, 2009. A December 2010 FBI memo on watchlisting guidance provides a little more detail on the "reasonable suspicion" standard, but not much:

> In order to nominate a subject for entry into the TSDB and all eligible supported systems, the FBI must have a reasonable suspicion to believe that the subject is a known or suspected terrorist (KST). To meet this standard, the FBI must have "articulable" intelligence or information which, based on the totality of the facts and taken together with rational inferences from those facts, reasonably warrants a determination that the subject is known or suspected to be (or has been) knowingly engaged in conduct constituting, in preparation for, in aid of, or related to terrorism or terrorist activities. There must be an objective factual basis for the nominator to believe that the individual is a KST. Mere guesses or "hunches" are not enough to constitute a reasonable suspicion that an individual is a KST.
>
> The Domestic Investigations and Operations Guide (DIOG) authorizes the initiation of a Preliminary Investigation based on any "allegation or information" indicative of criminal activity or threats to national security. Subjects of terrorism Preliminary Investigations must meet the reasonable suspicion standard for watchlisting. In order for such subjects to be watchlisted, the allegation or information used to predicate the investigation must have at least one source of corroboration that ties these subjects to terrorism or terrorist activities. The DIOG authorizes initiation of a Full Investigation based on "articulable factual basis" of possible criminal and national threat activity. The articulable factual basis used to open a terrorism Full Investigation will always meet the reasonable suspicion standard for watchlisting.
>
> Subjects of Guardian leads and assessments should not be submitted to TREX for watchlisting. In addition, the FBI will not nominate an individual based on single source information from unsolicited tips such as walk-ins,

write-ins, or call-ins, unless the subject meets the reasonable suspicion standard. Nominations should not be based on source reporting that is unreliable or not credible. Suspicious activity alone, that does not rise to the level of a reasonable suspicion, is not a sufficient basis to watchlist an individual.

Section 1.1. Watchlisting Standard – Reasonable Suspicion. FBI Memorandum to all field offices from Counterterrorism Front Office titled "Counterterrorism Program Guidance Watchlisting Administrative and Operational Guidance," Case ID # 3190-HQ-A1487636-CTD, Dec. 21, 2010 (hereafter "FBI Memo on Watchlisting Guidance"). This 29-page document was obtained through a Freedom of Information Act (FOIA) request dated June 7, 2011, that was submitted to the FBI by the Electronic Privacy Information Center (EPIC). The memorandum, part of a 92-page release made by the FBI dated Sept. 13, 2011, was subsequently posted on EPIC's website, http://epic.org/foia/fbi_watchlist.html (last visited June 15, 2012).

11. Healy and Brown interview, Dec. 4, 2009, *supra* note 10. Director Healy credited his general counsel, Jacqueline "Lyn" Brown, as having been instrumental in the drafting of this common standard for watchlist nominations.

12. The working group was composed of subject matter experts from the intelligence and screening communities (CIA, NSA, DOD, DOS, DHS, FBI, TSC, NCTC, and the Office of the Director of National Intelligence). The guidance document is classified as sensitive security information for official use only. It was approved in January 2009 by the Deputies Committee of the Homeland Security Council. It was then issued by the TSC and the White House Executive Secretariat. It was approximately twenty pages long and appeared in an appendix (Appendix 5 in March 2009) of the Watchlisting Protocol. The Watchlisting Protocol is a lengthy and detailed reference book used by TSC managers and analysts on a daily basis.

The working group's objective was to improve the definitional clarity of key terms in the relevant Homeland Security Presidential Directives. As noted above, terms such as "terrorism" and "terrorist activities," which are found in the HSPDs, are not always consistently defined in the U.S. Code. Likewise, successive HSPDs contain subtle differences in language. HSPD-6 refers to individuals "known or appropriately suspected" of various connections to "terrorism." HSPD-11 refers to individuals "known or reasonably suspected" of such connections and added the phrase "terrorist activities." HSPD-24, which concerns the use of biometrics in screening, refers to an "articulable and reasonable basis for suspicion" that an individual posed "a threat to national security."

This working group itself emerged out of one of the twice-yearly meetings of the TSC Policy Board, which is composed of the signatories to the TSC memoranda of understanding. The relationship of the working group to the Policy Board is roughly analogous to the relationship of the Deputies' Committee to its Policy Coordinating Committees (PCCs, which are now known as Inter-Agency Policy Committees, or IPCs). Since the Homeland Security Council no longer exists, these reevaluations are now conducted in the National Security Council. Author interview with Jacqueline "Lyn" Brown, General Counsel, Terrorist Screening Center, Mar. 8, 2010, Washington, D.C.; *see also* DEPARTMENT OF HOMELAND SECURITY OFFICE OF THE INSPECTOR GENERAL, ROLE OF THE NO FLY AND SELECTEE LISTS IN SECURING COMMERCIAL AVIATION 9 (July 2009) [hereafter "DHS 2009 OIG REPORT"]. The TSC issued new watchlisting guidance in July 2010. See FBI Memo on Watchlisting Guidance, *supra* note 10.

13. Is There a "Freedom to Travel"? That's the New Issue in Security Cases, 39 U.S. NEWS & WORLD REP. 39 (Sept. 9, 1955).

14. *See* 49 U.S.C. § 46110.

15. Memorandum of Understanding on the Integration and Use of Screening Information to Protect Against Terrorism, § 29, Sept. 16, 2003 (hereafter "TSC 2003 MOU").

16. Author interview with Richard Falkenrath, June 8, 2010, New York City (Kahn: "Now I understand it's a very consultative process with lots of detailees from the interested agencies at TSC. But do I understand that language to mean if and when there is ever a conflict where TSA says we want him on, and TSC doesn't agree, the deciding group is TSC, not TSA?" Falkenrath: "That was certainly our idea.").

17. Author's interview with Admiral James M. Loy, U.S.C.G. (ret.), Mar. 16, 2011, Washington D.C.

18. Falkenrath interview, June 8, 2010, *supra* note 16.

19. 49 U.S.C. § 114(e)(1) & § 114 (f).

20. 49 U.S.C. § 114(h)(1) & (2).

21. 49 U.S.C. § 114(h)(3)(A).

22. 49 U.S.C. § 114(h)(3)(B).

23. *See* Ch. 6, n. 130, for Falkenrath's description of this "squirrelly bit [about] who was going to own TSC."

24. Healy and Brown interview, December 4, 2009, *supra* note 10.

25. Kip Hawley, Assistant Secretary, Transportation Security Administration, Statement Before the House Committee on Homeland Security, Subcommittee on Transportation Security and Infrastructure Protection, Washington, D.C., Sept. 9, 2008 ("the TSC now provides 'one-stop shopping' so that every government agency is using the same TSDB"); Ms. Rossides' identical use of the phrase is found in the DHS 2009 OIG REPORT, *supra* note 12, at 41 (Memorandum from Gale D. Rossides, Acting Administrator, to Richard Skinner, DHS Inspector General, Mar. 17, 2009).

26. Timothy J. Healy, Statement before the Senate Committee on Homeland Security and Governmental Affairs, Washington, D.C., Mar. 10, 2010 (hereafter "Healy 2010 Testimony"). According to the Government Accountability Office, "[i]n general, a nominator is a department or agency that has determined that an individual is a known or suspected terrorist and nominates that individual to TIDE and the TSDB based on information that originated with that agency or another agency. An originator is a department or agency that has appropriate subject matter interest and classification authority, and collects terrorism information and disseminates it to other U.S. government entities." U.S. GOVERNMENT ACCOUNTABILITY OFFICE, TERRORIST WATCHLIST: ROUTINELY ASSESSING IMPACTS OF AGENCY ACTIONS SINCE THE DECEMBER 25, 2009, ATTEMPTED ATTACK COULD HELP INFORM FUTURE EFFORTS (GAO-12-476) 6 n.15 (May 2012).

27. *Id.*

28. A July 2009 report by the DHS Inspector General states that these "TSA subject matter experts . . . are detailed to the TSC from TSA's Office of Intelligence and Federal Air Marshal Service (FAMS)." DHS 2009 OIG REPORT, *supra* note 12, at 12; *see also* Brown interview, Mar. 8, 2010, *supra* note 12. This lends further support for the conclusion that TSC, not TSA, is truly in charge. "There was a core of people who were formally detailees," recalled Michael Jackson, Deputy Secretary of the Depart-

ment of Homeland Security from March 2005 through October 2007. "And it was not fair game for you to try to use that person to inflict your own policy views on the agency where they were working. They brought a general sense of what DHS was about or TSA was about over to that and to some degree represented the type of thinking and equities that were presumably resident at TSA. But they worked for this assignment and they took their daily operating orders from the head of the, well, if it was the FBI guy, for the agency." Author's interview with Michael Jackson, Mar. 14, 2011, Arlington, Virginia. Jackson also remembers sending "a bunch of loaners over and I suspect they weren't formally detailed. I just think they were the right type of people, some may be a lawyer, some may be intel office people, some may be FAMS who had intel training and field training, et cetera. But we essentially loaned them smart and capable generalists to go through the list." *Id.* Jackson is probably remembering the fallout of a July 2006 review when, with the help of ten federal air marshals assigned from DHS to TSC, the No Fly List was culled from 71,872 records down to 34,230 records by January 31, 2007. OFFICE OF THE INSPECTOR GENERAL, U.S. DEP'T OF JUSTICE, FOLLOW-UP AUDIT OF THE TERRORIST SCREENING CENTER 31–32 (Audit Report 07-41, Sept. 2007).

29. Healy 2010 Testimony, *supra* note 26.
30. *Id.*
31. Loy interview, Mar. 16, 2011, *supra* note 17 (Author: "So do I understand correctly that there was quite a lot of back and forth and conflict—for lack of a better word—but positive conflict. But in the end, at the end of the day, whether it's a decision in the first instance to watchlist or it's a decision to go back and take a look and see if redress is warranted, the final decision maker is TSC?" Loy: "Absolutely.").
32. *Id.*
33. Jackson interview, March 14, 2011, *supra* note 28.
34. U.S. DEPARTMENT OF JUSTICE OFFICE OF THE INSPECTOR GENERAL, FOLLOW-UP AUDIT OF THE TERRORIST SCREENING CENTER 31 (2007) (hereafter OIG 2007 Report) (Whether "records" includes multiple entries relating to a single individual is unclear.)
35. *Id.*, at 32.
36. *Id.*
37. *Id.*, at 33.
38. *Id.*, at 31 ("To assist the TSC in its review of the No Fly List, the DHS temporarily assigned 10 federal air marshals to the TSC"). This conflicts with the DHS Inspector General's report, which refers to subject matter experts "detailed" from TSA to TSC. Compare *supra* note 28. This may simply be a case of less than precise use of language. Regardless, the air marshals were there "[t]o *assist* the TSC in *its* review," which seems to capture a hierarchical relationship. OIG 2007 REPORT, *supra* note 34, at 31.
39. OIG 2007 REPORT, *supra* note 34, at 28, n. 41.
40. The description of Gray's allegations is taken from the Defendant's Opposition to Plaintiff's Motion for a Preliminary Injunction, Gray v. TSA, Case No. 05-11445-DPW, 2005 WL 3803814, at *5–8 (D. Mass. Sept. 20, 2005).
41. *Id.*, at *14–15 (internal citations omitted; emphasis in original).
42. DHS 2009 OIG REPORT, *supra* note 12, at 9.
43. *Id.*, at 42 (Memorandum from Rossides to DHS IG Richard Skinner, Mar. 17, 2009).

44. *Id.*, at 54.
45. Healy 2010 Testimony, *supra* note 26.
46. OIG 2007 REPORT, *supra* note 34, at 3 n.23.
47. Brown interview, Mar. 8, 2010, *supra* note 12.
48. FBI Memo on Watchlisting Guidance, Dec. 21, 2010, *supra* note 10.
49. *Id.*
50. Some history provided support for this conclusion. When the State Department controlled its own TIPOFF database back in the late 1980s and early 1990s, its criteria to start a file on an individual "included reasonable suspicion that the alien engaged in or might engage in terrorism, otherwise known as 'derogatory information' and sufficient biographical information for positive identification." THOMAS R. ELDRIDGE, ET AL. 9/11 AND TERRORIST TRAVEL: STAFF REPORT OF THE NATIONAL COMMISSION ON TERRORIST ATTACKS UPON THE UNITED STATES 89 (2004). The 9/11 Commission staff traced that "reasonable suspicion" standard back to the early 1980s, when it appeared in (and appeared to them to have been taken from) a confidential task force report that "suggested a border watchlist be created to improve national security. The task force suggested that the watchlist database hold names of those who may seek admission for criminal purposes. The reasoning was that since the database only compiled names of those who may seek admission, the higher standard of excludability need not be met." *Id.* at 110 n. 169.
51. Healy and Brown interview, Dec. 4, 2009, *supra* note 10.
52. 392 U.S. 1, 21 (1968).
53. Brown interview, Mar. 8, 2010, *supra* note 12.
54. 392 U.S. at 21 ("The scheme of the Fourth Amendment becomes meaningful only when it is assured that at some point the conduct of those charged with enforcing the laws can be subjected to the more detached, neutral scrutiny of a judge who must evaluate the reasonableness of a particular search or seizure in light of the particular circumstances.").
55. U.S. DEPARTMENT OF JUSTICE OFFICE OF THE INSPECTOR GENERAL, REVIEW OF THE TERRORIST SCREENING CENTER 30 (June 2005).
56. Press Conference Remarks by Secretary Acheson, *supra* note 9, at 41. A few years later, the head of the Bureau of Security and Consular Affairs began a public defense of passport procedures with the same argument: "Out of more than half a million passport applications made to the State Department last year, only about 450 were denied on substantive grounds. Only thirteen final denials were turn-downs on the ground of Communist activities." Roderic L. O'Connor, The State Department Defends, 41 SATURDAY REVIEW 11 (Jan. 11, 1958).
57. Healy 2009 Testimony, *supra* note 10.
58. Although the 9/11 Commission seized on the number twelve, the FAA and the TSA put the number of SDs in effect on September 11, 2001, at three and the number of names of individuals prohibited from air travel at sixteen. Internal TSA Memorandum on "TSA Watchlists" dated Oct. 16, 2002, from Claudio Manno, Acting Associate Under Secretary for Transportation Security Intelligence, to Associate Under Secretary for Security Regulation and Policy (ACLU FOIA Release, A1-009).
59. Internal TSA Memorandum on "TSA Watchlists" dated Oct. 16, 2002, from Claudio Manno, Acting Associate Under Secretary for Transportation Security Intelligence, to Associate Under Secretary for Security Regulation and Policy (ACLU FOIA Release, A1-010); Transportation Security Intelligence Service, *TSA Watchlists,* Unclas-

sified PowerPoint Slides dated December 2002 (ACLU FOIA Release, A1-002). This document is part of a Freedom of Information Act release obtained by the American Civil Liberties Union as a result of civil litigation, Gordon v. FBI, 390 F.Supp.2d 897 (N.D. Cal. 2004). *See* chapter 6, n. 106, for an explanation of document coding.

60. Transportation Security Intelligence Service, *TSA Watchlists,* Unclassified PowerPoint Slides dated Dec. 2002 (ACLU FOIA Release, A1-003); Internal TSA Memorandum on "TSA Watchlists" dated Oct. 16, 2002, from Claudio Manno, Acting Associate Under Secretary for Transportation Security Intelligence to Associate Under Secretary for Security Regulation and Policy (ACLU FOIA Release, A1-010).

61. Testimony of Edmond Soliday, Seventh Public Hearing of the National Commission on Terrorist Attacks upon the United States, Jan. 27, 2004, at 82.

62. OIG 2007 REPORT, *supra* note 34, at 31–32.

63. Healy and Brown interview, Dec. 4, 2009, *supra* note 10. On the Selectee List at that time were 13,903 people, of which 1,158 were U.S. persons. *Id.*

64. Jamie Tarabay, *The No-Fly List: FBI Says It's Smaller Than You Think,* National Public Radio (Jan. 26, 2011), http://www.npr.org/2011/01/26/133187841/the-no-fly-list-fbi-says-its-smaller-than-you-think. See also GAO 2012 Report, *supra* note 26 at 14 (reporting number of U.S. Persons on No Fly List "more than doubled" after post-Abdulmutallab initiative).

65. Carol Cratty, *21,000 people now on U.S. no fly list, official says,* CNN, Feb. 2, 2012. The article interchangeable refers to "people" and "names" on the list but seems to mean discrete individuals, saying the list "doubled over the past year."

66. OIG 2007 REPORT, *supra* note 34, at 7.

67. Seventh Public Hearing of the National Commission on Terrorist Attacks upon the United States, Jan. 27, 2004, at 28.

68. FINAL REPORT OF THE NATIONAL COMMISSION ON TERRORIST ATTACKS UPON THE UNITED STATES 393 (2004).

69. Seventh Public Hearing, *supra* note 67, at 37.

70. Testimony of Claudio Manno, Seventh Public Hearing of the National Commission on Terrorist Attacks upon the United States, Jan. 27, 2004, at 37.

71. Internal TSA Memorandum on "TSA Watchlists" dated October 16, 2002, from Claudio Manno, Acting Associate Under Secretary for Transportation Security Intelligence, to Associate Under Secretary for Security Regulation and Policy (ACLU FOIA Release, A1-011).

72. Author interview with C. Stewart Verdery Jr., July 20, 2009, Washington, D.C.

73. Author interview with Richard Falkenrath, June 8, 2010, New York City.

74. Memorandum for the Record, 9/11 Commission informal phone conversation with George Regan, Oct. 21, 2003 (quoted in Eldridge, *supra* note 50, at 86).

75. 49 U.S.C. § 114(h)(3)(A)–(B).

76. As noted in chapter 6, the Intelligence Community was not particularly enthusiastic about the FAA's security directives, or even the State Department's TIPOFF watchlist. As the staff of the 9/11 Commission observed, watchlisting was not seen as an "integral" tool for the work of the Intelligence Community, but rather "a chore off to the side" that "busy intelligence officials just have to remember to do." National Commission on Terrorist Attacks upon the United States Staff Statement No. 2, *Three 9/11 Hijackers: Identification, Watchlisting, and Tracking* 1–2 (2004).

77. Internal TSA Memorandum on "TSA Watchlists" dated October 16, 2002, from Claudio Manno, Acting Associate Under Secretary for Transportation Security

Intelligence, to Associate Under Secretary for Security Regulation and Policy (ACLU FOIA Release, A1-010, 0011); Transportation Security Intelligence Service, *TSA Watchlists,* Unclassified PowerPoint Slides dated Dec. 2002 (ACLU FOIA Release, A1-003).

78. Transportation Security Intelligence Service, *TSA Watchlists,* Unclassified PowerPoint Slides dated Dec. 2002 (ACLU FOIA Release, A1-002).

79. TSA, *Transportation Security Administration Aviation Watchlists: Congressional Staff Briefing,* TSA SSI PowerPoint dated Nov. 12, 2002 (ACLU FOIA Release, A1-017).

80. Healy 2010 Testimony, *supra* note 26.

81. Healy 2009 Testimony, *supra* note 10.

82. DHS 2009 OIG REPORT, *supra* note 12, at 11.

83. Homeland Security Presidential Directive 6 (HSPD-6), Sept. 16, 2003.

84. Docket # 44, Declaration of Christopher M. Piehota, Latif v. Holder, Case 3:10-cv-00750-BR, (D. Ore. Nov. 17, 2010), at ¶ 7 n. 2 (citing *Watchlisting Guidance,* July 2010, Appendix 1, Page 2); see also FBI Memo on Watchlisting Guidance, Dec. 21, 2010, *supra* note 10, at 4.

85. *Id.* (citing *Watchlisting Guidance,* July 2010, Appendix 1, Page 3); see also *supra* note 10, at 4.

86. Jacobellis v. Ohio, 378 U.S. 184, 197 (1964) (Stewart, J., concurring). The harm caused to law by such an unpredictable and subjective approach was later recognized by Justice Stewart himself. Paris Adult Theatre I v. Slaton, 413 U.S. 49, 84 (1973) (joining Justice Brennan's dissent).

87. Compare the definition used by the State Department to compile annual country reports on terrorism, 22 U.S.C. § 2656f (d)(2) ("the term "terrorism" means premeditated, politically motivated violence perpetrated against noncombatant targets by subnational groups or clandestine agents.") with the Federal Criminal Code, 18 U.S.C. § 2331 (5) ("the term "domestic terrorism" means activities that involve acts dangerous to human life that are a violation of the criminal laws of the United States or of any State; appear to be intended to intimidate or coerce a civilian population, to influence the policy of a government by intimidation or coercion, or to affect the conduct of a government by mass destruction, assassination, or kidnapping; and occur primarily within the territorial jurisdiction of the United States.") (internal outline omitted) and with federal immigration law, 8 U.S.C. § 1182 (a)(3)(B)(iii) ("the term 'terrorist activity' means any activity which is unlawful under the laws of the place where it is committed (or which, if it had been committed in the United States, would be unlawful under the laws of the United States or any State) and which involves any of the following: The highjacking or sabotage of any conveyance (including an aircraft, vessel, or vehicle); The seizing or detaining, and threatening to kill, injure, or continue to detain, another individual in order to compel a third person (including a governmental organization) to do or abstain from doing any act as an explicit or implicit condition for the release of the individual seized or detained; A violent attack upon an internationally protected person (as defined in section 1116(b)(4) of Title 18) or upon the liberty of such a person; An assassination; The use of any biological agent, chemical agent, or nuclear weapon or device, or explosive, firearm, or other weapon or dangerous device (other than for mere personal monetary gain), with intent to endanger, directly or indirectly, the safety of one or more individuals or to cause substantial damage to property; A threat,

attempt, or conspiracy to do any of the foregoing.") (internal outline omitted). All three definitions are referenced in the GAO's latest report on the TSC's involvement in terrorist watchlisting. See *supra* note 26 at 6–8.

88. Neil A. Lewis, Fate of Guantánamo Detainees is Debated in Federal Court, N.Y. TIMES, Dec. 2, 2004.

89. 49 U.S.C. § 44903(j)(2)(C)(v) ("The Assistant Secretary, in coordination with the Terrorist Screening Center, shall include on the No Fly List any individual who was a detainee held at the Naval Station, Guantanamo Bay, Cuba, unless the President certifies in writing to Congress that the detainee poses no threat to the United States, its citizens, or its allies. For purposes of this clause, the term 'detainee' means an individual in the custody or under the physical control of the United States as a result of armed conflict.").

90. CNN, *Detained Cat Stevens heading home,* Sept. 22, 2004.

91. ABC News, *Cat Stevens "In the Dark" Over No-Fly List,* Oct. 1, 2004. This claim has been disputed by many, among them Randy Beardsworth, who joined the DHS transition team in December 2002 to help organize operational aspects of border and transportation security: "Remember Cat Stevens was on the No Fly List. We make light of that now. Everybody in my office brought in *Morning has Broken.* Cat Stevens songs were popular, they were playing all over the place. So it was funny. But when we went back and said 'why was he on the No Fly List?' there were reasons that he would have been in the Terrorist Screening Database, but there were no reasons why he should have been on the No Fly List. That was one of the cases that drove us to say we need to make sure that we're adjudicating these lists." Author interview with Randy Beardsworth, Mar. 11, 2010, Washington D.C.

92. ABC News, *Cat Stevens deported amid terrorism fears,* Sept. 23, 2004.

93. CBS News, *Cat: Why Was I Banned From U.S.?,* Sept. 23, 2004.

94. Sara Kehaulani Goo, *Cat Stevens Held After D.C. Flight Diverted,* Sept. 22, 2004, at A10 (DHS Spokesman Dennis Murphy said that Stevens "is being detained on national security grounds.").

95. CBS News, *Cat: Why Was I Banned From U.S.?,* Sept. 23, 2004.

96. ABC News, *Cat Stevens deported amid terrorism fears,* Sept. 23, 2004.

97. Docket # 44, Declaration of Christopher M. Piehota, *supra* note 84, at ¶ 20 (italics added).

98. *Id.,* at ¶ 21 (italics added).

99. Jackson interview, Mar. 14, 2011, *supra* note 28. Use of this nickname has been difficult to corroborate, although Tuesday briefings of this sort certainly occurred. Kessler, *supra* note 5, at 224. Kessler also reports an interview with Fran Townsend, who emphasized how the President "oftentimes . . . will ask operational questions: Are agencies doing particular things to follow up?" *Id.* at 227. The nickname appears to be in use in the Obama Administration. *See* Jo Becker and Scott Shane, Secret "Kill List" Proves a Test of Obama's Principles and Will, N.Y. TIMES, May 29, 2012, at A1 (describing "Terror Tuesday" meetings).

100. Jackson interview, Mar. 14, 2011, *supra* note 28.

101. *Id.*

102. *Id.*

103. *Id.* (emphasis added).

104. DHS 2009 OIG REPORT, *supra* note 12, at 4.

105. Transportation Security Intelligence Service, *TSA Watchlists*, Unclassified PowerPoint Slides dated December 2002 (ACLU FOIA Release, A1-006).

106. U.S. GOVERNMENT ACCOUNTABILITY OFFICE, AVIATION SECURITY: TSA HAS COMPLETED KEY ACTIVITIES ASSOCIATED WITH IMPLEMENTING SECURE FLIGHT, BUT ADDITIONAL ACTIONS ARE NEEDED TO MITIGATE RISKS 5 (May 2009).

107. Pub. L. 108–458, § 4012(a)(1), 118 Stat. 3714–15, Dec. 17, 2004 (codified at 49 U.S.C. § 44903(j)(2)(A)–(C)).

108. 49 U.S.C. § 44903(j)(2)(C)(ii).

109. 73 FED. REG. 64019 (Oct. 28, 2008).

110. 49 C.F.R. § 1540.107.

111. U.S. DEPARTMENT OF JUSTICE OFFICE OF THE INSPECTOR GENERAL, REVIEW OF THE TERRORIST SCREENING CENTER'S EFFORTS TO SUPPORT THE SECURE FLIGHT PROGRAM 5 (August 2005).

112. 73 FED. REG. 64018, 64022 (Oct. 28, 2008) (49 C.F.R. § 1560.101).

113. http://www.tsa.gov/what_we_do/layers/secureflight/index.shtm (last visited June 20, 2012).

114. 49 C.F.R. § 1560.105(b)(1) ("Denial of boarding pass. If TSA sends a covered aircraft operator a boarding pass printing result that says the passenger or non-traveling individual must be placed on inhibited status, the covered aircraft operator must not issue a boarding pass or other authorization to enter a sterile area to that individual and must not allow that individual to board an aircraft or enter a sterile area.").

115. DHS 2009 OIG REPORT, *supra* note 12, at 4.

116. Leaving America is Easy—for Most, *supra* note 8.

117. EDWARD ALDEN, THE CLOSING OF THE AMERICAN BORDER 139 (2008).

118. FINAL REPORT OF THE NATIONAL COMMISSION ON TERRORIST ATTACKS UPON THE UNITED STATES 395 (2004).

119. *Id.*, at 400.

120. Jackson interview, *supra* note 28.

121. I put the question to Michael Jackson, describing how the MOU between these agencies indicates that TSC will make the final decision in all cases except where legal authority lies with TSA, for whom TSC makes a recommendation. Didn't recommendation in this context take on a euphemistic quality since, in practice, those recommendations are hard to distinguish from final decisions? "Right," Mr. Jackson responded, "So what's wrong with that?" Jackson interview, *supra* note 28.

122. *Id.*

123. Loy interview, *supra* note 17.

124. Jackson interview, *supra* note 28.

125. *Id.*

126. Both Michael Jackson, former DHS Deputy Secretary, and Admiral James Loy, former TSA Administrator, agree with this description. Jackson interview, *supra* note 28 (Author: "The idea is that we are an expert administrative agency. We've got checks and balances within, we've got fail-safes and switches, and when we say at the end of the day that all that has been done, that decision has to be given tremendous deference." Jackson: "I think that's true."); Loy interview, *supra* note 17 (Author: "But do I understand you correctly that other than those [informal, noninstitutional] con-

straints, what you felt was constraining you in the use of this security directive authority was your discretion?" Loy: "I think so.").

This is not to diminish efforts by these men and others to hear the critical opinions of their policy opponents outside of government. Both Jackson and Loy recounted a series of meetings at a retreat and conference facility at Wye River, Maryland, with representatives of the ACLU and various other civil liberties and privacy-rights advocates and groups. Both men described constructive exchanges of views about the appropriate limits to government use of databases. *Id.*

127. Kessler, *supra* note 5, at 160.

128. *Id.*; *See also* GARRETT M. GRAFF, THE THREAT MATRIX: THE FBI AT WAR IN THE AGE OF GLOBAL TERROR 17–19 (2011).

129. Graff, *supra* note 128, at 19.

130. Jackson interview, *supra* note 28.

131. "So the whole redress office was intended to be an intake valve, for complaints like T. Kennedy, you know, the famous Ted Kennedy thing, and to be able to then go back into that process and say, okay, so we have a T. Kennedy problem and what can we do about this thing? And this got, the redress office got progressively strengthened over time." Jackson interview, *supra* note 28.

132. *Id.*

133. "So, that is a totally hypothetical, and I'm going to say incredible, example because I have never known a case that was like that." Jackson interview, *supra* note 28. "Oh, I think those things, I think those conflicts happened. I won't say all the time but I'll say routinely." Loy interview, *supra* note 17. This disagreement may be more apparent than real. In a follow-up conversation, Admiral Loy stressed that the relevant officials in these two agencies "finally agreed all the time as to whether the name should go on or stay off the list (that was the job!). But it should also be recognized that such eventual agreement came only after thorough discussion where different initial opinions were often offered." E-mail correspondence with Admiral Loy, June 27, 2012.

134. Declaration of Christopher M. Piehota, *supra* note 84, at ¶¶ 7, 32–37.

135. DHS 2009 OIG Report, *supra* note 12, at 13.

136. Piehota Declaration, *supra* note 84, at ¶ 33.

137. *Id.*, at ¶ 33, n.11.

138. 5 U.S.C. § 552(b) & (c), 552a(j). The same is true of a FOIA request for watchlist information sent to TSA. 49 C.F.R. §§ 1520.5 & 1520.15(a). The TSA has successfully argued that it is statutorily exempt from disclosing information from watchlists, even those originating with other agencies, that it uses in security screening. *See* Barnard v. Dep't of Homeland Sec., 531 F. Supp. 2d 131 (D.D.C. 2008) (upholding TSA withholding of TECS watchlist information); Tooley v. Bush, No. 06-306-CKK, 2006 WL 3783142, at *20 (D.D.C. Dec. 21, 2006); Gordon v. FBI, 388 F. Supp. 2d 1028 (N.D. Cal. 2005).

139. Based on a number of similar details, it is likely that the episode Jackson referenced is described in more detail by former TSA administrator Kip Hawley. Hawley and Means, *supra* chapter 6 note 111, at 140–46. However, Hawley's account should be treated cautiously for the reasons previously stated. *Id.*

140. Jackson interview, *supra* note 28. Several requests to meet with the then current Officer for Civil Rights and Civil Liberties, Margo Schlanger, between March 2010

and March 2011 were unsuccessful. Two scheduled meetings were canceled by her office. A third meeting was canceled with the explanation that Ms. Schlanger lacked approval to meet with me. Efforts to meet with Francine Kerner, TSA General Counsel, were even less successful.

141. http://www.tsa.gov/what_we_do/civilrights/travelers.shtm.

142. Piehota Declaration, *supra* note 84, at ¶ 30. *See also* http://www.fbi.gov/terror info/counterrorism/redress.htm ("The TSC does not accept redress inquiries directly from the public."); *see also* DOJ 2005 OIG REPORT, *supra* note 111, at 23 ("According to TSA, the TSC will play a supporting role in the redress process and will not have direct contact with the public about these issues."). Although TSA operates a "blog" on which "Blogger Bob" and other anonymous TSA employees seek to give a human face to the agency, *see* http://blog.tsa.gov/, questions concerning the No Fly List are either redirected to the DHS TRIP website or to another web portal at which the individual may submit an electronic message to an unspecified unit of TSA. *See* http://www.tsa.gov/contact/index.shtm.

143. https://trip.dhs.gov/.

144. Healy 2009 Testimony, *supra* note 10.

145. Docket # 44, Defendants' Memorandum of Law in Support of Motion to Dismiss or for Summary Judgment, Latif v. Holder, Case 3:10-cv-00750-BR, (D. Ore. Nov. 17, 2010), at 13. The two laws in question are 49 U.S.C. § 44903(j)(2)(G) and 49 U.S.C. § 44926, both concerning the establishment of appeal procedures.

146. Piehota Declaration, *supra* note 84, at ¶ 35.

147. *Id.*

148. *Id.* In fact, the DHS specifically states: "The U.S. government does not reveal whether a particular person is on the terrorist watch list, which is administered by the Terrorist Screening Center." http://www.dhs.gov/files/programs/gc_1169699418061.shtm (under "More About Screening and Watchlists").

149. Docket # 44, Declaration of James G. Kennedy, Jr., Latif v. Holder, Case 3:10-cv-00750-BR, (D. Ore. Nov. 17, 2010), at ¶ 4.

150. If the complainant appeals one of its decisions (as communicated to the complainant by the TSA), the process is slightly different in the case of the No Fly List: the TSC Legal Department performs another analysis and a decision is made by the TSC Redress Appeals Board, which is comprised of TSC deputy directors. OIG 2007 REPORT, *supra* note 34, at 57. This time, however, the TSC makes only a recommendation to the TSA, which has the authority to make the final decision. *Id.*

151. Defs' Motion for a Stay of Proceedings or, in the alternative, for Summary Judgment, Scherfen v. Dep't of Homeland Security, 3:CV-08-1554, Ex. 1, pp. 49–50 (Jan. 2, 2009).

152. Scherfen v. U.S. Dep't of Homeland Security, No. 3:CV-08-1554, 2010 WL 456784, at *11 (M.D. Pa. Feb. 2, 2010) (internal quotations omitted).

153. *See, e.g.*, Named Defendants' Motion to Dismiss Petition for Review, Docket #18, Mohamed v. Holder, 11-1924 (4th Cir. Nov. 16, 2011), at 2 ("This Court should dismiss [because] despite repeated chances in both the district court and this Court, Mohamed has never named DHS or TSA as defendants, and has never identified a TSA order that he purports to challenge.").

154. Docket # 6, Declaration of Catrina M. Pavlik, Tooley v. Bush, 1:06-cv-00306-CKK, (D.D.C. May 1, 2006), at ¶ 21 ("The watch lists are incorpo-

rated into Security Directives and Emergency Amendments issued to air carriers and constitute SSI under governing regulations at 49 C.F.R. § 1520.5."); *see also* Defendant's Opposition to Plaintiff's Motion for a Preliminary Injunction, Gray v. TSA, 05-11445-DPW, 2005 WL 3803814, at *11 (1st Cir. Sept. 20, 2005); Gilmore v. Gonzales, 435 F.3d 1125, 1131 n. 4 (9th Cir. 2006) ("The No-Fly and Selectee lists are Security Directives."). The Security Directives that implement the No Fly List are exempt from standard notice-and-comment rulemaking. 49 U.S.C. § 114(l)(2)(A) exempts "a regulation or security directive [that] must be issued immediately in order to protect transportation security" from notice-and-comment rulemaking.

155. *Memorandum of Understanding on Terrorist Watchlist Redress Procedures*, § 4(C)(iii), Sept. 28, 2007 (signed by the heads of six departments or agencies), available at http://www.fbi.gov/terrorinfo/counterrorism/redress_mou.pdf.

156. 49 U.S.C. § 46110 ("[A] person disclosing a substantial interest in an order issued . . . in whole or in part under this part, part B, or subsection (l) or (s) of section 114 may apply for review of the order by filing a petition for review in the United States Court of Appeals for the District of Columbia Circuit or in the court of appeals of the United States for the circuit in which the person resides or has its principal place of business.").

157. Even when TSA has not escaped the jurisdiction of the federal district courts, it has argued that its Security Directives—since they contain "sensitive security information"—are privileged from civil discovery. At least one court has held that the Homeland Security Act of 2002, Pub. L. 107-296, § 1601(b), 116 Stat. 2135, 2312 (codified at 49 U.S.C. § 114(s)), created a privilege against civil discovery. Chowdhury v. Northwest Airlines Corp., 226 F.R.D. 608, 615 (N.D. Cal. 2004).

158. *Gilmore*, 435 F.3d at 1133 n. 7.

159. Federal Aviation Act of 1958, Pub. L. 85-726, § 1006(a), 72 Stat. 795, August 23, 1958. In 2003, Congress amended this section to add 49 U.S.C. § 114(l), under which the TSA issues security directives. Pub. L. 108-76, § 228, 117 Stat. 2532 (Dec. 12, 2003).

160. Ibrahim v. Department of Homeland Security, 538 F.3d 1250, 1256 (9th Cir. 2008) (footnote and citations omitted). Judge Kozinski's reference to notice-and-comment rulemaking reveals another reason why the TSA prefers this mixing of its Security Directives with TSC's No Fly List. *See* 49 U.S.C. § 114(l)(2)(A) ("Notwithstanding any other provision of law or executive order (including an executive order requiring a cost-benefit analysis), if the Under Secretary determines that a regulation or security directive must be issued immediately in order to protect transportation security, the Under Secretary shall issue the regulation or security directive without providing notice or an opportunity for comment and without prior approval of the Secretary."). Rahinah Ibrahim is a Malaysian citizen who, while on a student visa for graduate study at Stanford University, found herself on the No Fly List when she sought to return to her home country to attend a conference. As of this writing, she has not been permitted to return to the United States while her lawsuits against the DHS, TSC, and other agencies continue. *See* Ibrahim v. Department of Homeland Security, 669 F 3d 983 (9th Cir. 2012).

161. *Scherfen*, 2010 WL 456784 at *10–13 (M.D. Pa. Feb. 2, 2010); Tooley, 2006 WL 3783142 at *26 (D.D.C. Feb. 20, 2009), *aff'd on other grounds*, Tooley v. Napolitano, 586 F.3d 1006 (D.C. Cir. 2009); Green v. TSA, 351 F.Supp.2d 1119 (W.D. Wa. 2005).

162. *Ibrahim*, 538 F.3d at 1254–55 (footnote and citations omitted).

163. Docket # 44, Defendants' Memorandum of Law in Support of Motion to Dismiss or for Summary Judgment, Latif v. Holder, Case 3:10-cv-00750-BR, (D. Ore. Nov. 17, 2010), at 15–16.

164. *Id.*, at 16.

165. 49 U.S.C. § 114(f)(1)–(4). This hardly amounts to exclusive responsibility to identify and prevent threats to civil aviation or national security. Eleven other responsibilities in this section, uncited by the brief, suggest even greater collaboration.

166. 49 U.S.C. § 114(e)(1).

167. 49 U.S.C. § 114(h)(3).

168. 49 U.S.C. § 44903(j)(2)(E)(iii) ("The Secretary of Homeland Security, in consultation with the Terrorist Screening Center, shall design and review, as necessary, guidelines, policies, and operating procedures for the collection, removal, and updating of data maintained, or to be maintained, in the no fly and automatic selectee lists.").

169. *See, e.g.,* 49 U.S.C. § 44903(e) ("The Under Secretary has the exclusive responsibility to direct law enforcement activity related to the safety of passengers on an aircraft involved in an offense under section 46502 of this title from the moment all external doors of the aircraft are closed following boarding until those doors are opened to allow passengers to leave the aircraft. When requested by the Under Secretary, other departments, agencies, and instrumentalities of the Government shall provide assistance necessary to carry out this subsection"). Section 46502 is the offense of aircraft piracy.

170. 49 U.S.C. § 44903(j)(2)(C)(i) & (ii). None of the requirements listed in 49 U.S.C. § 44903(j)(2)(c)(iii) delegate authority over the watchlists compiled by the TSC to the TSA.

171. 49 U.S.C. §§ 44903(j)(2)(G)(i) and 44909(c)(6) (same for international passengers).

172. Piehota Declaration, *supra* note 84, at ¶ 36.

173. *Id.,* at ¶ 35; see *also supra* text accompanying note 146.

174. OIG 2007 REPORT, *supra* note 34, at 48 ("Exhibit 4-1").

175. *Id.*, at 51 (emphasis added).

176. Falkenrath interview, *supra* note 16.

177. Latif v. Holder, 686 F.3d 1122, 1127 (9th Cir. 2012) (quoting *Ibrahim v. Dep't of Homeland Security,* 538 F.3d 1250, 1255 (9th Cir. 2008)) (internal quotation marks omitted).

178. *Id.* at 1128–29 ("TSA simply passes grievances along to TSC and informs travelers when TSC has made a final determination. TSC—not TSA—actually reviews the classified intelligence information about travelers and decides whether to remove them from the List. And it is TSC—not TSA—that established the policies governing that stage of the redress process. . . . . Thus, because we would not be able to provide relief by simply amending, modifying, or setting aside *TSA's orders* or by directing *TSA* to conduct further proceedings [*i.e.,* the only jurisdiction granted to the appellate court under § 46110], we lack jurisdiction under § 46110 to address Plaintiffs' procedural challenge.") (emphasis in original).

179. *Id.,* at 1130.

180. Two petitions for review have been filed in the U.S. Courts of Appeals so far. *See* Kadirov v. TSA, et al., No. 10-1185 (D.C. Cir. filed July 12, 2010), and Mohamed v.

Holder, No. 11-1924 (4th Cir. filed Sept. 1, 2011). An index to the administrative record produced by the Government has been filed in both cases. In Kadirov's case, the index indicates that the record is composed of documents (mostly e-mails and electronic communications) from two agencies: TSC and TSA. *See* Document # 1286331 (filed January 5, 2011), Kadirov v. TSA. The Kadirov docket reports settlement discussions ongoing since July 2011. In Mohamed's case, the Justice Department filed the index under seal, preventing even a bare description of its contents. *See* Docket Entry # 32 (Dec. 23, 2011), Mohamed v. Holder.

181. Rep. John Dingell (D-MI), *Regulatory Reform Act Hearing on H.R. 2327*, Subcommittee on Administrative Law and Governmental Regulations of the House Committee on the Judiciary, 98th Congress 312 (1983).

Chapter 8

1. ERWIN CHEMERINSKY, CONSTITUTIONAL LAW: PRINCIPLES AND POLICIES 792–93 (3rd ed. 2006).

2. This phrase appears in a travel case, Haig v. Agee, 453 U.S. at 309–10, which cited to its use in a citizenship case, Kennedy v. Mendoza-Martinez, 372 U.S. 144, 160 (1963). Justice Jackson coined it in dissent in Terminiello v. Chicago, 337 U.S. 1, 37 (1949) ("There is danger that, if the Court does not temper its doctrinaire logic with a little practical wisdom, it will convert the constitutional Bill of Rights into a suicide pact").

3. BRUCE ACKERMAN, 2 WE THE PEOPLE: TRANSFORMATIONS 198 (1998) (observing that the Federalists of the Revolutionary Era "avoided any effort to define national citizenship, let alone to give it priority [over state citizenship]. Americans of their generation were profoundly uncertain whether the claims of national identity should trump more local commitments.").

4. U.S. Const., Art. I, § 2, cl. 2 (House of Representatives), Art. I, § 3, cl. 3 (Senate), Art. II, § 1, cl. 5 (President), XII Amend. (Vice-President).

5. *Id.*, Art. I, § 8, cl. 4.

6. *Id.*, Art. I, § 2, cl. 3. Until the passage of the Fourteenth Amendment, this decennial enumeration was marred by the fractional counting of African-American slaves. XIV Amend., § 2. "Indians not taxed" remained excluded in apportioning representatives.

7. *Id.*, XV Amend., XIX Amend., and XVI Amend., respectively.

8. *Id.*, XXIV Amend.

9. The text can also impede. The Privileges and Immunities Clause, for example, applies to citizens and noncitizen residents alike. *See* Hicklin v. Orbeck, 437 U.S. 518, 524 n.8 (1978); Zobel v. Williams, 457 U.S. 55, 73 n. 3 (O'Connor, J., concurring). I admit that such instances cloud my reliance on the canon of constitutional interpretation, *infra* at text accompanying note 25.

10. *See* JOSEPH STORY, 2 COMMENTARIES ON THE CONSTITUTION OF THE UNITED STATES §§ 1638, 1697–1700, 1804–6 (1851).

11. *See* Madison's notes for May 29, June 15, and June 18, 1787 concerning the Randolph Resolutions (the Virginia Plan). 1 THE RECORDS OF THE FEDERAL CONVENTION OF 1787, at 22, 244, 292 (Max Farrand, ed., 1937). The first reference to "subjects or citizens of other countries" is in notes of the Committee of Detail from late July. 2 THE RECORDS OF THE FEDERAL CONVENTION OF 1787, at 147 & 173.

12. Of course, slaves also toiled on earth (for they had no freedom to roam), which the Framers acknowledged in euphemistic terms. *See, e.g.,* U.S. Const., Art. I, § 2, cl. 3; Art. I, § 9, cl. 1; Art. IV, § 2, cl. 3.

13. For a brief discussion of the complicated relationship between the French Revolution, freedom of movement, and the passport, *see* JOHN TORPEY, THE INVENTION OF THE PASSPORT: SURVEILLANCE, CITIZENSHIP AND THE STATE 21–56 (2000).

14. Trop v. Dulles, 356 U.S. 86, 102 (1958).

15. Boumediene v. Bush, 553 U.S. 723, 848–49 (2008) (Scalia, J., dissenting) (emphasis added).

16. U.S. Const., Art. I, § 9, cl. 8.

17. *Id.* at § 10, cl. 1.

18. *Id.* at § 9, cl. 8. The Founders also feared the imposition of a foreign-born monarch and, through the Natural-Born Citizen clause of Article II, § 1, cl. 5, sought to "anticipate all the ways that European aristocracy might one day try to pervert American democracy." AKHIL REED AMAR, AMERICA'S CONSTITUTION: A BIOGRAPHY 165 (2005). Seeking to quell rising public anxiety about the same, some delegates to the Constitutional Convention even skirted the gag rule on their deliberations with the assurance published in a newspaper that "we never once thought of a king." *Id.* (citing MAX FARRAND, THE FRAMING OF THE CONSTITUTION OF THE UNITED STATES 173–75 (1913)). Professor Amar likewise interprets the thirty-five-year eligibility rule for the presidency as an inherently antiaristocratic requirement. *Id.* at 160–64.

19. Luther v. Borden, 48 U.S. 1 (1849).

20. Amar, *supra* note 18, at 277–80.

21. Daniel A. Farber & John E. Muench, The Ideological Origins of the Fourteenth Amendment, 1 CONST. COMMENT. 235, 269, 273–74 (1994).

22. Rebecca E. Zietlow, John Bingham and the Meaning of the Fourteenth Amendment, 36 AKRON L. REV. 717, 766 (2003); *see generally* Rebecca E. Zietlow, Belonging, Protection, and Equality: The Neglected Citizenship Clause and the Limits of Federalism, 62 U. PITT. L. REV. 281 (2000); but see Rogers v. Bellei, 401 U.S. 815 (1971), for a particularly narrow approach to the Clause.

23. "All persons born or naturalized in the United States and subject to the jurisdiction thereof, are citizens of the United States and of the State wherein they reside." U.S. Const., XIV Amend., § 1.

24. Dred Scott v. Sandford, 60 U.S. (19 How.) 393 (1856), held, *inter alia,* that descendants of slaves could not be U.S. citizens.

25. *See* James W. Fox Jr., Democratic Citizenship and Congressional Reconstruction: Defining and Implementing the Privileges and Immunities of Citizenship, 13 TEMP. POL. & CIV. RTS. L. REV. 453, 454 (2004) ("But it is dangerous to see the Citizenship Clause as only about overruling Dred Scott; this would be to view it too narrowly and too legally").

26. *See* Marbury v. Madison, 5 U.S. (1 Cranch.) 137, 174 (1803) ("It cannot be presumed that any clause in the constitution is intended to be without effect; and therefore such a construction is inadmissible, unless the words require it"); Hurtado v. California, 110 U.S. 516, 534 (1884); Prout v. Starr, 188 U.S. 537, 544 (1903). *But see supra* note 9.

27. *See, e.g.,* Amar, *supra* note 18, at 382 ("Read alongside Article I's prohibitions on

both state and federal titles of nobility, the citizenship clause thus proclaimed an ideal of republican equality binding on state and federal governments alike"). Kurt Lash has examined the phrase "privileges and immunities" as a term of art operating in this way. Kurt T. Lash, The Origins of the Privileges or Immunities Clause, Part I: "Privileges and Immunities" as an Antebellum Term of Art, 98 GEO. L.J. 1241 (2010). He has also examined John Bingham's own evolving understanding of "privileges or immunities" as protecting rights bestowed on citizens by the federal constitution. Kurt T. Lash, The Origins of the Privileges or Immunities Clause, Part II: John Bingham and the Second Draft of the Fourteenth Amendment, 99 GEO. L.J. 329 (2011).

28. Farber & Muench, *supra* note 21, at 235. Ironically, the authors imply as an aside that citizenship meant the right to travel abroad: "After the Civil Rights Act and the fourteenth amendment, citizenship would mean more than the right to an American passport when traveling abroad." *Id.* at 277.

29. *Id.*

30. *Id.* at 235, 247, 252.

31. William J. Rich, Taking "Privileges or Immunities" Seriously: A Call to Expand the Constitutional Canon, 87 MINN. L. REV. 153, 196 (2002) (arguing that 'privileges or immunities are rooted in other sources of positive law. . . . Reference to citizenship recognizes both the responsibility and the discretion vested with Congress"); Lash, 98 GEO. L.J. at 1258 ("just as different groups and institutions could have different 'privileges and immunities,' the citizens of various governments also had uniquely defined rights and advantages.").

32. CONG. GLOBE, 39th Cong., 1st Sess. 1757 (1866); *see also* Farber & Muench, *supra* note 21, at 268. Congressman Wilson similarly supported the civil rights bill, preveto, arguing that the rights it protected were those held by "citizens of the United States, as such." *Id.* at 265 (citing to CONG. GLOBE, 39th Cong., 1st Sess., 1117–18, 1294 (1866)).

33. CONG. GLOBE, 39th Cong., 1st Sess. 1757 (1866).

34. S. 306, 39th Cong., 1st Sess. (May 4, 1866).

35. Civil Rights Act of 1875, ch. 114, 18 Stat. 335 (1875), *invalidated by* The Civil Rights Cases, 109 U.S. 3 (1883).

36. *See* The Civil Rights Cases, 109 U.S. 3 (1883). Justice Harlan's dissent argued that the act was "appropriate legislation" enacted under Section 5 to enforce the provisions of the Fourteenth Amendment, including the Citizenship Clause. *Id.* at 46–47.

37. 2 CONG. REC. 4151 (1874).

38. 2 CONG. REC. app. 302, 304 (1874). Other prominent supporters of the bill followed suit. Senator Charles Sumner, for example, "whose persistence kept the idea of public accommodations rights in front of Congress, had advocated accommodations as a right of full citizenship since at least the 1860s." Fox, *supra* note 25, at 476.

39. Palko v. Connecticut, 302 U.S. 319, 325 (1937).

40. CHARLES J. BLACK, JR., STRUCTURE AND RELATIONSHIP IN CONSTITUTIONAL LAW 15–16 (1969).

41. *Id.*, at 62–63.

42. Transcript of Oral Argument at 25, *Saenz*, 526 U.S. 489 (No. 98-97). A similar point was made in the Government's brief.

43. For a brief survey of the contested meaning of citizenship, *see* Malinda L. Seymore, The Presidency and the Meaning of Citizenship, 2005 B.Y.U. L. REV. 927, 953–

68 (2005); *see also* PETER J. SPIRO, BEYOND CITIZENSHIP: AMERICAN IDENTITY AFTER GLOBALIZATION (2008); Will Kymlicka & Wayne Norman, Return of the Citizen: A Survey of Recent Work on Citizenship Theory, 104 ETHICS 352, 352–81 (1994).

44. William B. Allen, The Truth About Citizenship: An Outline, 4 CARDOZO J. INT'L & COMP. L. 355, 355 (1996). *See, e.g.,* the scholarly work of Linda Bosniak, Kenneth Karst, Leti Volpp, and many others. Professor Volpp briefly discussed the Ismails' case in an essay following the September 2006 conference "New Dimensions of Citizenship" at Fordham Law School. *See* Leti Volpp, Citizenship Undone, 75 FORDHAM L. REV. 2579 (2007).

45. Implicit, however, in my argument is that the right to travel is an undifferentiable right of citizenship. That is, the right inheres in citizenship no matter how citizenship is acquired, no matter where the citizen is resident, and without regard to dual citizenship. Concededly, even the text of the Constitution differentiates between types of citizens, only one category of which enjoy complete participatory rights in government. *See* U.S. Const., Art. II, § 1, cl. 5. Such a distinction may well have been more justifiable as a temporary provision at the birth of the nation than as a permanent impediment to equal citizenship. Some scholars have been more inclined than I to categorize citizenship within a framework based on national identity, especially in the context of counterterrorism. *See, e.g.,* Tung Yin, Enemies of the State: Rational Classification in the War on Terrorism, 11 LEWIS & CLARK L. REV. 903, 926–37 (2007). However, I think that such an exercise is too susceptible to abuse in an ever more globalized world, particularly during times of national crisis, to justify distinctions based on perceived national identity.

46. This would almost go without saying in a First Amendment context. *See infra* notes and text accompanying notes 52–54.

47. *See, e.g.,* Reginald Parker, The Right to Go Abroad: To Have and to Hold a Passport, 40 VA. L. REV. 853, 855–56 (1954); Right of Expatriation, 9 OP. ATT'Y GEN. 356, 358 (1859) ("Among writers on public law the preponderance in weight of authority, as well as the majority in numbers, concur with Cicero, who declares that the right of expatriation is the firmest foundation of human freedom, and with Bynkershoek, who utterly denies that the territory of a State is the prison of her people.").

48. *Id.,* at 857.

49. ALBERT O. HIRSCHMAN, EXIT, VOICE, AND LOYALTY: RESPONSES TO DECLINE IN FIRMS, ORGANIZATIONS, AND STATES 83, 97 (1970).

50. Crito: 51d, *in* THE COLLECTED DIALOGUES OF PLATO (Edith Hamilton & Huntington Cairns, eds. 1961). *But see* the severely statist limitations on foreign travel, notwithstanding praise for its beneficial effects, in Laws XII: 949e–952d, *id.* at 1495–98.

51. Aptheker v. Secretary of State, 378 U.S. 500, 519, 520 (1964) (Douglas, J., concurring).

52. New York Times v. Sullivan, 376 U.S. 254, 270 (1964) (extolling "a profound national commitment to the principle that debate on public issues should be uninhibited, robust, and wide-open, and that it may well include vehement, caustic, and sometimes unpleasantly sharp attacks on government and public officials"); Brandenburg v. Ohio, 395 U.S. 444, 447 (1969) ("[T]he constitutional guarantees of free speech and free press do not permit a State to forbid or proscribe advocacy of the use of force or of law violation except where such advocacy is directed to inciting or producing imminent lawless action and is likely to incite or produce such action.").

53. Chemerinsky, *supra* note 1, at 923–24; *Sullivan,* 376 U.S. at 276.

54. There is, of course, a well-established "national security" exception to the general rule against prior restraints. *See* Near v. Minnesota, 283 U.S. 697 (1931). But publishing in time of war "the sailing dates of transports or the number and location of troops," *id.* at 716, is more akin to the treason or immediate dangerousness that would be permissible grounds for the state to obstruct the traveler's plans, while speech in the form of political protest is more comparable to a constitutional right to travel.

55. Perez v. Brownell, 356 U.S. 44, 59 (1958), *overruled by* Afroyim v. Rusk, 387 U.S. 253 (1967).

56. *Perez,* 356 U.S. at 59.

57. Afroyim v. Rusk, 387 U.S. 253 (1967).

58. *Id.*, at 254.

59. *Id.* at 262, 268.

60. Trop v. Dulles, 356 U.S. 86, 93 (1958).

61. *Id.* at 88.

62. *Trop,* 356 U.S. at 92, 101.

63. *Id.* at 92–93. The opinion was joined by Justices Black, Douglas, and Whittiker. Justice Brennan concurred in a separate opinion.

64. *Trop,* 356 U.S. at 102.

65. Worthy v. U.S., 328 F.2d 386, 389 (5th Cir. 1964). The statute, 8 U.S.C. § 1185(b), at the time imposed a punishment of up to five years imprisonment and a fine up to $5,000.

66. *Id.* at 388 and 389, n. 1.

67. *Id.* at 393.

68. *Id.* at 393–94.

69. *Id.* at 394.

70. *Haig,* 453 U.S. at 307.

71. Transcript of Oral Argument, *Haig,* 453 U.S. 280 (No. 80–83).

72. *See, e.g.*, Parker, *supra* note 47, at 855–56 ("The totalitarian state typically demands that its subjects act at all times in the interest of the state. As a matter of fact, this attitude may be said to be the ultimate criterion of totalitarianism. Hence, under that form of rule the government has a right to expect that its subjects abroad will act always 'in the best interest' of their state, and consequently it is privileged to deny the right to go abroad to those not likely to be true agents for the totalitarian state.").

73. Phillippe C. Schmitter & Terry Lynn Karl, What Democracy Is . . . And Is Not, 2 J. OF DEMOCRACY 75, 77 (Summer 1991) ("*Citizens* are the most distinctive element in democracies. All regimes have rulers and a public realm, but only to the extent that they are democratic do they have citizens.") (emphasis in original).

74. Allen, *supra* note 44, at 368.

75. *Id.*, at 355.

76. Kenneth Diplock, Passports and Protection in International Law, 32 TRANSACTIONS GROTIUS SOC'Y 42, 44 (1947).

77. Magna Carta, at 31 (41 in British Library annotation), http://www.bl.uk/treasures/magnacarta/translation.html.

78. *Id.* at 42. This paragraph, among others, was omitted from the Charter of 1225 and later versions, but without apparent effect on the development of the common law on the matter. Admittedly, such a right waxes and wanes over the course of En-

glish legal history. Thus, for example, a statute enacted under Richard II provided for the forfeiture of all property of subjects (with a few exceptions, such as lords, selected merchants, and the king's soldiers) who "shall pass out of the said Realm without the King's special Licence." *See* 5 Ric. 2, 1381, Stat. 1, c. 2 (Eng.), reprinted in II Statutes of the Realm 18 ([1816] 1963). Although the statute was not repealed until 1606, *see* 4 Jac., 1606, c. 1, § 4, reprinted in IV Statutes of the Realm 1135 ([1819] 1963), Professor Baker observed that its force had weakened well before that time. *See* text accompanying note 57 at J. H. Baker, *Introduction*, I REPORTS FROM THE LOST NOTEBOOKS OF SIR JAMES DYER lxv (1994). For example, Dyer reports the holding of a divided court in a 1570 case at Queen's Bench that the departure from the realm of a subject without the Queen's license, "solely with the intent that he might live there free from the laws of this realm . . . is not any offence or contempt, for it is a thing indifferent to depart the kingdom; and the purpose and cause, which is secret in the heart, is not examinable." 73 Eng. Rep. 664 [3 Dyer 296a].

79. *See, e.g.*, JOHN BEAMES, A BRIEF VIEW OF THE WRIT NE EXEAT REGNO, AS AN EQUITABLE PROCESS WITH THE RULES OF PRACTICE RELATING TO IT 3–7 (2nd ed. 1824).

80. The contracted title of this writ may well be fully entitled *de securitate inveniendâ ne exeat regnum quod se non divertat ad partes exteras, sine Licentia Regis*. *See Memorandum*, Hilary Term, 1 Eliz., at 73 Eng. Rep. 361 [2 Dyer, 165b]. I translate the Latin into modern English as the writ of security contriving not to let him leave the kingdom who would separate himself to foreign parts without the King's license.

81. ANTHONY FITZ-HERBERT, THE NEW NATURA BREVIUM WITH SIR MATTHEW HALE'S COMMENTARY [*85] 192 ([1534] 7th ed. 1730). *See also* SIR MATTHEW HALE'S THE PREROGATIVES OF THE KING 270 & 296 ([c. 1660] D. E. C. Yale, ed. 1976).

82. Diplock, *supra* note 76, at 42 & 44. *See also* WILLIAM BLACKSTONE, I COMMENTARIES *265–66 ("By the common law, every man may go out of the realm for whatever cause he pleases, without obtaining the king's leave; provided he is under no injunction of staying at home: (which liberty was expressly declared in King John's great charter, though left out in that of Henry III.) . . .)." Acts of Parliament restricting the right in the past are noted, but "at present everybody has, or at least assumes, the liberty of going abroad when he pleases." *Id.* at *266. Likewise, royal prerogative is noted but circumscribed in practice by law. *Id.*

83. Beames, *supra* note 79, at 1. Beames sets forth a prehistory to the writ that extends from an initial interest in restricting the intercourse between English clerics and the Holy See, and other political concerns (such as treasonous subjects), to one designed to prevent debtors from escaping their obligations to creditors. *Id. passim* 1–24, but especially at 12, 16, n. 30, and 19. *See also* WILLIAM BLACKSTONE, I COMMENTARIES *265–66. The writ of *Ne exeat regno* was well known in the early United States (*see, e.g.*, The Passenger Cases, 48 (7 How.) 283, 357 (1849) (argument by counsel observing that "All the states of the Union constantly enforce the writ of *ne exeat*")) and, in fact, continues to be used in various forms in modern family law contexts.

84. Lash, *supra* note 27, 98 GEO. L.J., at 1258.

85. *Id.*

86. Charles E. Wyzanski, Jr., Freedom to Travel, ATLANTIC MONTHLY, Oct. 4, 1952, at 67.

87. *Id.*

88. Alan G. James, Expatriation in the United States: Precept and Practice Today and Yesterday, 27 SAN DIEGO L. REV. 853, 861–71 (1990).

89. Act of July 27, 1868, ch. 249, 15 Stat. 223, codified at 8 U.S.C. § 1481 note.

90. *Id.* at § 1.

91. *See* Universal Declaration of Human Rights, G.A. Res. 217A(III), U.N. GAOR, 3d Sess., U.N. Doc. A/810, at 71 (1948), Art. 13, § 2 ("Everyone has the right to leave any country, including his own, and to return to his country."). International Covenant of Civil and Political Rights, G.A. res. 2200A (XXI), 21 U.N. GAOR Supp. (No. 16) at 52, U.N. Doc. A/6316 (1966), 999 U.N.T.S. 171, *entered into force* Mar. 23, 1976, Art. 12, § 1 ("Everyone lawfully within the territory of a State shall, within that territory, have the right to liberty of movement and freedom to choose his residence."). The United States ratified this treaty on June 8, 1992 and the treaty entered into force three months later. *See* 138 CONG. REC. S 4781–84 (daily ed. Apr. 2, 1992); U.S. Ratification of International Covenant on Civil and Political Rights, 58 FED. REG. 45934-1 (Aug. 31, 1993). Ratification by the United States was subject to a declaration that the provisions of this article are not self-executing. *Id.*

92. International Covenant of Civil and Political Rights, *supra* note 91, Art. 12, § 2 ("Everyone shall be free to leave any country, including his own") and § 4 ("No one shall be arbitrarily deprived of the right to enter his own country"); International Convention on the Elimination of All Forms of Racial Discrimination, *entered into force* Jan. 4, 1969, Art. 5(d)(ii) ("The right to leave any country, including one's own, and to return to one's country"); Protocol No. 4 to the Convention for the Protection of Human Rights and Fundamental Freedoms, Securing Certain Rights and Freedoms other than those Already Included in the Convention and in the First Protocol Thereto, *entered into force* May 2, 1968, European Treaty Series No. 46, Art. 2, § 2 and Art. 3, § 2 ("Everyone shall be free to leave any country, including his own" and "No one shall be deprived of the right to enter the territory of the state of which he is a national").

93. *See, e.g.,* Correspondence dated October 18, 1974, between Secretary of State Henry A. Kissinger and Senator Henry M. Jackson regarding a wide variety of punitive measures and restrictions used by the Soviet Union to discourage or prevent emigration. *Reprinted in* Arthur W. Rovine, Contemporary Practice of the United States Relating to International Law, 69 AM. J. INT'L L. 382, 390–92 (1975). *See also Restrictions on International Travel,* Hrg. before the H. Comm. on Foreign Aff., Subcomms. On Int'l Econ. Policy & Trade, and on Int'l Operations, 101st Cong. 1 (1990) ("One of the more remarkable benefits of the recent changes in Eastern Europe has been the newly found freedom of its citizens to travel. Barbed wire and brick wall have been torn down, guard dogs and border patrols have been removed, and the people are at long last able to have contact with the rest of the world.") (Statement of Rep. Sam Gejdenson, Chairman).

94. Aptheker v. Sec'y of State, 378 U.S. 500, 520 (1964) (Douglas, J., concurring).

95. *See* Section 402(a)(1)–(3) in Title IV of the Trade Act of 1974, 19 U.S.C. § 2432, Pub. L. 93-618, 88 Stat. 1978 (Jan. 3, 1975).

96. Conference on Security and Co-Operation in Europe, Final Act, Helsinki, Aug. 1, 1975, at Co-Operation in Humanitarian and Other Fields, at 1(d) Travel for Personal

or Professional Reasons. *See also* SARAH B. SNYDER, HUMAN RIGHTS ACTIVISM AND THE END OF THE COLD WAR (2011).

97. *See, e.g.*, Woods v. Cloyd W. Miller Co., 333 U.S. 138, 141 (1948) (unanimously sustaining postwar rent controls, reaching the delicate conclusion that "the war power does not necessarily end with the cessation of hostilities"); Youngstown Sheet & Tube Co. v. Sawyer, 343 U.S. 579 (1952); Hamdi v. Rumsfeld, 542 U.S. 507 (2004).

98. *Haig*, 453 U.S. at 290 (quoting *Kent*, 357 U.S. at 127).

99. Majority Staff of H. Comm. on Homeland Sec., 110th Cong., The 2007 XDR-TB Incident: A Breakdown at the Intersection of Homeland Security and Public Health (Sept. 2007). It should be noted that the majority staff repeatedly refers to the "TSA no-fly list" and makes no mention of the Terrorist Screening Center. However, in testimony before a Senate subcommittee on June 6, 2007, CDC Director Julie Gerberding testified that officials from the TSA, DHS, and TSC were involved in placing Speaker on the No Fly List. HEARING OF THE LABOR, HEALTH AND HUMAN SERVICES, EDUCATION AND RELATED AGENCIES SUBCOMMITTEE OF THE SENATE COMMITTEE ON APPROPRIATIONS, THE IMPACT OF ONE TUBERCULOSIS PATIENT ON INTERNATIONAL PUBLIC HEALTH, JUNE 6, 2007. Dr. Gerberding expressed regret that the No-Fly order was not initiated faster, but praised the officials involved, who were "very helpful to us and stepped up to the plate to try to facilitate what we were trying to do, even though this is the first time they'd been in this situation of trying to use their authorities for an infectious disease." *Id.*

100. The 2007 XDR-TB Incident, *supra* note 99, at 20. It is possible that the Justice Department lawyers were from the TSC, although this is not at all clear in the staff report of the committee.

101. And to act rashly in doing so. Speaker subsequently filed a civil action against the Centers for Disease Control seeking damages for its alleged violation of the Privacy Act in publicly disclosing identifying private information about him from its system of records. The lawsuit survived a motion to dismiss, Speaker v. U.S. Dep't of Health and Human Services Centers for Disease Control and Prevention, 623 F.3d 1371 (11th Cir. Oct. 22, 2010), but failed to survive a motion for summary judgment, Speaker v. U.S. Dep't of Health and Human Services Centers for Disease Control and Prevention, No. 12-11967, 2012 WL 4052349 (11th Cir. Sept. 14, 2012).

102. Intelligence Identities Protection Act of 1982 § 601, 50 U.S.C. § 421 (2008). Congress passed the act as a direct response to Agee's case. *See* Robert W. Bivins, Silencing the Name Droppers: The Intelligence Identities Protection Act of 1982, 36 U. FLA. L. REV. 841, 843–45 (1984).

103. *See, e.g.*, Woods v. Cloyd W. Miller Co., 333 U.S. 138, 147 (1948) (Jackson, J., concurring) ("I would not be willing to hold that war powers may be indefinitely prolonged merely by keeping legally alive a state of war that had in fact ended.").

104. 381 U.S. 1, 3 (1965).

105. *Id.*

106. *Id.* at 13.

107. *Id.* at 14–15.

108. 468 U.S. 222 (1984).

109. *Id.* at 243.

110. Perez v. Brownell, 356 U.S. 44, 59 (1958), *overruled by* Afroyim v. Rusk, 387 U.S. 253, 268 (1967).

111. 18 U.S.C. § 2339B(a)(1).

112. Holder v. Humanitarian Law Project, 130 S.Ct. 2705, 2725 (2010).

113. *Id.* ("It also importantly helps lend legitimacy to foreign terrorist groups—legitimacy that makes it easier for those groups to persist, to recruit members, and to raise funds—all of which facilitate more terrorist attacks").

114. HSPD-6, Sept. 16, 2003.

115. MIKHAIL BULGAKOV, THE MASTER AND MARGARITA 222 (Mirra Ginsburg, trans. 1967) ("'They sent us sturgeon of the second freshness,' said the bar manager. 'My good man, that's nonsense!' 'What's nonsense?' 'Second freshness—that's nonsense! There is only one kind of freshness—first. And that's the last, too. And if the sturgeon is of the second freshness, that means it is rancid.'").

116. 4 WILLIAM BLACKSTONE, COMMENTARIES *21 ("Indeed, to make a complete crime, cognizable by human laws, there must be both a will and an act. For though, in *foro conscientiae*, a fixed design or will to do an unlawful act is almost as heinous as the commission of it, yet, as no temporal tribunal can search the heart, or fathom the intentions of the mind, otherwise than as they are demonstrated by outward action, it therefore cannot punish for what it cannot know.").

117. New York Times Co. v. U.S., 403 U.S. 713, 714 (1971); Near v. Minnesota ex rel. Olson, 283 U.S. 697, 716 (1931).

118. HARRY KALVEN, JR. A WORTHY TRADITION 403 (Jamie Kalven, ed. 1988).

119. Youngstown Sheet & Tube Co. v. Sawyer, 343 U.S. 579, 653 (1952) (Jackson, J., concurring).

120. Passport Refusals for Political Reasons: Constitutional Issues and Judicial Review, 61 YALE L.J. 171, 190 (1952) ("[T]he distinction between restriction to a jail, to a city, to a state, or to a nation is merely one of degree.").

121. Kalven, *supra* note 118, at 451 (emphasis in original).

122. Louis L. Jaffe, The Right to Travel: The Passport Problem, 35 FOREIGN AFF. 17, 18 (1956).

123. MARTIN BAUML DUBERMAN, PAUL ROBESON 388 (1989).

124. *Id.*

125. *Id.*

126. *Id.* at 389.

127. Kalven, *supra* note 118, at 451.

128. Aptheker v. Sec'y of State, 378 U.S. 500, 520 (1964) (Douglas, J., concurring).

129. United States v. Salerno, 481 U.S. 739 (1987). In *Salerno*, the Court extended to competent adult citizens a power to detain indefinitely upon a judicial finding of dangerousness that had only previously been enforced in time of active insurrection, on enemy aliens in time of war, the mentally incompetent, and juveniles. *Id.* at 748–49.

130. Transcript of Oral Argument, *Salerno*, 481 U.S. 739 (No. 86–87).

131. *Id.*

132. *Id.*

133. *Id.*

134. *Salerno*, 481 U.S. 749–50. It should be noted that the premise that the civilian criminal justice system is the appropriate analogue for preventive detention in this context is contested. Even if it is accepted, criminal procedure in a post-9/11 age may be in flux. *See* Robert Chesney & Jack Goldsmith, Terrorism and the Convergence

of Criminal and Military Detention Models, 60 STANFORD L. REV. 1079, 1079–1133 (2008).

135. *Salerno,* 481 U.S. at 751.

136. Demore v. Kim, 538 U.S. 510, 551–52 (2003).

137. DEPARTMENT OF HOMELAND SECURITY OFFICE OF THE INSPECTOR GENERAL, ROLE OF THE NO FLY AND SELECTEE LISTS IN SECURING COMMERCIAL AVIATION 27 (July 2009). Michael Jackson and Edmund "Kip" Hawley adopted a similar view of aviation security as a "system of systems" from the start of their work standing up the TSA. Author's interview with Michael P. Jackson, Mar. 14, 2011, Arlington, Virginia (describing management of a "system of systems"); KIP HAWLEY AND NATHAN MEANS, PERMANENT EMERGENCY: INSIDE THE TSA AND THE FIGHT FOR THE FUTURE OF AMERICAN SECURITY 179, 188, 231–32 (2011) (describing multilayered security networks); STEVEN BRILL, AFTER: HOW AMERICA CONFRONTED THE SEPTEMBER 12 ERA 236 (2003).

138. http://www.tsa.gov/what_we_do/layers/index.shtm. This graphic reproduces the one that appeared on this website on July 10, 2011. *See* http://web.archive.org/web/20110710142253/http://www.tsa.gov/what_we_do/layers/index.shtm. Sometime between that date and June 24, 2012, the second bar from the right ("International partnerships") was deleted from the TSA website graphic.

139. Docket # 44, Declaration of Sharon M. Raya, Latif v. Holder, Case 3:10-cv-00750-BR, (D. Ore. Nov. 17, 2010), at ¶ 6.

140. Shaughnessy v. United States ex rel. Mezei, 345 U.S. 206, 220 (1953) (Jackson, J., dissenting).

141. Paul Schemm (AP), *Yahya Weheli, American, Stranded Overseas Due to No-Fly List,* Huffington Post, June 17, 2010, available at http://www.huffingtonpost.com/2010/06/16/yahya-weheli-american-str_n_614902.html; Scott Shane, An American Abroad May Remain So Until He's Off the No-Fly List, N.Y. TIMES, June 16, 2010, at A6.

142. Shane, *supra* note 141.

143. Schemm, *supra* note 141; Shane, *supra* note 141.

144. Shane, *supra* note 141.

145. Peter Finn, Fairfax man returning from Yemen stranded in Cairo after landing on no-fly list, WASH. POST, June 17, 2010.

146. Shane, *supra* note 141.

147. *Id.*

148. *Id.*

149. Finn, *supra* note 145.

150. Shane, *supra* note 141.

151. *Id.*

152. *Id.*

153. *See* chapter 7, note 10.

154. *See* chapter 6, note 180.

155. *Id.*

156. Finn, *supra* note 145.

157. Karen Gray Houston, *Virginia Muslim Back After Being Detained In Egypt On U.S. No-Fly List,* Fox News Broadcast, July 19, 2010, http://www.myfoxdc.com/dpp/news/virginia-muslim-back-after-being-detained-in-egypt-on-us-no-fly-list-071810.

158. Markham Heid, Yahya Wehelie, WASH. EXAMINER, July 19, 2010, available at http://washingtonexaminer.com/local/yahya-wehelie.

159. Tom Fitzgerald, *Virginia Man Speaks Out After Being Stranded In Middle East*, Fox News Broadcast, July 20, 2010, video available at http://www.myfoxdc.com/dpp/news/virginia/virginia-man-speaks-out-after-being-stranded-in-middle-east-071910.

Chapter 9

1. U.S. v. Wunderlich, 342 U.S. 98, 101 (1951) (Douglas, J., dissenting).

2. Aaron H. Caplan, Nonattainder as a Liberty Interest, 2010 WISC. L. REV.1203, 1207 (2010) (internal citation omitted). Professor Caplan served as a plaintiffs' counsel in Green v. Transportation Security Administration, 351 F.Supp.2d 1119 (W.D. Wash. 2005) and Rahman v. Chertoff, 244 F.R.D. 443 (N.D. Ill. 2007).

3. The same, of course, cannot be said of the foreign visitor, who enters, remains, and departs the United States at the discretion of the state. Though Congress's plenary authority over immigration and naturalization is, of course, limited by the Constitution, no one but a citizen has a fundamental constitutional right to come and go across the country's borders.

4. Forsyth County, Georgia v. The Nationalist Movement, 505 U.S. 123, 136 (1992) ("A tax based on the content of speech does not become more constitutional because it is a small tax.").

5. *See, e.g.,* Defendants' Memorandum of Law in Support of Motion to Dismiss or for Summary Judgment, Latif v. Holder, 3:10-cv-00750-BR, at 24–28 (D. Ore. Nov. 17, 2010); Defendants' Memorandum in Support of Motion to Dismiss, Mohamed v. Holder, 1:11-cv-00050-AJT-TRJ, at 17 n. 9 (E.D. Va. Mar. 21, 2011).

6. Pub. L. No. 108-334, § 552, 118 Stat. 1298, 1319–20 (2004); Pub. L. No. 110-329, Div. D, § 512, 122 Stat. 3574, 3682–83 (2008). To the contrary, while questioning the director of the Centers for Disease Control about the unprecedented use of the No Fly List to attempt to stop an American citizen thought highly contagious with TB from returning to the United States in 2007, Senator Tom Harkin asked why the use of the No Fly List could not have happened faster. See *supra* chapter 8, note 99.

7. Consider the exasperation expressed by Judge William Alsup of the Northern District of California: "This action challenging the airport detention of plaintiff by police for being on the 'no-fly list' has reached a potential jurisdictional impasse. The Ninth Circuit earlier held that this Court has subject-matter jurisdiction over the action as against certain defendants [which included the Terrorist Screening Center] other than the Transportation Security Administration. On remand, however, it turns out that important evidence at the heart of the case is still under lock and key by TSA. The federal government asserts that this Court again lacks subject-matter jurisdiction, this time lacking jurisdiction to compel TSA to release the evidence." Ibrahim v. Department of Homeland Security, No. C 06-0545 WHA, 2009 WL 5069133, at *1 (N.D. Cal., Dec. 17, 2009).

8. Eugene Gressman, The Undue Process of Passports, 127 NEW REPUBLIC 13, 14 (Sept. 8, 1952).

9. In addition to the former government officials quoted in the Introduction, Justice Scalia could be added to this list, as suggested by an exchange with Georgetown Professor David Cole during a recent oral argument:

JUSTICE SCALIA: I think it's very unrealistic to compare these terrorist organizations with the Communist Party. Those cases involved philosophy. The Communist Party was—was—was more than a—than an organization that—that had some unlawful ends. It was also a philosophy of—of—of extreme socialism. And—and many people subscribed to that philosophy. I don't think that Hamas or any of these terrorist organizations represent such a philosophical organization.

MR. COLE: Your Honor, this—this Court accepted Congress's findings. Congress's findings were not that this was a philosophical debating society, but that it was an international criminal conspiracy directed by our enemy to overthrow us through terrorism.

Transcript of Oral Argument at 21, Holder v. Humanitarian Law Project, 130 S.CT. 2705 (2010) (Nos. 08-1498, 09-89).

10. This criticism can take another form that superficially seems based in science. Mrs. Shipley's analogy focuses us too much on Type I error—the false positive of innocent people incorrectly kept from traveling. But today the threat of Type II error is much greater—the false negative of people truly too dangerous to fly, but who are mistakenly allowed to board a plane. In Mrs. Shipley's day, so the argument goes, the harm of Type II error was minimal. One need only to recall the horror of September 11 to comprehend that such a world is gone forever.

This statistical argument is only superficially persuasive. First, it falsely assumes that the No Fly List is better at avoiding Type II error than at avoiding Type I error. But there is no science beyond the characterization of someone as a "known or suspected terrorist." As Jack Goldsmith observed of federal officials responsible for national security, "their incentives and responsibilities lead them to focus on the short term rather than the long term, and to minimize false negatives that might be the next 9/11 rather than false positives that will invite charges of exaggeration or mistake." JACK GOLDSMITH, THE TERROR PRESIDENCY: LAW AND JUDGMENT INSIDE THE BUSH ADMINISTRATION 191 (2007). Second, by suggesting greater danger, it implies that the No Fly List is essential for combating Type II error when other counterterrorism tools may actually do the job as well or better, but without raising constitutional concerns. Type II error is based on a prediction of future dangerousness. Not only terrorism but lots of social evils could be reduced by giving government the power to deny rights to those thought likely to abuse them or harm us. But our constitutional system recoils, and rightly so, against the grant of power to control citizens based on government predictions of their future behavior.

11. Scott Shane, Nuclear Fear of Cold War Now Applies to Terrorists, N.Y. TIMES, Apr. 16, 2010, at A13.

12. Benno C. Schmidt, Jr., A Nation Without Heretics, N.Y. TIMES, Feb. 21, 1988.

13. EDWARD ALDEN, THE CLOSING OF THE AMERICAN BORDER 244 (2008).

14. DAVID COLE, ENEMY ALIENS: DOUBLE STANDARDS AND CONSTITUTIONAL FREEDOMS IN THE WAR ON TERRORISM (2003).

15. WILLIAM J. KROUSE, TERRORIST IDENTIFICATION, SCREENING, AND TRACKING UNDER HOMELAND SECURITY PRESIDENTIAL DIRECTIVE 6, CRS Report for Congress 17 (CRS Report 32366) (2004).

16. ALDEN, *supra* note 13, at 238.

17. U.S. GOV'T ACCOUNTABILITY OFFICE, VISA WAIVER PROGRAM: DHS HAS IMPLE-

MENTED THE ELECTRONIC SYSTEM FOR TRAVEL AUTHORIZATION, BUT FURTHER STEPS NEEDED TO ADDRESS POTENTIAL PROGRAM RISKS (GAO-11-335) 21 n. 24 (2011).

18. Judgment of 3 September 2008 of the Court of Justice of the European Union in Joined Cases C-402/05 P and C-415/05 P Kadi and Al Barakaat International Foundation v. Council and Commission [2008] ECR I-6351 *(Kadi I)*; and Judgment of 30 September 2010 of the General Court (Seventh Chamber) of the European Union in the Case T-85/09 *Kadi v. Commission (Kadi II)*; Gráinne de Búrca, The European Court of Justice and the International Legal Order After Kadi, 51 HARV. INT'L L.J. 1, 9, 17–19 (2010).

19. Author interview with Richard Falkenrath, New York City, June 8, 2010.

20. In the context of the No Fly List, this distinction was first made by Professor Aaron Caplan, and should be attributed to him. Caplan, *supra* note 2, at 1206.

21. KIP HAWLEY AND NATHAN MEANS, PERMANENT EMERGENCY: INSIDE THE TSA AND THE FIGHT FOR THE FUTURE OF AMERICAN SECURITY 231–32 (2012).

22. *See* the discussion, *supra*, in chapter 6.

23. *See, e.g.*, Danielle Keats Citron, Technological Due Process, 85 WASH. U. L. REV. 1249 (2008) (examining effects of automation bias and computer systems on traditional due process protections and advocating both technological and legal solutions to protect notice and hearing rights); Peter M. Shane, The Bureaucratic Due Process of Government Watch Lists, 75 GEO. WASH. L. REV. 804 (2007) (exploring a variety of pre- and post-watchlisting procedures).

24. *See, e.g.*, Life After 9/11: Issues Affecting the Courts and the Nation, 51 U. KAN. L. REV. 219 (2003); Robert M. Chesney, State Secrets and the Limits of National Security Litigation, 75 GEO. WASH. L. REV. 1249 (2007).

25. Nat'l Fed. of Indep. Business, et al. v. Sebelius, 567 U.S. __ (2012), Nos. 11-393, 11-398, and 11-400, slip. op. at 65 (Scalia, Kennedy, Thomas, and Alito, J J., dissenting).

26. FINAL REPORT OF THE NATIONAL COMMISSION ON TERRORIST ATTACKS UPON THE UNITED STATES 384 (2004).

27. *Id.*
28. *Id.*, at 385.
29. *Id.*
30. *Id.*, at 389, 393.

Bibliography

N.B. This bibliography collects the citations to books, articles of an academic or argumentative nature, and government reports that are referenced in the text. Judicial opinions referenced in the text are identified in the Table of Cases. Newspapers, magazines, and other sources of factual information are not referenced here. Nor are constitutions, treaties, statutes, regulations, opinions of the Attorney General, executive orders, internal government memoranda, official letters, presidential proclamations, joint resolutions of Congress, and other miscellaneous sources such as interviews and correspondence with current and former government officials and primary source materials obtained at archives and through Freedom of Information Act releases. References to these materials may be found in the endnotes.

Books

Ackerman, Bruce. We the People: Transformations (1998).
Alden, Edward. The Closing of the American Border (2008).
Amar, Akhil Reed. America's Constitution: A Biography (2005).
Beames, John. A Brief View of The Writ Ne exeat Regno, as an equitable process with the rules of practice relating to it (2nd ed. 1824).
Black, Charles L., Jr. Structure and Relationship in Constitutional Law (1969).
Black's Law Dictionary (9th ed., Bryan A. Garner, ed.).
Blackstone, William. Commentaries.
Böcker, Anita, Kees Groenendijk, Tetty Havinga, & Paul Minderhoud, eds. Regulation of Migration: International Experiences (1998).
Brater, Enoch. Arthur Miller: A Playwright's Life and Works (2005).
Brill, Steven. After: How America Confronted the September 12 Era (2003).
Bulgakov, Mikhail. The Master and Margarita (Mirra Ginsburg, trans. 1967).
Chafee, Zechariah, Jr. Three Human Rights in the Constitution (1956).
Chemerinsky, Erwin. Constitutional Law: Principles & Policies (2006).

Cole, David. Enemy Aliens: Double Standards and Constitutional Freedoms in the War on Terrorism (2003).
Davies, Norman. Europe: A History (1996).
Douglas, William O. The Douglas Letters: Selections from the Private Papers of Justice (Melvin I. Urofsky, ed. 1987).
Duberman, Martin Bauml. Paul Robeson (1989).
Farrand, Max. The Framing of the Constitution of the United States (1913).
Farrand, Max, ed. The Records of the Federal Convention of 1787 (1937).
Fitz-Herbert, Anthony. The New Natura Brevium with Sir Matthew Hale's Commentary ([1534] 1730).
Freedom to Travel: Report of the Special Committee to Study Passport Procedures of the Association of the Bar of the City of New York (Fifeld Wokum, chairman, 1958).
Goldsmith, Jack. The Terror Presidency: Law and Judgment inside the Bush Administration (2007).
Gottfried, Martin. Arthur Miller: His Life and Work (2003).
Graff, Garrett M. The Threat Matrix: The FBI at War in the Age of Global Terror (2011).
Hawley, Kip, & Nathan Means. Permanent Emergency: Inside the TSA and the Fight for the Future of American Security (2012).
Hellman, Lillian. Scoundrel Time (1976).
Hirschman, Albert O. Exit, Voice, and Loyalty: Responses to Decline in Firms, Organizations, and States (1970).
Hobsbawm, Eric. The Age of Extremes: A History of the World, 1914–1991 (1994).
Hunt, Gaillard. The American Passport: Its History and a Digest of Laws, Rulings, and Regulations Governing Its Issuance by the Department of State (1898).
Kalven, Harry, Jr. A Worthy Tradition (Jamie Kalven, ed., 1988).
Kamen, Martin D. Radiant Science, Dark Politics: A Memoir of the Nuclear Age (1985).
Kemper, Donald J. Decade of Fear: Senator Hennings and Civil Liberties (1965).
Kessler, Ronald. The Terrorist Watch: Inside the Desperate Race to Stop the Next Attack (2007).
Koestler, Arthur. The Ghost in the Machine (1976).
Kraus, Theresa L. The Federal Aviation Administration: A Historical Perspective, 1903–2008 (2008).
Kurland, Philip B., & Ralph Lerner, eds. The Founders' Constitution (1987).
Mencken, H. L. A Mencken Chrestomathy (1949).
Mosley, Leonard. Dulles: A Biography of Eleanor, Allen, and John Foster Dulles and Their Family Network (1978).
Newman, Robert P. The Cold War Romance of Lillian Hellman and John Melby (1989).
Orwell, George. Essays (John Carey, ed. 2002).
Plato. The Collected Dialogues of Plato (Edith Hamilton & Huntington Cairns, eds. 1961).
Reports from the Lost Notebooks of Sir James Dyer (1994).
Rollyson, Carl. Lillian Hellman: Her Legend and her Legacy (1988).
Smith, Paul H., et al., eds. Letters of Delegates to Congress (1976–2000).

Smith, Rogers M. Civic Ideals (1997).
Snyder, Sarah B. Human Rights Activism and the End of the Cold War (2011).
Spiro, Peter J. Beyond Citizenship: American Identity After Globalization (2008).
Story, Joseph. Commentaries on the Constitution of the United States (1851).
Stuart, Graham H. The Department of State: A History of Its Organization, Procedure, and Personnel (1949).
Torpey, John. The Invention of the Passport: Surveillance, Citizenship and the State (2000).
Tribe, Laurence. American Constitutional Law (2000).
Wright, William, and Lillian Hellman: The Image, the Woman (1986).
Yale, D. E. C., ed. Sir Matthew Hale's The Prerogatives of the King ([c. 1660] 1976).

Articles

Allen, William B. *The Truth About Citizenship: An Outline*, 4 Cardozo J. Int'l & Comp. L. 355 (1996).
Bivins, Robert W. *Silencing the Name Droppers: The Intelligence Identities Protection Act of 1982*, 36 U. Fla. L. Rev. 841 (1984).
Boudin, Leonard B. *The Right to Travel: A Significant Victory*, 181 The Nation 95, 96 (July 30, 1955).
Caplan, Aaron H. *Nonattainder as a Liberty Interest*, 2010 Wisc. L. Rev. 1203 (2010).
Chesney, Robert M. State Secrets and the Limits of National Security Litigation, 75 Geo. Wash. L. Rev. 1249 (2007).
Chesney, Robert, & Jack Goldsmith. *Terrorism and the Convergence of Criminal and Military Detention Models*, 60 Stanford L. Rev. 1079 (2008).
Citron, Danielle Keats. Technological Due Process, 85 Wash. U. L. Rev. 1249 (2008).
Comment. *Passport Refusals for Political Reasons: Constitutional Issues & Judicial Review*, 61 Yale L.J. 171 (1952).
Conference Proceedings of the 2002 Tenth Circuit Judicial Conference, *Life After 9/11: Issues Affecting the Courts and the Nation*, 51 U. Kan. L. Rev. 219 (2003).
de Búrca, Gráinne. *The European Court of Justice and the International Legal Order After Kadi*, 51 Harv. Int'l L.J. 1 (2010).
Diplock, Kenneth. *Passports and Protection in International Law*, 32 Transactions of the Grotius Society 42 (1947).
Evans, Alona E. *Aircraft Hijacking: Its Cause and Cure*, 63 Amer. J. Int'l L. 695 (1969).
Farber, Daniel A. *National Security, the Right to Travel, and the Court*, Sup. Ct. Rev. 263 (1981).
Farber, Daniel A., & John E. Muench. *The Ideological Origins of the Fourteenth Amendment*, 1 Const. Comment. 235 (1994).
Fox, James W., Jr. *Democratic Citizenship and Congressional Reconstruction: Defining and Implementing the Privileges and Immunities of Citizenship*, 13 Temp. Pol. & Civ. Rts. L. Rev. 453 (2004).
Gaidis, Henry L. *Lithuanian FBI Connection*, Bridges: Lithuanian American News Journal 4–6 (November 2009).
Goldstein, Justin. *Getting "Delisted": The Independent Socialist League's [Ultimately] Successful Challenge to the "Attorney General's List of Subversive Activities," 1948–1958*, 52 Amer. J. of Legal History 143 (Apr. 2012).

Gressman, Eugene. *The Undue Process of Passports*, 127 New Republic 13 (Sept. 8, 1952).
Gressman, Eugene. *Have You the Right to Travel Abroad?* 127 New Republic 14 (Sept. 15, 1952).
Horlick, Gary N. *The Developing Law of Air Hijacking*, 12 Harv. Int'l. L. J. 33 (1971).
Hurwitz, Leon. *Judicial Control Over Passport Policy*, 20 Clev. St. L. Rev. 271 (1971).
Jaffe, Louis L. *The Right to Travel: The Passport Problem*, 35 Foreign Aff. 17 (Oct. 1956).
James, Alan G. *Expatriation in the United States: Precept and Practice Today and Yesterday*, 27 San Diego L. Rev. 853 (1990).
Johnson, Calvin H. *The Dubious Enumerated Powers Doctrine*, 22 Const. Comment. 25 (2005).
Kymlicka, Will, & Wayne Norman. *Return of the Citizen: A Survey of Recent Work on Citizenship Theory*, 104 Ethics 352 (1994).
Lash, Kurt T. *The Origins of the Privileges or Immunities Clause, Part I: "Privileges and Immunities" as an Antebellum Term of Art*, 98 Geo. L. J. 1241 (2010).
Lash, Kurt T. *The Origins of the Privileges or Immunities Clause, Part II: John Bingham and the Second Draft of the Fourteenth Amendment*, 99 Geo. L. J. 329 (2011).
Parker, Reginald. *The Right to Go Abroad: To Have and to Hold a Passport*, 40 Va. L. Rev. 853 (1954).
Passport Denied: State Department Practice and Due Process, 3 Stan. L. Rev. 312 (1951).
Passport Refusals for Political Reasons: Constitutional Issues and Judicial Review, 61 Yale L.J. 171 (1952).
Pauling, Linus. *My Efforts to Obtain a Passport*, 8 Bull. of the Atomic Scientists 253 (Oct. 1952).
Pound, Ezra. *The Passport Nuisance*, 125 The Nation 600 (Nov. 30, 1927).
Reale, Egidio. *The Passport Question*, 9 Foreign Affairs 506 (1931).
Rich, William J. *Taking "Privileges or Immunities" Seriously: A Call to Expand the Constitutional Canon*, 87 Minn. L. Rev. 153 (2002).
Riesman, David, Jr. *Legislative Restrictions on Foreign Enlistment and Travel*, 40 Columbia L. Rev. 793 (1940).
Rogers, Alan. *Passports and Politics: The Courts and the Cold War*, 47 The Historian 497 (Aug. 1985).
Rovine, Arthur W. *Contemporary Practice of the United States Relating to International Law*, 69 Am. J. Int'l L. 382 (1975).
Ryan, James G. *Socialist Triumph as a Family Value: Earl Browder and Soviet Espionage*, 1 American Communist History 125 (2002).
Schmitter, Phillippe C., & Terry Lynn Karl. *What Democracy Is . . . And Is Not*, 2 J. of Democracy 75 (Summer 1991).
Scott, James Brown. *Editorial Comment*, 24 Amer. J. Int'l L. 556 (1930).
Seymore, Malinda L. *The Presidency and the Meaning of Citizenship*, 2005 B.Y.U. L. Rev. 927 (2005).
Shane, Peter M. *The Bureaucratic Due Process of Government Watch Lists*, 75 Geo. Wash. L. Rev. 804 (2007).
Stephen, John E. *"Going South"—Air Piracy and Unlawful Interference with Air Commerce*, 4 Int'l Lawyer 433 (Apr. 1970).
Strantz, Nancy Jean. *Aviation Security and Pan Am Flight 103: What Have We Learned?* 56 J. Air L. & Com. 413 (1990).
Volpp, Leti. *Citizenship Undone*, 75 Fordham L.Rev. 2579 (2007).

Wambaugh, Eugene. *Book Review,* 51 Harv. L. Rev. 942 (1938).
Wytrwal, Joseph A. *Lincoln's Friend: Captain A. Bielaski,* 14 Polish American Studies 65 (1957).
Wyzanski, Charles E., Jr. *Freedom to Travel,* Atlantic Monthly 66 (Oct. 4, 1952).
Yin, Tung. *Enemies of the State: Rational Classification in the War on Terrorism,* 11 Lewis & Clark L. Rev. 903 (2007).
Zietlow, Rebecca E. *Belonging, Protection, and Equality: The Neglected Citizenship Clause and the Limits of Federalism,* 62 U. Pitt. L. Rev. 281 (2000).
Zietlow, Rebecca E. *John Bingham and the Meaning of the Fourteenth Amendment,* 36 Akron L. Rev. 717 (2003).

Government Documents

Answer to Attack on Passport Operations, 26 Dep't of State Bull. 110 (1952).
Confidential Instructions, August 8, 1918. Control of Foreign Travel. Issued for the Guidance of Officials Connected with the Administration of the Act of May 22, 1918 (Public No. 154) (1918).
Department of State Historical Division, The Department of State, 1930–1955: Expanding Functions and Responsibilities (January 1955).
Eldridge, Thomas R., et al. 9/11 and Terrorist Travel: Staff Report of the National Commission on Terrorist Attacks Upon the United States 79 (2004).
Elias, Bart, William Krouse, & Ed Rappaport. *Homeland Security: Air Passenger Prescreening and Counterterrorism,* CRS Report for Congress (Mar. 4, 2005).
Explanation of Passport Procedures: Press Conference Remarks by Secretary Acheson, 27 U.S. Dep't of State Bull. 40, 41 (July 7, 1952).
Final Report of the National Commission on Terrorist Attacks upon the United States (2004).
Government Accountability Office, Aviation Security: TSA Has Completed Key Activities Associated with Implementing Secure Flight, but Additional Actions Are Needed to Mitigate Risks (GAO-09-292) (2009).
Hearing of the Labor, Health and Human Services, Education and Related Agencies Subcommittee of the Senate Committee on Appropriations, The Impact of One Tuberculosis Patient on International Public Health, June 6, 2007.
Krouse, Wm. J. Terrorist Identification, Screening, and Tracking Under Homeland Security Presidential Directive 6, CRS Report for Congress (RL32366) (2004).
National Commission on Terrorist Attacks upon the United States, Staff Statement No. 2, *Three 9/11 Hijackers: Identification, Watchlisting, and Tracking* (2004).
Report of the President's Commission on Aviation Security & Terrorism (1990).
Stuart, Graham H. *Safeguarding the State Through Passport Control,* 12 Dep't St. Bull. 1066 (1945).
U.S. Department of Homeland Security Office of the Inspector General, Role of the No Fly and Selectee Lists in Securing Commercial Aviation (2009).
U.S. Department of Justice Office of the Inspector General, Review of the Terrorist Screening Center (2005).
U.S. Department of Justice Office of the Inspector General, Review of the Terrorist Screening Center's Efforts to Support the Secure Flight Program (2005).

U.S. Department of Justice Office of the Inspector General, Follow-up Audit of the Terrorist Screening Center (2007).

U.S. Department of Justice Office of the Inspector General, The Federal Bureau of Investigation's Terrorist Watchlist Nomination Practices (2009).

U.S. Department of Justice Office of the Inspector General, A Review of the FBI's Investigations of Certain Domestic Advocacy Groups (Sept. 2010).

U.S. Government Accountability Office, Terrorist Watchlist: Routinely Assessing Impacts of Agency Actions since the December 25, 2009, Attempted Attack Could Help Inform Future Efforts (GAO-12-476) (May 2012).

Table of Cases

Abu Ali v. Ashcroft, 350 F.Supp.2d 28, 66 (D.D.C. 2004): 264n133
Afroyim v. Rusk, 387 U.S. 253 (1967): 214, 215, 319n55, 319nn57–59, 322n110
Aptheker v. Sec'y of State, 378 U.S. 500 (1964): 74, 75, 76, 124, 263nn90–91, 264n122, 272n111, 287n209, 318n51, 321n94, 323n128
Attorney General of New York v. Soto-Lopez, 476 U.S. 898 (1986): 258n15, 261n71
Barnard v. Dep't of Homeland Sec., 531 F. Supp. 2d 131 (D.D.C. 2008): 311n138
Bauer v. Acheson, 106 F.Supp. 445 (D.D.C. 1952): 245n2, 246nn16–17, 284n172
Bearden v. United States, 320 F.2d 99 (5th Cir. 1963): 288nn12–13
Bearden v. U.S., 403 F.2d 782 (5th Cir. 1968): 288n15
Bell v. Maryland, 378 U.S. 226 (1964): 260n59
Bivens v. Six Unknown Named Agents of Federal Bureau of Narcotics, 403 U.S. 388 (1971): 255n75
Blake v. McClung, 172 U.S. 239 (1898): 259n35
Boudin v. Dulles, 136 F.Supp. 218 (D.D.C. 1955): 286nn192–193
Boudin v. Dulles, 235 F.2d 532 (D.C. Cir. 1956): 286n194
Boumediene v. Bush, 553 U.S. 723 (2008): 316n15
Brandenburg v. Ohio, 395 U.S. 444 (1969): 318n52
Bray v. Alexandria Women's Health Clinic, 506 U.S. 263 (1993): 263n89
Briehl v. Dulles, 248 F.2d 561 (D.C. Cir. 1957): 245n18, 263n118, 271n98, 276n47
Browder v. United States, 312 U.S. 335 (1941): 277n62
Califano v. Aznavorian, 439 U.S. 170 (1978): 262n88
Chowdhury v. Northwest Airlines Corp., 226 F.R.D. 608 (N.D. Cal. 2004): 313n157
City of Houston v. FAA, 679 F.2d 1184 (5th Cir. 1982): 72, 262n77, 262n85
The Civil Rights Cases, 109 U.S. 3 (1883): 317nn35–36
Clancy v. Office of Foreign Assets Control, 559 F.3d 595 (7th Cir. 2009): 262n88
Corfield v. Coryell, 6 Fed. Cas. 546 (C.C.E.D. Pa. 1823): 61, 68, 258nn17–18, 260n52
Crandall v. Nevada, 73 U.S. 35 (1867): 62, 63, 67, 68, 74, 75, 259n25, 259–60nn38–48
Dayton v. Dulles, 237 F.2d 43 (D.C. Cir. 1956): 124, 286n194
Dayton v. Dulles, 357 U.S. 144 (1958): 124, 287nn207–208
Demore v. Kim, 538 U.S. 510 (2003): 226, 324n136
Dennis v. United States, 341 U.S. 494 (1951): 113, 250n75, 282n127, 282n131
Dickerson v. City of Gretna, No. 05-6667, 2007 WL 1098787 (E.D. La. 2007): 261n71
Dixon v. Love, 431 U.S. 105 (1977): 262n75, 262n83

335

Dulles v. Nathan, 225 F.2d 29 (D.C. Cir. 1955): 285nn184–189
Duncan v. Cone, No. 00-5705, 2000 WL 1828089 (6th Cir. 2000): 262n75
Edwards v. California, 314 U.S. 160 (1941): 64, 68–69, 74–75, 259nn31–33, 260n49, 260n57
Forsyth County, Georgia v. The Nationalist Movement, 505 U.S. 123 (1992): 325n4
Gibbons v. Ogden, 22 U.S. (9 Wheat.) 1 (1824): 259n30
Gilmore v. Gonzales, 435 F.3d 1125 (9th Cir. 2006): 258n14, 312n154, 313n158
Girouard v. U.S., 328 U.S. 61 (1946): 277n64
Gordon v. FBI, 390 F.Supp.2d 897 (N.D. Cal. 2004): 296n106, 306n59
Gordon v. FBI, 388 F. Supp. 2d 1028 (N.D. Cal. 2005): 311n138
Gray v. TSA, Case No. 05-11445-DPW, 2005 WL 3803814 (1st Cir. Sept. 20, 2005): 305n40
Green v. Anderson, 811 F.Supp. 516 (E.D.Cal.,1993): 261n63
Green v. TSA, 351 F.Supp.2d 1119 (W.D. Wash. 2005): 313n161, 325n2
Haig v. Agee, 453 U.S. 280, 309 (1981): 215, 245n17, 245n19, 262n88, 264nn119–121, 287n209, 315n2, 319nn70–71, 322n98
Hamdi v. Rumsfeld, 542 U.S. 507 (2004): 322n97
Hicklin v. Orbeck, 437 U.S. 518 (1978): 315n9
Holder v. Humanitarian Law Project, 130 S.Ct. 2705 (2010): 323nn112–113, 325n9
Hurtado v. California, 110 U.S. 516 (1884): 316n26
Ibrahim v. Department of Homeland Security, No. 06-545, 2009 WL 5069133 (N.D. Cal. Dec. 17, 2009): 325n7
Ibrahim v. Department of Homeland Security, 538 F.3d 1250 (9th Cir. 2008): 196, 200, 313n160, 313n162, 314nn177–179
Ibrahim v. Department of Homeland Security, 669 F.3d 983 (9th Cir. 2012): 196, 313n160, 325n7
Jacobellis v. Ohio, 378 U.S. 184 (1964): 308n86
Kadi and Al Barakaat International Foundation v. Council and Commission, [2008] ECR I-6351 *(Kadi I)* Judgment of 3 September 2008 of the Court of Justice of the European Union in Joined Cases C-402/05 P and C-415/05 P: 327n18
Kadi v. Commission (Kadi II) Judgment of 30 September 2010 of the General Court (Seventh Chamber) of the European Union in the Case T-85/09: 327n18
Kadirov v. TSA, et al., No. 10-1185 (D.C. Cir. filed July 12, 2010): 314n180
Kennedy v. Mendoza-Martinez, 372 U.S. 144 (1963): 245n19, 315n2
Kent v. Dulles, 357 U.S. 116 (1958): 27, 75, 76, 123, 124, 245n18, 262n87, 263n97, 268n40, 271n98, 276n47, 286n200, 287n210, 322n98
King v. New Rochelle Municipal Housing Authority, 442 F.2d 646 (2d Cir. 1971): 261n71
Latif v. Holder, No. 3:10-cv-00750-BR, 2011 WL 1667471 (D. Ore. May 3, 2011): 32, 249n67
Latif v. Holder, 686 F.3d 1122 (9th Cir. 2012): 314nn177–179
Lemmon v. People, 20 N.Y. 562 (1860): 258n20
Luther v. Borden, 48 U.S. 1 (1849): 316n19
Marbury v. Madison, 5 U.S. (1 Cranch.) 137 (1803): 316n26
Mem'l Hosp. v. Maricopa County, 415 U.S. 250 (1974): 261n71
Miller v. Reed, 176 F.3d 1202 (9th Cir. 1999): 262nn75–76, 262n78, 262n81
Mohamed v. Holder, No. 11-1924 (4th Cir. filed Sept. 1, 2011): 314n180
Nathan v. Dulles, 129 F.Supp. 951 (1955): 120–22, 285nn179–181

Cases • 337

Nat'l Fed. of Indep. Business, et al. v. Sebelius, 567 U.S. ___ (2012): 327n25
Near v. Minnesota, 283 U.S. 697 (1931): 319n54, 323n117
New York v. O'Neill, 359 U.S. 1 (1959): 257n10
New York Times v. Sullivan, 376 U.S. 254 (1964): 318n52, 319n53
New York Times Co. v. U.S., 403 U.S. 713 (1971): 323n117
Olmstead v. United States, 277 U.S. 438 (1928): 243n1
Oregon v. Mitchell, 400 U.S. 112 (1970): 260n59
Palko v. Connecticut, 302 U.S. 319 (1937): 317n39
Paris Adult Theatre I v. Slaton, 413 U.S. 49 (1973): 308n86
Paul v. Virginia, 75 U.S. (8 Wall.) 168 (1868): 258n19, 259n35
Perez v. Brownell, 356 U.S. 44 (1958): 213, 214, 319nn55–56, 322n110
Pesnell v. Arsenault, 490 F.3d 1158 (9th Cir. 2007): 255n75
Phillippi v. CIA, 546 F.2d 1009 (D.C. Cir. 1976): 254n72
Prout v. Starr, 188 U.S. 537 (1903): 316n26
Rahman v. Chertoff, 244 F.R.D. 443 (N.D. Ill. 2007): 325n2
Ramos v. Town of Vernon, 353 F.3d 171 (2d Cir. 2003): 261n71
Redpath v. Kissinger, 415 F.Supp. 566 (1976): 264n133
Regan v. Wald, 468 U.S. 222 (1984): 221–23, 287n209
Robeson v. Acheson, 198 F.2d 985 (D.C. Cir. 1952): 247nn36–37
Robeson v. Dulles, 235 F.2d 810 (1956): 247n41
Roe v. Anderson, 134 F.3d 1400 (9th Cir. 1998): 261n63
Rogers v. Bellei, 401 U.S. 815 (1971): 316n21
Saenz v. Roe, 526 U.S. 489 (1999): 63, 67–69, 71, 74, 211, 257n10, 261nn60–62, 261nn64–67, 261nn69–70, 317n42
Scherfen v. Department of Homeland Security, 2010 WL 456784 (M.D. Pa. Feb. 2, 2010): 247n26, 247nn31–32, 312n152, 313n161
Scott v. Sandford, 60 U.S. (19 How.) 393 (1856): 208, 316nn24–25
Shachtman v. Dulles, 225 F.2d 938 (D.C. Cir. 1955): 285n190
Shapiro v. Thompson, 394 U.S. 618 (1969): 258n15, 261n71, 262nn72–73
The Slaughter-House Cases, 83 U.S. 36 (1872): 61, 67–68, 208, 258n21, 259nn25–27, 260nn50–51
Smith v. Turner & Norris v. Boston (The Passenger Cases), 48 U.S. (7 How.) 283 (1849): 259nn28–30
Speaker v. U.S. Department of Health and Human Services, 623 F.3d 1371 (11th Cir. Oct. 22, 2010): 322n101
Speaker v. U.S. Dep't of Health and Human Services Centers for Disease Control and Prevention, No. 12-11967, 2012 WL 4052349 (11th Cir. Sept. 14, 2012): 322n101
Terminiello v. Chicago, 337 U.S. 1 (1949): 245n19, 315n2
Tooley v. Bush, No. 06-306-CKK, 2006 WL 3783142 (D.D.C. Dec. 21, 2006): 311n138, 313n161
Tooley v. Napolitano, 586 F.3d 1006 (D.C. Cir. 2009): 313n161
Town of Southold v. Town of East Hampton, 477 F.3d 38 (2nd Cir. 2007): 72, 262n75, 262n84
Trop v. Dulles, 356 U.S. 86 (1958): 214, 215, 319nn60–64
Tutor-Saliba v. City of Hailey, 452 F.3d 1055 (9th Cir. 2006): 262n75, 262n82
Twining v. New Jersey, 211 U.S. 78 (1908): 259n42
Urtetiqui v. D'Arcy, 34 U.S. (9 Pet.) 692 (1835): 264n126

U.S. ex rel. Keefe v. Dulles, 222 F.2d 390 (1955): 264n133
U.S. v. Bland, 283 U.S. 636 (1931): 277n64
U.S. v. Dennis, 183 F.2d 201 (2d Cir. 1950): 250n74
U.S. v. Guest, 383 U.S. 745 (1966): 69, 257n10, 259nn34–35, 259n42
U.S. v. Hayat, Verdict, No. 2:05-CR-00240-GEB (E.D. Cal. Apr. 25, 2006): 252n38, 253nn42–44
U.S. v. Macintosh, 283 U.S. 605 (1931): 277n64
U.S. v. Miller, 152 F.Supp. 781 (1957): 250n82, 281n116
U.S. v. Salerno, 481 U.S. 739 (1987): 226, 323nn129–134, 324n135
U.S. v. Schwimmer, 279 U.S. 644 (1929): 277n64
U.S. v. Wunderlich, 342 U.S. 98 (1951): 325n1
Ward v. Maryland, 79 U.S. 418 (1870): 258n19
Western Center for Journalism v. Cederquist, 235 F.3d 1153 (9th Cir. 2000): 255n75
Woods v. Cloyd W. Miller Co., 333 U.S. 138 (1948): 322n97, 322n103
Worthy v. Herter, 270 F.2d 905 (1959): 77, 263nn111–113, 263nn115–117, 287n206, 287n209
Worthy v. United States, 328 F.2d 386 (1964): 319nn65–69
Youngstown Sheet & Tube Co. v. Sawyer, 343 U.S. 579 (1952): 322n97, 323n119
Zemel v. Rusk, 381 U.S. 1 (1965): 76, 79, 221, 223, 263n107, 264nn122–25, 264n132, 266n13, 283n142, 287n209
Zobel v. Williams, 457 U.S. 55 (1982): 261n71, 315n9

Index

Abdel-Rahman, Omar, 135, 179
Abdulmutallab, Umar Farouk, 162, 172
Acheson, Dean, 23, 34, 155, 157, 169, 171
Addington, David, 4
Adee, Alvey, 97, 272n5, 276n45
Advanced Passenger Information System (APIS), ix, 135, 138, 173
Afroyim, Beys, 214
Agee, Philip, 78, 215, 220
Air Transportation Security Act of 1974, 131
Alden, Edward, 184
Archibold, Randal, xi
Arpey, Gerard, 293n66
Arriza, John, 10, 134
Ashcroft, John, 44
Atta, Mohamed, 5
Aviation and Transportation Security Act of 2001, 139

Baker, Stewart, 14
Baruch, Bernard M., 157
Bauer, Anne, 19–21
Bearden, Leon, 127
Beardsworth, Randy, 15, 53, 142, 152, 309n91
Bielaski, Alexander Bruce, 100–101, 272n1
Bielaski, Ruth. *See* Shipley, Ruth
biometrics, 6, 106, 238
Black, Charles L., 74, 210, 259n40, 260n57

"Bojinka" Plot, 293n69
Boudin, Leonard, 121
Boyle, Brian, 177
Brandeis, Louis D., 1
Browder, Earl, 277n62
Bucella, Donna, 147, 151, 153, 171
Burke, David, 294n85
Burke, Thomas R., 296n106
Bush, George W., 137–38, 180, 188, 298n131, 298n133
Butterworth, Bruce, 293n67

Carpenter, J. Henry, 112
CBP. *See* Customs and Border Protection
Chafee, Zechariah, 82, 257n9
Chemerinsky, Erwin, 33
Cheney, Richard, 4, 295n93
Chertoff, Michael, 163, 180
CIA (Central Intelligence Agency), 146, 149
citizens, 8, 206, 318n45
  history of travel rights for, 216–19
  No Fly List inclusion of, 171–72
  passports denied to, 171
  referenced in text of Constitution, 206–7
  See also Citizenship Clause
Citizenship Clause, 70, 71, 206
  democratic theory and, 212–16
  drafting history of, 208–10
  interpretation, 206
Clark, William, 120

CLASS. *See* Consular Lookout and Support Systems
Cofresi, Roberto, 127
Cold War, 33–35, 92–94, 110–19, 218, 235–37
Commission, 9/11. *See* 9/11 Commission
Communists, 7, 9, 33, 34–35, 125, 182, 236
Constitution, United States
  absence of right to travel in text of, 58
  balancing test for international travel and, 75–79
  citizens referenced in text of, 206–7
  Citizenship Clause (*see* Citizenship Clause)
  domestic travel and, 60–73
  Due Process, 205, 233
  fundamental interests analysis, 261n71
  international travel and, 73–80
  Interstate Commerce Clause, 63–65
  intrastate travel and, 261n71
  "mode of transportation" and, 71–73, 234
  "not a suicide pact," 8, 205
  Privileges and Immunities Clause, 60–63
  Separation of Powers, 79–80
  structural protection for travel in, 65–68
Consular Lookout and Support Systems (CLASS), ix, 135
Cuba. *See* Hijacking
Cummings, Arthur M., 297nn113–15
Customs and Border Protection (CBP), 184

Dahl, Francis Wellington, 129, 289n22
D'Amuro, Pasquale, 297n113
DHS. *See* Homeland Security, Department of
DHS Office for Civil Rights and Civil Liberties (CRCL), 14, 46–48, 50, 190
Dingell, John, 201
DOS. *See* State, Department of
Douglas, William O., 124, 218, 225, 232, 260n49, 260n57

Dulles, Eleanor, 110
Dulles, John Foster, 97, 98

Elkarra, Basim, 40
Emergency Detention Act (1950), 93, 271n99
expatriation, 213–14

FAA (Federal Aviation Administration)
  "Authority to Refuse Transport," 128
  Intelligence Division, 131, 132–33, 143
  Security Bulletins, 132
  Security Directives, 3, 4, 10, 133–39, 141–42, 143, 160, 171–73, 181, 294n83, 306n58
  suicide hijacking, threat assessment of, 287n3
  Transportation Security Administration and, 139
Falkenrath, Richard A., 2, 139, 145, 161, 175, 198, 238, 295n103, 297nn129–30, 304n16
FBI (Federal Bureau of Investigation), 13, 175
  Inspector General criticism of, 3
  No Fly List and, 139–44
  Transportation Security Administration and, 139–42
  Watchlisting Guidance Memo (2010), 302n10
Federal Air Marshal Service (FAMS), 162, 164
Flynn, Cathal "Irish," 137, 287n3, 292n65, 293n67
Foreign Airport Security Act of 1985, 131
Franks, Howard L., 289n26
Fried, Charles, 226

Gerberding, Julie, 322n99
Glomar response, 254n72
Goldsmith, Jack, 4, 52
Graham, John Gilbert, 129, 289n27, 290n29
Gray, Robert, 165
Green, Joyce Hens, 177

Gressman, Eugene, 35, 117
Guay, J. Albert, 289n27

Hand, Learned, 33–34
Hasan, Nidal Malik, 10
Hawley, Edmund "Kip," 29, 162, 239, 256n85, 296n111
Hawley, John Steven, 292n65, 293n67
Hayat, Hamid, 44
Hayat, Umer, 44
Hazmat List, 5, 244n15
Healy, Timothy J., 1, 3, 4, 5, 15, 147, 158, 162, 163, 166, 171, 176, 191, 228, 252n31, 255n75
Hellman, Lillian, 113
Helsinki Final Act, 219
Henning, (Senator) Thomas, 122–23
hijacking, 126–30
    aircraft piracy, crime of, 126, 128, 288n6, 289n23
    Cuba, hijackings to, 128, 129
    early effect on security, 129–31
    Pan Am 103, 130
    suicide and, 129, 287n3
    TWA 847, 131, 143
Homeland Security, Department of (DHS), 13, 139
    Office for Civil Rights and Civil Liberties, 14, 46–48, 50, 190
    Redress and (*see under* redress)
    Traveler Redress Inquiry Program (TRIP), 2, 191–92, 197–201
    TSC and, 148
Homeland Security, Office of, 138, 139
Homeland Security Act of 2002, 139
Homeland Security Council, 138, 145, 147, 164, 165, 168, 176, 303n12
Hoover, J. Edgar, 9, 12, 26, 225
HSPD-1, 295n94
HSPD-6, 147, 148, 160–61, 238, 297n129, 303n12
HSPD-11, 148, 303n12
HSPD-24, 148, 303n12
Hull, Cordell, 88, 89, 91, 106, 108

Ibrahim, Rahinah, 313n160
Ibrahim v. DHS, 196

Intelligence Community, 13
Intelligence Reform and Terrorism Prevention Act of 2004, 181
Internal Security Act (1950), 93, 94, 117
Ismail family, (*see generally in chapter* 2), 225, 227, 240, 241

Jackson, Michael, 2–3, 15, 53, 138, 164, 179–81, 184–85, 186, 187, 190, 243n4, 245n28, 295n103, 296n105, 304n28, 310n121, 310n126, 311n131, 311n133
Jackson, Robert H., 69, 224, 228
Jackson-Vanik Amendment, 218
Japanese-American internments, 9

Kaczynski, Ted, 10
Kalven, Harry, 224, 225
Kamen, Martin, 112
Kennedy, (Senator) Edward "Ted," 29, 187
Kennedy, Joseph, 106
Kerner, Francine, 312n140
Kerry, Bob, 295n89
Knaeble, Raymond, 31
Knight, Frances, 119, 120
Koestler, Arthur, 125, 154
Kozinski, Alex, 196, 199

Latif, Ayman, 31, 200, 248n56
Latif v. Holder, 30, 199–200
Lehman, John, 136, 173
Longmire, Lee, 292n60
Loy, James, 136, 161, 163, 185, 305n31, 310n126

Magna Carta, 216
Manno, Claudio, 140, 173, 174, 175, 291n45, 292n48, 292n50, 294n83
Mass, Julia Harumi, 42–43, 46–48
McCarran, (Senator) Pat, 115
McCarran Act, 94, 117
McCleod, R. W., 122
McVeigh, Timothy, 10
Meissner, Doris, 134
Miller, Arthur, 35, 112, 125
Miller, Mark E., 297n113

342 • Index

Mineta, Norman, 138, 295n103
Morse, (Senator) Wayne, 35, 112, 119
Moussaoui, Zacharias, 143
Musarra, Larry, 27–28

Nansen Passport, 268n51
Nathan, Otto, 120–21
National Counterterrorism Center (NCTC), ix, 145, 148–49
  "Liberty Crossing" location, 148
  TTIC, 146–47, 298n133
Nationality Act (1940), 90, 269–70nn77–78
NCTC. *See* National Counterterrorism Center
Ne exeat Regno, 217
Neutrality Act (1939), 89–90, 108
9/11 Commission, 134, 136–37, 143, 151, 173–74, 184, 240–41, 306n58
Nixon, Richard M., 128
No Fly List, x, 5, 13
  citizens rarely placed on, 171–72
  control by TSC of, 160–66 (*see also* Terrorist Screening Center)
  criteria for inclusion on, 166, 168
  FBI and, 139
  "reasonable suspicion," 169–71, 306n50
  scope, expansion of, 173–81, 237
  size, expansion of, 3, 164, 172–73, 237
  standards governing, 164, 166–71
  TSA and, 162–64 (*see also* Transportation Security Administration)
  Watchlisting Guidance Memo (2010), 302n10
  See also redress
No Gun List, 5
nominators and originators defined, 304n26

Orlemanski, Stanislaus, 109, 280n89
Orwell, George, 92
Osmus, Lynne, 292n65, 293n67

Palmer Raids, 9
Pan Am 103, bombing of, 130, 132, 143. *See also* hijacking

Parenti, Drew S., 43, 46, 48, 51, 252n31, 255n75
Passport Act (1926), 86–89, 276n50
Passport Division, Department of State, 11, 100, 107, 109–10, 114–15
  Board of Passport Appeals, 117–19
  legal standard used by, 158
  Neutrality Act (1939) and, 90, 270n78, 270n80
  number of files, 12, 154
  publicly known location, 14
  Red Card system, 182
Passports
  Cold War, 33–35, 73, 92–94, 110–19, 218, 235–37, 262n88
  denials, small number of, 171, 306n56
  history of (*see generally in chapter* 4)
  World War I, 83–85, 99
  World War II, 88–92, 105–10
Pauling, Linus, 35, 112, 119, 125, 250n78, 281nn107–108
Persaud, Stephen, 249–50n68
Piehota, Christopher, 179, 189, 197–98
Pistole, John S., 297n113
Pombo, Richard, 40
Pound, Ezra, 86, 267n39

Rauh, Joseph, 113, 281n119
Redd, John, 146, 186, 299n140
redress, 184, 234
  DHS and, 190
  jurisdiction of courts over, 195–200
  litigation and, 195, 196, 199–200, 234 (see also *Ibrahim v. DHS; Latif v. Holder;* Scherfen, Erich)
  sample letters, 49, 193–94, 197
  TRIP and, 23–25, 191–94, 248n54
  TSA and, 189, 190–91, 192, 197
  TSC and, 189, 191–92, 198, 199 (chart)
Ridge, Tom, 138, 160
Riggins, John, 5
right to travel
  Constitution and (*see generally in chapter* 3)
  democracy and, 212–16
  history and, 216–19

international law and, 218–19
strict scrutiny, 8, 219–28
Robeson, Paul, 26–27, 111–12, 122, 125, 225
Roemer, Timothy, 136, 174
Roosevelt, Franklin Delano, 12, 109
Rossides, Gale, 162, 165
Rover, Leo, 111
Ryan, Mary, 134

Scalia, Antonin, 207, 226, 325n9
Scherfen, Erich, 22–25, 192
   DHS TRIP letter to, 23–25, 193–94
Schlanger, Margo, 311n140
Scott, McGregor, 15, 44–45, 47–48, 50–51, 254n62
Secure Flight, 4, 30, 181–84, 183 (chart), 248n55
Security Directives. *See under* FAA (Federal Aviation Administration)
Selectee List, x, 22
September 11, 2001, attacks of, 136–37
Shachtman, Max, 121
Shahzad, Faisal, 10
Shipley, Ruth B., (*see generally in chapter 5*), xi, 11, 92
   "a wonderful ogre," 12
   Conference for the Codification of International Law, delegate to, 273n14
   criticism, responses to, 103–4, 116
   Distinguished Service Medal, 98
   early career, 97, 99, 102–5
   early life and education, 97
   Eleanor Dulles and, 110
   Emergency Program, 105–10
   family, 97, 272n1
   Franklin and Eleanor Roosevelt and, 100, 109
   Lillian Hellman and, 113
   Loyalty Security Appeals Board, chair of, 273n14
   paternalism of (re: ballerinas), 103
   Pat McCarran and, 115
   Paul Robeson and, 26
   picture of, 11, 98
   Red Card system, 182
   retirement, 119
SME (Subject Matter Experts). *See under* Terrorist Screening Center
Soliday, Edmond, 293n66
Souter, David, 226
Soviet Union, 7, 12, 218
Speaker, Andrew, 220, 322n101, 325n6
State, Department of (DOS), 13, 146, 148
   shoebox, watchlist kept in, 4, 10 (*see also* TIPOFF)
Stettinius, Edward, 92
Stevens, Cat, 29, 178–79, 248n52
Stevens, Ted, 29
Stewart, Potter, 177
Subversive Activities Control Act (1950), 34–35, 93

Tallman, Richard, 199
Tashima, A. Wallace, 199
Tenet, George, 143–44
Terrorism, definitions of, 308n87
Terrorism Information, definition of, 152, 177
Terrorist Identities Datamart Environment (TIDE), x, 146, 147
Terrorist Screening Center (TSC), 3, 5, 145
   anonymity of analysts, 14
   authority over watchlisting, 162–63, 165, 167 (chart)
   Call Center, 149–50
   creation of, 147
   FBI location, 13, 147, 148
   "funnel and sieve," 13, 149
   legal foundation, 13, 148
   legal standard used by, 158
   Memorandum of Understanding (2002), 149
   Memorandum of Understanding (2003), 160, 299n138, 300n160, 300n162
   multiagency nature, 13, 147, 148, 299n146
   NCTC (TTIC) and, 148, 149, 162
   Policy Board, 303n12
   PowerPoint, 5–6, 149, 150

Terrorist Screening Center (*continued*)
  Subject Matter Experts (SME) at, 162–63, 164–65
  undisclosed location, 14, 148, 156
  Watchlisting Guidance Memo (2010), 302n10
  Working Group, 158, 303n12
Terrorist Screening Database (TSDB), x, 5, 10, 13, 135, 147, 149, 150–53, 166
TIDE. *See* Terrorist Identities Datamart Environment
TIPOFF, x, 10, 134, 135, 136, 137, 146, 148, 149, 173, 174, 294n78. *See also* Consular Lookout and Support Systems
Townsend, Fran, 180, 309n99
Transportation Security Administration (TSA), 13
  creation of, 139
  delegation of watchlisting power to TSC by, 162, 165, 167 (chart)
  functions delegated by Congress to, 161
  FBI and, 139–43
  No Fly List, early use by, 139–42, 162, 296n105
  Office of Civil Rights and Liberties (OCRL), 190–91
  Office of Transportation Security Redress (OSTR), 191, 192
  Secure Flight, 4, 30, 181–84, 183 (chart), 248n55
  Security Directives, acquires authority to issue, 139, 181, 296n105
  Subject Matter Experts (SME) (*see under* Terrorist Screening Center)

Travel Control Act (1918), 83–85, 90–91, 108
Traveler Redress Inquiry Program (TRIP), 2, 191–92, 197–201. *See also* redress
Travers, Russell E., 156, 299n139
Trop, Albert, 214
Trumbull, Lyman, 209
TSA. *See* Transportation Security Administration
TSC. *See* Terrorist Screening Center
TSDB. *See* Terrorist Screening Database
TTIC. *See* National Counterterrorism Center
TWA 847, 131, 143. *See also* hijacking
Type I and Type II error, 326n10

USA PATRIOT Act, 138

Verdery, Stewart, 174
Violent Gang / Terrorist Organization File (VGTOF), x, 174
Volpp, Leti, 318n44

Warren, Earl, 207, 214
Washburn, Steven, 31–32
Waxman, Seth, 211
Wehelie, Yahya, 230–31, 240
Winder Building, 14, 114, 115, 156, 191
Workum, Fifield, 266n14, 285n178
World Trade Center, 1993 bombing of, 134, 135
Worthy, William, 77, 214, 263n111

Zemel, Louis, 221